To 'Mac'

With Best. Wishes

Jimmy Eaten

Mac - thanks for all your hard work
during the Centenary

Christie

The North Irish Horse

A Hundred Years of Service

THE NORTH IRISH HORSE

A HUNDRED YEARS OF SERVICE

by

Richard Doherty

SPELLMOUNT
Staplehurst

British Library Cataloguing in Publication Data:
A catalogue record for this book is available
from the British Library

Copyright © Richard Doherty 2002

ISBN 1-86227-190-9

First published in the UK in 2002 by
Spellmount Limited
The Old Rectory
Staplehurst
Kent TN12 0AZ

Tel: 01580 893730
Fax: 01580 893731
E-mail: enquiries@spellmount.com
Website: www.spellmount.com

1 3 5 7 9 8 6 4 2

The right of Richard Doherty to be identified
as the author of this work has been asserted by him
in accordance with the Copyright, Designs
and Patents Act 1988

Typeset in Palatino by MATS, Southend-on-Sea, Essex
Printed in Great Britain by
Biddles Ltd, Guildford and King's Lynn

Contents

List of Maps

Note to maps

Four maps are included in this volume, one covering the First World War and the remainder covering the Second World War. Their purpose is as a guide only and it has not been possible to note on these maps every place that is mentioned in the text.

Foreword by

His Grace The Duke of Westminster OBE TD DL

Eaton Hall · Chester

The North Irish Horse has earned a unique reputation in its century of service. As the Regiment looks back over the hundred years since its formation, it can reflect with pride on many achievements. In two world wars and in the years of peace since 1945, the Horse has achieved a name for reliability, steadfastness and originality of thought.

During the Second World War, the Regiment became a byword for excellence in Tunisia and Italy. Although there was distrust between armour and infantry in the early days of the war, such distrust was never felt by the infantry units supported by the Horse. A Regiment that was capable of putting a troop of Churchill tanks on the heights of the Djebel Ang, taking the enemy completely by surprise, was one that the infantry knew could be trusted fully. And in Italy, at the breaking of the Hitler Line, the Horse, although suffering its worst-ever day for casualties, worked so well with the Canadian infantry that, subsequently, the Regiment was given the right to wear the Maple Leaf of Canada as a dress distinction.

Today the Regiment exists as a Squadron of the Queen's Own Yeomanry and a Squadron of Royal Signals. It has done well to survive the many cuts in the Territorial Army since the 50s; and its reputation in high places has done much to ensure that survival.

In its centenary year the Regiment's deeds are now enshrined within the covers of a book that tells the story of the gallant Horsemen who have done their duty so well on so many battlefields.

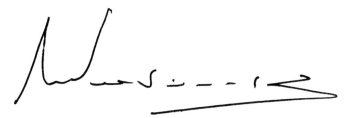

The Duke of Westminster OBE TD DL

vii

Introduction

Britain's Army is an unusual body. To begin with it is a collection of contra-dictions, operating with the most modern of equipment and ideas but cherishing traditions that are, sometimes, as old as the Army itself. Indeed, some regiments claim to be older than the Army; and that is a contradiction of the first order. The Honourable Artillery Company, the Coldstream Guards and the Royal Scots lay claim to histories that reach back before 1660, the accepted date of birth of the Army. And they are not alone.

It is the existence of such contradictions that makes the study of military history so fascinating. Each regiment has its own traditions and its own history, all of which are held dear by those who serve and those who have served. Far from being a huge organisation with a common ethos, the Army is a collection of smaller bodies each of which claims a form of moral independence. Thus it is that individuals have, traditionally, not so much joined the Army as joined a specific element of that Army. This has been especially so in the case of the Army's cavalry and infantry regiments – and the term cavalry, although archaic, is still very much in use – today's steads are heavy metal monsters of tanks or armoured cars; and in the near future the British cavalry will probably imitate its American cousins and take to the air in helicopters.

The Regiment that is the subject of this book is one hundred years old and it holds a special place in the military history of the United Kingdom, and of Ireland. It is an Irish regiment, formed in 1902, although its roots go back to the beginning of the Boer War, and it is also a cavalry regiment that distinguished itself as a cyclist regiment in the Great War and as a tank regiment in the Second World War. It has always been a reserve forces' unit, being today part of the Territorial Army, and was the very first such unit to arrive in France in August 1914 and to see active service in the Great War. It can boast a record that was second to none in the Second World War; and that from a Regiment that existed only on paper in the 1930s with but one combatant officer.

The Regiment is the North Irish Horse which, as it marks its centenary, can look back with pride on the achievements of its soldiers in two world wars and can also reflect that it has performed so well in the post-war years as a TA unit that it has survived a series of defence reviews that have reduced the Army, including the TA, to a shadow of the organisation that existed fifty years ago.

My earliest memories of the North Irish Horse are of armoured cars and scout cars – Daimlers and Dingos – parked outside my parents' front door at weekends in the 1950s. The man responsible for parking them was our next-door neighbour, Jimmy McFeely, known as 'Toby' to his friends, who was a TA soldier in the Horse. Jimmy McFeely had soldiered with my father during the war when both were Gunners in 9th (Londonderry) HAA Regiment but, as a younger man, he was able to soldier on with the TA into the 1960s. Some forty years ago, Jimmy McFeely made me a present of his cap badge. I have it still, the angel harp polished so much that the silver plating has worn through to show the brass beneath.

Although well worn and worth nothing, that badge has always been something special to me: a memory of a good neighbour, now dead, and of the days when it was possible to take armoured cars or scout cars engaged in driver instruction to his home where a welcome cup of tea might be enjoyed, but also a sign of pride in a Regiment that developed its own special ethos and culture as 'The Horse' and whose soldiers proved themselves more than ready when called upon in two world wars. Writing their story has been fascinating and a privilege. It is a good story, a story of duty well done and hardships endured in conditions that were often appalling. There is a common perception that the First World War was especially horrific. I have always believed that the Second World War was equally horrific and writing this book has strengthened that belief.

It must have required a special kind of courage to go into battle in a tank, knowing all too often that German anti-tank guns were more than a match for your machine and its armour, and knowing what the results of a direct hit on a tank could be. Nerve-wracking indeed was the ordeal of the tank-man who waited for the 'clunk' as an anti-tank shell hit home, or for the glowing area of metal in the armour of his tank that told him his life was almost over and a shell was burning its way through his only protection. And what an experience it must have been to have had to remove the re-mains of a dead comrade from the interior of a tank that had taken a direct hit.

That special courage was shown by the men of the North Irish Horse in Tunisia and Italy, and especially at the battle for the Hitler Line, the worst day for casualties in the Regiment's history. The men of the Horse were trained well and they worked together well as a Regiment. They who were tried in the furnace of war can justifiably hold their heads high and I know that those who wear their badge today are proud of their forebears and keen to uphold the special traditions and ethos of the North Irish Horse that were created by such men of courage.

Acknowledgements

The work of researching for this book was carried out by a team of dedicated North Irish Horsemen. Chief among them was James Eaton. He was supported ably by the late Michael Bexon, who served in the Regiment during the Second World War, Donald Hunt, another veteran of those days, and James Leslie. To each of them is due the thanks of all who have an interest in the history of the Regiment since without their efforts this book would not have been possible.

Thanks are also due to all those who supported the idea of a history of the North Irish Horse, and here one must mention the late Robin Griffith MC and Bar, who made a bequest in his will to help defray the costs of producing the regimental history. Colonel Dan Christie, Honorary Colonel of the North Irish Horse, has been a most enthusiastic supporter of the project and that enthusiasm and support are much appreciated.

His Grace the Duke of Westminster kindly wrote the Foreword to the book for which I am most grateful.

Photographs were lent by a number of people whose names are noted in the captions; thanks are also due to each of them and to the regimental archive from which several of the photographs are taken. Bracken Anderson, a former member of the Regiment, provided some of his excellent illustrations for use in the book and I thank him for his kindness in so doing.

The staff of the Public Record Office at Kew were most helpful in the search for regimental war diaries as were the staff of the Reading Room of the National Army Museum at Chelsea where the Lummis Files are held on behalf of the Military Historical Society and from which information on Richard West VC was obtained.

A special word of thanks is due to my publishers, Spellmount Ltd, for undertaking this project with their typical professionalism and enthusiasm and their customary high standards of production.

Finally, I must also thank my wife, Carol, and children, Joanne, James and Catríona for their constant support.

Richard Doherty
July 2002

CHAPTER I

Early Days

This book is a history of one regiment, the North Irish Horse, which was raised in 1902 as the North of Ireland Imperial Yeomanry but which belongs to a tradition that is much older. In Britain the Yeomanry regiments trace their roots back to 1794 when units of yeomanry cavalry were raised as part of the defences against a feared French invasion. In Ireland the Yeomanry could trace their heritage back a little further to the creation of a volunteer force to defend the country in the absence of an adequate garrison of regular soldiers.

When the American War of Independence broke out most army units serving in Ireland – their number had totalled 12,000 in 1770 – were sent to reinforce the army in North America, or in other theatres. France declared war on Britain in 1778 and thus was born the threat of invasion. Although a Militia Act was passed that year there was no money to activate this new organisation. However, John Paul Jones' raid into Belfast Lough in April, during which he captured a Royal Navy warship, increased the fear of invasion and was one of the factors that led to the raising of the Irish Volunteers. Recruited by the local gentry, this force was designed to defend Ireland against possible invasion; the French attack on Carrickfergus in 1760 was still fresh in many minds. High Sheriffs, Grand Juries and magistrates were largely responsible for raising the Volunteers although officers were elected by their men. Lord Charlemont was elected as their commander.

The Volunteers soon became a political force, refusing to subordinate the rights of the citizen to the duties of the soldier. Lord North, the prime minister, became one of their targets; the movement supported the removal of English restrictions on Irish commerce. By 1781 the Volunteers were almost wholly beyond the scope of official influence and were responsible for the creation of an independent Irish parliament, as well as the ending of many trade restrictions. The administration had little choice but to incorporate the Volunteers into plans for the defence of Ireland and artillery was allotted to them.

In 1793 a new Militia Act was passed in the Irish parliament, money was made available and home defence Militia battalions were raised in every

1

county, with soldiers enlisted by ballot. The Volunteers were disbanded compulsorily that same year. However, the threat of French invasion had not receded and this led to the raising of yeomanry cavalry in England in 1794. Volunteer Irish cavalry and infantry units were raised by an act of the Dublin parliament in September 1796. Forty-nine cavalry, later to be re-named yeomanry, troops had been raised in Ulster by 20 December; the Fermanagh and Toome troops were commanded by Lord Cole and The Hon C O'Neil respectively. A troop normally consisted of a captain and two lieutenants, commissioned by the Lord Lieutenant of Ireland, and about forty men with a permanent sergeant and trumpeter attached; troops were grouped under the command of a regular brigade major. In addition to providing his own horse, each man had to undertake nine days' training, for which he was paid; he was also paid for full-time duty.

A French invasion fleet that arrived in Bantry Bay in 1796 was thwarted by the Royal Navy and fear of inclement weather, but in the summer of 1798 – the year of the United Irishmen's rebellion – the French planned another invasion. A small force under General Humbert landed on 23 August at Killala Bay in County Mayo, entered Ballina quickly and took Castlebar. A British force of approximately 4,000 was routed in what became known as the 'Castlebar Races'. The French, with their Irish supporters, then set off for Dublin by a roundabout route but were surrounded and forced to surrender at Ballinamuck, ten miles from Longford, on 8 September, when their flag was captured.

A number of yeomanry troops were engaged in this brief campaign. Killala was re-taken, with yeomanry help, on 23 September, which brought the rebellion in Connaught to an end. The invasion had been planned badly, the second part of the force not sailing until 16 September. This consisted of ten ships carrying 3,000 troops; amongst those on board was Wolfe Tone, one of the United Irishmen's leaders. This fleet was intercepted and attacked by the Royal Navy off Donegal on 12 October when all but three of its ships were captured and escorted to Buncrana in Lough Swilly.

The Londonderry Yeomanry, under Sir George Fitzgerald-Hill, was in Buncrana to guard the French prisoners. Sir George, who knew Wolfe Tone, saw him, recognised him and Tone was arrested. Although two further French contingents sailed in October, no landing attempts were made. Yeomanry were also employed in the suppression of the rebellions in the summer of 1798. A number of small, uncoordinated insurrections broke out around Dublin on 23 and 24 May. By the end of the month, however, the rebels had scattered to the hills and the threat to the capital was over. The most serious and determined effort was made in County Wexford, lasting from 26 May until the recapture of Wexford town on 22 June. These two outbreaks of violence in the south were led and carried out mainly by Roman Catholics.

There were also risings in Ulster, led by and involving Presbyterians. On 7 June Henry Joy McCracken, of Belfast, led a force against Antrim town but was driven off. Henry Monro, of Lisburn, posed a more serious threat in County Down, occupying Saintfield on 9 June from where 7,000 insurgents marched on Ballynahinch. However, Monro's force was defeated on 13 June; McCracken and Monro were executed. In common with Tone they had wanted to create an Irish republic where Catholic, Protestant and Dissenter would be equal in every way and would unite in the common name of Irishman.

One result of the rebellion was the abolition of the Irish parliament. The Act of Union, joining Great Britain and Ireland as the United Kingdom of Great Britain and Ireland, and admitting Irish members of parliament to Westminster, as well as abolishing the Irish parliament, received Royal Assent on 1 August 1800 and came into force on 1 January 1801, the first day of the nineteenth century.

The Irish Yeomanry, raised by an act of the Irish parliament in 1796, remained in being under new Westminster legislation, the Yeomanry Act for Ireland 1802, which laid down conditions of service but did not include compulsory drills or training, the Yeomanry only being subject to the articles of war when called out for regular service. The Act also decreed that a yeoman who failed to hand in all his kit on discharge was liable to a fine of £10, a sum calculated to ensure the return of firearms.

The number of Yeomanry units started to fall in the early 1800s and their role became increasingly that of 'aid to the civil power'. Those units remaining in Ireland were popular among the Protestant population and the honour of belonging offset the low pay which, in January 1826, was fixed at eleven pence per day, less than 5p in modern money, with permanent trumpeters, usually retired soldiers, being paid ninepence-farthing per day. Brigade majors continued to control the groups of units and reported directly to the War Office. Strictly enforced orders forbade yeomen from taking part in political parades, particularly on 12 July. Although there is a perception of the Yeomanry as an exclusively Protestant force it is interesting to note among the officers of the Lawyers' Corps in Dublin the name of one Daniel O'Connell, later to become famous as 'the Liberator' and one of the greatest political figures of nineteenth-century Ireland.

By 1830 the number of units had declined, reflecting the pattern in Britain where the peace that followed the final defeat of Napoleon at Waterloo in 1815 allowed large reductions in the forces. Not surprisingly, the Exchequer began to raise objections to the call-out of the Irish Yeomanry. Matters were brought to a head by an injudicious call-out of Yeomanry at Newtownbarry in 1832. Permanent members were discharged compulsorily in March 1834 and all Yeomanry units appear to have been disbanded by 1845, not to be re-raised until 1900 and then for a very different purpose.

The Boers of the Transvaal and the Orange Free State declared war on Great Britain on 11 October 1899. Three widely separated Boer columns immediately invaded Natal, while other columns moved against Kimberley and Mafeking, which, together with Ladysmith, were besieged while the Boers continued their march southwards. On 10 December a British attack to retake Stromburg Junction in Cape Province failed and further failures to relieve Kimberley and Ladysmith led to that week becoming known as 'Black Week'. In this first phase of the war a professional army had been defeated by Boer farmers. That this could have happened at all created waves of horror and shock throughout the United Kingdom and led to the immediate despatch of Field Marshal Lord Roberts VC, Commander-in-Chief in Ireland, to take command in South Africa.

A decision to recruit yeomanry squadrons for service in South Africa[1] was also taken, although a War Office Committee of six yeomanry officers and one regular reported that 'it would not be possible, in the time available, to train the new force in the use of both the arme blanche [cold steel] and the rifle'. Twelve months was required to train a recruit to take his place in the cavalry, as against six for an infantryman. Accurate rifle shooting ability and good horsemanship were requirements for potential yeomanry recruits. In a break with cavalry tradition, neither swords nor lances were to be issued to the new units. A minor recommendation proposing the title Imperial Yeomanry rather than Yeomanry Cavalry was also accepted.

The Imperial Yeomanry Committee was constituted by an Army Order on 4 January 1900. An amateur but powerfully influential and effective body that drew its membership largely from distinguished Yeomanry colonels, supported by leaders of other disciplines, it organised, recruited, equipped, mounted, trained and arranged transportation to South Africa for 10,000 officers and men of the first contingent within four months. This remarkable achievement indicated considerable dedication, commitment and professionalism. Perhaps not surprisingly, the committee's reward was to be taken over and disbanded by the War Office.

Details of the force were published in the press on Tuesday 26 December. Pay was to be at the rate of one shilling and three pence per day, just over 6p in today's currency, with recruiting to start immediately. Initially, volunteers were sought from the thirty-eight Yeomanry regiments, but others who were good shots and competent horsemen would be considered. Six squadrons were raised quickly in Ireland including 46th Squadron (1st Belfast), 54th (2nd Belfast) and 60th (North Irish). Although the Dublin Castle administration raised objections to such recruiting, stating that there was no legislation under which yeomen could be recruited in Ireland, these were side-stepped by volunteers signing on for one year's service in South Africa and accepting the 'Queen's shilling'. Initial training in Belfast's Victoria Barracks was followed by a move to the Curragh in County Kildare. Shamrock was presented for the first time, instituting the tradition, to Irish regiments (Yeomanry included) on Saint Patrick's Day 1900, by special order of Queen Victoria, in recognition of the gallant service of Irishmen fighting in South Africa.

Four squadrons, including 46th and 54th, together with 45th (Dublin) and 47th Squadrons, formed the 13th (Irish) Battalion Imperial Yeomanry, commanded by Lieutenant-Colonel B E Spragge. Masters of foxhounds provided most of the officers for 45th Squadron, known as the Irish Hunt Squadron. The ranks were filled by either hunt members, all thirty-two counties being represented, or by sons of Dublin professional men; the squadron was commanded by Captain the Earl of Longford. One of the troopers of the Irish Hunt Squadron was Richard Annesley West, who was to win the Victoria Cross in 1918.

The Earl of Donoughmore raised 47th Squadron – the Duke of Cambridge's Own – in London from rich men-about-town who paid £130 each to provide their own horses, uniforms and passage to South Africa. They also donated their pay to the Soldiers' Widows' and Orphans' Fund, as did all officers in the battalion. The Ulster Squadron's officers included the Earl of Leitrim, Sir John Power (the whiskey baronet) and James Craig, later Lord Craigavon. The battalion became known as the 'Millionaires' Own'. The 60th (North Irish) and 61st (South Irish) Squadrons became part of 17th Battalion.

Thirteenth Battalion disembarked at Cape Town on 8 April and the two Belfast squadrons, following further training at Maitland Camp near Cape Town, joined the other two squadrons at Bloemfontein on 15 May. Eight days later, the battalion entrained for Kroonstad, from where it set out immediately to march to Lindley to join General Colvile. Arriving at Lindley on the 27th, the battalion found Colvile gone and the town deserted. Colvile was later told by Lord Roberts that he 'might go home'.

The yeomen had marched into a trap to be surrounded quickly by a large Boer force and besieged. Appeals for help from Colvile were refused. The four-day siege was brought to a premature conclusion when a corporal of 47th Squadron raised a white flag. Although the corporal's companions shot him, the lieutenant in charge of this sector of the line considered himself honour-bound by the man's action and surrendered. Since the Duke of Cambridge's Own were holding a hill that dominated the whole position, Colonel Spragge had little choice but to surrender as well. Given the battalion's pedigree, this news was greeted with some hilarity in the London clubs.

The battalion lost twenty-one killed and forty-two wounded, 410 being taken prisoner and, in spite of many attempts by the British to retrieve the situation, the Boers succeeded in getting their prisoners away. On the third day of their march, the prisoners reached the small town of Reitz where they were able to rest, obtain fresh food and purchase sheepskins to keep themselves warm. Twenty-four lightly wounded and sick were left there under the care of Trooper Fitzgibbon, a third-year Trinity medical student in 45th (Hunt) Squadron, a son of Mr Justice Fitzgibbon. Thirty-six hours later, the fit prisoners started the march to the prison camp at Noightgedacht, on a bend of the Crocodile river in the Transvaal. The officers, with two exceptions, were conveyed by cart, the men having to march the two hundred miles.

Lieutenants James Craig, 46th Squadron, and Lord Ennismore, 45th Squadron, removed their badges of rank and marched with their men. The journey to Noightgedacht took a month and, on arrival at the primitive camp, they were met by Lieutenant-Colonel Spragge, looking very spick and span, who berated severely both Craig and Ennismore for their misbehaviour in sharing their men's fatigue and discomfort on the march. The prisoners, badly clothed and half-starved, were released by the Boers on their withdrawal from the Crocodile river, due to the imminent arrival of the British on 29 August 1900.

After a period of rest and re-equipment, the subsequent seven months were spent chasing lightly laden and quick-moving Boer commandos across the length and breadth of the country before the battalion returned to camp to begin training the second contingent of Imperial Yeomanry. These men had received no training in Ireland prior to coming to South Africa, but were paid at the rate of five shillings (25p) a day, a princely sum in comparison to the pay of the original volunteers. At the beginning of May 1901, the original 13th Battalion sailed for home.

Seventeenth Battalion included 50th Hampshire Carabiniers, 60th North Irish, 61st South Irish and 65th Leicestershire Yeomanry Squadrons. The North Irish Squadron, commanded by Captain R L Moore, of Molenan House, Londonderry, was the only squadron to embark on SS *Galeka* equipped with helmets in lieu of slouch hats. Their cap badge was the Red Hand of Ulster on a white shield; the South Irish badge was in the form of a shamrock. The battalion, as well as 18th Battalion 1st Sharpshooters, landed at Beira in Portuguese East Africa on 11 May to join the Rhodesian Field Force and, from June until early December, 17th Battalion marched across, down and then halfway back up Southern Rhodesia. Entraining at Bulawayo, they moved south, first to Orange River Station and then De-Aar, both in Cape Colony. On 21 December they joined in the hunt for the elusive Boer generals Hertzog and Brand, a quest that was to take the two Irish squadrons the length and breadth of Cape Colony.

Going into action for the first time, things started badly for the battalion. On 22 December forty-four men (fifteen from 60th and twenty-nine from 61st) and Lieutenant Murland were taken prisoner. Two men from 60th, four men from 61st, and Lieutenant-Colonel T J de Burgh, the commanding officer, were slightly wounded. De Burgh had been the first Squadron Leader of 61st (South Irish) Squadron. The prisoners and lightly wounded were allowed to withdraw and, next day, walked twenty miles, arriving at De-Aar a day later to rest and refit. This small composite squadron remained in De-Aar until 16 February when they replaced the Berkshire Yeomanry Squadron in 10th Battalion. Once again, the next three weeks were spent in chasing the commandos of Hertzog and Brand.

On 7 March the battalion entrained for Aliwal North, just inside Cape Colony, and a three-week, two-hundred-miles sweep up the western boundary of Basutoland and back. During this period, the battalion carried out the commander-in-chief's scorched earth policy, burning crops, and bringing cattle, sheep, horses and families back into internment camps. The first three weeks of April were the most satisfying for this composite half-squadron which joined a company of Bethune's Mounted Infantry. One day, near Dewetsdorp, contact was made with a Boer commando and, after a running fight, eighty-six prisoners were taken. Soldiers of 61st Squadron recognised some of their captors of 22 December; one Boer had a pair of field glasses purloined from a comrade of that time.

On 24 April they reached Smithfield and re-joined their original squadrons whom they had not seen since 22 December. These men had joined Lieutenant-Colonel H de b de Lisle's column. De Lisle was a most successful but unorthodox column commander, and his column spent until the end of March scouring Cape Colony in the hunt for Hertzog and Brand but, although they came close on many occasions, they were never able to engage the commandos in battle. After that, they marched to Springfontein to meet and train their successors, the men of the second untrained contingent, moving to Smithfield on 24 April to join those already there.

The two squadrons spent two weeks on column work in the south-eastern district of the Orange Free State, during which they emptied large quantities of grain into the Caledon river, before returning to Smithfield with a large convoy of Boer women, children and sheep under escort. On 8 May they returned to Springfontein to finish training the new Yeomanry, and there received orders for their return home; eight days later they sailed from Cape Town

No account of the activities of the second contingent while serving with the Ulster Squadrons has been discovered.

A decision to raise a third contingent for service in South Africa was made in December 1901. Six new squadrons were raised in Ireland, two of them, 133rd and 134th, in Ulster. The latter, also known as D Squadron, was commanded by Captain James Craig who had served in 46th Squadron of the first contingent. These six squadrons formed 29th Battalion Imperial Yeomanry, known as the Irish Horse. The new volunteers were trained at home before being sent out to The Cape. Twenty-ninth Battalion consisted of thirty-one officers and 725 NCOs and men, commanded by Lieutenant-Colonel Lord Longford. They sailed on SS *Bavarian* from Queenstown (now Cobh) in County Cork, on 10 May 1902 and arrived in South Africa just as the war was ending. Longford, as a captain, had raised and commanded 45th (Hunt) Squadron and had been severely wounded at Lindley on 31 May 1900. His battalion saw no active service, returned home in October and was demobilised in November.

There is some confusion as to whether these units were Imperial Yeomanry battalions or regiments, companies or squadrons, but battalion seems to have been the normal term. The term squadron would appear to have depended upon the whim of the commanding officer, although an Army Order early in 1900 designated the term squadron, with four troops in each and each division of four men to be termed a section.

The discharge certificate, Army Form B 128, issued to Trumpeter F C Stewart on 25 November 1902, bears three different rubber stamps, viz.

XXIX Bn. I.Y. Irish Horse
O/C 134th Co. I.Y. Irish Horse
Commanding 'D' Sqn. Irish Horse

the second and third being signed James Craig.

The terms battalion and squadron have been used throughout this account, in view of the wording appearing on the war memorial erected inside the City Hall in Belfast.

To the Memory
of the officers, non-commissioned officers and other ranks
of the Ulster Squadrons, the 46th, 54th, 60th & those of the 29th Battn.
(Irish Horse) raised in the 9 counties of Ulster with Belfast H.Qrs. who served
as volunteers and fell in the South African War.
1899 – 1902

At the beginning of the Boer War there were many who predicted that it would be over by Christmas; after all, what chance had a makeshift army of farmers against the Army of the greatest empire the world had ever seen? However, the war revealed many shortcomings in the command, training and equipment of that Army. The Boer forces, consisting entirely of dedicated volunteers, were made up largely of farmers, born horsemen and natural marksmen, expert at judging distance in the clear air and wonderful visibility of their country. If they did not 'kill for the pot' they went hungry. Initially, the British woefully under-estimated distance in these strange conditions whereas Boer volunteers were used to the conditions and, armed with modern, accurate, long-range rifles firing smokeless ammunition and machine guns, proved to be a formidable foe.

Time-honoured cavalry, infantry and artillery tactics proved expensive, and certainly not effective. The guerrilla tactics adopted by the Boers from November 1900 onwards forced new tactics on the British. Protracted warfare revealed the lack of trained reserves and shortcomings in the logistic system. Purchasing commissions scoured the world for the necessary supplies and replacement mounts to keep the army in the field, horses being bought from as far away as South America.

In all, over 100,000 volunteers, 35,625 of them Imperial Yeomen, sailed from the United Kingdom, together with almost 20,000 from the Dominions, to serve in South Africa; these were in addition to the regular soldiers who fought in the war. Those volunteers who came from Ireland were the forebears of two famous regiments of cavalry, one of which, The North Irish Horse, the subject of this book, is still in existence.

When the South African war ended the bureaucrats saw an opportunity to reduce spending on the Army. However, sixteen new yeomanry regiments were raised, two of which were formed in Ireland as the North of Ireland Imperial Yeomanry and the South of Ireland Imperial Yeomanry, these being sanctioned on 7 January 1902.

There were difficulties in raising both regiments, with legal objections being voiced against the raising of any yeomanry regiment in Ireland, but these were finally overcome by adding a new section to the Militia and Yeomanry Bill which became law on 24 December 1902, more than a year after King Edward VII had approved the raising of the two Irish regiments.

Commanding the North of Ireland regiment was the Earl of Shaftes-bury, who had resigned his commission in 10th Royal Hussars in 1899 before joining the Dorset Yeomanry.[2] The Earl was gazetted as a lieutenant-colonel, commanding the North of Ireland Imperial Yeomanry, on 12 March 1902 although authority to begin recruiting for the regiment was not granted by the Commander-in-Chief, The Duke of Connaught, until 21 January 1903. Shaftesbury would command the North of Ireland Imperial Yeomanry until 1912, by which time the regiment had become the North Irish Horse, and was appointed its Honorary Colonel in June 1913. Captain R G O Bramston-Newman, 7th (Princess Royal's) Dragoon Guards,[3] from County Cork, was the first adjutant and senior NCOs from regular cavalry regiments became permanent staff instructors (PSIs). On 7 December the Duke of Abercorn KG, CB became the Regiment's first Honorary Colonel.

Recruiting for the North of Ireland regiment began on 17 February 1903 and in the course of that year four squadrons were formed with Regimental Headquarters and A Squadron, the Headquarter Squadron, based at Skegoniel Avenue in Belfast; the other squadrons, B, C and D, were raised in Londonderry, Enniskillen and Dundalk respectively.[4] The latter town's Blackrock camp was the location for the Regiment's first annual camp, from 28 July to 12 August 1903. On 27 July, the day before departing for that first camp, the Regiment provided a dismounted guard of honour for King Edward VII at Belfast's Balmoral Showgrounds. The guard was commanded by Major R D Perceval-Maxwell, who commanded A Squadron, and included Second-Lieutenant The Honourable R W H O'Neill, second son of Lord O'Neill, who later became Lord Rathcavan, and forty men from A Squadron.

A number of reports of that first camp appeared in newspapers. On 31 July the *Northern Whig* noted that an artilleryman had been kicked by a charger, presumably a North Irish horse, and that, on the following day, a horse broke loose, brought down tents and had to be destroyed. It is not known if the same horse was involved in both incidents. That the horses were not as disciplined as the soldiers is suggested by another report that stampeding horses knocked down a little girl. Towards the end of camp, the same newspaper reported that Lord Chesham, Inspector General of Yeomanry, had inspected the Regiment on 8 August and had been highly pleased with its appearance, the physique of the men and the splendid condition of the horses. Chesham's report notes that

> The men of this Regiment are of the best class to be found for mounted troops. The riding is good, mounting and dismounting are done very quickly. The men take an interest in their work and are keen and intelligent. The shooting is satisfactory. In the very short time since the raising of the Regiment the men are as fit to go on active service as the best of the IY raised in December 1899. In a short time they should be as fully efficient as the best of the Imperial Yeomanry.

This was high praise indeed for a young regiment at its first camp and must have compensated to some extent for the poor weather during camp. At its next camp, held at Finner, near Bundoran in County Donegal, from 20 June to 7 July 1904, press reports indicated that the Regiment was almost up to full strength. On that occasion it was able to train on a four-squadron basis.[5] The third camp was held at Donnelly Hollow at the Curragh in County Kildare, then the second home of the Army after Aldershot. On this occasion the South of Ireland Imperial Yeomanry were also at camp at the Curragh and it is believed that there were both training and social contacts between the two regiments. Until the outbreak of war in 1914, the Regiment held a camp each year, the culmination of the annual training programme and an opportunity to show its mettle as a full unit.

In December 1905 Balfour's Conservative government resigned to be succeeded by a Liberal administration led by Sir Henry Campbell-Bannerman, in which the post of Secretary of State for War was held by a lawyer, Richard Haldane. He immediately set about an Army re-organisation that would allow for a British Expeditionary Force of seven divisions to serve in any European war and bring about greater efficiency. Although overall manpower was to be reduced by 35,000 this was really a paper exercise since many units were undermanned.

Haldane recognised the feebleness of the auxiliary forces – Yeomanry, Volunteers and Militia – and thus the most far-reaching of his reforms was the decision to replace these with a new home defence force, intended to be much more efficient than its predecessors. Although raised and administered on a county basis, it would be organised as a reserve army of fourteen divisions and a cavalry brigade. Haldane's Territorial and Reserve Forces Act was passed in 1907 and came into effect on 1 April 1908; the Territorial Force and the Special Reserve replaced the previous forces. However, the new structure did not apply in Ireland, where the Volunteer organisation had not existed. Irish militia battalions were renamed Special Reserve and would survive on the Army List until 1953.[6] The two Imperial Yeomanry regiments were renamed North Irish Horse and South Irish Horse and were also included in the Special Reserve. Both regiments were disbanded as yeomanry on 7 July 1908 and re-raised as Special Reserve on the 8th under their new names.

This new arrangement gave both Irish regiments precedence over the Territorial Force's yeomanry regiments in the Army List, being placed after the regular cavalry regiments but before the Territorial Force regiments. For the North Irish and South Irish Horse, their new Special Reserve status included a commitment to overseas service in time of war, which entailed the maintenance of an enhanced composite squadron in each regiment, known as the Expeditionary Squadron, with a manpower establishment of six officers and 154 other ranks, compared to the normal establishment of six and 112. (A similar enhanced company was maintained in the Irish infantry SR battalions.) The Expeditionary Squadrons and Companies were to be on forty-eight hours' notice for overseas service. Each Yeomanry regiment was to retain the same establishment of 476, the appointment of second-in-command was abolished[7] since it was envisaged that the squadrons would serve independently on mobilisation – as they did – and new weapons were issued, including the SMLE rifle,[8] Maxim machine guns and binoculars. The uniform was unchanged save for badges and buttons which reflected the new names, but new recruits would now receive regular Army breeches; the older soldiers continued to wear their Imperial Yeomanry breeches with white welts on the outside seam until they wore out, thus marking themselves out as 'senior men'. Annual training was to be

11

increased from a maximum of eighteen to twenty-four days and the role of the Yeomanry regiments was defined as providing divisional cavalry squadrons for an expeditionary force.

In 1909 a Regimental band was formed and made its first public appearance at Ormeau Park in Belfast on Thursday 10 June, followed by a second appearance in the city, at Alexandra Park, a week later. The twenty-four strong band then attended annual training at Murlough Camp, near Dundrum in County Down.

King Edward VII died in 1910 and was succeeded by King George V, whose coronation was held on 22 June 1911. On Coronation Day soldiers of both the North Irish Horse and South Irish Horse lined Piccadilly, west of Hamilton Place, on the route taken by the royal procession. The bands played a selection of music in the middle of the lined streets prior to the procession's arrival. As the procession approached, the bands joined the ranks lining the route and then played the National Anthem. A second procession was held on the 23rd, known as Royal Progress Day, and the same soldiers again lined the route. For this duty men were paid two shillings a day for 22 and 23 June; they were also paid the same rate for the 21st and 24th if they were more than 100 miles from home. Naturally the Irish soldiers qualified for the enhanced payment although some lost buttons from the backs of their tunics while at 'the present' outside St George's Hospital as several nurses snipped them off as souvenirs. The Coronation Medal was awarded to Major the Honourable A Hamilton-Russell, the RSM, Mr J E Pittaway, and Trooper J Adams. Involvement in the coronation procession meant that annual training that year was brought forward and took place in May.

The Earl of Shaftesbury retired as commanding officer on 31 December 1912 and was succeeded by Lieutenant-Colonel E A Maude. The Regiment's Adjutant, Captain Edward Mungo Dorman of 4th Dragoon Guards, wrote an account of the annual camp – held at Dundrum that year – for the *Army Review*. His account gives a good insight into life at camp and the type of soldier who enlisted in the Regiment, as well as interesting snippets of information, such as the pay drawn by the various ranks while at camp. (A squadron sergeant-major was paid four shillings and four pence per day, a squadron quartermaster-sergeant received three shillings and four pence, a sergeant two shillings and eight pence, a farrier-sergeant two shillings and ten pence, a corporal two shillings and a trooper a shilling and two pence.[9]) In addition each man received a messing allowance of a shilling per day as well as his bread and meat ration and was allowed forage plus six shillings and eight pence per day for his horse. Of the soldiers and their officers, Dorman wrote

> As regards their usefulness on service, taking into consideration their average intelligence, education, and present training, they would

12

apparently be best employed as divisional cavalry. The men are at present only armed with a rifle, and would, therefore, if taken by surprise, and if they did not have time to dismount, be absolutely at the mercy of a cavalry soldier with a sword or lance. It is this lack of another arm which considerably curtails their scope of action, and makes them feel at a disadvantage with a Regular cavalryman. . .

As regards the officers, the Regiment is extremely fortunate in having a large proportion of ex-Regular cavalry officers, who have also intimate association with the country. The commanding officer has commanded the regiment since its creation. The four squadron leaders, two of the captains, and the senior subaltern are also ex-cavalry officers. The remainder of the officers nearly all live in Ireland, and are in close touch with the men.

This is in marked contrast to some of the Yeomanry regiments in Britain where the best commands were often held not by an ex-cavalry officer but by a local dignitary, as a result of which ex-cavalry officers were less inclined to join the Yeomanry. Lord Lovat summed up the situation when he wrote that the officers had to be taken from two categories:

The men of influence in the country and the men financially sufficient to be able to help your squadrons to go, and, secondly, you want to get the other officers who, if it comes to war, would be ready to help, and who would really do the work of the squadron, and who, as a rule, are not so rich.

It would seem that, in terms of leadership, the Irish regiments were better served than their counterparts in Britain.

On 3 January 1913 the Duke of Abercorn, Honorary Colonel of the North Irish Horse, died. A full-dress dismounted party of forty men from the North Irish Horse represented the Regiment at his funeral, held at Baronscourt on the 7th. The cortege was led by four pipers of the Princess Victoria's Regiment (Royal Irish Fusiliers), who played 'Lord Lovat's Lament'. In succession to the Duke, the Earl of Shaftesbury, the Regiment's first commanding officer, became honorary colonel on 7 June 1913, an appointment he would hold until 1946. In 1913 also, the two Irish Horse regiments were joined in the Special Reserve by King Edward's Horse, which had been raised as 4th County of London Yeomanry (The King's Colonials) in 1901 but was now transferred out of the TF Yeomanry.[10]

That year's annual camp, held at Finner in Donegal, was visited by the Inspector General of Cavalry whose report was complimentary in some respects but noted that there were aspects upon which the Regiment needed to improve. These latter aspects included the scouts' 'powers of appreciating and reporting a situation' although one despatch rider was considered to be 'exceptionally good at this'.

In 1914 the North Irish Horse went to annual camp once again, returning to County Down and Donard Lodge near Newcastle. They did so in a situation of international uncertainty that, before long, was to lead to war. The training of the peacetime years was soon to be put to the harshest judgement of all, that of war. Less than a month after the Regiment returned from camp the First World War had begun.

NOTES

1   Terms of enlistment for the existing thirty-eight yeomanry regiments entailed service in defence of Great Britain only; there were no yeomanry regiments in Ireland at this time.
2   Dorset Imperial Yeomanry from 1901.
3   This regiment was renamed 7th Dragoon Guards (Princess Royal's) in 1921, a year before it was amalgamated with 4th Royal Irish Dragoon Guards to form 4/7th Royal Dragoon Guards. It is now part of The Royal Dragoon Guards, a new regiment created on the amalgamation of 4/7th with 5th Royal Inniskilling Dragoon Guards in 1992.
4   An attempt was made to raise a squadron in Ballymena, which would have been designated B Squadron, in March 1903 but this was unsuccessful and the Londonderry squadron assumed the designation.
5   One of the recruits for A Squadron in 1904 was W P McArthur, a medical student at Queen's College, Belfast, who was to become Lieutenant-General Sir William McArthur KCB, DSO, OBE, MD, Colonel Commandant of the Royal Army Medical Corps from 1946 to 1951.
6   This gave rise to the newly formed TA battalions of the Irish regiments having higher ordinal designations than elsewhere in the UK; 5th Royal Inniskilling Fusiliers, 6th Royal Ulster Rifles and 5th Royal Irish Fusiliers were indicators that 3rd, 4th and – in the case of the Rifles – 5th SR Battalions were still on the Army List.
7   The Marquess of Hamilton, who had been second-in-command, continued to serve, appearing in the Army List as the senior major.
8   Short magazine Lee Enfield, known to all who used it as the 'Smelly'.
9   These sums equate to 22p, 17p, 13p, 14p, 10p and 6p respectively. Only the penultimate figure is exact as a modern penny is the equivalent of 2.4d.
10 Two regiments of King Edward's Horse served in the Great War with 2 KEH being disbanded in 1917. The regiment was disbanded on 31 March 1924.

CHAPTER II
The Green Fields of France

On 28 June 1914, the anniversary of the Turkish defeat of the Serbs at the Battle of Kosovo in 1349, Austria's Archduke Franz Ferdinand, heir to the Habsburg crown, and his wife were on a state visit in Sarajevo. An attempt to assassinate the Archduke failed when a bomb that was intended to kill him bounced off his car. However, two of his aides were injured and Franz Ferdinand later asked to be driven to the hospital where the injured men were being treated. That concern cost him his life, and that of his wife. His driver took a wrong turn on the journey to the hospital and, by chance, Gavrilo Princip, a colleague of the men who had bungled the earlier bomb attack, was given the opportunity to fire at the Archduke. Princip's shots killed both Franz Ferdinand and his wife.

The double murders in Sarajevo created tension throughout Europe and provoked an Austrian declaration of war on Serbia. Thus began the chain of events that led to the outbreak of the First World War. Russia came to the aid of Serbia and Germany to that of Austria. By the end of July preparations for war were underway in Serbia and Austria. Diplomatic efforts to prevent the Balkan crisis from worsening into war were to no avail. Russia began partial mobilisation on 29 July and Germany prepared to declare war on Russia, which it did two days later. Then, on 3 August, Germany declared war on France. German troops marched on France and, in so doing, violated the neutrality of Belgium, which Britain had guaranteed. On Sunday 4 August the United Kingdom declared war on Germany and orders were issued for the mobilisation of the British Expeditionary Force (BEF).

Among the units assigned to the BEF was the Expeditionary Squadron of the North Irish Horse. Over the next four years the Regiment would win eighteen battle honours and lose twenty-seven officers and 123 men killed in the Great War. One of those officers, Captain Richard West, would win the Military Cross, the Distinguished Service Order and Bar, and the Victoria Cross, the last as a posthumous award. But that was all in the future on that August bank holiday Sunday when the orders for mobilisation were issued.

Units and formations of the Expeditionary Force were stationed throughout the United Kingdom, with many of them in Ireland where their principal embarkation port was Dublin. When the order to mobilise was received, North Irish Horse headquarters despatched pre-written telegrams to the members of the Expeditionary Squadron. Its soldiers were ordered to report immediately to their respective squadron headquarters before concentrating at Regimental Headquarters in Belfast. On the Monday, orders were issued to the remainder of the Regiment to report, not later than noon on 9 August, to their respective squadron headquarters.

Major Lord Cole, of the pre-war C Squadron, commanded the Expeditionary Squadron, which was redesignated A Squadron and which left Belfast by train on 7 August, bound for Dublin and embarkation. The squadron was at full strength with six officers and 154 other ranks. In Dublin A Squadron was joined by the Expeditionary Squadron of the South Irish Horse, now to be known as B Squadron and commanded by Major I W Burns-Lindon, a former King's Royal Irish Hussar and the first adjutant of the South of Ireland Imperial Yeomanry. On 17 August the two squadrons sailed from Dublin's North Wall quay on board SS *Architect* for Le Havre where they disembarked two days later. By so doing they achieved the distinction of being the first non-regular units to land in France.

Under Lord Cole as troop leaders in A Squadron were Lieutenants D A W Ker and R D Ross, and Second-Lieutenants T W G J Hughes and Lord Jocelyn. Captain E C Herdman, of the Londonderry Squadron, was second-in-command. As with the officers, the soldiers were drawn from the various squadrons to create this composite squadron and efforts were made to keep men from the same pre-war squadrons together as far as possible in the same troops. The composite squadron was soon to have its first taste of war, giving them – with their South Irish comrades – the additional distinction of being the first reserve forces units to see action.

In the meantime the remainder of the Regiment assembled in the various squadron locations and moved into temporary accommodation in their local agricultural showgrounds, although the lack of facilities in Belfast necessitated a move to Antrim for both the Belfast Squadron and RHQ. And it was at Antrim that a second composite squadron was formed for the BEF. This was C Squadron, commanded by Major Lord Massereene and Ferrard DSO, of the pre-war A Squadron, which sailed for France on 20 August, landing on the 22nd. Among the troop leaders of C Squadron was Lieutenant Richard Annesley West. RHQ continued to enlist further men for the Regiment and to train them prior to moving to France either in additional formed squadrons or as reinforcements. Three more squadrons of North Irish Horse were sent to France, landing there on 2 May 1915, 17 November 1915 and 11 January 1916; in all seventy officers and 1,931 men of the Horse went to war.

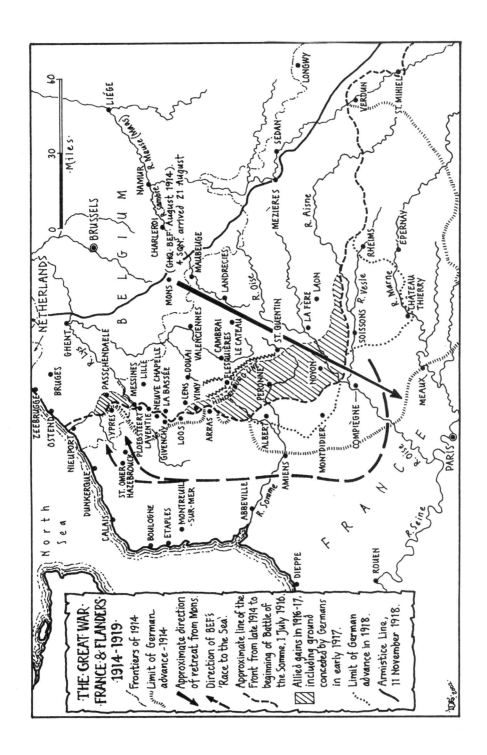

THE·GREAT·WAR·
FRANCE·&·FLANDERS·
1914-1919·

···· Frontiers of 1914.

········ Limit of German
advance·1914·

→ Approximate direction
of retreat from Mons.

← Direction of BEF's
'Race to the Sea'.

--- Approximate line of the
Front from late 1914 to
beginning of Battle of
the Somme, 1 July 1916.

▨ Allied gains in 1916-17,
including ground
conceded by Germans
in early 1917.

········ Limit of German
advance in 1918.

╱ Armistice Line,
11 November 1918.

0   30   60
·Miles·

On landing in Le Havre both A and B Squadrons moved to a temporary camp from which, on 21 August, they entrained for Busigny and then marched the three miles to Le Cateau and General Headquarters of the BEF to be designated as GHQ Troops and assigned to the protection of GHQ. Since the soldiers of the North Irish Horse had returned from annual camp only three weeks before, their mounts were fit and the men well versed in their duties and the role of a divisional cavalry squadron.

When the Irish Horse squadrons arrived at Le Cateau, the Belgian army was engaged in a desperate defence of its country. Such was the tenacity of that defence that the German strategy for the rapid defeat of France – the Schlieffen plan – was knocked out of kilter. The Schlieffen plan had envisaged a rapid flanking movement through Belgium into France to threaten Paris and roll up the French armies from the flank and the rear, defeating the French before the Russians had time to complete their mobilisation; the German armies could then march east and defeat the Russians in their turn. That was the plan; but the courage of the Belgians and then of the BEF was to write *finis* to that plan in the late summer and early autumn of 1914.

As the Belgian army was forced into an even smaller redoubt, the commander of the French Fifth Army, General Lanrezac, planned to attack the German forces to his front. The BEF was on the left flank of Fifth Army and Sir John French, its commander, agreed to comply with the French plan. Orders were issued for an advance towards Mons to begin on 21 August. The BEF moved forward, the Cavalry Division probing ahead, with I Corps on the right flank and II Corps on the left. No contact was made with German troops that day but, on the morning of the 22nd, a bright, clear summer day, the BEF and the German army met.

Near the village of Casteau, north of Mons, C Squadron, 4th (Royal Irish) Dragoon Guards were the first British troops to encounter the enemy and the first British shot of the war was fired by an Irish cavalry-man – Corporal Edward Thomas, a native of Nenagh in County Tipperary. Later in the day the BEF infantry reached the Mons–Condé canal on either side of Mons where they prepared to stay the night before resuming their march on the morrow. However, at 8pm GHQ learned that Lanrezac had decided both to abandon his advance and to retire in the face of German pressure; the French withdrawal was to begin at 9pm. Sir John French had no option but to order the cancellation of the following day's advance. He deployed the Cavalry Division to II Corps' left flank and prepared to meet the inevitable German assault.

On the morning of Sunday 23rd the BEF was ordered to hold its positions for twenty-four hours before withdrawing if that became necessary. I Corps faced eastwards in defence of the flank left open by the French withdrawal while II Corps faced north. The BEF's open left flank was covered by the cavalry who took up position before dawn after a long night march. Between the BEF and the sea there were only some French territorial troops.[1] A Squadron was detailed to escort the Commander-in-Chief. Two troops of A Squadron were detached on the 24th to join 4th Division, which was arriving from England; the remaining two troops stayed with GHQ. The next day the two detached troops found themselves in good company, supporting 2nd Battalion Royal Inniskilling Fusiliers. During the confusion of that night's withdrawal, the Horsemen found themselves with 3rd Division, whose cavalry – A Squadron 15th The King's Hussars – had been virtually wiped out at Blangies. Next morning the half squadron was pressed into service to strengthen 3rd Division's rearguard, where they remained until rejoining 4th Division on the 28th and becoming part of the rearguard of that formation. The withdrawal continued under a blistering sun until Brie-Compte-Robert was reached on 5 September. On the following day, in a reversal of role, the half squadron acted as advance guard to 4th Division's counter-attack, a role carried out until Signy Signale was reached on the 8th. On the 9th the exhausted half squadron marched to Coulommiers, where they rejoined GHQ. The march to the Aisne was going well.

While A Squadron was thus engaged, B Squadron was attached to I Corps. II Corps was heavily engaged on the line of the Mons–Condé canal but I Corps and the Cavalry Division did not see so much action. Led by cavalry, the Germans attacked under cover of early morning mist and, in spite of their courageous stand, the BEF's soldiers were eventually forced to give ground. They had taken a heavy toll of the foe; the German cavalry had withdrawn quickly as soon as they came under fire while their infantry suffered horrendous casualties in the face of the disciplined and withering British rifle fire, still, and for many years to come, known as musketry.[2] But weight of numbers told and the BEF blew the canal bridges as they withdrew to stronger positions on high ground south of the canal.

There was to be no stand on that high ground. With the French army still withdrawing, a great gap of fifteen miles had opened on the BEF's right flank which forced GHQ to issue orders for a general withdrawal in an effort to regain contact with Fifth French Army and thus avoid being cut off and surrounded. I Corps' line of withdrawal was east of the ten-miles-long forest of Marmal while II Corps was to retire west of the forest with both corps making contact again the next evening – the 25th – near Le Cateau. In spite of that plan, it was eight days before I and II Corps again came in contact. In those days, and subsequently, the BEF fought for its very existence and the Irish Horse squadrons had their first taste of war in Europe with A and B Squadrons being joined by C Squadron, the second NIH squadron, which landed in Le Havre on 22 August.

C Squadron was to join GHQ at Le Cateau but its orders were changed and it joined 5th Division as its divisional cavalry squadron in lieu of A Squadron 19th Hussars, which was transferred to the Cavalry Division on

24 August. The first record of C Squadron with 5th Division indicates the Squadron's presence with 15 Brigade on 1 September as that brigade withdrew southwards; the Squadron was acting as rearguard. By now the German thrust was beginning to lose its impetus and by the 5th the Franco-British retreat had ceased. The Battle of the Marne, which began on 6 September, lasted until the 10th and the Germans were forced, in their turn, to withdraw. On 11 September British troops crossed the Ourcq river and the Aisne was crossed two days later. Thus began the Battle of the Aisne which lasted until the 28th and during which C Squadron North Irish Horse suffered its first casualties; Trooper William Moore was killed in action on 15 September while Lieutenant Samuel Barbour Combe, of Donaghcloney, County Down, was wounded and succumbed to his injuries on 1 October. The Battle of the Aisne could be compared to a struggle between two tired heavyweights, neither of whom could gain a decisive advantage. Since the Allies failed to break the German line north of the Aisne and along the Chemin des Dames, it can also be seen as the beginning of the period of stalemate that was to lead to trench warfare along a front that stretched from the North Sea to the Swiss frontier.

However, the battle had yet to resolve itself into that phase of grinding attrition that was to become the hallmark of the Great War and further efforts were being made to break the deadlock, including the transfer of the BEF to the still open northern flank, which move began on 1 October. The idea was that cavalry could operate on the northern flank, the BEF would be close to its supply ports on the Channel coast, and its lines of communication would not be entangled with those of the French. However, the Germans were also aware of the potential advantages of the northern flank and so began the 'race for the sea'. A Squadron entrained at Fère-en-Tardenois on 8 October and rejoined GHQ at Abbeville the next day.

By now the BEF included an additional corps – III Corps, with 4th and 6th Divisions but the latter was transferred to II Corps to replace 5th Division and C Squadron remained with 16 Brigade until 12 October when it began its northward march, regaining contact with GHQ and joining up with A Squadron, now at St Omer, where they would remain until April 1915. Unfortunately, not all of the war diaries for the period have survived – there is no diary for C Squadron prior to October 1915 – and there are no other known records that would allow the historian adequately to tell the Regiment's story in this tumultuous period.

By mid-October most of Belgium was under German control but the BEF had occupied Ypres, key to the remaining channel ports, on the 13th, the day that the Germans entered Lille. As both British and German forces raced for the sea, British troops reached the Lys river on 19 October but lacked the strength to force a crossing; their opponents had local superiority in manpower and artillery. The British march to the north was virtually complete by the 21st, just in time to meet a strong German thrust for Ypres and the channel ports. A Squadron had moved from St Omer to Bailleul, which was reached on the 18th, where it came under command of the Assistant Provost Marshal (APM) and was detailed to undertake police and traffic control duties from Messines to Estaires. In a confused and fluid situation, with the cavalry manning the front line being forced back while infantry units were being pushed into the line as soon as they arrived, the Horse helped bring cohesion to the overall picture. The Squadron was then ordered back to St Omer, reaching there on 25 October, to resume the role of GHQ Troops.

Such duties were undemanding when compared to life in the line. Great emphasis was placed on ceremonial cavalry drill to which, as a reserve unit, the Regiment was unused; its mounted drill had been based on that of mounted infantry rather than of cavalry. Cavalry drill had now to be learned as a high standard of turn-out for both men and horses was demanded and it seemed as if an inordinate amount of time was being spent saluting officers, both those resident at GHQ and those visiting. Officers and men had to learn sword drill although swords had neither been issued to nor used by the soldiers before the war; officers at least had some experience with them. There was one change that was welcome: the awkward bucket for the rifle, which held the weapon butt-down, was replaced by the cavalry bucket, which held the rifle muzzle-down.

By the end of October the Regiment had gained its first battle honours: Retreat from Mons, Marne 1914, Aisne 1914 and Armentières 1914.[3] It had also suffered its first casualties: in addition to Trooper Moore and Lieutenant Combe, two other men, Trooper the Honourable Harry St G L Scott and Corporal Edmond Buchanan, a Donegal man, lost their lives during October 1914 while many others were wounded.

At home in Ireland recruiting for the Regiment had intensified and B Squadron moved from its home in Derry to Antrim on 12 December where it joined D Squadron. In that month also, E and F Squadrons were formed at Antrim under the command respectively of Majors H Waring and R G O Bramston-Newman. B Squadron, commanded by Major Lord Farnham, was attached to 59th Division in Hertfordshire from August 1915. D Squadron had already left Antrim to join 51st (Highland) Division in Bedford, whence it left for France, disembarking at Le Havre on 2 May 1915. Both 51st and 59th Divisions were Territorial Force formations; the Highland Division was a first-line TF division while 59th was second-line. F Squadron also moved from Antrim in the first half of 1915 and joined 33rd Division at Ripon in Yorkshire before moving to Salisbury Plain. It left Netheravon on 16 November, arrived at Le Havre on the 17th and then moved to the Bethune area where it appears to have remained until the end of the year. E Squadron left Antrim for Ripon and 34th Division in

June 1915 before moving to Salisbury Plain; it did not embark for France until January 1916. The divisions to which E and F Squadrons were attached were both part of what was known as K.4, the fourth new army raised as a result of Kitchener's famous 'your country needs you' appeal for volunteers.

As additional squadrons of both North Irish Horse and South Irish Horse arrived in France, the two regiments assumed their distinct identities although there were to be many parallels in their experiences of war in the years that lay ahead. One of these was their employment as divisional and, later, corps cavalry. This meant that there was little involvement either at regimental or squadron level in the major actions of 1915 and early 1916, nor do most of the surviving war diaries give us much of a picture of what life was like on such duties. An exception is that of E Squadron, which, having landed in France on 12 January 1916, marched from a transit camp near Blendeques to Estaires on the 23rd, a journey described as 'a good day's march' by the war diarist. However, the following day was less pleasant as E Squadron 'cleaned up after [the Westmorland and] Cumberland Yeomanry'. Many days show little activity although that was probably not how the soldiers saw it at the time. Others indicate that training was taking place or that the Squadron was on the move; on Saint Patrick's Day it marched to Croix du Bac and three days later we are told that the GOC was 'pleased with [the] Squadron'.

Guard duties had been carried out at bridges and other vital points and there was much training as well as that old military catch-all of 'fatigues'. On 20 February a sergeant and twenty men were detached for duty with the APM while another sergeant and eleven men were performing guard duties at Bac St Maur bridge. The following day forty-five men were provided for fatigues at a nearby brickworks, leaving two men 'to water and feed 143 horses'. Such was the manpower situation that the diarist felt compelled to write, on 23 February, that the 'Squadron has ceased to exist from a military or fighting point, due to fatigues'. Six days later he commented on an improvement – 'now have 19 men to put into action'.

This was the lot of many cavalry regiments at this stage of the war. The war of movement in which cavalry would play a leading role was nowhere to be found in France and Flanders. And so the cavalry were assigned to other tasks. As the Earl of Anglesey, the historian of the British cavalry, noted, the cavalry were being used for every odd job where there was no one else to carry it out.

> The resulting working parties were often far from pleasant. Trench-digging parties were peculiarly repulsive since 'they were generally on ground that had already been fought over, and dead bodies in varying stages of putrefaction', as the 5th Dragoon Guards found, 'were lying about all over the place'. In July, 1915, the 12th Lancers

took part in building 'defensive works around La Clytte which after a trifling set-back when one redoubt was found facing the wrong way were so well done that Plumer ordered them to be known as "the 12th Lancer works"'.

When infantry reserves marching to the front on 1 July 1916, the opening day of the Somme campaign, met cavalry troops, one foot soldier called out to the horsemen that they had broken their 'neutrality at last'. Cavalry soldiers were frustrated at this turn of events, one officer describing the wait for a breakthrough as 'like staying somewhere for Ascot and not going to the races'. Preparing for a possible cavalry action meant more physical work to create cavalry tracks across ground that had been ravaged by artillery fire and was otherwise impassable to men on horseback, as well as bridges over the rear trenches, and the filling-in of sections of the front-line trenches. It was hardly a surprise, therefore, when the cavalry was ordered to form pioneer battalions in November 1916; but it was a move that was not calculated to improve the morale of the cavalry soldiers.

By mid-1916 there were two regiments of North Irish Horse in France and a third at home in Antrim. In France 1st North Irish Horse was formed from A, D and E Squadrons on 10 May. On 25 May F Squadron was redesignated as B, the original B becoming F, whilst still at home, and, apparently, it returned to Antrim. Major Lord Farnham, to be promoted lieutenant-colonel, was posted away and was taken prisoner on 21 March 1918 while commanding 2nd Battalion Royal Inniskilling Fusiliers. The creation of 2nd North Irish Horse was announced on 11 May and the Regiment was formed on 21 June on joining X Corps. Its three squadrons were the Service Squadron 6th Inniskilling Dragoons[4], renamed A Squadron, and B and C Squadrons North Irish Horse. It appears that the depot in Antrim may have adopted the title 3rd North Irish Horse but there is no documentary evidence to support this conjecture.

The two regiments in France were to assume the role of corps cavalry regiments following a re-assessment of the divisional cavalry function in the light of the massive growth in army strength in France and the development of the corps organisation as a result of which

Much of the independence of action and movement formerly belonging to the Division has now passed to the Corps. It has been found necessary therefore to reconsider the organization and distribution of the mounted troops hitherto allotted to Divisions.

The allotment of these troops was originally made with a view to providing the Divisional Commander with a small mobile force under his immediate control for reconnaissance, protective and escort duties, and on the assumption (originally correct) that the Division would be moving independently, or with one or more roads allotted to its exclusive use.

These conditions are unlikely to recur; any future movement will be by corps, marching and fighting in depth on a comparatively narrow front. The mounted troops belonging to the Corps must therefore be assembled under the direct control of the Corps Commander and organized as Corps units.

All divisional cavalry squadrons were re-assigned to produce corps cavalry regiments, each including a headquarters and three squadrons, with one regiment being allocated to each corps. By now there were some seventeen corps with more than fifty infantry divisions. A similar re-organisation applied to divisional cyclist companies, which were formed into three-company battalions with one battalion to each corps; the corps cyclist battalions were also to provide the home for corps machine-gun batteries.

On 10 May 1st North Irish Horse formed at Grouches, north-east of Doullens, to become the cavalry regiment of VII Corps, which included 37th, 46th (North Midland) and 56th (London) Divisions. Lieutenant-Colonel Lord Cole commanded 1st North Irish Horse while Brevet Colonel Goring, late of 3rd Hussars, assumed command of 2nd North Irish Horse which was to be the corps cavalry regiment for X Corps, made up of 32nd, 36th (Ulster) and 49th Divisions, and which officially came into being on 5 July on the arrival of the CO, Second-in-command, Adjutant and Quartermaster from England. The new organisation brought little demonstrable change for the officers and men of the two North Irish Horse regiments as their routine and duties remained very much as they had been under the previous dispensation. Bridges and stores dumps were still being guarded, prisoners escorted and some patrol duties carried out in addition to providing stretcher bearers and burying parties. These last two duties could be both unpleasant and dangerous as Nos. 2 and 4 Troops of A Squadron 2nd North Irish Horse discovered in early July 1916.

Nos. 2 and 4 Troops were supporting 36th (Ulster) Division on 1 July. On the 1st their task was to escort prisoners but on the 2nd they were detailed to provide stretcher-bearers and to bury the dead. As they performed these tasks they were shelled heavily and one man was killed and three wounded. The following two days were spent 'waiting for orders' and on the 5th they carried out salvage work before receiving orders that afternoon to rejoin the Regiment at Toutencourt. Shellfire caused the horses to bolt but the troops reached Senlis late that evening having suffered four men severely injured and six slightly wounded. Sixteen horses had been killed or wounded and two were missing. During the entire Somme campaign, which lasted until mid-November, the North Irish Horse lost only two men dead: Trooper William James Finlay, B Squadron, a 19-year-old Belfastman, was killed on 23 June, during the preparatory phase for the opening of the offensive, while Trooper Thomas Wright, a 22-year-old from Coleraine, died on 28 July from wounds received six days earlier.

The pattern of life on divisional and corps cavalry duties was one that did not appeal to many of the officers and men who felt that they had volunteered for a more active part in the war and so applied for transfers to other units. Among the officers who left the Regiment was Richard Annesley West who, in July 1915, had already moved to the North Somerset Yeomanry with the temporary rank of major and would later, in January 1918, move again, this time to the newly created Tanks Corps with which he would win his posthumous Victoria Cross. Of the 150 officers and men of the North Irish Horse who lost their lives during the Great War, the majority perished while serving with other units.

Another change in the Regiment's order of battle came at the end of August 1917 when 2nd North Irish Horse was converted to infantry and over 300 men from the NIH squadrons were absorbed by 9th Bn Royal Irish Fusiliers, which adopted the title 9th (NIH) Bn Royal Irish Fusiliers. The final entries in the regimental war diary note that 'Men of the late X Corps Cavalry Regiment [were] undergoing training in infantry work' on 29 and 30 August and that 'All officers with the exception of C.O., Adjutant and Q'master came under orders of C.O. 36 I.B.D.' on 31 August. From that date X Corps had no cavalry regiment as 2nd North Irish Horse were not replaced in the role. Of the 300 men who transferred to the Royal Irish Fusiliers, one in six lost their lives fighting as infantrymen; fifty of the names on the Regimental Roll of Honour are of men who died while serving with 9th (NIH) Bn Royal Irish Fusiliers; this represents one third of the Regiment's dead of the Great War.

During 1917 the corps cavalry routine continued for 1st North Irish Horse with many working parties, guard duties, traffic control duties and prisoner guard duties. There were also many moves, including a move from XIX Corps to V Corps. Some of the working parties were detached to 16th (Irish) and 36th (Ulster) Divisions, where the soldiers would have felt at home. And in the hope that a breakthrough might occur in which the cavalry could carry out their role of exploitation, cavalry training continued to be carried out whenever possible. At the beginning of 1918 the name of Lord Cole disappears from the war diary and, from 15 February, Major The Honourable A Hamilton-Russell took over command as a temporary lieutenant-colonel and remained in command until the Regiment converted to a cyclist regiment.[5] The first intimation of this change of role was received on 18 February and a day later the Regiment received a letter from the CinC British Armies in France expressing his appreciation of the Regiment's service as a mounted unit.

In the closing days of February the Regiment began handing in the stores such as saddlery and other cavalry equipment that it held as a mounted unit and most of the horses were transferred to 2nd Cavalry Division's remount depot at Marseilles. This must have been a particularly poignant time for both officers and men as the bond with the horses would have been very strong, especially with those who had 'been out since fourteen' and who had, therefore, been with the Horse since pre-war days. Since the establishment of a cyclist regiment was some twenty-five per cent lower than that of a cavalry regiment, there would also be goodbyes to many officers and men. However, a cyclist regiment could deploy the same number of rifles as a cavalry regiment since there was no need for men to hold horses when riders dismounted. A cyclist squadron included four officers and ninety-five men, compared to the six officers and 134 men of a cavalry one. Command of a cyclist regiment devolved on a major rather than a lieutenant-colonel with captains commanding the squadrons, each of which consisted of three troops of some twenty-eight to thirty men apiece. Cyclist regiments retained a small number of horses, principally for transport purposes; their standard mount was a specially designed folding bicycle with heavy-duty tyres for use on rough surfaces.[6]

Training for the new role continued into March and a new designation was given to the Regiment on the 19th; it was now 5th Cyclist Regiment (North Irish Horse), commanded by Major The Honourable A Hamilton Russell, but squadron designations remained unchanged as A, D and E. An officer and twenty-eight men of the Cyclist Corps were posted in that same day and the Regiment began training on the Lewis machine gun in anticipation of the issue of that weapon as a replacement for the Hotchkiss. But there was to be no time for lengthy training either in the new role or with the new weapon; on the morning of 21 March the Germans launched Operation MICHAEL, a major offensive designed to defeat the British and French armies in detail before sufficient American ground forces could arrive in France to turn the tide of war against Germany. Operation MICHAEL was possible since Russia had collapsed and sued for peace, allowing Germany to move much of its eastern front army to the western front. Out of the misty dawn of that spring morning the first thirty-two-division wave of German infantry struck at the Allied positions which had been subjected to an artillery and mortar bombardment from 10,000 guns and mortars on a forty-three-mile-long front. Covering an area of 150 square miles, this bombardment was not to be equalled in Europe until the Red Army's assault on Berlin in 1945.

Third British Army, in which the Horse was serving, held a twenty-eight-mile-long front from Arras to the Flesquières salient with fourteen infantry divisions in well prepared and defended trenches; V Corps held the army's southern flank. On that right, or southern flank, was Fifth

Army, of twelve infantry and three cavalry divisions, holding a forty-two-mile-long front, recently taken over from the French army and with poorly prepared defensive positions. The boundary between Third and Fifth Armies was on the southern face of the Flesquières salient. It was on this front held by the two armies that three German armies – Seventeenth, Second and Eighteenth – fell on that March morning. The North Irish Horse was ordered to stand to and be ready to move at short notice.

Regimental HQ moved back to Murlincourt on the 22nd and squadrons were detached to divisional HQs. On the following day Fifth Army began to disintegrate under the weight of the German onslaught but Third Army, although forced to give up some ground, continued to hold firm until the morning of the 24th when the salient was abandoned following the decision of the six battalion commanders of the Royal Naval Division to withdraw, although they had no orders to do so. Thus began the great retreat of spring 1918. Third Army pulled back its right flank but, simultaneously, had to try to stretch southwards to regain contact with Fifth Army and prevent a German breakthrough in the gap between the armies. Reinforcements had arrived for Third Army and, although Bapaume was evacuated on the night of 24 March and Albert on the 26th, the army was able to stabilise its front and prevent the Germans achieving their objective in that sector – the capture of Arras. Against stout and determined resistance, doughtier than they had expected, the German attack ground to a standstill on 5 April as their high command began to prepare for a fresh offensive against the Ypres salient, which was to begin on 9 April.

In the confused fighting of those days the Regiment suffered a number of casualties. On 23 and 24 March nine men were wounded, of whom five were from A Squadron, two from E Squadron and the others were Army Cyclist Corps (ACC) personnel. On the 26th, when RHQ moved to Terramesnil, some twenty-two miles west of Villers au Flos, three men were killed, two of whom were from A Squadron and the third from E.

By 27 March RHQ had moved to Rubempre where it would remain until 11 April. Two gallantry awards had also been won and these – the Military Medal to two men of A Squadron – were announced on 3 April. Until the 9th the Regiment was employed chiefly as corps guides, on traffic control duties Corps HQ duties and as 'runners' to V Corps' heavy artillery. Casualties were light with one man killed and three wounded; two of the latter were attached ACC soldiers.[7] The manner in which the Regiment discharged these duties brought a special commendation from the Assistant Provost Marshal, who described their work as 'splendid', and another from the corps commander, who indicated his belief that 'the comparatively light losses in guns and transport suffered by the V Corps [was due] very largely to their self sacrificing devotion to duty'.

On 11 April RHQ made another move, this time some four miles westwards to Naours. This was to be a more permanent home, RHQ residing there until 7 August. It was also a period in which there were no fatal casualties and the Regiment saw no direct action against the enemy, although some men were wounded in the course of their duties. Those duties included traffic control, providing guides and 'runners' as well as men for various Corps HQ tasks. On the 17th the traffic posts were withdrawn and road patrols ceased and, next day, the Regiment began training in dismounted action, scouting, map reading, use of the Lewis gun, bombing, musketry and various tactical schemes in conjunction with 12th Machine Gun Squadron. Regimental strength is shown as 358 all ranks on 26 April.

Throughout the next two months the Regiment carried out a range of duties similar to those they had already been performing. On 12 May they learned that about thirty men of 9th (NIH) Bn Royal Irish Fusiliers had been captured during the March fighting and subscriptions were sought to pay for parcels to be sent to those men. July saw a continuation of the routine of earlier months with the addition of men being employed on a working party with Army Divisional Signals.

There was an efflux of men from the Regiment between April and July; nine officers were posted away, the majority going to the Royal Field Artillery (RFA)[8]; between early March and early October thirty-eight men were posted to cadet schools in Britain for officer training. In September the commanding officer was posted to the RFA; two days earlier, on 6 September, Major Finlay, E Squadron Leader, had been posted to the Royal Scots Greys. By then, however, the Regiment had been involved in action during the BEF offensive that began on 8 August 1918. This began the campaign known as the 'hundred days' during which the BEF played the major role in the Allied assault on the German armies that was to lead to the armistice of November and the German surrender.

The Regiment's training programme continued until it moved forward in preparation for the BEF offensive. As early as 14 August an officer and thirteen men from A Squadron were attached to 64 Brigade of 21st Division for patrol duties and, two days later, Trooper W McClelland[9] was killed in action. On the day that Trooper McClelland was killed the Corps commander, Lieutenant-General Shute, inspected the North Irish Horse and explained the role that they would be expected to play in the offensive. The Regiment would be acting as vanguard to V Corps, with one squadron attached to each of the three divisions, and they would be used entirely for tactical work, keeping in touch with the enemy as he withdrew. In essence this was the old divisional cavalry role of scouting or reconnaissance. A Squadron, under Captain Kirkpatrick MC, would be attached to 21st Division, E Squadron, under Major I A Finlay, to 38th Division, and D Squadron, under Captain H E L Montgomery, to 17th Division. The commanding officer would act as liaison officer between

17th and 21st Divisions and the adjutant would fulfil the same role with 17th and 38th Divisions. Training continued, with an officer and five men of E Squadron undergoing a course of instruction in pigeon carriers and the squadrons receiving instruction in semaphore signalling.

On 20 August two officers and sixty-seven men, with the Regiment's complement of nine Lewis guns, were detached to 62 Brigade of 21st Division to take part in an attack that was due to start on the morning of the 21st. Between the 21st and month's end thirteen men of A Squadron were detached to 64 Brigade for patrol duties; on the 21st three men of A Squadron were killed and another three gassed. Second-Lieutenant J A O'Neill and a soldier of D Squadron were wounded and another man gassed on the same day while E Squadron also suffered three wounded. Next day Lieutenant Cleaver of A Squadron was gassed and two men of the squadron were wounded.

On the 22nd E Squadron reported for duty with 38th Division and A and D Squadrons reported to their respective divisions the following day. RHQ moved forward to Beaussart and the Lewis guns of both D and E Squadrons were ordered to return to their squadrons. Between the 24th and 31st the squadrons were engaged on patrol duties with their divisions and RHQ moved forward again, to Hamel on the 25th and Courcelette on the 26th. In the patrol actions that were taking place casualties were being suffered. Trooper George Gill, of Belfast, and Trooper Adam Kelly, from Keady in County Armagh, both from A Squadron, lost their lives on the 26th as did Trooper John McVea, another Belfastman, and Trooper F Livingston, both of E Squadron. Each squadron also suffered seven wounded. There were further casualties, including Major Finlay who was hospitalised on 30 August and, as noted earlier, was posted to the Royal Scots Greys on his discharge from hospital.

When Major Finlay was admitted to hospital Lieutenant Donald O'Neill Hodson, the senior subaltern of E Squadron, took command of the squadron and performed those duties until 20 September. In so doing he earned the Military Cross:

> For conspicuous gallantry and devotion to duty in command of a squadron. On coming under heavy fire from a party of the enemy in concealed positions, he at once attacked them, capturing eighteen, and killing the remainder. Later, during an attack, he organised three Lewis-gun teams to protect the flank, and thus caused a flanking movement by the enemy to be repulsed. He rendered very valuable service.

Hodson's was not the sole Military Cross won by the Regiment in those days. Lieutenant Edward Arthur Atkinson, of A Squadron, also earned this gallantry decoration:

For conspicuous gallantry and good leadership during the advance from 22nd August, 1918, to 1st September, [1918], near Le Burgue. When the left flank of a battalion was severely threatened, realising the situation, he, of his own initiative, led forward three Lewis gun teams under heavy fire and brought them into action, nullifying the attempts of the enemy, and enabling the battalion to hold its positions.

On 1 September Lieutenant Atkinson, with six men, was detached to V Corps Lewis Gun School. By that date RHQ was at Martinpuich and each squadron was maintaining a separate war diary, indicating that they were operating independently with their respective divisions. On 8 September RHQ, now at Lechelle, received a letter from Major-General T A Cubit of 38th (Welsh) Division, expressing his appreciation of the work carried out by E Squadron in support of his division.

> I am deeply grateful for the magnificent assistance rendered to this Division by the squadron of V Corps Cyclists, North Irish Horse, during the past sixteen days. They have been gallant to a degree, unflagging in energy, and although placed under different Brigadiers almost daily, have never failed to supply me with early and accurate information.
>
> I desire especially to place on record my appreciation of the manner in which this sqn, on the 4th inst, took forward ammunition to the troops of the 114th Bde through a very heavy HE and gas barrage, across the Canal du Nord.
>
> I shall be very happy to forward any recommendations for immediate awards that the Squadron Commander may see fit to submit.

Five men of E Squadron were also awarded the Military Medal; the notification of those awards was received on the 19th. Eight days later came news that the Military Medal had also been awarded to three men of A Squadron.

On 10 September the commanding officer was posted to the Royal Field Artillery and Captain Kirkpatrick MC, of A Squadron, assumed command of the Regiment. Subsequently Major A E Phillips, of the Royal Welsh Fusiliers,[10] took over command. At the end of September A Squadron relieved E Squadron in support of 38th (Welsh) Division. Until then A Squadron had been working with 21st Division and had assisted in the capture of Beaulincourt at the beginning of the month; had assisted the three brigades on reconnaissance work and as runners from the 10th to the 15th; and had moved with the advance of 64 Brigade on the 18th. On that day one troop recce'd forward to Villers-Guislain which was found to be occupied, and patrols were sent to contact 51 Brigade. Subsequently a party carried ammunition forward for the two battalions that were to take Villers-Guislain.

Much of E Squadron's service for September is summarised in Major-General Cubit's letter while D Squadron was also commended by a divisional commander who noted that:

> When all forward telephone lines were cut and the Power Buzzer out of action the [cyclists] riding down the Fins–Gouteaucourt road maintained communications from the forward battalions to the Dessart Wood report centre.
>
> During the check on the Canal du Nord they were used to maintain liaison with troops on right and left and were most useful.
>
> The cyclists were of the greatest use, their keenness was most marked and they carried out the tasks allotted to them in a most competent manner.

During patrolling work on 2 September E Squadron lost Private Alexander Blair, a Belfastman, killed in action.

In October two members of the Regiment died: Lieutenant Harold Kellock, from Totnes in Devon, and who had been attached to 13 Battery of 17th Brigade Royal Field Artillery, died in a base hospital on the 6th while Trooper John Evans, from Welshpool, who was wounded on the 22nd, died three days later. A total of thirty-four men were wounded or gassed during the month. Both A and D Squadrons had a comparatively quiet month, with the former suffering only two men wounded in the closing days of the month while D had no casualties. E Squadron had a very different experience and suffered the majority of the Regiment's casualties, including the death of Trooper Blair. On 2 September the squadron recce'd the Canal du St Quentin and on the following day had fifteen men gassed. Patrols were carried out in front of the Hindenberg line on the 6th and, although 33rd Division, to which the squadron was attached, was relieved that day, E Squadron remained in the trenches for three days. E Squadron moved up with 99 Brigade to just behind Malincourt on the 10th to carry out patrol work but came back to Hurpevent for a rest two days later. A move to Bertry, about five miles west-south-west of Le Cateau, followed on 17 October and on the 23rd came an attachment to 100 Brigade for a new attack.

The enemy were located in Englefontaine on the 24th and an attack was put in. Two Lewis-gun teams of E Squadron were sent to occupy the village until relieved by infantry. Heavy shelling brought the squadron back to Poix du Nord next day and, on the 26th, 33rd Division was relieved by 38th and E Squadron marched back to Troisville and rejoined the Regiment, three miles west of Le Cateau.

During the first three days of November A Squadron was operating with 113 and 114 Brigades of 38th (Welsh) Division. On the 4th two troops were in the Forêt de Marmal with 38th Division when Trooper J Culley was killed. Moving to Grand Patures the following day the Squadron joined 33rd Division, which was also joined by half of E Squadron that same day. There was a further move, to Sarbaras, on the 6th and, next day, A Squadron provided the advance guard for 99 Brigade and was heavily engaged; Trooper C Elder was killed in this action; he was to be the Squadron's last fatal casualty of the war. Returning to Sarbaras on 8 November, A Squadron then moved forward to Dimechaux on the 9th to join 113 Brigade of 38th (Welsh) Division with which it advanced to Hestrud and then to Eccles over the next two days, forming an outpost line between Hestrud and Cousoire. And it was there that the war ended for A Squadron; the outpost line was withdrawn with the cessation of hostilities and the Squadron returned to Dimechaux where it remained until moving to rejoin the Regiment at Pont du Nord on the 19th.

Early November also saw D Squadron engaged in action at Berlaimont and Limont Fontaine before establishing an outpost line from Orchies to Quievelon, which it was holding when hostilities ended. E Squadron was split between 21st and 33rd Divisions and was also in action at Limont Fontaine at this time. The Squadron had been withdrawn from the line to rest when hostilities came to an end. RHQ moved from Troisville to Poix du Nord on the 4th and then to Aulnoye, making a final move to Beaufort on the 9th where it was located when the guns finally fell silent at the eleventh hour of the eleventh day of the eleventh month. In those closing days the RHQ order book notes the final deaths during the war: as well as Privates Culley and Elder, Trooper H Brennan of RHQ and Trooper C R Woodside of D Squadron both died in hospital, as did Trooper J Johnston while Lance-Corporal D Hill died from injuries sustained on 1 November.[11] The order book also notes the award of the Victoria Cross to the late Captain, Acting Lieutenant-Colonel R A West DSO*, MC, late of the Regiment, but serving with the newly formed Tank Corps at the time of his death.

The Tank Corps won four Victoria Crosses in the course of the war, the fourth of which was awarded to Richard Annesley West for actions near Courcelles on 21 August and at Vaulx Vraucourt on 2 September 1918. As we have already noted, West remained with the North Irish Horse until July 1915 when he transferred to the North Somerset Yeomanry with the temporary rank of major. Born in Cheltenham on 26 September 1878, he was the son of Augustus George West of White Park, County Fermanagh; his mother, Sara, was the daughter of Canon Richard Booth Eyre, rector of Eyre Court in County Galway. Richard West had already served in the South African War of 1899–1902, at first as a trooper in the 45th Irish Hunt Company, Imperial Yeomanry before transferring to 2nd Bn Kitchener's

Fighting Scouts with whom he was commissioned. He remained in South Africa after the war and was Assistant Adjutant of the Transvaal Horse Artillery Volunteers, serving with them until 1912. In that year he went on to the Transvaal Reserve of Officers. West joined the North Irish Horse on the outbreak of the Great War and was gazetted lieutenant on 11 August 1914. He made his transfer to the Tank Corps in 1917, by which time he was already a holder of the DSO, awarded for his actions with the North Somersets on 11 April 1917.

On 8 August 1918, as a major commanding a company of 6th Light Tank Battalion, he earned an immediate award of the Military Cross. Then, on 21 August, came the first of the two actions that earned him the VC. He was also awarded a Bar to the DSO for his actions on 21 August:

> For conspicuous gallantry near Courcelles . . . In consequence of this action being fought in a thick mist, this officer decided to accompany the attack to assist in maintaining direction and cohesion. This he did mounted, until his horse was shot under him, then on foot until the final objective was reached. During the advance, in addition to directing his Tanks, he rallied and led forward small bodies of Infantry lost in the mist, showing throughout a fine example of leadership and a total disregard of personal safety.

His commanding officer having been killed, West took command of the battalion and, next day, was appointed acting-lieutenant-colonel. West had two horses shot from under him during the action and was fortunate to escape unscathed himself. The citation for his Victoria Cross notes of this day that:

> during the attack on Courcelles, the infantry having lost their bearings in the dense fog, this officer at once took charge of any men he could find. He reorganized them and led them on horseback through the village on to their objective in face of heavy machine-gun fire. . . . Throughout the whole action he displayed the most utter disregard of danger, and the capture of the village was in great part due to his initiative and gallantry.

He was on horseback again on 2 September when it was planned that a battalion of light tanks should exploit an initial attack by infantry and heavy tanks. To keep himself apprised of the battle's progress, West, now commanding 6th Light Tank Battalion, went forward to the front infantry positions where he would have the advantage of being aware immediately of any enemy counter-attack. When he arrived with the foremost infantry he learned that the battalion had suffered severe casualties to its officers and that its flanks were exposed. The possibility of the battalion giving way before the Germans was very real and, to prevent this, West rode out in front of the soldiers, ignoring heavy rifle and machine-gun fire. He rallied the men and ordered NCOs to take the place of the officers who had been killed or wounded. In spite of severe pressure from the enemy, Richard West's leadership restored the situation at the front.

Riding up and down in front of the battalion, West exhorted the soldiers to stand their ground, calling, 'Stick it men, show them fight, and for God's sake put up a good fight'. Those were probably the last words he spoke. He was then struck by a burst of machine-gun fire and fell to the ground. Richard West was dead.

In the light of such bravery there could be little doubt that West would receive a posthumous Victoria Cross. The award was gazetted on 30 October and his VC, his DSO and Bar, and Military Cross were all presented to his widow in the ballroom of Buckingham Palace on 15 February 1919. By that time, Maud Ethel West had given birth to their daughter, Gertrude Annesley, on 17 November 1918. Richard Annesley West was buried in Mory Abbey Military Cemetery.

It soon became clear that the war was over; on 13 November the Regiment received a supply of boot blacking and button polish for sale in the canteen. Over the next few days some of the impedimenta of war was handed in, including tents and the anti-aircraft mountings for Lewis guns.

The end of hostilities saw the Regiment near Le Cateau, not very far from where its squadrons had begun the war over four years earlier in August 1914. In the course of the conflict, Europe's bloodiest, the Regiment had seen its role change dramatically; there had been little opportunity for divisional cavalry, or corps cavalry, to operate in their intended role and it was really only when the Regiment became a cyclist battalion that it saw action in the reconnaissance role – and then only because the war had changed from being static to being one of movement. It had been very different from the war for which the Regiment, and the entire British Army, had trained but, nonetheless, the Regiment and its soldiers had acquitted themselves well. Now peace beckoned; but the circumstances in which the Great War had ended would sow the seeds for a further war with Germany, and one that would be even more bloody. It would also be one in which the North Irish Horse would play a signal part, using one of the new weapons devised to break the trench deadlock of the Great War.

NOTES

1   Territorials in the French army were not the equivalent of British Territorials who were part-time volunteer soldiers. Instead, French Territorials were men who had passed through the regular army and the reserve over an eleven-

year period and then became soldiers of the Territorial army and reserve for a further fourteen years. In addition the Territorials also included some men who were not considered fit for full compulsory service.

2 Such was the rate of fire from the British infantry that the Germans believed they were coming under machine-gun fire. However, there were only two machine guns per battalion of 1,000 men in the BEF.

3 Battle Honours were not allocated until after the war and were decided upon by a War Office committee.

4 This squadron had been formed on 2 October 1914, from volunteers of the Inniskilling Horse of the Ulster Volunteer Force. The Colonel of the Inniskilling Dragoons, and the War Office, had given permission for the squadron to bear the title of the Inniskillings and, until 1919, the squadron took precedence in the Army List immediately after the Dragoons. The Inniskillings did not take kindly to being re-assigned as a squadron of 2nd North Irish Horse and maintained their Inniskillings' identity.

5 Captain T W G J Hughes, who had gone to France with A Squadron in 1914, commanded the Regiment as an acting lieutenant-colonel from 15 January to 1 February.

6 A similar machine was to surface in the Second World War and, although it is thought of mainly as an item of equipment for airborne soldiers, it was issued to infantry battalions involved in the invasion of Normandy. One of those battalions was 2nd Royal Ulster Rifles.

7 It appears that the attached Cyclist Corps soldiers lived a separate existence from the men of the North Irish Horse as none of their fatal casualties are listed on the NIH War Memorial in Belfast.

8 1918 saw an expansion in the number of artillery regiments as artillery now dominated the battlefield and there was an increased need for horsemasters.

9 There is no official record to show Tpr McClelland's Christian name, nor his home.

10 In 1922 the regiment adopted the spelling Welch for its title.

11 The regimental war memorial notes the death of Trooper W Hillocks on 10 November. He was not with the Regiment and died in the British Cavalry Base Depot.

CHAPTER III
The One Man Regiment

Although the guns fell silent on the Western Front on that November Monday morning at 11 o'clock, the war did not end officially until the Treaty of Versailles was signed in June 1919. In those intervening months of a peace that awaited ratification, the North Irish Horse remained in France; but much of the panoply of war had disappeared, beginning with the handing in of the Regiment's Lewis guns during the first week of December 1918.

Between 7 and 10 December the Regiment moved to Vignacourt, some ten miles north-west of Amiens, where it was to stay until June 1919. Echoes of war were still present with the news of the awards of decorations to a number of officers and men. On 10 December the awards of two Military Medals and a Bar to the Military Medal to members of A Squadron were noted in the regimental order book, followed by four to men from D Squadron on the 28th, while the award of the Distinguished Service Order to Major Phillips followed at the beginning of January 1919.

However, the Regiment could also see further signs of peace; on 12 December the first 'key' worker was demobilised and reveille was put back by thirty minutes to 7.00am daily. Normal peacetime soldiering began with a routine of fatigues, PT, route marches and other training. January saw a victory concert and further demobilisation, including that of Major Phillips, who was succeeded as commanding officer by Captain Grant who had been commissioned into the North Irish Horse in April 1909.[1] Those entitled to the 1914–15 Star were given permission to wear the ribbon of that medal on their tunics on the 13th.[2] The order book indicates the weather conditions prevailing at the end of the month when it noted an order that 'No snowballs are to be thrown at the drivers of passing vehicles'. By 31 January the Regiment was preparing to reduce to a cadre of three officers, five senior ranks and twenty-seven other ranks, who would be responsible for the eventual rundown of the North Irish Horse and its departure from France. That rundown was well underway with a further two officers and 106 men, including the regimental sergeant-major, being demobbed during February; awards of the Military Medal to four senior ranks were noted in the order book.

During March and April the Regiment continued to run down and weekly orders replaced daily orders. The last entry in the regimental order book was made on 13 May by Captain Grant, 'commanding V Cyclist Regiment (NIH)'. On 11 June North Irish Horse finally said goodbye to France when the rear party of an officer and seven soldiers left Vignacourt for Pembroke dock. At the same time the regimental depot in Antrim closed and the men remaining there were transferred to the Curragh, where they took part in peace celebrations before being demobbed. Tragically by then Ireland was involved in its own war, the so-called Anglo-Irish war, or the war of independence. For old soldiers there would be little peace in Ireland over the new few years and many who had thought they were coming home to put war behind them would find it again on their doorsteps; some would lose their lives as terrorists defined them as British spies and murdered them, often in horrendous circumstances.

As the Regiment said farewell to its soldiers it also bade a farewell to the horses that it had continued to hold; these were transferred to 8th King's (Royal Irish) Hussars. On 22 July Lord Massereene and Ferrard DSO, one of the early squadron leaders,[3] was 'disembodied'. The Regiment had ceased to exist as a fighting unit and, by 1920, was itself classed as 'disembodied'. This state of existence, strange to the layperson and suggestive almost of something supernatural, meant that the Regiment's name continued to be shown in the Army List. In August 1920 the Army List included the names of the Honorary Colonel, Honorary Chaplain, a Brevet-Colonel (E A Maude), six majors, six subalterns and the quartermaster. These officers had no peacetime training commitments.

In 1921 the Territorial and Militia Act changed the name of the Territorial Force to Territorial Army, a tribute to the contribution that the 'Saturday night soldiers' had made during the Great War, while the Special Reserve was to be known as the Militia; these changes were to come into effect from 1 October. In the Army List of October 1921 there is a section headed 'Cavalry Special Reserve – Irish Horse' which is subdivided North Irish, South Irish. A year later the heading was 'Cavalry Militia', with precedence after the Remount Service, which followed the junior cavalry regiment, 17th/21st Lancers. By now only the North Irish Horse and King Edward's Horse appeared; South Irish Horse had been disbanded on 31 July 1922 with the Irish infantry regiments territorially linked with the Irish Free State.

That year of the disbandments also saw the dedication of a chapel in Westminster Cathedral, the metropolitan cathedral of the Roman Catholic Church in England and Wales, to the dead of the late war who had served in the Irish regiments. In this Chapel of St Patrick and the Saints of Ireland the badges of the Irish regiments are displayed on the walls and a Roll of Honour for each regiment is also held in the Chapel.[4] The badges have been refurbished recently.

King Edward's Horse was disbanded in 1924, leaving North Irish Horse as the sole cavalry militia regiment on the Army List. It was also the only militia regiment that had not been placed in Suspended Animation. This year saw the first reunion of the North Irish Horse, which was held in Thompson's Restaurant, Belfast on 28 February and at which it was agreed that a memorial to the Regiment's dead should be erected. A sum of £500 'had been allocated from certain funds for the purpose, and a committee had the matter in hands'.

The memorial took the form of a window in Belfast City Hall and was unveiled and dedicated on 30 April 1925, on which day the second regimental reunion was held. The Earl of Shaftesbury performed the unveiling while the Moderator of the Presbyterian Church, the Right Reverend R W Hamilton MA, dedicated it. A contemporary press cutting described the window as dignified and simple and possessing beauty in both its composition and colour scheme. To one side of the window a brass plate records the names of those men of the Regiment who died on service. A second memorial window, dedicated to those who fell in the Second World War, was installed beside this window and dedicated on 28 October 1962.

Brevet Colonel Maude retired in July 1925 and by the beginning of 1930 the Army List included only the names of the Honorary Colonel, the Earl of Shaftesbury, Honorary Chaplain, Reverend W A Stack of Tullycorbet in County Fermanagh, Major Sir Ronald D Ross Bt, MC, and Captain T W G J Hughes; all officers below the rank of lieutenant-colonel had to retire on their 50th birthday and this had removed a number of those who had been listed previously. Maude died on 31 August 1932. Retirement took Hughes off the list in April 1934, leaving the Regiment with only three men: Honorary Colonel, Honorary Chaplain and Major Ross. The latter remained the sole combatant officer until he, too, retired in 1938. Those years from 1934 to 1938 when Ross was the only combatant officer gave rise to a regimental soubriquet: The One Man Regiment.

That soubriquet occasioned an unusual tribute to the Regiment. In the early 1930s Moss Brothers produced an amusing 'Unofficial Army List', illustrated with line drawings and cartoons, a publication in which the North Irish Horse was one of the few non-regular units listed. The Regiment's entry, under 'Cavalry, Militia', included basic details of the uniform, the information that there was an Honorary Colonel and an Honorary Chaplain and a poem celebrating the Regiment's unique establishment.

Have ye ivver heard the story of that famous Oirish Rigimint,
The loikes of which was never seen from Larne to Donegal,
And they look so foine in green and whoite, though faith Oi'll give ye just a hint
There's not a Captain in it nor a Corporal at all:

There's a Colonel, and begorra, there's an honorary Chaplain, too,
That's there to tache the bhoys to be a credit to the corps,
And if they had some shquadrons, sure 'tis foine they'd look and illigint
With their green plumes all a-wavin' and the Colonel to the fore.

They never sound reveille, faith they haven't any thrumpeterr,
And there's divil a liftinint or a sargint in the force,
But when the bugle blows for the bhoys to go to war,
They'll be riding off to glory on the North Oirish Horse.

The status of the Regiment led to a question being tabled in the House of Commons on 14 July 1936 when Captain Balfour MP asked the Secretary of State for War if he would state the duties of the clergyman appearing in the Army List as the Honorary Chaplain of the North Irish Horse, 'How many Church Parades had been held in the last two years for Officers and ORs and whether the attendance had been voluntary or compulsory?' In his response the Secretary of State for War, Mr Duff Cooper, described the Regiment as being in a state of suspended animation with one officer only. That officer was Major Ross, who was then MP for Londonderry at Westminster. Balfour followed up with a question on the duties of that single officer to which Duff Cooper responded that he took his place on the Army List as being the sole member of this unit but did not give a true answer to the question posed, although that might not be considered unusual for a politician. It is quite possible that the original question was planted deliberately, perhaps by the Earl of Shaftesbury, to draw attention to the Regiment and keep its name in the public mind. If that is so, it certainly seems to have succeeded; three years later, the Regiment was recruiting once again.

As part of an accelerated programme of Army expansion in the wake of the 1938 Munich crisis, the Army's eight yeomanry armoured-car companies were increased to regimental strength while seven Territorial Army infantry battalions were converted to battalions of the Royal Tank Corps.[5] Five months later, in April 1939, the Royal Armoured Corps (RAC) was formed as the parent formation for all armoured units in the Army, including the Royal Tank Regiment. On 12 April all TA units were ordered to raise duplicate units while a further five Royal Tanks TA regiments were formed by splitting some recently raised tank battalions.

Munich had galvanised Britain's politicians who now realised that Hitler meant business; rapid expansion of the armed services was imperative. This enormous task must have appeared almost impossible in the case of the North Irish Horse, represented in the Army List only by the Earl of Shaftesbury, its Honorary Colonel, and the Honorary Chaplain. With no trained personnel the Regiment had to expand from being a 'one man regiment' to a fighting force of almost 700. That it did this was an achievement in itself; to have produced at the same time one of the RAC's finest fighting regiments of the Second World War was quite amazing. Much credit must be due to the fact that most of the Regiment's officers and men were volunteers whose pride in Ulster and in Ireland ensured that everyone was determined to make province and country a credit to the war effort.

On Thursday 4 May Prime Ministers Neville Chamberlain, in Westminster, and Lord Craigavon, in Stormont, announced the re-activation of the North Irish Horse as a Supplementary Reserve light tank unit.[6] In Great Britain the Supplementary Reserve – the old Special Reserve or Militia renamed – included individuals, or sub-units of specialist corps but Northern Ireland had full regiments. In addition to the North Irish Horse, there were three Royal Artillery regiments[7] and supporting sub-units. Legally, supplementary reservists were First Class Army Reservists who could be ordered to full-time service without a proclamation in parliament, as was needed for the TA.

The County Antrim Territorial Association, formed on 1 April 1937 to raise, organise and administer the first two territorial sub-units to be raised in Northern Ireland, was also given responsibility for the Supplementary Reserve and, in June 1939, the Association established a special sub-committee[8] to re-form the Horse. Local newspapers reported that the regiment would be commanded by Sir Basil Brooke Bt, CBE, MC, DL, MP, formerly of 10th Royal Hussars (Prince of Wales's Own), with Lord Erne, formerly Royal Horse Guards, as his second-in-command. Several potential officers were also named as was the fact that Armagh, Dungannon and Enniskillen would each host squadron headquarters and recruiting would begin shortly. Brooke's appointment was short-lived; pressure of public duties forced him to stand down; he was to become Northern Ireland's prime minister during the war. Major Sir Ronald Ross Bt, MC, MP, who had been the Regiment's single combatant officer for four years, was appointed to command in his stead.

NOTES

1   Grant served with C Squadron from August 1915 to March 1916 and was later with 1st North Irish Horse.
2   The 1914–15 Star was awarded to original members of D and F Squadrons while those who went to France with A and C Squadrons as members of the original BEF received the Mons Star.
3   He had commanded the Belfast Squadron from 1907 to 1914 and C Squadron from August to December 1914. Subsequently he was CO of the Westmorland and Cumberland Yeomanry (June 1916 to September 1917) as an acting lieutenant-colonel.
4   There is also a memorial to the Royal Irish Constabulary, one of only two

    memorials to that force in the British Isles. The second RIC memorial is also in London, in St Paul's Cathedral.

5   The Royal Tank Corps was later redesignated Royal Tank Regiment and its battalions became regiments.

6   Conscription was also introduced at this time but did not apply to Northern Ireland.

7   These were 8th (Belfast) and 9th (Londonderry) Heavy AA Regiments as well as 3rd (Ulster) Searchlight Regiment; all were part of 3rd (Ulster) AA Brigade.

8   Lord O'Neill, Lord Massereene and Ferrard DSO, Captain D C Lindsay and Captain A O' C Chichester MC.

CHAPTER IV

Once More unto the Breach

On 31 August 1939 the reconstitution of the North Irish Horse as a light armoured regiment (wheeled) was authorised by the War Office, and on 6 September authority to recruit was given while, two days later, it was decided to raise and equip the Regiment to war establishment. By Special Army Order dated 11 September the Regiment was transferred from the Cavalry of the Line to the RAC, the rapid expansion of which was causing a very serious shortage of instructors, especially as there were few former members with armoured vehicle experience. In the case of the North Irish Horse, lack of accommodation in Northern Ireland, which had had no active reserve forces units heretofore, led to a decision to enlist a select few to train as instructors thereby forming the nucleus of the new Regiment. Twelve recruits from the six counties plus the cities of Belfast and Londonderry were selected, all of whom survived the war. After twenty years in limbo the North Irish Horse was alive again.

Captain O C Smith-Bingham, 17th/21st Lancers, the newly appointed Adjutant, one staff sergeant and one sergeant from the Derbyshire Yeomanry arrived in Belfast on 9 September to be joined a day later by two East Riding Yeomanry corporals; both yeomanry regiments had been Royal Tank Corps armoured-car companies since 1920. The following were gazetted, as acting captains: Lord O'Neill, formerly 8th King's Own Royal Irish Hussars, C N L Stronge MC (later Sir Norman Stronge Bt)[1], R C Newton (formerly Royal Air Force) and A R Booth. Seven second-lieutenants were gazetted shortly afterwards. The Marquis of Ely was attached to 2nd Royal Sussex for signalling instruction and others were attached to 2nd South Wales Borderers at Londonderry's Ebrington Barracks for instruction in regimental duties. Also joining were Sergeants Fowler and Wells, 17th/21st Lancers, and Lieutenant (QM) M T McDonald MBE, 7th Royal Tanks, as Quartermaster. Twenty-nine recruits were undergoing training in Palace Barracks, Holywood, County Down.

The continuing huge expansion meant that everything for the Army was in short supply, including uniforms; recruits received only denim working overalls and a khaki side hat, *sans* cap badge, and civilian gasmasks in cardboard boxes. Even boots were in short supply. Twenty-four men went to the Armoured Fighting Vehicles School in Dorset wearing second-hand uniforms provided by the East Lancashires. In such circumstances personnel looked more like farmers or golfers than soldiers. This lack of a clear identity was indicated in a letter to the press from Colonel Ross, dated 4 October.

Sir,

Although general recruiting for the North Irish Horse (Royal Armoured Corps) cannot be opened until instructing staff has been assembled . . . a number of men have already been specially enlisted.

These men are naturally anxious to wear, as soon as possible, the badge of the Regiment so particularly associated with this Province. Owing to the Regiment being in abeyance since the last war, no regimental badges or buttons are immediately available. If any of my old comrades in the Regiment have in their possession any regimental badges or buttons which they could give for the use of the men in the new Regiment, I should be most grateful. Any such badges or buttons should be sent to:

North Irish Horse Regimental Headquarters,
Victoria Barracks,
Belfast.

At much the same time *The Daily Mirror* told its readers.

The North Irish Horse will begin recruiting on 10 November in Armagh, Fermanagh and Tyrone.
Fifty men, the nucleus of the unit, already have undergone a training course, and a further thirty to forty will start a similar course next week.

Newspaper advertisements sought 20- to 38-year-old volunteers; weekly pay ranged from fifteen to thirty-five shillings (75p to £1.75) for troopers and £2.10s.0d. (£2.50) to £3.15s.0d. (£3.75) for sergeants. Rates increased according to trade and qualifications and for married soldiers; a married man with one child would receive an additional £1.10s.0d. (£1.50). Recruits were enlisted at fortnightly intervals and, although the recruiting area had been defined as Armagh, Fermanagh and Tyrone, young men from all over Northern Ireland, as well as many from across the border, deluged recruiting offices, such was the Regiment's reputation. After careful screening, suitable applicants were interviewed by a senior officer. Many recruits were sons or nephews of former Horsemen with barristers, bankers, civil servants, newspapermen and solicitors among them. At least one in ten came from southern Ireland and there were two Canadians; all were volunteers. Such careful selection and screening paid rich dividends when the regiment arrived in Tunisia in 1943. A regiment of skill, character and courage was being created, maintaining the high standards set by Lord Shaftesbury in 1903.

On 21 October it was decided to concentrate the Regiment in Enniskillen and it moved by train to Enniskillen's Castle Barracks in early November; photographs of the departure appeared in the next morning's newspapers. In Enniskillen well-wishers cheered them on their way to their new quarters – publicity for further recruits was more important than secrecy in the 'phoney' war then underway. But those quarters were in direct contrast to the townspeople's warm welcome; cold, draughty and cramped conditions probably contributed to a tonsillitis epidemic that later swept the Regiment. With only ninety men guard duties were frequent, the guard being issued with rifles without ammunition; the fire picket received pick helves.

In mid-November the first corporals were promoted and fifty-three recruits arrived. To emphasise the shortage of equipment and uniforms, Second-Lieutenant J A Coey, a troop leader with C Squadron in France twenty-three years earlier, rejoined in London Scottish uniform, still bearing sergeant's chevrons. By month's end regimental strength was close to 200, thus reducing the frequency of guard and other duties. Lack of equipment led to the purchase of a private car and three civilian lorries for instructional use but this situation eased in late November when six Morris 15-cwt trucks, plus a water and wireless truck, a wireless van, a Humber Utility staff car and ten motorcycles arrived.

Fitness and sports played a big part in regimental life with rugby and soccer teams being fielded every Saturday. The rugby team's prowess was established first with the former Irish captain, Sergeant Sammy Walker, who had captained the British Lions, leading the way. Trooper Norman Hewitt, from the famous Ulster rugby family, Sergeants Bertie Sidebottom and Harry Irwin, and Trooper Desmond Patrick were other famous Ulster names to strengthen the regimental team, which was reinforced by a number of ex-Malone RFC players. Soccer was not forgotten, Troopers Joe Lester, Frank Peacock and Irish international Sergeant Willie Pollock ensuring that their sport was kept in the regimental limelight.

Since uniforms were still in short supply, newcomers wore civilian clothes for some time after joining but regimental spirit and camaraderie were much in evidence. Although recruits were eager to learn there was a 'language problem', caused by the inability of English PSIs[2] to attune to the nuances of Irish accents. Finding a gunnery class thirsty work, an English instructor asked Trooper Wilson from Ballymoney to 'Fetch me some char from the cookhouse.' Wilson quickly returned, not with the expected tea but a chair. Sergeant McLaughlin, another north Antrim man, reported his troop on parade one morning as 'Ten men present, two sick, two on fatigues, and yin mon absent, Sir.' The Squadron Sergeant-

Major, needless to say from England, was quite mystified by 'yin mon'. So as not to lose face at the time he later enquired from a friend the meaning of 'yin mon'.

The New Year of 1940 brought the first visit from the GOC Northern Ireland, Major-General R V Pollock CBE, DSO. A Galwegian, Pollock expressed pleasure at the progress made and high standards achieved and brought two pieces of good news: uniforms would be more freely available, and armoured cars would arrive in mid-January. The 'new' cars duly appeared; they were of Great War vintage. Already twenty-three years old, the Rolls Royce cars were crewed by three men, armed with a Vickers machine gun, weighed almost four tons, had a top speed of 45 mph, very poor brakes and were fitted with a No. 11 wireless set. Nonetheless, these were armoured cars and the Horse was an armoured-car regiment; there was now more sense of purpose.

On 18 January the Regiment formed into three sabre squadrons, plus HQ Squadron, to create a unit more recognisable as an armoured-car regiment. Captain Lord O'Neill continued as A Squadron Leader with Second-Lieutenant J P Herdman as his second-in-command; B Squadron was commanded by Captain Booth with Second-Lieutenant K G Pomeroy; C Squadron's Leader was Captain Sir Norman Stronge Bt, assisted by Captain Coey, now minus sergeant's chevrons and Captain Newton commanded HQ Squadron with the marquis of Ely as second-in-command. The North Irish Horse did not lack support from the nobility. Squadron locations were HQ Squadron at Castle Barracks; A Squadron at County Hall; B Squadron at the McArthur Hall and C Squadron at the Orange Hall.

With the new organisation and the arrival of armoured cars, the Regiment was able to start training for its primary role but equipment shortages continued; two airguns were purchased and a pellet range constructed for firing practice, while Bren guns were also borrowed. What wonderful propaganda this would have made for the enemy. However, it was not unusual in the rapidly expanding Army; 3rd (Ulster) AA Brigade's gunners were having to make do with a handful of guns and wooden practice rounds.

The training programme included driving, there being many fewer people who knew how to drive in 1939. Occasionally this could lead to comical incidents, such as that recalled by Walter Mitchell. Squadron Sergeant-Major Wells, urgently needing a temporary driver, approached a class learning the mysteries of the internal combustion engine. 'Anyone here a driver?' Silence descended on the group. The SSM repeated his request in more earthy terms. Trooper Johnny Wesley spoke up: 'I am, but not that kind of machine'. 'They're all the same. Report to Castle Barracks and Move!' Johnny Wesley mounted the truck at Castle Barracks and gazed in mystification at the vehicle; he had never driven one like this before. 'Now's your chance to learn,' bellowed the sergeant major. Somehow Wesley started the truck, drove towards the heavy wooden doors and, with a crash heard on the main street, came to rest amongst the wreckage. Fortunately, he was uninjured. Exasperated, Wells enquired: 'What sort of driver do you think you are?' 'I'm an engine driver on the Donegal railway!'

Dick Dawson recalled an incident during driving instruction when a sergeant took a soldier out and explained pedantically every dial and lever before allowing the man to start up. The soldier drove away smoothly, using the gears to perfection in a superb demonstration. An amazed sergeant asked foolishly, 'Have you driven before?' Trooper Casey, in a broad southern Irish accent, replied, 'Yes, Sergeant, I used to drive a London fire-engine'.

The training routine was interrupted on 24 May 1940 when an IRA bomb exploded in Enniskillen's main street, close to the Officers' Mess. The mobile column, and all armoured cars, was ordered to 'stand to'; the guard was issued hurriedly with five rounds per man and instructed not to use it under any circumstances. Thereafter everyone had to live in, with not less than fifty per cent of the personnel permanently in barracks. All guards were doubled and ammunition issued and loaded at guard mounting. (On one occasion an accidental discharge during the inspection of arms at County Hall was immediately followed by a similar report from Castle Barracks.) Foot parties had to consist of at least four armed men and no single vehicle movements were allowed but these restrictions were rescinded before the end of the month. However, a grim warning was issued on 27 May: 'The enemy may invade Northern Ireland by air or sea and attacks by lightly armed mobile troops assisted by the IRA and 5th Column may be expected.'

That warning coincided with the BEF's evacuation from France. Training was now geared to use of the rifle and infantry training. Road-blocks were constructed on all roads into Enniskillen; blockhouses were built and manned at night. Rumours abounded with telephonists from the local exchanges being the main source of information; one rumour suggested that the Regiment would soon move to Portrush.

Rumour became fact when orders were received to move to Portrush on 4 July 1940 and the move was complete four days later. The main party moved by rail but the journey took much longer than expected as the main line ran through County Donegal in neutral Éire. Since this had to be avoided, a circuitous route around much of Northern Ireland was followed. That sudden move to Portrush, on the north Antrim coast, upset many holidaymakers, whose hotel bookings were cancelled to accommodate soldiers. Regimental HQ was established at the Landsdowne Hotel overlooking the East Strand; A Squadron was based at the Windsor Hotel in Main Street. B Squadron was located in the Orange

Hall and C Squadron was based initially in the Station Cafe before moving to nearby Portstewart. Other hotels and guesthouses were used as extra billets but Trooper Alfie Roberts did best of all, being billeted in his own home. Daily mobile patrols were carried out along the coast to Magilligan Point. Army efficiency seemed to have excelled itself with pillboxes built in the nearby sandhills from sandbags that had been filled and brought all the way from Enniskillen. The shortage of mobile equipment was exacerbated by the fall of France, when so much material had been abandoned. Only a hundred men were required to man the regimental vehicles. As a temporary expedient, twenty-eight civilian lorries were requisitioned, still bearing owners' names and liveries while requisitioned private cars were used to create a communication troop in HQ Squadron. The latter were eventually replaced by Humberettes, classified as light armoured cars, the arrival of which allowed exercises to be carried out farther afield to develop map-reading skills.

Practising night convoy driving led to a story that acquired legendary status in the Regiment. C Squadron lined up for one such exercise and, since few vehicles were equipped with wireless, Major Coey ordered that, to maintain contact, the vehicles would follow his tail light, which he would switch on before moving off. Coey then returned briefly to Squadron HQ. Arriving back to start the exercise, he found not a single vehicle in sight. Apparently a wireless message had been received from RHQ to move off and C Squadron followed what they thought was the squadron leader's tail light. However, the light belonged to a bread van, the driver of which did not stop until he got home to Bushmills. Next day Major Coey addressed C Squadron and told them that 'The trouble with you fellows is that you'd follow a red light to hell!'

By early 1941 squadron exercises over two–four days were quite commonplace and boredom was creeping in. At the end of one such exercise A Squadron's Humberettes were first home to Portrush, which upset Robin Griffith, an armoured-car troop leader. His drivers were Stanley Jackson from Strabane, George Dunn from Dublin and George Beattie, who was the oldest, with First World War ribbons, and an unwilling accomplice in his juniors' pranks. They schemed for the armoured cars to close up on the Humberettes on the long stretch leading downhill into Portrush, build up an unstoppable speed and shoot past the unsuspecting Humberettes – highly dangerous but great fun for the young bloods. Unfortunately for them, Lord O'Neill found out about this; thereafter, each troop took turns to arrive home first.

In one artful exercise a squadron would act as the 'fox' and be sent about thirty miles away while the other two tried to prevent the 'fox' returning to base. As well as improving map-reading, this also advanced wireless communications. Training started to become more professional and warlike on 19 April when A Squadron moved to Ballykinlar in County

Down to convert to Valentine tanks; the remainder of the Regiment followed in July. Meanwhile many NCOs and men were attending gunnery courses at Lulworth in Dorset, an aspect of armoured training that needed improvement.

The North Irish Horse were pleased to be moving on to train for a more effective role. Ballykinlar was a complete contrast to Enniskillen and Portrush, with the camp in the country and hardly a local person in sight. Perhaps this helped to stiffen the Regiment from the easier and more pleasant mode of life. For the first time since annual training in 1914, the complete Regiment was accommodated together. By coincidence, that earlier occasion had been at Lord Annesley's Donard demesne at nearby Newcastle. The Regiment occupied a recently erected Nissen hut camp, west of the modern Hore-Belisha Abercorn Barracks and within easy walking distance of Miss Sandes' Soldiers' Home.[3] 'Liberty trucks', 3-ton lorries, were laid on in the evenings for off-duty soldiers, due to the camp's remote location.

In early 1941 the War Office had announced the conversion of the North Irish Horse to an armoured regiment. A shortage of Cruiser tanks meant that the Regiment was issued with Valentines with A Squadron receiving their first tanks on arrival at Ballykinlar. In July the remainder of the Regiment joined A Squadron who claimed that all the tanks were 'runners' which they could crew effectively.

The Regiment's Valentines were 'tired' Mk 1s, powered by 135 hp AEC petrol engines, with a two-man turret mounting a good co-axial machine gun and the 2-pounder. Since the Valentine required a three-man crew, as did the armoured cars, personnel remained together, although drivers had to be trained to handle the much larger and more cumbersome vehicles. The No. 11 wireless set was still in use, but operators now had to learn gunnery as well. Commanders had to deal with the tank's size and capability; due to the driver's very limited field of vision, commander/driver cooperation was essential. The driver sat in a very cramped space at the centre front and steered with two levers. Tracks broke frequently and were slow and difficult to mend, although later models overcame this problem. Initial driving instruction was carried out on flat and relatively firm ground at the back of the dunes before moving on to the roads, which became noticeably wider. Advanced driving was attempted in the sandhills and the foothills of the Mournes, but conditions were bad. The gunner/wireless operator sat on the left of the turret with the commander on the right. At the rear of the turret was the wireless set.

A Squadron welcomed the rest of the Regiment. Whilst on detachment they had built a strong sense of self-reliance and unity, which would stand them in good stead in Tunisia and Italy, where squadrons fought and lived on their own for long periods. B and C Squadrons immediately started individual training, whilst A Squadron moved on to squadron training, limited almost entirely to roads because of the unsuitability of the country, where tanks frequently became bogged down and were difficult to recover. The squadron also laid on a demonstration for the Brigadier General Staff of III Corps and a number of other staff officers which consisted of building a ramp at Newcastle railway station and driving the tanks up the ramp onto the flat trucks of a waiting train where they were shackled down.

Between 4 and 10 August a composite squadron under Captain Ketchell took part in Exercise SUMMIT in the Mournes. This was of little tactical use as the Valentines bogged down regularly, but it was a valuable exercise in recovery work. Sergeant Harry Irwin's tank sank to turret level when ordered off a hillside track by an umpire and recovery took forty-eight hours. The second exercise did not take place until September when arable land could be used with much better results.

HQ Squadron, which was not so heavily involved in training for the new role, sent some men to assist with the harvest. Soldiers were happy to do this, as were the local farmers who had extra help at minimal cost. Some farmers responded better than others. Mary Ann McSwiggan recognised a bargain when she saw one, and treated the troops very well. Paddy Smith also owned a pub; many of those sent to help him were also his customers, and he did not forget this 'when day was done'. One lance-corporal recalled with amusement his 'employer' observing that the lance-corporal's stripe had not been earned for tying corn.

On 18 October the Regiment left Ballykinlar to move 'overseas', to Westbury, a small market town, on Salisbury Plain in Wiltshire. RHQ was established in the Town Hall with B Squadron in the nearby village of Upton Scudamore. Initially residents were aghast on learning that an Irish regiment was in their midst as some rumbustious Irish labourers had been engaged on war construction work nearby. However, good relations were soon established, and the inevitable marriages took place, notably Sammy Walker and Trooper George McDowell of C Squadron who wed local girls. The latter settled in Westbury after the war.

Only six days after their arrival the Regiment was inspected by Major-General Sir Oliver Leese Bt, CBE, DSO, commanding the newly formed Guards Armoured Division. Imagination quickly linked the inspection with the possibility of joining this new division. This proved to be pure speculation, although the North Irish Horse served under Leese as commander of Eighth Army in Italy in 1944. The uncanny 'nose' of an inspecting officer to find the Achilles' heel appeared again on this occasion. Inspecting a Valentine, General Leese checked the fire extinguisher, only to find it full of petrol rather than Pyrene fluid. The crew had discovered Pyrene to be good for removing stains from uniforms while the petrol-filled extinguisher was an excellent tool for removing grease and hard-packed oil from inaccessible engine parts. Leese was not impressed.

RHQ and HQ Squadrons moved to Rood Ashton Hall, some three miles to the north, a large country manor set in extensive, heavily wooded demesne, with a mile-long drive and its own church. B Squadron took over HQ billets, whilst part of A Squadron took over a large country house, purported to have been used by Hanging Judge Jeffries while dispensing justice in that area. On 25 November Queen Mary, who had taken up wartime residence at Badminton, inspected the Regiment before taking tea at Rood Ashton Hall. The inter-communication troop commanded by Lieutenant T M Batchen, a Dubliner, gave a demonstration of armoured mobility, using the woods to great effect.

In wartime England church bells were to be rung only for a German invasion. Some happy Horsemen returning from Trowbridge decided to ring the bells of the Rood Ashton estate church in a noisy and uncoordinated way, before creeping unchallenged to their huts. The guard commander took no action, rightly assuming it to be a false alarm. However, Southern Command, lacking local knowledge, sprang into action and a massive search for German parachutists began. The North Irish Horse slept. Next morning there was uproar; generals, brigadiers and Special Branch descended upon Rood Ashton. Colonel Dawnay was involved and harsh words flew in all directions. The CO's anger was aroused when the Regiment was described as a bunch of Irish rebels. As a result, heads rolled from field officers downwards, and the price had to be paid by all. The culprits were never discovered. Their names were the war's best kept secret. Since this incident made it clear that the anti-invasion plans were not as effective as had been thought, these were modified but thankfully never used for their correct intention.

At Westbury the Regiment learnt that it would convert to the Churchill I-tank Mk IV to become an infantry tank regiment. Drivers and wireless-operators went on appropriate courses to the RAC schools at Bovington in Dorset and North Irish Horse came under command of 34 Army Tank Brigade, commanded by Brigadier J N Tetley, of the famous Yorkshire brewing family, a TA officer. North Irish Horse, the senior regiment in the new brigade, would be the only cavalry regiment to fight as a Churchill unit throughout the war. The brigade's other regiments were 147 RAC (10th Hampshires) and 153 RAC (8th Essex). Tanks had individual markings consisting of regimental, squadron and troop signs, plus names of Irish towns and villages, viz. A Squadron, *Ardmore* and *Antrim*, B Squadron, *Blackrock*, C Squadron, *Castlederg*; HQ Squadron used names beginning with the letter D.

The stay at Westbury ended on 28 January 1942 with a move to Ogborne St George, twenty-five miles to the north-west and a modern, brick-built army camp that backed onto the Downs to provide a superb training area. This camp included a spacious hall, which served for concerts, dances and church services as occasion demanded, and a dining hall large enough to accommodate the entire Regiment at one sitting. Superb workshops allowed fitters to work under the best conditions possible, with a convenient tank park close by. The parade ground could take the entire Regiment quite comfortably.

The arrival of Churchill Mk Is caused an immediate problem as this tank required a five-man crew, necessitating a large increase in fighting personnel. About one hundred reinforcements were posted from all parts of England and quickly absorbed. Sixty years on, an English Branch of the Regimental Association flourishes still. The 40-ton Churchill tank seemed a veritable monster. Thickly armoured where it mattered, it had two 75-gallon fuel tanks, plus an auxiliary 32½-gallon-tank, held on by two quick-release straps and intended merely for use on approach marches. The Churchill was very thirsty, as crews knew only too well when carrying 4-gallon petrol cans to refill one.

The crew included commander, wireless-operator/loader, gunner, driver and co-driver. At first the armament consisted of the ludicrous 2-pounder gun, mounted co-axially in the turret with the Besa medium machine gun but later replaced by the 6-pounder. A further, even later, improvement was the 75mm gun and, in some cases, the 95mm howitzer. The 75mm could be used as an artillery piece for indirect fire or, with armour-piercing (AP) shells, against enemy tanks. A second Besa was mounted in the hull for forward firing by the co-driver. A major improvement was the replacement of the No. 11 wireless set by the No. 19 set, a radio receiver/transmitter set designed by Pye Radio Works at Cambridge for use with armoured vehicles. The No. 19 set included three systems: the A-set for regimental use, the B-set for short-range communication (visual) and the intercommunication system for use between the tank crew. Used correctly, the set was a good one.

Crew duties are self-explanatory: driver and co-driver worked closely on maintaining the tank; the co-driver often helped out with driving on approach marches and, since each crew had to be self-sufficient, was often the cook as well. The wireless operator doubled as loader for the main gun, having to be very wary of the recoil in such a confined space; its speed and power could remove an arm. The commander had to be the driver's eyes, direct the gunner on targets and range-find them, as well as carrying out the tactical plan. Stowage was always an important task, making best use of the confined space. Larger crews meant much extra training, most of it on the nearby Downs. On 26 February the tanks, with the necessary administrative personnel, moved to Linney Head ranges at Castlemartin in Pembrokeshire to fire the 2-pounders. Although Linney Head was wet and cold this did not prevent the gunnery practice being carried out in near war-like conditions.

The Reconnaissance Troop Humberettes were replaced by Daimler scout cars, known as Dingos, small, low, fast, purpose-designed vehicles with some armour plating. A rear-mounted engine with a fluid flywheel presented a constant servicing headache but the five-speed gearbox allowed the vehicle to travel as fast in reverse as forwards. The Dingo had good cross-country performance and was equipped with a Bren gun while some carried the now-universal No. 19 wireless set. Second-Lieutenant P Francis became Recce Troop Leader.

Supplies were the responsibility of the two echelons. A – the forward – Echelon's main task was to bring forward supplies of petrol in 4-gallon containers, very heavy to carry to the tanks, ammunition for both machine guns and main armament, rations, water and mail. A Echelon linked up with the much larger B – rear – Echelon, which carried extensive supplies of all main requirements. B Echelon was also responsible for bringing forward, daily, the Regiment's many requirements from supply points well behind the front line. A Echelon's task of carrying supplies of petrol and ammunition to the front line, often under fire, could be quite unpleasant.

The following story from Lyle Craig illustrates some of the difficulties encountered and the pitfalls that could take place.

Sergeant Major Fowler was charged with . . . taking supplies out to the tanks on the Downs late one evening. Two problems faced him, to arrive at the correct rendezvous with all his trucks. It sounds easy, BUT, to make sure all his trucks stayed with him, he placed John McXxxxx from North Antrim in the back of his own truck, with instructions to bang on the roof of his truck if the convoy stopped or fell behind. After about twenty minutes not a sound from his man in the back, Mr Fowler decided to stop and see if all was well. Not a truck in sight! He went to the back of the truck expecting to find his man asleep. The man was wide awake.

'Why didn't you let me know when the convoy stopped?'

'But, sir, it never started.'

The new infantry tank regiment role was taken a step further when B and C Squadrons went to Devon for training with infantry. B Squadron was attached to 9th Royal Warwicks in 61st Division and C Squadron to 103 Marine Brigade near Exmouth where their arrival did not endear them to the local community; driving from the railway station to the Marines' camp, the tank tracks tore up all the newly-laid 'cat's eyes'. Night driving in wartime was difficult at the best of times as headlights had shields placed over them, which allowed only limited light to shine on the road, to deter detection from the air. The 'cat's eyes' were an enormous help. Both squadrons found this spell, the first time they had been completely separated from the Regiment, a welcome break from daily training on familiar ground. Training and weather were both better at Perranporth but C Squadron committed another gaffe when, during an approach march on a very dark night, they committed the unforgivable sin of straying across a golf course. Daylight revealed a few churned fairways.

Another move took place in June, this time to Didlington in Norfolk for II Corps' Exercise SCORPION, which revealed a whole new dimension in organisation and administration, plus the horrors of their implementation. On a lower plane a new lesson was learned; petrol cookers should not be used for a 'brew up' in railway carriages. As a result of this being tried, one carriage was completely destroyed by fire. Fortunately, the train was stationary and the fire did not spread but the coach was so badly damaged that it had to be uncoupled. Although there were no casualties, the loss of much personal kit proved good training for the Quartermaster's department.

One exercise objective was the dispersal of vehicles and their camouflage against air attack, which was carried out effectively, except for the Light Aid Detachment (LAD). As Lord O'Neill discovered, fitters were always a law unto themselves. Mail had been delivered and, standing in the middle of a clearing, Alex Holmes held the *Banbridge Chronicle* in his outstretched arms reading aloud items of interest to an avid group of listeners. Lord O'Neill appeared and did not like what he saw: 'The Lord was not pleased, indeed he was exceeding wrath.' Another lesson had been learned, at no cost, save loss of face on one hand and temper on the other.

To add realism, and keep pressure on the troops twenty-four hours a day, a Junior Leaders' Regiment was employed to make nightly attacks. Hand-picked and enthusiastic young men, they had many successes but when they attacked the Recce Troop, under Sergeant Walford, they found them well on their toes. However, other squadrons had been caught napping, literally.

Wartime service life included long periods of inactivity to counter which a directive was laid down to arrange discussion groups. Many subjects were explored, including the conduct of Belfast shipyard workers, who downed tools every morning and evening to watch and jeer at the arrivals and departures of ferries packed with troops, going or returning from leave.

At Didlington the Regiment was back to Nissen huts, in marked contrast to Ogborne St George, in a camp widely dispersed among the thick forests that were a feature of the flat, bleak countryside. On arrival there was an acute shortage of beer in the local hostelries; landlords displayed notices reading 'RCs only', which dismayed a number of staunch Protestants. While they remained thirsty, their feelings were somewhat appeased on learning that the reference was to 'regular customers only'. So isolated and unattractive was the camp that any excuse to get away was welcomed. A six-day working week was instigated with Saturdays and Sundays becoming normal working days. One twenty-four-hours off-duty period was allowed each week, with Sunday afternoons set aside for regimental route marches, which increased steadily in length.

Excitement mounted at the end of June when it was learned that full mobilisation had to be completed by 28 July. Everything started to move quickly and the Regiment was transferred to 1st (Mixed) Division, which had served as an infantry division in France and, subsequently, in a home defence role. It was now one of the new 'mixed' divisions, a concept devised to provide an integrated infantry and tank force. The idea did not work in practice; although 4th Division served as such in the Tunisian campaign it was found that the formation lacked the necessary reserve provided by the third infantry brigade and the concept was abandoned.

Most 2-pounder-armed Churchill Mk Is had been replaced by Mk IIIs with the 6-pounder in a distinctive welded turret. To bring the Regiment up to strength, thirty-four more men were drafted in, including some conscripts who also experienced the problem encountered with English instructors in the early days in Northern Ireland; an inability to understand Ulster dialects. One man, later to become an enthusiastic and useful member of the Regiment, applied for a transfer to another RAC regiment, claiming that he could not understand a word that was said.

On Tuesday 28 July an advance party of twenty tanks from B and C Squadrons, plus some other vehicles and crews, left for the combined training centre at Castle Toward, near Dunoon on the Firth of Clyde, to train crews in driving on and off landing craft. The tedium of a twenty-hour train journey was relieved by the splendid service of the WVS, who provided tea and sandwiches at the longer halts at larger stations. These ladies, with other voluntary organisations, did wonderful work in the war, which was much appreciated by the Forces. Eventually the train arrived at Wemyss Bay, where the tanks were unloaded, driven across the hard and on board the landing craft, for the short journey across the firth.

The loading of tanks onto LCTs was quite a thrilling task, especially the first time. As the tank went up the ramp the bows dipped under the weight, then the gentle slope increased rapidly as the tank moved inboard and weight transferred aft. The bows rose rapidly, causing the incline to level off, and the final part of the journey was downhill. Such a tight fit was the Churchill on these craft that the air louvres on each side had to be removed before loading the tank.

The next few days were spent waterproofing the tanks as they would encounter depths greater than the normal forty inches of water through which they could wade. This task completed, C Squadron spent a week practising loading the tanks onto LCTs. The tanks had to be reversed on.

At first, loading was done on gentle sloping, sheltered beaches, gradually moving onto steeper and more open ones. Finally, there was loading in the dark, followed by a night at sea, a dawn landing and advance inland for the whole squadron. A Squadron followed C, but B Squadron's training was cancelled at the last minute.

This interlude was much enjoyed, despite atrocious weather and mud. Liberty trucks were available for off-duty personnel and some good times enjoyed in Dunoon, which was packed with holidaymakers. Scottish hospitality abounded and it was noticed that more and better food was available than in England. The splendid views reminded the men very much of Ulster. Another novel feature was the MacBrayne steamers, the normal form of transport between the little ports, and to Rothesay and the Isle of Bute.

Following the return from Scotland there was a hectic training programme of field firing and anti-aircraft practice at Stiffkey on the Norfolk coast, and then, farther along the coast at Brancaster, practice with the anti-tank rifle and Bren gun. About this time the Dieppe raid took place and the Churchill was used in action for the first time. Although the raid was unsuccessful, many valuable lessons were learned about the tank. August's closing days were devoted to individual tests in gunnery, map-reading, wireless, gas and first aid. Great credit was due to the instructors for the very high standard attained at these tests.

On 6 September the North Irish Horse transferred from 34 to 25 Army Tank Brigade, in 43rd (Wessex) Infantry Division, replacing 11th Royal Tanks. The other two regiments in 25 Brigade were 51st Royal Tank Regiment (formerly 7th Leeds Rifles) and 142nd Regiment, Royal Armoured Corps (142 RAC), formerly 7th Suffolks.[4] The brigade was commanded by Brigadier R H Maxwell, who had commanded 7th Suffolks during conversion to Churchills and re-badging as 142 RAC in November 1941.

Stanford, not far from Didlington, saw a series of infantry cooperation exercises in September which were much more realistic than anything heretofore; live ammunition was used for the first time. Another hint that the long training period was nearing its end with the 'real thing' nigh came when eighty men joined as first-line reinforcements to provide battle casualty replacements. Officer strength was increased to war establishment with the arrival of seven newly commissioned troop leaders, including three former North Irish Horse men, Second-Lieutenants J Maxwell, R E Perioli and H E Irwin. Harry Irwin had been one of the original men at Holywood.

On 24 September the Regiment changed to its new war establishment with a full complement of Churchill Mk IIIs and all-new ancillary vehicles. A further 'work-up' phase took place when the squadrons moved to Minehead in Somerset for a fortnight's firing with their main weapons. By now Recce troop had re-equipped with tracked carriers, increasing their cross-country performance; only four of the ten carriers were equipped with wireless sets. The carriers could also be used in the replenishment chain; in country unsuitable for the wheeled echelon vehicles, carriers could deliver petrol and ammunition.

News of Eighth Army's offensive and the victory at El Alamein was a real morale booster; the Regiment and the entire nation followed Eighth Army's advance with great enthusiasm. Since Dunkirk a huge re-armament programme had been carried out and the Battle of Britain had been won in the air, but otherwise little progress had been made against the Germans, whose star was in the ascendant. That was now changing. Morale was further raised by news of Operation TORCH, the Anglo-American landings in Morocco and Algeria on 8 November 1942.

Next day North Irish Horse set out on its final exercise in Britain and, on its return, preparations began for the move to their last camp in England. This move proved anti-climactic. The Regiment assumed that four months' intensive training was the prelude to active service. Instead, they moved to Clavering Hall outside Wickham Market in Suffolk on 16 November. On the 17th Captain Griffith, with 110 men, left to help farmers harvest their sugar beet crop.

Clavering Hall proved much more compact with better accommodation than at Didlington. Wickham Market is ten miles inland from the coast, and about the same distance north of Ipswich. With the tempo of training not so intense, nightly runs into Ipswich were allowed for off-duty personnel. After the initial shock of not going on active service, the troops engaged on beet pulling felt quite pleased with their contribution to the war effort; they felt that they had really accomplished something, as well as being well rewarded by the farmers. Sugar cane had to be imported, taking up valuable space in ships which could be put to better use. The first twenty-seven days of December passed quietly as the agricultural work parties returned.

At Wickham Market, Major Stratton assumed command of HQ Squadron and was succeeded as Adjutant by Captain Mackean. Christmas leave was given in the normal way, trying to allow as many men as possible to visit home. Those on early leave completed their allotted time at home, but those on late leave were not so lucky and were recalled by telegram as the result of a warning order for overseas' service on 28 December. With Colonel Dawnay on leave at home in Waterford and the second-in-command, Major Lord O'Neill at Senior Officers' School, Major Rew put all the necessary arrangements in hand. The Regiment was at full strength having been put on twenty-eight days' notice of mobilisation in June.

A message from the Prime Minister to the Secretary for War, Minister of War Transport and the CIGS, dated 31 December 1942, read:

I am not satisfied with the dates given for sending the brigade of Churchill tanks to Tunis. A strenuous effort must be made with full battle urgency to have this brigade embarked complete in the convoy which leaves about January 17. If the Ministry of War Transport can produce the ships, a very grave responsibility will fall upon the War Office if they are not able to load this brigade, which has already once been mobilised, in time.

This left no one in any doubt of the urgency of the situation. Intense activity followed, with round-the-clock packing of stores, and 3-tonners were loaded as the packed stores became available while tanks were stowed with personal equipment and comforts tucked away carefully inside. Hatches were greased and all maintenance completed. There were not enough hours in the day to carry out the tremendous job of sending a regiment overseas.

The first train carrying tanks and carriers left on 4 January, followed by trains on successive days, bound for Birkenhead, Cardiff and Swansea. B Echelon's vehicles moved in separate convoys on 5 and 6 January to the South Wales ports. The move was completed; the Regiment had done a magnificent job to get everything away in such a short time.

Most soldiers were granted a short embarkation leave of six days including travelling time, although men from southern Ireland were allowed an extra day for travel. With security of the utmost importance, each man had to sign a declaration not to disclose that he was on embarkation leave. Having had Christmas leave so recently might arouse some suspicion, so they were to say that they had been awarded the extra leave as a reward for harvesting the sugar beet crop so quickly.

The Regiment left Wickham Market in great secrecy by troop train on the evening of 20 January. Tanks had been sheeted down for the rail journey and were re-sheeted immediately on arrival at the docks. Another security measure was the removal of all regimental badges from uniforms; badge-less side caps replaced berets. Next morning, the train reached Liverpool and the Regiment de-trained on the dockside station, well away from the public gaze. Of 25 Army Tank Brigade's other regiments, 51st Royal Tanks left Liverpool on 19 January and arrived in Bone on 2 February while 142 RAC sailed from Gourock on 24 January, arriving at Algiers on 1 February.

For many the next fortnight seemed the longest of their lives. The seemingly never-ending sea journey to an unknown destination in a rolling ship, mostly spent in hammocks, suffering from seasickness, was enough to make men wish never to leave dry land again. Embarking 770 men from the North Irish Horse aboard HMT *Duchess of York* was a long and dreary business with troops guided along endless passages and down steep companionways, leading to confusion as soon as individuals later tried to find their way about. Besides the North Irish Horse, who formed the majority of the 'passengers', also on board were the headquarters personnel of 25 Army Tank Brigade and some Canadians, as well as an ENSA party of Polish ballet dancers.

After casting off, the ship lay in the Mersey for a day, when she moved northwards to join a fast convoy. The *Duchess* was stripped of all luxury accommodation to make as much room as possible. Hammocks were slung and the uncomfortable journey began. The ship was almost flat bottomed to allow for her peacetime trade on the St Lawrence river. Once in the Atlantic she pitched and rolled horribly. The stench of vomit and the lack of air below decks made the sleeping quarters very uncomfortable. Bad seasickness left the men with the feeling that land could not come too soon. Food, for those well enough to eat, was superior to army rations except for the bread, which later in the voyage became infected by weevils. The dining room had been converted to self-service and meals were served round the clock on a rota basis.

Sunday 24 January saw *Duchess of York* meet up with the convoy and escort force, which included an aircraft carrier. As the convoy passed the coast of Northern Ireland many familiar places could be recognised, such as Rathlin Island, Whitepark Bay and Inishowen Head. Memories came flooding back of the war's early days and the re-forming of the Regiment. Men sang with great feeling as their homeland gradually faded into the distance. Two men could see their homes as they passed along the coast. Many thoughts went through the minds of the soldiers: where were they going? would they ever see their beloved Ulster again?

The incredibly boring journey passed without any enemy interference, but the weather was very bad in the Atlantic so that men could rarely get on deck for exercise. Incessant rolling and pitching made life a nightmare. If they did get on deck visibility was so poor that the nearest ship could hardly be seen. As was customary with wartime convoys they went far out into the Atlantic to avoid the dreaded U-boats before turning south. At last the 'Drunken Duchess', as she was nicknamed, headed east when the convoy split in two, the other half heading south round the Cape. Soon the lights of Gibraltar were spotted and before long they were sailing through the narrow straits. Street lights were visible on the Rock and on the North African coast and cars could be seen driving along the roads with full headlights, a sight unknown at home since 1939, when black-out was enforced. They passed through the straits at 2.20am on Sunday 31 January, now knowing that their destination was North Africa.

Next day some beautiful views could be seen; Spain's snow-capped Sierra Nevada mountains glistened in the sunlight, while the grim outline of the Atlas mountains dominated the African vista. The sea was now calm to the relief of the men who had suffered debilitating seasickness.

Then came the official announcement: the troops would land at Algiers next day and the North Irish Horse would have to march seventeen miles to camp. At last they knew something.

Algiers was a spectacular sight, bounded by the lighthouse and the Cap du Nord to the west, and to the east by the green ribbon of Cap Matifou, where orange groves and palm trees contrasted with white, red-roofed bungalows. As soon as the ship anchored, it was surrounded by a bevy of small craft, manned by Arabs offering fruit and other delicacies for sale. Trade was carried on with much shouting and merriment, payment being made in local currency following a pay parade when francs were issued.

As *Duchess of York* weighed anchor to move alongside the quay for disembarkation, the evidence of German bombing was clear to see, the harbour being littered with the masts of sunken ships. By 3.30pm the regiment was clear of the ship and at 4.45 the long march began. *Duchess of York* was sunk on a subsequent voyage to North Africa; it happened close to the coast and the ship went down slowly, allowing nearly all aboard to be rescued.

The cobbled streets of Algiers proved unpleasant for feet for the first few miles. However, the Regiment had not come all this way to be defeated by a few cobblestones. They persevered, and on reaching the outskirts of the town the surface improved somewhat. All the good work of route marches in England was negated by the seasickness and lack of exercise on board ship. Gradually the miles passed and the march, aided by whistling and singing, was completed shortly before 10pm. All were glad to bed down in wine vat buildings with stone floors for the first night on foreign soil.

During the years of preparation the Regiment had undergone many changes, not least of which was the transformation to an army tank regiment. Effective instructors and officers had guided it and, by the time of the move to Tunisia, the latter included many original members of the Regiment who had been commissioned. There had been changes in command; Sir Ronald Ross, who had succeeded Sir Basil Brooke, was admitted to hospital and had to relinquish command; on 24 January 1940 the Earl of Erne assumed temporary command, handing over to Major J A L Powell, 4th Queen's Own Hussars, who was appointed commanding officer and promoted Lieutenant-Colonel. On 12 April the Earl of Erne departed on attachment to 12th Royal Lancers, now in France with the British Expeditionary Force[5] while Captain Sir Norman Stronge Bt relinquished his commission at about this time due to ill health.

In early May Second-Lieutenant R D Morton, whose father had been born and lived in County Tipperary, joined. Bob went through the whole war with the North Irish Horse and was a most popular member. He had served with the Inns of Court Regiment,[6] a London TA unit, before the war, attended the first Officer Cadet Training Unit (OCTU) at Sandhurst and was the first volunteer officer to join the Regiment from OCTU. June saw the first of the earliest recruits, now senior NCOs, posted to OCTU from which they would return as troop leaders in December. Some officers who would become famous for their exploits in North Africa and Italy joined as second-lieutenants, including W H Ketchell, P Welch, G P Russell and R J Griffith, all of whom had been at OCTU at Blackdown and later became squadron leaders.

At the end of June another southern Irishman arrived. Major David Dawnay, destined to become a regimental legend, had served in France with 10th Royal Hussars and arrived at Enniskillen as second-in-command. From an old County Waterford family, Dawnay was married to Lady Katherine Beresford, daughter of the marquis of Waterford, who had raised the South of Ireland Imperial Yeomanry. Lady Katherine did splendid work for the Regiment during and after the war, helping dependants of those who had lost their lives. Both David Dawnay's and Lord O'Neill's fathers had been killed in action on the same day, 6 November 1914, whilst serving together in France, in 2nd Life Guards. Lord O'Neill was to lose his own life in action with the North Irish Horse.

The stories of two officers who joined the North Irish Horse are a little out of the ordinary. Second-Lieutenant W H Mackean joined from 525th Coast Regiment, Royal Artillery. Wanting more active service than might be found in a coastal defence unit, he had to resign his TA commission and obtain a Supplementary Reserve commission before his transfer could be finalised. Mackean had made a little bit of history in September 1939 when he gained the distinction of firing what was possibly the first shot of the war, when a ship coming into Belfast harbour failed to observe the correct recognition procedure and he was ordered to fire a round across its bows. That round was certainly the first fired by the British Army.

Captain R H Bowring first met the Regiment at Ballykinlar as a Staff Captain (Agriculture) who came over to encourage a 'Dig for Victory' campaign. Impressed with what he saw, in common with Lieutenant Mackean, he felt he could better aid the war effort with the North Irish Horse. Before the war Dick Bowring had been a troop leader in the Duke of Lancaster's Own Yeomanry whose role on mobilisation had been to be ready to ride into Manchester with 650 horses and provide aid for the civil power, following the expected air raids. When his unit was converted to 77th Medium Regiment, Royal Artillery in 1940, Captain Bowring did not like what he saw; hence his job in Northern Ireland. He also had to resign his TA commission and transfer to the Supplementary Reserve.

Another arrival at this time was Second-Lieutenant W R Hern, a great horseman who, after the war linked up with another Horse officer, Mike Pope, as his assistant trainer but later launched out on his own. Success followed success; he trained winners of all the classic races and became the Queen's trainer. In July Captain J Rew, 16th/5th Lancers, joined as

Adjutant in succession to Captain Smith-Bingham while four more candidates went to OCTU and ten soldiers were transferred to the infantry, having been found unsuitable for the RAC. Among newly commissioned officers to arrive was Second-Lieutenant P M B (Peter) Pope whose two brothers were later to join him. December saw the arrival of ten new officers from OCTU. Five were returning, namely R S Hutton, R S H Sidebottom, T M Batchen, E S Robinson and S Walker. Newcomers included C M Thomas, P C M Sinclair and W G Lavery. Soon after this, another famous name was to join as chaplain, the Reverend E M Hughes, a native Welsh speaker.

When Major Dawnay was promoted and posted to command 2nd Battalion Reconnaissance Corps, Major Lord O'Neill became second-in-command. Padre Elwyn Hughes was posted to 53rd (Welsh) Divisional Battle School. Padre Hughes had earned the respect and admiration of all ranks. His Celtic background provided an insight to the vagary of the Ulster character. A popular member of the Officers' Mess, and a welcome visitor to the Sergeants' Mess, he had built up a wonderful rapport with the men and was sadly missed.

Early in November Colonel Powell was posted to command 2nd Battalion Reconnaissance Corps, allowing David Dawnay to return to his beloved North Irish Horse where he learned that Padre Hughes had been posted away and applied immediately for his return. This was refused. Nothing daunted, Dawnay re-applied direct to the Corps Commander but was admonished for improper procedure, and received another refusal. There was great delight, therefore, when the telephone rang in the orderly room one afternoon in mid-January announcing Padre Hughes' request for transport to collect him from the station, at which he had just arrived, to rejoin the Regiment. He served with and encouraged the North Irish Horse for the remainder of the war. 'D. D.', as the CO was universally known, was quite determined and, with the uncompromising support of the Colonel of the Regiment, succeeded in obtaining the very best.

In wartime conditions all letters had to be censored, from which it became evident that the soldiers were unhappy about the small number of Irish officers serving with the North Irish Horse. After all it was an Irish regiment; some rude comments were also made about the ability of some English officers. As a result of this, or was it coincidence? five troop leaders were posted out.

Further senior changes within the Regiment included the Quarter-master, Lieutenant (QM) McDonald MBE, being posted to the War Office and succeeded by Lieutenant (QM) F Marks, 23rd Hussars. Fourteen new officers posted in from OCTUs included Second-Lieutenants J J H Pyl, D R King and R B M King (no relationship), who became Sir Richard in 1976. R B M King was later joined by his brother B E S King. All three Kings were awarded the Military Cross while serving with the Regiment in Italy. Also arriving was Second-Lieutenant M B (Mike) Pope to join his brother P M B (Peter), who had already been with the Regiment for seven months. However, Peter was injured during Exercise LIMPET and did not return. The third Pope brother, Barry, joined in Italy in late 1944. Mike's later exploits with the Regiment and, after the war, in the racing world were to make him a household name. While C Squadron was in Scotland Captain Crofton and Lieutenant R J Adams, who was to achieve post-war fame as a rally driver, were also posted, leaving Lord O'Neill as the only original officer from Enniskillen days.

The Regiment's strength had increased steadily. By mid-February 1940 there were over 300 soldiers with eleven armoured cars. Between 5 and 9 March a recruiting tour was carried out in County Antrim with the Rolls Royce armoured cars, the first time the vehicles had been seen outside Fermanagh. Regimental strength was now 425 all ranks, just seventy-five short of the target. By the end of April regimental strength was 496, almost on target. Since every recruit was a volunteer, this added to the camaraderie; esprit de corps was growing also, helped to an extent with the opening of the Sergeants' Mess and a NAAFI at Enniskillen. It may also have been assisted by the shared, and unpleasant, experience of a plague of tonsillitis during the first winter of war. Gargling twice a day – the prescribed treatment – did little to halt the epidemic, which reached such serious proportions that the Orange Hall in Enniskillen was turned into a reception centre to deal with the afflicted. The North Irish Horse quickly became an effective and cohesive force, with an air of pride and confidence in what had been achieved in its first five months.

Sport had also helped build the sense of belonging and distinction was gained when Sergeant Sammy Walker was chosen to represent the Army against France in Paris. The subsequent return of Bertie Sidebottom and Sammy Walker from OCTU boosted greatly the rugby side that, since there were no pitches in Portrush, played all fixtures away during the Regiment's time in the resort. General Carton de Wiart arranged a needle match between North Irish Horse and 7th Gloucestershire Regiment, reputed to be the champion Army side serving in Northern Ireland.[7] As wartime conditions prevented many attending, Lieutenant Griffith improvised a commentary system over radio for those unable to be present. Sammy Walker was the hero of the day, kicking three penalties and two drop goals (worth four points in those days) to win.

When France fell there was a real threat of invasion of Ireland, to meet which troop strength in Northern Ireland was increased. Posted into the province was 61st Division, commanded by that famous soldier, Major-General Carton de Wiart VC, CB, CMG, DSO, late 4th Royal Irish Dragoon Guards; the division's headquarters was established at Ballymena.

Towards the end of July 1940, Carton de Wiart[8] inspected the Regiment and congratulated them on their smartness and the high standard of the vehicles. Also keen on the fitness of his men, he was delighted with the daily PT parades, the weekly rugby and soccer matches and the boxing that took place in the regiment.

There were, of course, many other visitors, including the Duke of Gloucester who came a few days after the move to Ballykinlar. Not least of the visitors was the Honorary Colonel, the Earl of Shaftesbury, who made his first visit to his Regiment for almost twenty-five years on 26 August 1941 when an early celebration of the second anniversary of the re-forming took place. On 26 September 1940 the Duke of Abercorn KG, KP, Governor of Northern Ireland, had visited his old Regiment on the first anniversary of the enlistment of the first twelve volunteers of the re-raised regiment. The Earl of Shaftesbury also visited during the stay at Westbury, as did Lieutenant-General G LeQ Martell CB, DSO, MC, Commander Royal Armoured Corps.

Shortly before the departure from Wickham Market, the Earl of Shaftesbury came to say farewell. During this visit, which turned out to be his last, he made a most heartening speech, which was greatly appreciated by all ranks. That speech was recalled, in a special and personal way, at the regimental ninetieth birthday lunch held in Belfast in January 1992, attended by the present Earl of Shaftesbury, grandson of the Regiment's founder.

At the luncheon, held at Belfast Castle, the ninth Earl's ancestral home, which is now owned by Belfast City Council, an Old Comrade, Corporal Joe Lavery, sent his apologies but asked that a personal letter be read out, which was pertinent to the occasion. An extract from the letter read as follows:

> One thing which very much caught my attention was his regret at not being able to come with us, although he said, 'The glory of the cavalry charge is gone forever' and went on to say, 'Please do remember that, although I am not with you, I shall be following your movements with great interest, wherever you are'. His speech finished with these words, 'Whilst I am here on the Home Front, if there is anything I can do, for any of you, don't hesitate to write to me, my address will be easily remembered: Lord Shaftesbury, House of Lords, London'.

Joe Lavery went on to say that, before leaving Wickham Market, 'My young wife wrote to say she was very worried about an unpayable hospital bill. When the Padre was unable to help either in England or North Africa, I remembered Lord Shaftesbury's words and wrote to him in desperation. Imagine my delight when I received a letter from my wife to say

Dear Joe,

I have great news for you. One morning recently, whilst making the breakfast, a knock came at the door, and on opening it, there stood an elderly gentleman, dressed in a dark grey suit and wearing an Anthony Eden hat. He asked me if I were the wife of Joe Lavery, serving with the North Irish Horse in North Africa? I said I was and invited him in. He asked me for the unpaid hospital account. He went on to say he was Lord Shaftesbury, and for me to give the account to him, and not to worry any more about it. He sat down and had a cup of tea with me and then shook hands and left.

The secretary then continued, 'Gentlemen, these are the kind of men, who over the years have made Britain Great, and a cause worth fighting for'.

When Lord Craigavon, who, as James Craig, served with the Imperial Yeomanry in the Boer War, and who had been prime minister of Northern Ireland since 1921, died on 24 November 1940, the North Irish Horse provided the armoured car that towed the gun carriage bearing his coffin with Sergeant John Maxwell driving and Second-Lieutenant Mackean commanding the car on foot. A second armoured car brought up the rear of the procession.

There had been many memorable moments in the long months before departing for Tunisia. There was the episode, recalled by Walter Mitchell, on 10 May 1940, the day that the Germans invaded the Low Countries and Captain Coey carried out a snap inspection of the barrack-rooms. With a few minutes to spare before going on traffic duty at the main gate, Walter watched incredulously as Coey used his walking stick's crook to pull bottles and many other non-military items from under bunks. Walter went on duty at the main gate, from where he could watch the captain tearing the men off a strip about their appearance. Coey continued: 'Today the Germans have invaded Belgium and Holland, and what are you doing about it? Your barrack-rooms are the worst I have ever seen, and your appearance on parade this morning is beyond belief. You call yourselves soldiers? And look at that policeman leaning against the gate with his hands in his pockets!'

Tom Hamilton recalled a famous Court Martial case:

A regular army sergeant had been in charge of the Sergeants' 'booze' from the Province to Westbury. On arrival there was a considerable discrepancy between the original quantity and the amount which arrived in Westbury. Not surprisingly the Sergeant was court-martialled, requesting Second-Lieutenant R S H Sidebottom, a solicitor in civilian life, to defend him. I was unfortunate enough

to be a shorthand writer and had to do the transcript of the proceedings.

Surprisingly Mr Sidebottom seemed to be suggesting that there
was a far larger quantity of beer missing than appeared on the charge
sheet. The Judge Advocate representing pointed out that surely he
was making the case even worse for the accused.

'Certainly not, Sir. I am demonstrating beyond doubt that the stock
figures are so unreliable that no one knows how much, if any, of the
beer was missing.'

The accused got off, much to his own, and everyone's, surprise.

Lyle Craig recalled two stories of Norfolk days.

Two requirements of a Liberty truck driver were that he must drink
no alcohol and must immobilize the truck by removing the rotor arm.
B Squadron personnel went to King's Lynn for an afternoon and
evening out. The driver liked a drink but the long wait proved too
much for him. When the troops returned late in the evening – no
driver. The sergeant in charge of the party was renowned for his
resourcefulness, guessed what had happened to the driver. Posting
two men to keep watch, he removed the rotor arm from the only other
vehicle in the car park, which happened to be an MP's jeep, knowing
that they never practised the removal of the rotor arm.

The sergeant started the truck and drove his men back to camp.

Later the MPs picked up the driver, who had imbibed to his heart's
content and was out to the world. Before putting him in a cell for the
night, they searched him and discovered the rotor arm.

Next day the MPs put him in a jeep and drove him back to
Didlington. They went straight to the truck, removed the distributor
cap – no rotor arm. The sergeant, grateful for the rotor arm, had
removed it the night before and thrown it away. The MPs were
intrigued by this chain of events and interviewed the sergeant in
question. However, they were further confused when the sergeant
declared he knew nothing about motor vehicles and must have
driven home without the rotor arm.

Nothing more was heard of the case.

In the Horse there was a 'throw-away' expression: 'To hell we'll give them
rice' which was used frequently for situations with no rice content
whatever. For example, if a tank driver wanted distilled water and none
was available he might use the said expression and put in ordinary water.
This expression came about in the following way:

The lance corporal in the cookhouse in C Squadron was allocated a number of fatigue men each day. In C Squadron it was customary to display the menu for the following day on a blackboard and this was usually the job for one of the fatigue men. When one, George D, had this to do the dessert consisted of tapioca and he asked Christie C if he would spell it for him. This request was beyond Christie's educational limits, so after some thought he remarked to George, 'To hell, we'll give them rice.'

Overall, memories were of happy times. Portrush had been a happy place, which had seen much hard work but also much pleasure. A number of men married local girls; some were able to find accommodation and 'live out' and quite a number had families living nearby. A reminder of the affection in which the North Irish Horse is held can still be seen at the North Irish Horse Inn at nearby Dervock. In 1968 William McLernon, who served in C Squadron, purchased the premises which he turned into a lasting memorial to the Regiment with the regimental badge displayed above the front door. The Inn is full of memorabilia of great interest and well worth a visit. Past members who make themselves known are asked to sign the visitors' book.

All of the training and preparation had been done against the background of a gloomy war situation. First there had been the defeat of France and the evacuation of British troops from the mainland. Then the glimmer of hope that came with successful operations in Libya and east Africa faded with the Greek campaign and the subsequent evacuation of Crete. An Axis offensive in North Africa followed with British forces pushed back into Egypt, although the port of Tobruk held out in a siege that would last until November. Then, in June 1941, Germany invaded Russia and made rapid progress while Japan came into the war with the attack on Pearl Harbor in December, followed by a lightning campaign in the Pacific and Far East, in which British arms suffered heavily. As the Regiment sailed to war the tide had begun to turn; the US Navy had defeated the Japanese at Midway, Eighth Army had defeated the Axis Panzer Armee at El Alamein and the Germans were stalled at Stalingrad.

Before moving on to follow the North Irish Horse in action this is an appropriate time to look at the development of British tanks. Britain's tank technology led the world in the 1920s but fell behind in the next decade, especially when Germany began re-arming. During this period many British prototype tanks were produced and found wanting, usually being too small, too lightly armoured and under-gunned. In 1936 Christie-type suspension, an American innovation in 1928, was used for British tanks and proved much superior to previous systems. Well into the North African campaign, the authorities persisted with the 2-pounder gun, which was little better than a peashooter, for British tanks that were out-gunned by the German PzKw MkIIIs and IVs.

Matilda was the first British tank to be used with success in the war. Weighing 26 tons, with 75mm of armour at the front, it was armed with the ubiquitous 2-pounder and was an I-, or infantry-support tank, intended to be used in conjunction with infantry, with cruiser tanks operating independently. This splitting of roles – not something the Germans practised, or understood – proved a major drawback in action. The European war would be almost over before a truly good British tank design emerged in spite of many senior figures, including Montgomery, expressing frustration with the old two roles concept.

Valentine, so called because it was offered to the War Office on 14 February 1938, Saint Valentine's Day, was another I-tank. Initially fitted with the out-dated 2-pounder, later models carried the heavier 6-pounder, or 75mm, gun and some mounted a 3-inch howitzer for close-support work. Although difficult to drive, Valentine was reliable and sturdy and well liked by its crews; it also had the distinction of earning Soviet praise; they received Canadian-built Valentines and described them as the best tanks they had received from any of their Allies. The North Irish Horse were to become familiar with the Valentine and also with a later I-tank, the Churchill, the prototype of which, A-20, was built in Belfast by Harland and Wolff. It was, of course, the tank with which they went to war.

NOTES

1 Sir Norman Stronge served with 10th Royal Inniskilling Fusiliers – the Derrys – in the Great War. He was subsequently an honorary colonel of a Royal Irish Fusiliers battalion. Sir Norman was a Unionist MP and was Speaker of the Northern Ireland House of Commons. With his son James, a reserve constable in the RUC GC, he was murdered by republican terrorists at his Tynan Abbey home in County Armagh.
2 Permanent Staff Instructors.
3 An Irish charitable organisation created for the welfare and comfort of servicemen, where excellent, well cooked meals at reasonable prices were available, as well as a games room and quiet reading room.
4 A number of infantry battalions were converted to armour and became numbered regiments of the Royal Armoured Corps in the same fashion as 7th Suffolks.
5 On 23 May Lord Erne died from wounds received whilst on active service. Colonel Powell, eight officers and thirty NCOs and men attended a memorial service at Crom Castle, the earl's home, on 14 June. Queen Mary, the Queen Mother, attended a simultaneous service at Badminton.
6 Known as 'The Devil's Own', a soubriquet shared with the Connaught Rangers.
7 The general won his VC while serving with 8th Glosters on the Somme.
8 Carton de Wiart subsequently went to Yugoslavia with the British military mission. His aircraft developed engine failure near Bardia in Libya and he

and the crew made their way ashore only to be taken prisoner and transferred to a PoW camp in Italy from which Carton de Wiart made several unsuccessful attempts to escape. Later, he was flown with the Italian General Zanussi to Portugal to take part in negotiations for the Italian armistice. This amazing man, who considered himself Irish and retired to live in Ireland, ended his military career as Sir Winston Churchill's personal representative to General Chiang Kai-Shek in Chungking.

CHAPTER V

Tunisia: Baptism of Fire

On 8 November 1942 Allied troops landed at Casablanca and Oran on the Atlantic coast of French north-west Africa and at Algiers on the Mediterranean coast in Operation TORCH. With the Italo-German army in full retreat after the Battle of El Alamein, the Allied strategic objective was to trap the enemy in a pincer movement, with the newly arrived forces providing the second arm of the pincer. Although the initial landings took the Axis command by surprise, the Germans recovered quickly and were soon reinforcing North Africa; fresh troops arrived by sea and air, elements of Panzer Armee Afrika moved into Tunisia and Luftwaffe strength was built up in the region. Hitler was adamant that Africa would not be given up and his insistence on continuing the struggle there would cost the Axis a manpower loss equivalent to that of Stalingrad.

The first German troops to arrive in Tunisia were the men of Fallschirmjäger Regiment Nr. 5 (5th Parachute Regiment) under the redoubtable and experienced Oberstleutnant Walter Koch while General Walter Nehring, who had been on his way to rejoin Rommel's command, was diverted to Tunisia as theatre commander. Within two weeks of the initial TORCH landings over 20,000 German and Italian troops had also deployed to Tunisia and great stores of ammunition and equipment had been shipped in. With typical German efficiency, the Axis forces prepared to do battle on two fronts.

The initial British advance, by Blade Force, reached Beja and Djebel Abiod before it ran into enemy opposition. First Army was able to probe to within twelve miles of Tunis before it was repulsed by the Axis forces. At Tebourba the Germans beat off an attack by 78th Division. There was also heavy fighting at Medjez, which the German Paras captured from French troops, supported by some Americans before the Germans withdrew in the face of an attack led by American armour. Crossing to the far side of the Medjerda river the Germans established a new defensive line. That German withdrawal was a surprise to the Allies and indicated that the enemy may have believed the attacking Allied force to be much stronger than it was.

Then the weather intervened; on 7 December the winter rains began and the ground became a morass of cloying mud. The roads were little better and movement became almost impossible. Allied aircraft were grounded but the Luftwaffe, with all-weather airfields, was able to fly and Allied troops had the most unpleasant experience of an enemy with local air supremacy. Land communications were disrupted and the 'dash for Tunis' had to be abandoned. Against that, the Germans also lost the opportunity to defeat First Army. There was a new German commander in Tunisia, General Jürgen von Arnim, who commanded the newly created Fifth Panzer Army; Nehring had lost the confidence of Kesselring.

There was fighting throughout December and into the first months of 1943. By mid-February the weather began to improve, just as the North Irish Horse arrived in the country. Tanks were unloaded at Algiers, Philippeville and Bougie and crews were disappointed to find that many personal items stowed in the tanks had been pilfered by dock workers in Britain and in Africa. Some tanks did not arrive until 21 February as the ship carrying them had been forced to return to England and came out with a later convoy.

The main regimental party moved from Algiers to Philippeville, now Skikda, by sea, leaving a composite party at Algiers. At Philippeville there was a delay unloading the tanks as the ships were too heavily laden to enter the harbour and part of their cargoes had to be transhipped by lighters, a slow task that was performed under regular attacks by the Luftwaffe. At last, on 17 February, Major Rew and six tanks set off for Le Kef while the Regiment moved two days later, with the tanks travelling by rail and transporters and the men by road. A Squadron travelled by train and reached Le Kef on the 24th where the main regimental party had arrived four days earlier. Twenty-five miles inside the Tunisian border, Le Kef, an important road communication centre, was the main administration base for First Army. It is sixty-five miles west of Medjez el Bab, which nestles below the mountainous ranges guarding the approach to Tunis which both sides sought to hold; the high ground was easily defensible and provided magnificent observation.

But the operational situation was fraught and the Regiment was being committed to action almost piecemeal. German offensives in recent days had hit the Allies hard. Rommel, the Desert Fox, was now in Tunisia with Panzer Armee Afrika and his reputation was worth many extra troops. On 21 February came the news that the Germans had pushed through the Kasserine Pass and were advancing on Thala. To counter this threat 6th Armoured Division was deployed to meet the Germans and a small force was created to defend Le Kef; command of this devolved on Brigadier R H Maxwell, commander of 25 Tank Brigade. Under his command Maxwell had tanks from North Irish Horse and 51st Royal Tanks, those of 142 RAC, with a North Irish troop, having been sent to Sbeitla on the 19th.

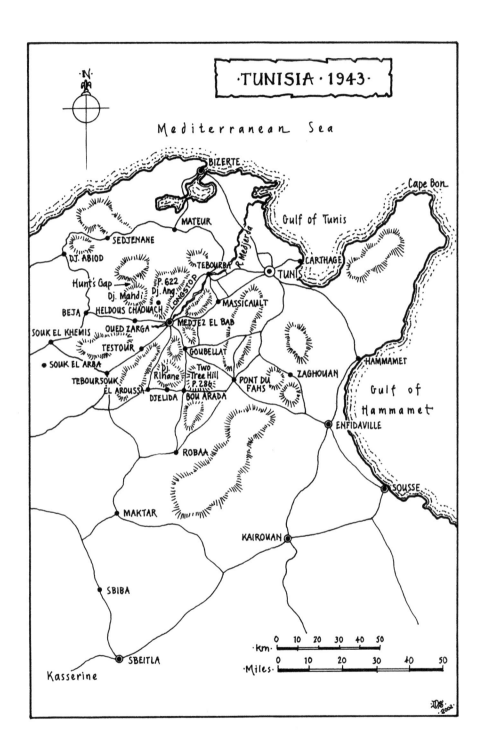

·TUNISIA·1943·

N

Mediterranean Sea

BIZERTE

Cape Bon

MATEUR

Gulf of Tunis

SEDJENANE

DJ. ABIOD

TEBOURBA

CARTHAGE

Hunt's Gap

P. 622

Dj. Ang.

TUNIS

Dj. Mahdi

LONGSTOP

BEJA

HELDOUS CHAOUACH

MASSICAULT

SOUK EL KHEMIS

OUED ZARGA

MEDJEZ EL BAB

TESTOUR

GOUBELLAT

SOUK EL ARBA

Dj.
Rihane

Two
Tree Hill
P. 286

ZAGHOUAN

HAMMAMET

TEBOURSOUK

EL AROUSSA

PONT DU
FAHS

DJELIDA

BOU ARADA

Gulf of

Hammamet

ROBAA

ENFIDAVILLE

MAKTAR

SOUSSE

KAIROUAN

SBIBA

·km·

·Miles·

SBEITLA

Kasserine

The nine North Irish Horse tanks and the available tanks from 51st Royal Tanks were placed under command of Lieutenant-Colonel C W M Timmis, 51st Royal Tanks, while a scratch infantry force, including North Irish Horse headquarters personnel, was commanded by Lieutenant-Colonel Dawnay. Some tanks from 6th Armoured Division's workshops at Le Kef were used as pillboxes under command of Major E V Strickland MM, 25 Brigade Headquarters Squadron. This defensive arrangement lasted until 24 February, during which time Le Kef was dive-bombed three times; very little damage was done and the Regiment suffered no casualties. By the 24th the Germans had been driven back through the Kasserine Pass; the Regiment returned to harbour.

On 18 February the Allied command in Tunisia had been restructured and 18 Army Group – First and Eighth Armies – was created with General Sir Harold Alexander as its commander-in-chief. Alexander inherited chaos with nationalities, corps and divisions mixed together. Units had been rushed forward indiscriminately to plug gaps created by Rommel's advance through the Kasserine Pass and order had yet to be restored. Now another German general was about to strike.

Von Arnim launched his multi-pronged offensive, Operation OCHSENKOPF (Oxhead), at dawn on 26 February with major attacks directed on Tebarka through Sedjenane, Beja through Sidi Nsir–Hunt's Gap and from Tebourba to Medjez el Bab. That morning Colonel Dawnay was ordered to accompany Major-General Evelegh of 78th Division to view the battle that had just started. Returning to Le Kef, he was told that he was wanted urgently at brigade headquarters where he found that Major Rew, acting second-in-command,[1] had already received orders: North Irish Horse was to move immediately ninety miles to the north-east where a strong German battlegroup under Colonel Rudolf Lang, with some seventy-five tanks, including fourteen Tigers, twelve MkIV Specials and about fifty MkIIIs of 10th Panzer Division, supported by the equivalent of three infantry battalions, was thrusting down the Mateur–Beja road to Beja, a major communications centre vital to First Army's line of supply. The main British position on this axis was at Hunt's Gap,[2] where the valley narrowed to under a mile, which was held by 128 Brigade of the newly arrived 46th Division.

At Sidi Nsir, some twelve miles in front of Hunt's Gap and midway between Mateur and Beja, stood 5th Hampshires and their supporting gunners, 155 Battery of 172nd Field Regiment. Kampfgruppe Lang hit them early on the morning of the 26th and tried to bludgeon its way through. An epic defence ensued as the little garrison was assailed by tanks, mortared, bombed, shelled, and shot up by fighters. The defenders knocked out many tanks before being overrun late that evening; only about 120 Hampshires and nine gunners made their way back to brigade headquarters. This gallant defence had two effects: it drew the sting from the German attack and allowed the garrison at Hunt's Gap to complete their preparations – and for the North Irish Horse to be rushed forward. Rain poured down during the night, delaying the German advance and keeping their tanks roadbound next day.

Colonel Dawnay issued orders for North Irish Horse to make best speed through the night to Beja; the tanks had to be in position by first light. Churchills normally moved over long distances either by rail or road transporters, thus saving wear and tear on tracks and engine and much petrol. However, with no transporters available, the unprecedented night road march of some ninety miles took place. Dawnay left for Beja at 7.30pm with his intelligence officer, Lieutenant Francis, and Captains Sinclair and Finch Noyes, reconnaissance officers of A and B Squadrons respectively. Arriving at about 1 o'clock next morning, he went immediately to 46th Division's headquarters and met Brigadier Maxwell, who took him to the divisional commander, Major-General Freeman-Attwood. Dawnay learned that the situation was grave; Sidi Nsir had fallen. It was vital that the tanks be in position by first light. He would come under command of 128 Brigade, and was told which locations the squadrons would occupy.

Meanwhile the Regiment, consisting of a total of twenty-seven tanks, left harbour at 8pm, on the hilly winding road leading through Souk El Arba. Incessant heavy rain made the road surface treacherous and crews were soaked quickly, adding to the discomfiture of drivers and commanders who strained to keep sight of the dim convoy light of the tank ahead. By 3am Military Police reports suggested that it would be impossible for the tanks to reach Beja before first light. Then came a further setback: at a Bailey bridge the leading tank's crew was told the bridge would not bear a Churchill's weight. However luck was on their side in the form of a sapper sergeant who had been present at user trials of the Bailey bridge conducted by the North Irish Horse in England during which the bridge had carried a Churchill tank. Eventually they were allowed to proceed and arrived at Beja soon after first light, thus completing one of the most memorable marches ever undertaken by Churchills. As echelon vehicles carrying petrol had been diverted during the night by the Military Police, the only fuel immediately available was that carried in each squadron's White half-track. Tanks were refuelled 'at the double', a difficult task for tired tank crews operating on hot engine decks and exhausts.

Beja, a charming town of white houses, is about twenty-five miles west of Medjez el Bab. Just behind Beja stands a small ruined castle, from which can be seen the main Medjez el Bab–Tunis road and two valleys, one swinging north to Djebel Abiod, while the other vanishes between the hills leading to Hunt's Gap. The road between Sidi Nsir and Hunt's Gap, overlooked on both sides by rugged mountains, is narrow and twisting, following the railway. At Hunt's Gap the mountains close in. The Gap was held by 1/4th and 2/4th Hampshires with 1/4th on the right flank and 2/4th holding the valley floor and the left flank. The depleted 2/5th Leicesters, from 139 Brigade, recently engaged at Thala, had been brought up from reserve during the battle at Sidi Nsir and inserted on the right of the railway line between B and C Companies of 2/4th Hampshires.

By 9am the squadrons were in position with B Squadron on the right west of Djebel Munchar. No. 1 Troop joined a cold, wet and hungry platoon of Leicesters; a 'brew-up' and rations were quickly provided. A Squadron moved to a position that became known as the 'Loop', a saucer-like depression with its low point in the front right corner where the railway line disappeared up the valley. Tanks were able to take up good hull down positions; A Squadron joined B Company, 2/4th Hampshires. This position was the key to the defence of Beja. It blocked the defile, which was defended by an anti-tank obstacle and mines extending as far south as Djebel Munchar, and by hilly and mined country to the north. Had the enemy succeeded in forcing a way through, their armour would have debouched into rolling country and nothing could have saved Beja. Had the town fallen, the Allies might have had to withdraw fifty miles.

About midday a strong force of enemy tanks advanced down the road until they ran foul of the minefield in front of B Company's positions. Hurribombers[3] knocked out two tanks while anti-tank guns halted another pair. The attack was stopped. A Squadron, aware of the noise of battle, could see nothing of it from their positions on the reverse slope while B squadron was an impotent observer.

An observation post of 2/4th Hampshires on the left flank at 'Spion Kop' reported German infantry debussing from vehicles in the road and deploying through the hills, obviously building up for a co-ordinated attack on the defences. A Squadron, ordered to deal with this party of German infantry, decided to carry out a recce in force up the road in front of the Loop, towards battalion headquarters of 2/4th Hampshires, between 'Black Rocks' and 'Spion Kop'. No. 2 Troop commanded by Lieutenant Ballantyne undertook this task. Major Ketchell and Lieutenant Ballantyne led in a scout car followed by the troop leader's tank, commanded by Corporal Mitchell, Corporal Barbour's tank, and Sergeant Allen's. Corporal Mitchell recounted:

> . . . the hill rose steeply on the left, and fell equally sharply to the right. The faster scout car went out of sight. The road forked, the right-hand track descending into a pleasant sunlit valley. Milling about were quite a number of light-coloured tanks. I ordered the driver to stop while I studied the situation. We continued along the upper road where the road straightened. I looked around but could see only the troop corporal's tank. I called up the missing tank on the wireless but

received no reply. We saw no enemy infantry and on our return discovered that Sergeant Allen's tank had been hit by the enemy, but fortunately no one had been injured. My short stay at the fork in the road had been long enough to attract the attention of the Germans.

Sergeant Allen remembered that his tank was fired on after he passed the track junction; his driver reported that he had no steering or brakes. Looking around, Allen saw the engine decks aflame; the tank had been struck on the right side of the engine compartment. On the drive to Beja the right petrol tank had been used first and, on replenishing, the petrol, fortunately, was put in the left tank. The Churchill came to rest in a small cutting where it remained until darkness fell. It was then towed by Corporal Barbour's tank to a safer position nearer the Loop.

No one who was present will ever forget the fantastic electrical storm, accompanied by torrential rain, that occurred that night with tongues of blue flame issuing from the tops of the aerial rods. Captain Sinclair's tank, which had a track blown off by a HE shell earlier in the day, was repaired in the dark by Corporal Jackson and his ARV[4] (armoured recovery vehicle) crew. Captain Sinclair, the two No. 2 Troop tanks and the ARV then withdrew to rejoin the squadron, which had moved back to harbour near Sidi Mimech.

Next morning dawned sunny and bright. A Squadron returned to the Loop to resume their previous day's position, but Major Ketchell continued along the road to where Sergeant Allen's tank had been left the night before. The tank had no wireless but the turret could be traversed by hand and the guns were still intact. Allen was horrified to see the approaching Churchill knocked out by an 88mm, presumably fired from the disabled Tiger, ditched beside the railway line. At this stage he did not know who was in the tank or what the damage was.

Ketchell's tank had been hit in the turret, severely wounding him in the head and killing his wireless operator, Sergeant Patrick Walters, from southern Ireland, and gunner Trooper John Nursey, from Norwich. With no wireless to report the event, Trooper Samuel Johnston and Lance-Corporal Cecil Moriarty, driver and co-driver, had the unpleasant task of evacuating their squadron leader under heavy fire and bringing him back to the Loop for which both received the Military Medal. The loss of the squadron leader, plus the fact that Captains Griffith and Sinclair were not present, left Lieutenant Hern temporarily in command; Griffith, the second-in-command, arrived from Beja soon afterwards and took over.

When reports came through of enemy movement in the valley Major Rew was ordered to leave one troop near Munchar and move the remainder of his squadron to a position near Ksar Mezouar station, to the right rear of A Squadron. Sergeant Allen had a grandstand view of this attack.

An armoured German column brought up in the rear by two Tiger tanks started to advance up the valley towards The Loop position. I engaged the Tigers, Corporal Milligan, the gunner, claimed a hit ... My tank was then hit on the track guard which jammed the turret, moments later a further hit was sustained on the mantlet, the Churchill's 'Achilles Heel', which put the gun completely out of action. . . . The remainder of the crew joined the driver and co-driver, Troopers Hill and Hinds, who had earlier dismounted the forward Besa. From a small gap they had fired eight or nine belts at German infantry moving along the railway. . . . it kept the enemy's head down, and let them know that our left flank was defended. The Tigers stopped below my position while the rest of the tanks continued towards the Loop where they were met by a barrage from our 5.5s, being beyond the range of 25-pdrs.

Second-Lieutenant Harry Irwin, commanding Recce Troop, did invaluable work in providing extra observation posts throughout the day and brought artillery fire on to this concentration of German tanks. Corporal Cox and his driver, Trooper Maguire, were sent out to report enemy movements in the area, taking their carrier as far as was judged safe before moving on foot to an observation position where they spotted enemy tanks. A report was radioed from the carrier to RHQ and artillery fire brought to bear. The men returned to their observation post where they corrected the fire at intervals for about two hours; two enemy tanks were destroyed and several others, already disabled, were more heavily damaged. To send their reports they took it in turn to cover the 300 yards to the carrier under heavy machine-gun and small arms fire and their OP was under frequent heavy mortar fire. Their conduct throughout was exemplary and inspiring and both received the Military Medal.[5]

About the same time Lieutenant Hern had a shot at one of the enemy MkIVs and holed it through the turret before his tank was struck and he was wounded by a ricochet in the back of the neck and evacuated. Colonel Dawnay then ordered that no tanks were to go forward to engage the enemy, but should wait for them to show themselves. The Germans attacked throughout that day and, although their tanks made no progress, their infantry enjoyed considerable success, B and C Companies, 2/4th Hampshires coming under greatest pressure. In their waterlogged slit trenches, the Hampshires stubbornly held out until late afternoon when their positions were finally overrun.

Captain Griffith wrote:

That afternoon the C.O. came up to A Squadron's position. . . . I explained the tactical situation to him and said that we must not risk losing this position and therefore must stay there and keep the tanks manned all night. The tanks were not using much petrol, just enough to keep the batteries charged for wireless communication.

This remarkable decision, though unorthodox, proved tactically sound. A Squadron were to man the front line without infantry in front of them, or in direct support, for almost sixty hours. Each tank had enough compo rations to last the crew three days; other requirements could be brought up by carrier and scout car.

Trooper Dennis Farmer, a wireless operator in No. 5 Troop, A Squadron noted that

> Life at the 'Loop' was always rather fraught, especially when one had to leave the tank for any reason. Survival also entailed a high degree of athleticism during periods of re-supply. Crew members had to sprint back and forth between the visiting supply vehicles and the tanks, encumbered on the return journey by anything from a 12-volt battery, belts of ammunition, 6-pdr rounds or tins of petrol, one in each hand.

Being left 'in the line' without infantry made the tanks rather vulnerable. Signal wire was put to good use with old petrol cans strung on it and the wire placed around the squadron to act as a trip wire and early warning of any night attack. During the night each tank was given 'fields of fire' on fixed lines with both guns firing at intervals, at the commander's discretion, to make life more difficult for the Germans. A feature of each day was the 'Stonk' carried out before and after dusk in which each tank emptied belt after belt of Besa into the surrounding hillsides, hoping to deter the opposition from venturing forward during the dark hours. One humorous incident which occurred involved two of A Squadron's main characters, Sergeant Des Kennedy and Corporal Cowan (Cowsy) Watson. This pair were frequently at odds with each other, even if sometimes tongue in cheek, and delighted in exchanging abuse and insults. For several days at the Loop they shared the same turret as part of a composite crew. Kennedy was not a fan of the nightly 'Stonk'. After a day of considerable argument in the tank, realisation came that, at any moment, they could end up as figures on a casualty list. They then decided that in future they would at least try to be civil to each other. The 'Stonk' commenced with no order for Cowsy to fire. Increasingly concerned about this, he enquired politely several times if he should do so, pointing out that every other tank was firing away – and questions would surely be asked at some future date if he did not join in! Each enquiry was met with a negative response. Finally, in some state of exasperation, came the threat 'Desmond I am now going to fire like everybody else – so give the bloody order!' A moment of reflection brought the classic reply. 'Alright then

Cowan – if you think you must – but fire the Besa because the six pounder hurts my head!!'

The enemy attacked D Company, 2/4th Hampshires on the left flank at 4.30 the next morning under cover of thick mist. When the mist cleared they were in occupation of most of the Black Rocks ridge. A counter-attack was unsuccessful. Meanwhile enemy machine guns managed to work round to the rear of battalion headquarters, bringing it under close fire, forcing a move farther up the hill into A Company's positions. The enemy now held Djebel El Kermate, known as 'Spion Kop', in force and overlooked A and B Squadrons' positions. Successive attacks to regain the high ground were unsuccessful. The divisional commander asked for the use of the corps reserve, which consisted of only one infantry battalion, 8th Argyll and Sutherland Highlanders.

During the morning of 1 March Captain Griffith went forward on foot, entered a Tiger, one of six German tanks abandoned the previous evening and brought back valuable information, including maps and a wallet, which were sent back to 128 Brigade HQ, plus fresh eggs, English cigarettes and Cadbury's chocolate. He was also keen to recover the damaged Tiger tank, but was ordered not to do so, although Corporal Jackson removed the 88mm gun's sighting gear. The tanks were later destroyed by sappers. Earlier there had been a misunderstanding while Griffith was examining the knocked-out tanks and the artillery was ordered to bombard the area; the order had to be countermanded hurriedly. Throughout the day the Germans put down intense mortar fire at intervals and, just before last light, tanks were again seen manoeuvring in the valley but artillery fire dispersed them.

Subsequently Captain Griffith was awarded the Military Cross, the citation for which noted that he:

> very coolly and competently organized the defence of this area. He remained in command until March 5th, and during this period was responsible for holding the position by day and night. Captain Griffith displayed marked powers of leadership and initiative. The position was frequently under fire and Captain Griffith went out many times on foot to locate the enemy guns and to secure valuable information of enemy tanks and infantry movements. Captain Griffith played a very valuable part in the stopping of tank thrust on Beja.

That morning C Squadron arrived from Beja. Major Welch was immediately sent forward to reconnoitre the Loop with the idea of relieving A and B Squadrons that night. Meanwhile, however, the Regiment was ordered to send three troops to Sedjenane, forty-five miles away by road. Welch and his reconnaissance officer, Captain Robinson, left immediately in a scout car, the three troops moving throughout the night. The other two troops of the squadron under Captain Morton were sent to Sidi Ameur.

Next morning enemy armour and infantry began manoeuvring around Guessa Farm, which C Company, 2/4th Hampshires had evacuated during the night, and prepared to attack Montagne Farm, held by a company of 2/5th Leicesters. This attack was launched during the afternoon and was witnessed by B Squadron at Ksar Mezouar station. Enemy infantry were seen advancing and B Squadron thought the farm was lost. Suddenly it was realised that the enemy were surrendering. It was a moment of great relief. Shortly afterwards these prisoners were on their way back to brigade headquarters; they stated that the artillery fire had been more severe than that experienced in Russia and they could stand no more. Enemy armour then withdrew out of range, never to return. During the day the remaining two troops of B Squadron and the four RHQ tanks arrived at Beja. B Squadron's tanks were sent forward immediately to Major Rew, while the RHQ tanks were left in reserve at Beja where they were dive-bombed heavily during the day but without casualties. A and B Squadrons were now complete, a total of thirty-six tanks.

Lieutenant Pope, No. 4 Troop, B Squadron, recalled his arrival at Le Kef.

We were perched on our tanks, loaded on tank transporters. The rain poured incessantly and the night was pitch dark as we made our way along the hilly winding road from Boujie which was as slippery as glass. The drivers of these loaded transporters, weighing seventy tons, were fantastic, no praise can be too high for them. At last we arrived at Le Kef, freezing cold, soaked to the skin and very hungry. Immediately we were ordered to proceed to Beja and be prepared to go straight into action. The journey seemed to take forever with petrol dangerously low. On reaching Beja we carried the four gallon cans, in great haste, to the tanks and filled up. We were warned there was a major crisis and we must press on with all speed as soon as we had re-fuelled. I led the column of six tanks with instructions to go straight along the road until I came to a guide in a scout car on the left hand side. . . . The road was straight and rolled on and on, up and down hill, mile after mile, with hardly a landmark. I wondered whether we should ever see the scout car, or perhaps he had been killed or captured and we would drive into an ambush without firing a shot in anger! At long last we saw our guide, flashing his signal light and waving us down. He repeated the orders we had received and added, 'Tell your crews to stay in their tanks, the enemy have an observation point on the highest land in the area and can see every movement we make.' The latter statement proved correct when I had to answer an urgent call of nature. I hopped out of the tank and had hardly dropped my trousers when a shell landed dangerously close with an almighty bang. Scrambling back into the tank I gave orders immediately that all further ablutions, however urgent, would have to wait until after dark!

. . . my feet and ankles were now throbbing madly and I had to take my boots off. Dusk came eventually and when safe a hasty evacuation took place to relieve bursting bladders. By this time my legs were in a terrible state and my crew insisted I must hand over command to my Sergeant and have medical attention. Before I ever got to hospital I heard that Major John Rew had been killed. This was a terrible shock. He was a great man, ever cheerful. Shortly before leaving England I had attended his wedding to his beautiful wife.[6] It was diagnosed I had phlebitis and had to lie still with my legs in the air for a long time.

At 10am on 3 March 8th Argylls, three companies up, attacked the high ground on the left. The two companies on the left were successful but intense mortaring and machine-gun fire prevented the company on the right reaching its objective. During the afternoon, the divisional commander ordered Colonel Dawnay to send a troop to support the stalled Argyll company. Lieutenant Ballantyne's No. 2 Troop A Squadron was again selected for the task. The attack was to be made up the same track as used on the previous Sunday, the objective being to keep the enemy's heads down by fire, while the Argyll company launched its attack. It was known that the road was mined and guarded by a small enemy anti-tank gun.

Sergeant Allen and his crew had returned that morning in a replacement tank. Ballantyne, whose tank had engine trouble, took over No. 3 Troop Leader's tank and crew from the acting troop leader, Sergeant Best. The attack started at 5.30pm, the order of march being Corporal Barbour, Lieutenant Ballantyne and Sergeant Allen. An artillery concentration and smoke programme were carried out as planned but the smoke was ineffective. The enemy reacted immediately with very accurate machine-gun and mortar fire, causing the Argylls many casualties and forcing them to take cover while the sappers' carrier was hit and ditched, one sapper being wounded, the remainder going to ground. Ballantyne called for more smoke from Captain Griffith before ordering the troop to advance. When Corporal Barbour's tank reached the minefield the RE officer, who was acting as Barbour's co-driver, advised that they should not go on, but the troop leader decided to continue. Barbour's tank was blown up. Although further mines exploded in sympathy, the other two tanks were able to struggle past the disabled tank. Sergeant Allen engaged an anti-tank gun in a farmyard and then followed Lieutenant Ballantyne. When Allen's tank was hit on the left track by a mortar bomb, the tank swerved off the road and dropped ten or fifteen feet below the road, coming to rest facing a farm two-to-three hundred yards away. Sergeant Allen engaged the farm with both machine guns.

Lieutenant Ballantyne, showing great determination and initiative, continued alone to his objective. He reported that no infantry were in sight, the Argylls having been unable to make progress, and was then ordered to return. Nothing further was heard on the wireless. The tank was seen abandoned the next day and, from subsequent inspection, it was obvious that it had been mined as it was returning. Lieutenant Ballantyne and his temporary crew, Lance-Corporal McKee, Troopers Armstrong, Robbins and Wilkes, were taken prisoner. Trooper Robbins recounted how he was captured.

> When the tank blew up having gone over a mine, I was temporarily deafened . . . We had to evacuate the tank and were promptly taken prisoner. Unfortunately I got separated from the remainder of the crew and never saw them again. Soon afterwards I was very lucky when heavy shelling started. I never heard a thing because of my temporary deafness but a German realized what was up and hurled me into a nearby ditch and flung himself on top of me, thus saving my life.

On 22 November 1944 the *Belfast Telegraph* reported:

> An Ulster soldier hiding from the Germans for over a year . . . has arrived home. He is 30 years old Trooper Cecil Armstrong, North Irish Horse, son of Mr and Mrs M. Armstrong, Tempo, County Fermanagh. Trooper Armstrong . . . related some of his experiences to a 'Belfast Telegraph' representative. After being captured he was kept for six weeks with some 700 prisoners in a filthy building that had been used as a rubber factory in Tunis. It was crawling with lice and the camp to which they were taken in Arezzo in Italy seemed luxurious by comparison. After some months, he was sent to another camp where he worked at brick making and from which he escaped. 'I took to the woods and hills around,' said Trooper Armstrong. 'The Germans offered a reward for my capture. I had to be careful of the Fascists though, they were worse than the Germans.' While alone for some months, cut off from the outside world, the trooper improved his knowledge of Italian and was soon able to read somewhat imperfectly the single page Italian newspapers. Also, he compiled a little book, in which he described in detail the many thrilling incidents since leaving the camp. This book he later destroyed when he thought recapture was imminent. Smoking was another problem and most of the tobacco was raw leaf. He even tried smoking dried

leaves. Then came the day of liberation. The Allied troops were about five miles away. He came out and saw six Bren carriers of a patrol along a road and dashed to meet them. 'As I had grown a beard, my clothes were in rags and my feet bare, the South Africans were doubtful until I showed prisoner of war letters and told them about my unit,' said the Trooper.

The crews of the other two tanks remained in their vehicles until after midnight when, having decided that it was impossible to effect recovery that night, Colonel Dawnay gave the order to immobilise and evacuate.

On the afternoon of 4 March A and B Squadrons were still in the Loop area when the Ksar Mezouar station area was mortared heavily. Major John Rew, commanding B Squadron, was killed by the blast from a mortar bomb. Trooper Hughes, his gunner, recalled the moment he was hit. 'Major Rew had his head and shoulders out of the turret. He was hit in the forehead by shrapnel from a mortar bomb. He fell down dead on top of my back in the turret. This was my first experience of the horrors of war.'

Until then, mortars had been considered a noisy nuisance; thereafter they were treated with much more respect. Enemy guns then joined in and quickly hit and destroyed a gun tractor. Crews of nearby carriers and scout cars took cover in scattered slit trenches. The citation for the award of the Military Cross to Second-Lieutenant Irwin for leadership and devotion to duty records:

> He rounded up the crews under continuous heavy fire and safely evacuated them and their vehicles. He showed complete disregard for his personal safety. While employed on observation duties since 27 February, he has amply demonstrated initiative, enterprise and resource, on many occasions under heavy mortar and machine-gun fire.

Captain Russell took over B Squadron and was promoted to major. The Regiment had lost two squadron leaders within four days but it speaks volumes for their training that captains were able to take command of squadrons with no loss of efficiency.

During the night 4–5 March, 2/4th Hampshires were relieved by 8th Argylls and moved back to Beja to rest and re-organise. That morning Major Strickland MM, who had been Brigade HQ squadron leader, arrived to take over A Squadron, an event described by Captain Griffith.

> I saw the CO coming up the road towards me accompanied by a smallish man wearing a beret with the RTR badge, in full service dress and Sam Browne. The Colonel introduced him as Major Strickland, who was to take over as 'A' Squadron Leader. Major

Strickland, or 'Strick' as he was always known, had won the M.M in France in 1940. A professional through and through, he was to play an important part in the Regiment during the campaign and later still, to command it at the Hitler Line battle. The CO had met Major Strickland on the ship going out to North Africa and had asked for him specially as a replacement for Major Ketchell. 'Compo' rations played a big part in life, whilst in action. There were three types, A, B and C. Type A contained extra 'goodies' such as chocolate and tinned fruit. Major Strickland discovered that only B and C types were coming forward to A Squadron. He changed that very quickly!

Since the early days in Northern Ireland the Regiment had functioned very much as a family, growing, as families do, to become a full active unit. Casualties, so soon, had a dramatic effect on the sense of loss. As they became battle-hardened, this sense of loss eased a little. Thus these quotations from the then Captain Griffith give an idea how they were overcome.

The men are tired out, needing to be withdrawn as soon as possible. Some of the soldiers' feet are swollen in their boots. 'Strick' got us out more quickly than I thought possible.

He considered it important that I, the second-in-command, should look after the day to day running of the Squadron while he commanded in battle. He felt that not being used to the Irish ways that is the best way of running things. 'Strick' added that he required a good supply of Craven 'A' cigarettes!

I think as an Englishman[7] he had rather an Irish attitude to life. Certainly the soldiers thought the world of him. This was not always their attitude to all English officers in the Regiment, although good ones always won their respect. I am afraid that we on the Celtic fringe always tend to be a little suspicious until we get to know them better.

Trooper Moore, Major Strickland's gunner, wrote:

When in action crews always slept together. A waterproof sheet would be attached to the tank to form a bivouac. One night, after a period when there had been little time for sleep, Major Strickland's tank was parked on a slope. His blankets were placed on the low side. Inevitably, nature and gravity took its course and Major Strickland rolled outside the cover. It had been a beautiful night when we went to bed, but later on heavy rain poured down. It was some time before the rain woke him to find he was drenched to the skin. Thereafter if the tank was parked for the night on a slope, his blankets were always placed on the high side!

This was typical of the team spirit pervading the crews. Strickland was equally pleased to come to the North Irish Horse as he noted in a letter to his wife: 'These men are magnificent, particularly in action of which we have seen quite a bit. Most are Irish Volunteers and consequently a cut above others. We will do well.'

On 6 March 46th Division's commander ordered two simultaneous operations for the next day. The first was by 2nd Parachute Battalion, on its way north to help stem Colonel Witzig's paratroop regiment, spearheading the German assault on Sedjenane. The Paras were to drive east of the Beja–Djebel Abiod road to clear the enemy from the high ground north of Sidi Mimech. The second operation by a company of 2/4th Hampshires, supported by Lieutenant Pyl's No. 2 Troop B Squadron, was to occupy Zouave Bend. At midnight on the 6th, No. 2 Troop moved off from Sidi Mimech and two and a half hours later arrived at Chemical Corner, about halfway along the road north from Beja to Djebel Abiod. At 3am the Hampshires arrived. The plan was to advance to Zouave Bend, where the road turned to run southward through the hills back to Hunt's Gap.

Joined by the Paras, who had successfully completed their first task, the force started at 6am, the paratroopers moving through the hills south of the road. At 11 o'clock the Hampshires and tanks were west of La Forestiere farm, just south of Zouave Bend with No. 2 Troop reduced to two tanks, one having broken down. The infantry fanned out and advanced, supported by the tanks; by noon the farm had been taken without a shot being fired. Immediately the Hampshires began digging in, the tanks providing flank protection. Half an hour later, heavy mortar and machine-gun fire rained down on the farm, forcing the infantry to withdraw with casualties. The tanks covered the withdrawal and endeavoured to locate the enemy.

Lieutenant Pyl's tank was hit several times by anti-tank fire from positions north of the farm but Pyl made three journeys in his tank, collecting the Hampshires' company commander and some wounded and carrying them back to safety while Sergeant Tommy McAughtry covered this operation. During the afternoon Pyl and McAughtry took forward two infantry officers and two other ranks in their tanks and put them back in the farm before taking up hull down positions. Shortly afterwards more heavy fire came down and the position was finally evacuated at 5pm. The force arrived back at Chemical Corner two hours later. This was the last active engagement carried out by either A or B Squadron at the Loop.

On the evening of 7 March tactical reconnaissance reported the remnants of enemy armour were withdrawing north-east. Following devastating losses, German tanks were not to re-appear in the area but their infantry retained the high ground until finally driven off by First Army's early April offensive. During the battle the German infantry had failed to operate at night or to attempt any outflanking movements with their tanks; two squadrons of Churchills had fought in a very small area by day and night for nine days, for a period manning the front line in the absence of defending infantry; and the artillery had been outstanding with Lieutenant-Colonel Graham acting as local Commander Royal Artillery. Information from his own observation posts, the North Irish Horse and the infantry, produced excellent results.

A and B Squadrons withdrew from Hunt's Gap and the Ksar Mezouar area on the evening of the 8th, leaving a couple of troops in observation posts. Sergeant Graham, No. 5 Troop A Squadron was the last tank in the column. Complete wireless silence had been ordered. Soon the roar of Vauxhall Twin-Six engines and the clatter of tracks were the only sounds disturbing the cool night air. As the driver accelerated away from a corner into comparative safety, the engine spluttered and stopped. Frantic efforts failed to persuade it to restart. They were stuck and alone, the drone of the other engines fading in the distance. Trooper Farmer, the wireless operator, the man best spared, and also the youngest crew member, was ordered to walk to Beja for assistance. The long and lonely journey was fraught with danger and enlivened by many alarms and excursions. Not until he was approaching Beja station did he come across the first friendly face – that of a military policeman who asked for Farmer's name and number and the reason for his being where he was before, satisfied, directing him to follow the white tapes across the marshalling yards to the squadrons. After a most welcome mug of tea, he returned triumphant with the fitters to his broken-down tank.

Less C Squadron, the Regiment remained east of Beja during the rest of the month while troops rotated in the position around Ksar Mezouar farm. On several occasions a troop was sent back to Sidi Ameur.

On 16 March a counter-attack force of tanks, infantry, anti-tank guns and artillery commanded by Major Lord O'Neill was established about two miles east of Sidi Mimech, tanks for this being supplied on a rota basis by the various troops. Major Randolph Churchill, the Prime Minister's son, joined the Regiment as an observer on 19 March. His short stay was remembered clearly by all and his departure was not mourned. On one occasion Trooper Parkinson acted as wireless operator to the celebrated guest during a recce in a carrier. Heavy shelling forced them to shelter in a smelly old farm building. When they came out of the filthy place they found themselves covered in fleas and had to strip naked to douse themselves liberally with AL63. Parkinson recalled, 'not a pretty sight – him not me!'

During the early hours of 21 March two troops of A Squadron under Captain Griffith moved back into the Loop position following a report, that turned out to be false, of enemy armour in the area. They remained for thirty-six hours and had a most unpleasant time, being mortared and shelled most accurately by enemy infantry occupying the high ground to the north.

No. 1 Troop C Squadron was finally withdrawn from Sidi Ameur to rejoin the Regiment at Beja on the 28th.

The northern flank of Von Arnim's OCHSENKOPF offensive was directed at Djebel Abiod, an important lateral road communication centre, where the attacking force included four German regiments, each the size of a small British brigade. The British front line, held by the depleted 139 Brigade[8] – 5th Sherwood Foresters and 16th Durham LI – of 46th Division, was east of Sedjenane, in positions taken at the end of November in the first unsuccessful dash for Bizerte. On 26 February the Germans flung themselves at the Foresters and DLI, who had to give ground. Reserves, which were limited, consisting of No. 1 Commando and 6th Lincolns,[9] rushed to strengthen the defences of this vital northern road. The Lincolns, of 138 Brigade, were brought up from the Medjez el Bab area. They and the rest of their brigade were serving with 78th Division, which was also reduced temporarily to two brigades, the Guards' Brigade not having returned from the defence of Sbiba. The *Thin Red Line* was very stretched with divisions and brigades horribly mixed up. C Squadron's change of plans resulted directly from this command chaos. Second Coldstream were ordered north to Tamara at the same time. The Germans were approaching Sedjenane rapidly; their advance had not been checked.

Major Welch and Captain Robinson, his reconnaissance officer, left Beja in a scout car to drive north. At Tamara he met the Lincolns' CO, under whose command he was to operate, and carried out a reconnaissance. Nos. 1, 2 and 4 Troops left Beja at 7pm, arriving at Tamara at 4am on Tuesday 2 March. Captain Morton with Nos. 3 and 5 Troops left for Sidi Ameur at the same time. The road taken by Major Welch and his three troops from Beja ran northwards to Djebel Abiod where it forked, left to Tebarka on the coast, right for Sedjenane. On the approach road a towering viaduct dominates the valley. Young green corn and spring wild flowers looked very beautiful against the red soil of the area. The valley leads to the heavily wooded, scrub-covered Tamara gorge after which the road follows the railway until the bleak salt flats, which herald the approach of Sedjenane, are reached. At Sedjenane, a small village, the main east–west road is joined by a road leading northwards towards Cap Serrat and by a track leading up into the mountains to the south. It also has a railway station, really more of a siding, for the products of the nearby mines.

The enemy had infiltrated through the positions of the Foresters, 1 Commando and the DLI during Monday's fighting. The Lincolns and Major Welch's tanks were to hold Sedjenane as a firm base. On approaching Sedjenane at first light, Welch moved two troops to the village; the third was sent up on the Mansour Ridge to guard the left flank. All troops were in position at 9am. The troop on the right of the road was in a bad position due to difficult ground and Germans managed to infiltrate right up to it but were checked by Besa fire. Otherwise the day was quiet and the enemy made no progress. At dusk the troops were ordered to return to harbour. While retiring, the right flank troop, No. 4, stopped to help pull out a bogged carrier and got caught by darkness. Taking a wrong turning, two tanks, those of Lieutenant Williams and Sergeant McIlveen, went over a small cliff by a pit mineshaft and could not be recovered. Luckily, both crews escaped unscathed and returned to harbour on the troop's third tank. During the day Trooper McClean was reported as missing; subsequently it was learned that he had been captured.

In the early hours of Wednesday, 1 Commando began retiring. They reported the Lincolns were still in Sedjenane, and surrounded. The commander of 139 Brigade ordered C Squadron to advance at first light to clear the village. Such was the disorganisation of the defence that neither infantry nor artillery support was available. C Squadron advanced, with No.1 Troop under Lieutenant Norris leading, and all went well until the outskirts of the village where the leading tank, Sergeant Ingram's, was knocked out by a 50mm anti-tank gun, which penetrated the front plate and started an ammunition fire. The blazing tank was evacuated; Lance-Corporal Denis O'Farrell, the wireless operator, and the drivers, Troopers James Ryan, and Leslie Isherwood, were killed by sniper fire, before they could reach cover. Lance-Corporal Robert Hazeldine, the driver of the second tank, was also killed while assisting Sergeant Ingram's crew to escape.[10] Ingram was wounded but was carried to safety by his gunner, Trooper Dines, who was wounded later in the day. Sergeant Ingram recovered and was later commissioned and served with A Squadron in Italy.

The remaining tanks opened fire on the village and the enemy, except for snipers, retired. Realising that there was no infantry support, the Germans began infiltrating back, sniping increased and heavy mortar and artillery fire was brought down on the tank positions. Eventually one depleted platoon of infantry, about twenty-five in numbers, arrived but was unable to provide any help due to the intense fire. Casualties included the Royal Artillery forward observation officer (FOO), who had been given the use of a tank. At 3pm the Lincolns' adjutant contacted Major Welch to advise him that his battalion was about to retire and asked for cover. The squadron leader advanced towards the village and ordered the tanks to give all possible assistance to the Lincolns. A troop was ordered to move up on to the Mansour Ridge to cover this withdrawal.

While the infantry were withdrawing, Lance-Corporal Kennedy, Major Welch's gunner, volunteered to go forward on foot and drive the FOO's tank back. He had to cover 100 yards under heavy mortar fire before entering the tank where he found the FOO slumped across the gunner's seat, and took him for dead. Otherwise the tank was empty and Kennedy started it, turned it around and drove back to the regimental aid post where he left casualty and tank before returning on foot to the squadron leader's tank. On his way an infantryman told him that a tank crewman was lying injured in a mortar pit. Kennedy reported back to Major Welch, who ordered his driver to move forward in the direction of the mortar pit. Both Welch and Kennedy dismounted to investigate and found Trooper Ward badly wounded and unconscious. The major did not think much could be done for him but Corporal Kennedy suggested that they try to drag him out of the pit; if successful, Kennedy would try to carry Ward on his back to the waiting tank. Ward was a big lad, as were the lance-corporal and the squadron leader. They managed to get him out, the lance-corporal knelt down and the major dragged the injured man on to his back. The tank was about fifty yards away and the mortar fire heavy; that made them run all the faster. Ward was laid on a tank track cover. Corporal Hutchman, the wireless operator, and the by-now-exhausted gunner wanted to stay with Ward and hold him on. As there were low branches as well as rough ground to contend with on the way back to the RAP, Major Welch would not allow this since he thought Ward was too far gone and dared not risk any further casualties. The RAP was reached with Ward still on board. He later made a complete recovery but was unable to return to the Regiment. It is incredible how many severely wounded men, who looked to be beyond medical aid, the RAMC were able to return to health. Lance-Corporal Kennedy was awarded the Military Medal for his coolness and determination that afternoon.

The fire brought down by the two troops covering Sedjenane was effective. A number of Germans were killed or wounded; the Lincolns were able to withdraw and came back through the woods on the right, protected by smoke from the squadron leader's tank. Major Welch remained in his observation position for another half hour and, seeing no further movement by the Lincolns, moved back to Mansour Ridge; the troop there was sent farther back. The remaining two troops were ordered to retire to Mansour Ridge, having been on the outskirts of the village for over ten hours.

The squadron was ordered to harbour in the Nefza area. On their way back they destroyed numerous abandoned petrol and ammunition dumps and recovered an abandoned 6-pounder anti-tank gun. No.1 Troop tried to pull out some further guns but one of their tanks bogged down and had to be destroyed, putting an end to recovery work. Just as it was getting dark, the squadron came back through the Coldstream Guards who, in common with C Squadron, were recently arrived in the area and had taken up a firm base east of Tamara. The majority of the

Foresters, DLI, Lincolns and 1 Commando were back safely. During the day the squadron suffered four killed, and five wounded. Casualties not already listed were Troopers Durrant and Shaw, both wounded.

The squadron was held in reserve until Sunday 7 March, the time being used to assimilate knowledge gained from the first two days in action, to bring up Captain Morton and Lieutenant Whelan's No. 5 Troop from Sidi Ameur and obtain replacement tanks, four out of twelve having been lost. Following the death of Major Rew and the promotion of Captain Russell, Lieutenant Bertie Sidebottom, No. 3 Troop Leader, C Squadron, was promoted and appointed reconnaissance captain in place of Captain Robinson, who transferred to HQ Squadron, as second in command.

Although expecting to be withdrawn from the line for a well earned rest, 1 Parachute Brigade was ordered to move at very short notice on 5 March from the Bou Arada area on First Army's right flank to Tamara on the left flank; 2nd Parachute Battalion became involved with B Squadron on 6 March, during their move north. On 7 March C Squadron was placed under command of the Parachute Brigade which moved forward, in cold pouring rain that continued for days, to the firm base established on the evening of Wednesday the 3rd by the Coldstream. At noon on the 8th, a composite troop commanded by Lieutenant Williams, supported by Captain Sidebottom, was ordered to advance to support 2 Para. They had been ordered to drive out the Germans who were attempting to infiltrate between 2 Para in Cork Wood and 1 Para farther north on Death Ridge. The four tanks supported the paratroopers into the south-west corner of the wood where the troop leader's tank became bogged. Trooper Jack Neilson dismounted and, under heavy machine-gun fire, coolly supervised the towing out. With the road cleared and the enemy driven into the north-west corner of the wood, Captain Sidebottom was asked to take his tanks farther up the road where he found a good position. The paratroopers then bolted the Germans out of the wood, giving the tanks a most successful and gratifying shoot, as the enemy crossed open ground. It was a change to be the giver rather than the receiver of fire. The number killed was not ascertained, but the paratroopers took 157 prisoners. The troop withdrew to harbour at dusk.

Next day General Allfrey, commanding V Corps, ordered a reconnaissance in force and detailed two troops of tanks to support two platoons of infantry. The tank force was subsequently reduced to one troop, commanded by Lieutenant Williams, with Major Welch in a close-support tank. Eventually the force started to advance at 2.15pm with the infantry on the right and the tanks completely roadbound on the left. The tanks' advance had not gone very far when Lieutenant Williams' tank struck a mine; Sergeant Hewitt's point tank, borrowed from No. 3 Troop, had safely passed over this previously unlocated minefield. Sergeant Johansen, in the reserve tank, got past after lifting mines, but was too late to support the point tank, which was found on fire approximately 600 yards ahead.

Meanwhile Major Welch continued to support the infantry in the wood on the right who were initially successful, taking about twenty-five prisoners and gaining useful information. Throughout the afternoon, the road was under very heavy mortar and artillery fire and, in due course, the infantry commander decided to retire under cover of smoke from the squadron leader's tank. Sergeant Johansen's tank then withdrew successfully, picking up Lieutenant Williams' crew en route. Both tanks returned to harbour. Sergeant Norman Hewitt, Lance-Corporal Henry Hutchinson, both from Belfast, and Trooper Robert Currie from Antrim had been killed and Troopers Johnston and Harrison taken prisoner when the point tank was hit.

At first light No. 5 Troop returned to support the Parachute Brigade who were coming under increasing pressure in their positions on heavily forested hilltops. Totally roadbound, the troop engaged in a number of small actions where supporting Besa fire was provided. An encouraging incident occurred when tanks of 10th Panzer Division attacking 2 Para were dive-bombed by their own Stukas; this saved the battalion. No. 5 Troop remained in position during the night and were relieved by Second-Lieutenant Perioli at first light. Just before noon on 11 March, No. 2 Troop supported the right flank of 1 Para with Besa fire in a counter-attack eastwards in the area about Ahmed Baleus. A number of enemy infantry bolted but the total number of casualties was never ascertained due to the dense nature of the scrub. In the early afternoon No. 4 Troop, with Captain Morton in his close-support tank, supported 2 Para with Besa fire from the high ground north of Rag Bou Krachiba. The Paras were successful in driving the Germans back and some one hundred dead and wounded enemy were found. Troopers McKerrow and Smith were wounded during the day.

No. 5 Troop relieved No. 2 Troop next morning and was detailed for an anti-tank role, covering the main road leading back to Djebel Abiod. German pressure was building up. No. 1 Troop was withdrawn to a defensive position covering the approaches to Djebel Abiod. The following morning No. 2 Troop relieved No. 5 Troop in the anti-tank role on the main road in the Tamara area. By now the Germans were using the equivalent of a division against 1 Parachute Brigade and the corps commander ordered the Foresters forward to take Djebel Bel and relieve the pressure on the Paras, but they were unsuccessful and suffered many casualties.

The Germans maintained relentless pressure on the ground and in the air. Nos. 5 and 2 Troops continued in the anti-tank role on alternate days until Saint Patrick's Day. Lieutenant Whelan's No. 5 Troop was withdrawn to Djebel Abiod before dark. Enemy pressure was proving too great and it was decided to withdraw to a line running roughly north-west to south-east through Djebel Abiod. The Foresters, who had replaced 3 Para at Tamara, withdrew during the night, as did 2/5th Leicesters, covered by 1 Para. A general withdrawal continued during the next day, No. 2 Troop helping cover the withdrawal of 139 Brigade and 2 Para back to the stop line at Djebel Abiod. C Squadron suffered no casualties during this trying time and earned praise from all the units they had supported. On Sunday 14 March Padre Hughes was on his way north from the Beja area, to take a service with C Squadron, when he and his driver were shot up very accurately by an enemy aircraft. Both men evacuated their car quickly and suffered great discomfort in the comparative safety of a nearby ditch. It was reported, and never denied, that the Padre turned to his driver and said 'for what we are about to receive may the Lord make us truly thankful'. The Padre got a lift to the C Squadron harbour, took his service there and returned in time to conduct a memorial service for the late Major Rew in B Squadron lines. The Padre was popular; every man in the Regiment was glad he escaped uninjured.

Colonel Dawnay wrote the following tribute to Major John Rew.

> I feel that I must pay some small tribute, however inadequate, to John Rew, whose death is so deeply mourned by all in the North Irish Horse. I first met him in Portrush when he arrived . . . as adjutant and it was not many days before it was apparent that here was a man of exceptional character and personality. John was born a leader of men, whether as adjutant or squadron leader, he commanded the complete trust, respect and affection of all. With his terrific laugh and voice and his unfailing cheerfulness he was the life and soul of the Regiment. A more generous and kinder man I have yet to meet. No commanding officer could have a more loyal and conscientious squadron leader. A keen disciplinarian, he had the priceless gift of being able to deal severely with offenders yet at the same time holding their friendship and respect. He was scrupulously fair and his integrity beyond all suspicion or doubt. During his few days in the fighting line John had confirmed his reputation as an inspiring, determined and cool commander. He was killed instantly by a shell when directing the defence of a vital area. He set a magnificent example; his task well done. I shall always treasure my friendship with him and know full well how much I have gained from it. His death is an irreparable loss to the Regiment and his friends. The devotion of his squadron to him will always remain in my memory. His name will always serve as an inspiration to me and my Regiment.

Meanwhile the Regiment, less C Squadron, was having a much quieter time in the Beja area. Some changes in appointments and inter-squadron postings were made: the recently promoted Captain Sidebottom was appointed Adjutant; Captain C M Thomas from the first-line re-inforcements became C Squadron reconnaissance captain; Lieutenant Norris was transferred from C Squadron to RHQ and appointed Intelligence Officer in place of Lieutenant Francis who had been posted as IO, 25 Tank Brigade HQ. Captain Mackean, the former Adjutant, went to A Squadron as reconnaissance captain, taking over the position held by Captain Sinclair, who had become second-in-command of B Squadron, following the death of Major Rew.

The situation on the northern sector had been stabilised and the German advance halted. Saturday the 20th was spent in active patrolling and improvement of defensive positions. During the night No. 2 Troop supported a company of 2 Para in a moonlight attack on Nefza station. It was very difficult to see but Second-Lieutenant Perioli successfully joined up and gave all possible help into the station. Although 2/5th Leicesters had reported that the station was occupied, no enemy were found and a strong patrol was driven off down the railway line. The troop returned to harbour, well pleased with the night's work.

On active service, death and destruction are never far away. On the afternoon of 21 March C Squadron's A Echelon vehicles, while driving up the Beja–Djebel Abiod road on the daily re-supply run, were mortared by a party of Germans who had infiltrated unseen through the eastern hills overlooking the road. The 3-ton lorry containing SQMS Alexander Brown was blown off the road and he was killed instantly.[11] Trooper Denis McFaul, from Antrim, subsequently died of wounds and Lance-Corporal Fitzpatrick and Trooper Irwin were wounded.

C Squadron remained in harbour until the 27th when the tanks started to move forward in mid-afternoon. Less 128 Brigade, but with 1 Parachute Brigade under command, 46th Division launched a major counter-offensive late that evening to drive the Germans back to their start line of 26 February. The assault, starting at 10pm, was led by 1 Parachute Brigade and made swift progress. C Squadron, under 138 Brigade, was to advance on the right of 1 Parachute Brigade; 36 Brigade from 78th Division was in reserve.

C Squadron had a very difficult night march to a rendezvous south-east of Djebel Abiod and was delayed by a minefield which was eventually cleared by sappers; the Lincolns were joined on time. At 6am on the 28th Lincoln personnel mounted the tanks and the advance started along a difficult road, little better than a track, in the direction of the mine situated in the hills to the right of and overlooking Sedjenane. The tanks quickly came under fire and the infantry dismounted. The Lincolns continued their advance up a steep hill and were supported by the tanks until a steep-sided wadi was reached. Although the tanks had to halt they continued to support the infantry as they fought their way up the hill. At least two enemy machine-gun posts were accounted for and five prisoners taken due to the tanks' supporting fire. During the next two days the squadron was held in reserve. No. 3 Troop, now commanded by Second-Lieutenant Mann, which had remained undisturbed at Sidi Ameur, was ordered to rejoin the Regiment at Beja.

On 31 March C Squadron moved to the main Djebel Abiod–Sedjenane road to join 36 Brigade who were making slow but steady progress towards Sedjenane; the brigade had been told that the town must be taken that night. Nos. 4 and 2 Troops supported 8th Argylls and No. 5 Troop supported 6th Royal West Kents. The tanks linked up with their infantry just beyond the Tamara gorge; the Argylls were advancing along the main road to Sedjenane; the West Kents, on their right, were pushing up the track to the mine overlooking the village. Mines and constant air attacks made for slow going; Allied air superiority was still a few weeks off – what a difference this would make. Lieutenant Williams' tank received a direct hit from a bomb but none of the crew was injured and the tank was safely evacuated, despite being heavily strafed by three Messerschmitts. No. 2 Troop took the lead and supported the Argylls as far as the woods west of Sedjenane. All troops were stopped at nightfall. The Argylls re-captured Sedjenane during the night.

Next day No. 2 Troop was able to enter Sedjenane after sappers had improved the entrance and exit of a ford, the bridge at the entrance to the village having being blown. Complete success had been achieved. The Germans had never intended to leave Sedjenane, but leave they did; the panic of their going was obvious with abandoned rifles and ammunition, clothing, mosquito nets, personal belongings and family photographs being found. In a roofless building was a complete officers' mess, with tables laid and food ready to serve. The road east of the village was mined very heavily, making progress slow and the entire area was subjected to heavy air attacks throughout the day. No. 5 Troop continued its advance towards the mine, which was captured by the Lincolns just before they got there. That evening, whilst returning to harbour, Sergeant Bell's tank, No. 2 Troop, was blown up on a mine; the driver, Trooper Carter, and Lieutenant Dickens, a Canadian travelling in the co-driver's seat, were wounded by the explosion. Sergeant Bell's wireless operator that day was also a Canadian; both were members of the Churchill-equipped 1 Canadian Tank Brigade, a number of whom had been attached to 25 Tank Brigade to gain battle experience prior to the invasion of Sicily, in which 1st Canadian Division was to be involved.

Friday 2 April was a good day. The Germans having withdrawn during the night, 138 Brigade had taken over the lead from 36 Brigade and made very good progress. With the aid of French Goums, 1 Parachute Brigade also made good headway northwards towards Cap Serrat. First Army had regained in seven days all the territory the Germans and Italians required twenty-three days to capture. All C Squadron troops were allowed to withdraw into a large wood east of Sedjenane on 3 April where they remained in reserve until the 12th, when all but Lieutenant Whelan's No. 5 Troop returned to Beja. No. 5 Troop was left under temporary command of II (US) Corps, which had taken over from the British 46th Division in the northern sector. On 13 April Major Welch and his three troops, now under command of 12 Infantry Brigade of 4th (Mixed) Division (two infantry brigades and 21 Tank Brigade equipped with Churchills), was ordered to Ksar Mezouar but was not used and was withdrawn the next day. Lieutenant Whelan's troop rejoined the Regiment at Oued Zarga on the 14th, soon to be followed by Major Welch and Nos. 1, 2 and 4 Troops. The Regiment was complete in one location for the first time since early January.

NOTES

1 Lord O'Neill had remained in Bône, marshalling the last boatload of tanks and vehicles.
2 Named after Lieutenant-Colonel G B Hunt, commanding officer of 49th LAA Regiment, who had reconnoitred the area as a possible defensive position in November 1942. Hunt's son, J C V Hunt OBE, TD, DL, commanded the Royal Yeomanry from 1979 to 1982.
3 Hawker Hurricane fighters equipped to carry bombs and carry out ground attack missions.
4 A Churchill fitted with a dummy turret, lifting equipment and a powerful winch.
5 Trooper Michael Maguire MM was commissioned subsequently and earned the Military Cross with the Horse in Italy in April 1945. Born in Lancashire of Irish descent, he became a barrister after the war and was a prominent QC.
6 General Sir Cecil Blacker GCB, KCB, CB, OBE, MC, Colonel 5th Royal Inniskilling Dragon Guards 1972–81, married Mrs Rew in 1947.
7 In fact, Strickland had family connections in County Kerry.
8 The brigade's other battalion, 2/5th Leicesters, had been deployed to Thala to counter Rommel's February attack.
9 The 'Royal' title was granted to both the Lincolns and Leicesters in 1946.
10 O'Farrell and Ryan were from southern Ireland while Isherwood and Hazeldine were from Lancashire.
11 SQMS Brown was a resident of Belfast but had been born in Stirlingshire.

CHAPTER VI

The Final Phase in Tunisia

The Ten Peaks country of the Oued Zarga sector has been described as 'mountainous country [that] . . . was essentially infantry terrain with hills large enough to swallow up a brigade'. Tanks could operate only in small numbers; wheeled transport was almost impossible and supply practicable only by mules. This was the area that 78th Division was to clear, with North Irish Horse supporting Brigadier Howlett's 36 Brigade, thus re-opening the Beja–Medjez el Bab[1] road, a vital first step before launching the assault on Tunis. The divisional attack, supported by a tremendous artillery bombardment, started at 4.30am on 7 April. On the right of the ten-mile front was 11 Brigade with 36 Brigade in the centre and the Irish Brigade on the left; 36 Brigade attacked with 5th Buffs and 8th Argylls up and 6th Royal West Kents in reserve.

Lying south-east of Hunt's Gap, the Ten Peaks are a series of very steep hills, each of which had to be wrested from German control before the Allies could reach Longstop Hill, the gateway to Tunis. Most were so steep that the tanks could be re-supplied only by the use of Lieutenant-Colonel Hume Dudgeon's (of Irish post-war equestrian fame) 4th Transport Group of mules.[2] In a mechanised war such beasts of burden still had an important part to play in mountainous areas. Using tanks in this terrain amazed the Germans, who never dreamt that tanks could scale these heights; but Churchills were the only tanks on either side that could do so, although First Army commanders were slow to appreciate and capitalise on the Churchill's agility. To counteract this, the Germans mined liberally any place where tanks might appear.

On the night of 6–7 April the Regiment, less C Squadron HQ and four troops held in reserve at Sedjenane, reached Oued Zarga heights and began moving forward at 3.30am. Spike Milligan, who served with 19 Battery, 56th Heavy Regiment RA, refers to the North Irish Horse, in typical manner, in his account of the Tunisian Campaign, *Rommel? Gunner who?*

'Hello'? said Chater (Lieutenant-Colonel Chater Jack, DSO, MC) 'Right'. He put the phone down. 'Gentlemen, The North Irish Horse are going in'. He looked at his watch. 'Dead on time', he grinned.

Milligan also describes the tanks fighting their way up the mountain to his front.

Two troops under Captain Finch Noyes, sent to help 5th Buffs finish the successful attack on Djebel el Nahel, worked round the right flank to send the enemy fleeing while Major Russell successfully took three troops of B Squadron to Point 259 and onwards to Oued Bouneb, forcing an enemy withdrawal. Although two tanks were damaged on mines, no casualties were sustained. In Phase two, A and B Squadrons were to cross Oued Bouneb near Italian Farm, A Squadron supporting the Argylls and B the West Kents onto their objectives. With the infantry delayed by mines, the advance started ninety hours late but was completed successfully; an hour and a half later Chaouach was also in Allied hands. In the attack on Chaouach a deep wadi had to be crossed. This had been mined but a gap was cleared. However, the forming-up area on the other side was much more concentrated than was healthy for tanks and, as A Squadron formed up, Stuka divebombers arrived. All tank crews 'closed down' hastily and, after a few moments, bombs could be heard dropping but the sound seemed not too close. Major Strickland recalled that:

> I raised my flaps carefully and looked out and was amazed and delighted to see our Spitfires in amongst the Stukas and causing havoc. Bombs were being jettisoned in all directions, no direct hits were scored; the shrapnel from the bombs proved ineffectual against the tanks' armour plate. The tank crews waved their thanks to the Spitfire pilots.

Spitfires shot down eight Stukas. At long last the RAF were gaining the upper hand in Tunisia. After the attack Walter Mitchell saw one-and-a-half-inch-deep holes in the armour. He recalled an incident during this action when a 16-year-old Austrian youth was captured. Conscripted into the German army the youth had deserted his tank and 'climbed up the mountain to join us. We took him on board. He was a very enthusiastic "fan" of ours and was delighted as we fired at the last wave of Stukas'.

A Squadron continued up the lower slopes, wiping out many machine-gun posts that were delaying the infantry, and taking more prisoners. To the Germans' horror, but the delight of the infantry, the tanks continued to climb and climb until, at the top, they were halted by a deep ravine. This housed the local German HQ but they evacuated rapidly, leaving behind much equipment and very valuable operational orders. The squadron remained on the hilltop, dominating Chaouach and the low ground to the north. German reaction was to bring four Tigers to guard the east side. Although the Churchills opened fire, the range was too great for the 6-pounder; the 88s returned fire but the angle was too steep for them to engage the mountaintop Churchills.

On 8 April the Buffs attacked Point 667, the highest point in Tunisia, with A Squadron supporting them as far up the slopes as possible. When the Buffs reached Oued el Djeb, they were stalled by determined opposition. Moving up to assist, A Squadron was shelled by British artillery. The Buffs resumed their advance and two troops of A Squadron, under Captain Mackean, crossed the defile after removing mines. Mackean's small force reached a white house on the uppermost slopes of Point 667, spotted enemy tanks in the valley below and called down heavy artillery fire. This tank deployment was thought to be a German delaying tactic, in the hope that the Churchills would go forward to meet them.

About noon B Squadron took up hull-down positions on Oued el Djeb's south side and suffered dive-bombing and machine-gun attacks but had much Besa shooting. Before last light the two A Squadron troops were withdrawn and the squadron harboured on the western slopes of Mergueb Chaouach. RHQ and B Squadron returned to the morning's assembly position. Lance-Corporal Moriarty and Trooper Leathem were wounded during the day.

The Buffs met an early morning counter-attack on Point 667 on 9 April with two troops of A Squadron under Lieutenant Hern supporting them from an area near the 'white house'; the enemy were driven back. Tanks were again seen in the valley and artillery fire was directed on to them. Following a midday foot recce by Colonel Dawnay, B Squadron was ordered to advance through a defile and take up hull-down positions on the far side of Point 667, from where they saw an abandoned enemy gun and, after checking for booby traps, towed it back. At 3.30pm another enemy counter-attack was beaten off by the Buffs. Shortly after 5pm Major Strickland returned on foot from a visit to his two troops near the 'white house' and reported eight Tigers in good hull-down positions in the valley below, with MkIIIs and IVs forward as bait. The CO arranged for artillery fire on these tanks; his own tanks also fired. A hit on a MkIV was claimed.

About this time Trooper Parkinson and his mates, stripped naked, were washing their clothes when they heard an enemy aircraft approach. They dived for the nearest cover, a cactus hedge, with the plane almost overhead. It dived, banked sharply and, as it pulled away, they could see the pilot's grinning face: a German with a sense of humour. They spent the next few hours pulling thorns out of each other on this day of frequent dive-bombing and air machine-gun attacks. Subsequently the Regiment withdrew to the western slopes of Chaouach. Lance-Sergeant Burke (HQ) and Craftsman Pearce (LAD) were wounded during the day.

On 10 April all available tanks were brought forward from Beja and by first light A and B Squadrons were positioned near the 'white house'. Supported by No. 1 Troop C Squadron, the Irish Brigade was to advance from Djebel el Mahdi and seize Djebel Oum Guernat; the North Irish

Horse, less C Squadron, would engage any enemy tanks found in the valley. A force of spare tanks, two troops of anti-tank guns, a section of 17-pounders and one section of sappers under Major Lord O'Neill was left as a firm base on the northern side of the defile that crosses Oued el Djeb.

Much German transport was observed moving north-east, indicating a withdrawal. A Squadron advanced cautiously onto Point 361, which was clear, and B Squadron then advanced north-west to Point 391. Realising the Irish Brigade's attack could be helped, the CO ordered A and B Squadrons to advance on a two-front basis to Djebel Rmel. A minefield delayed A Squadron, but B moved quickly and engaged the enemy with Besa fire from high ground west of Djebel Rmel from which the enemy retreated; Djebel Rmel was occupied. Meanwhile, A Squadron had negotiated the minefield and moved southeast of Der Rmel farm.

The Irish Brigade attack was completely successful with many enemy seen leaving El Guernat and nearby features when A and B Squadrons occupied the Rmel feature. C Squadron's troop led by Lieutenant Mann 'Sailed up the Djebel Guernat as if it was the last furlong at the Maze', according to Brigadier Nelson Russell, the Irish Brigade commander.

These positions were to be held until 6th Black Watch, from 12 Brigade of 4th Division, arrived. At about 5pm the enemy emplaced a 50mm anti-tank gun in a hut at the northern end of the Rmel. In dealing with this gun, B Squadron suffered casualties: one of Lieutenant Brown's tanks was penetrated by a 50mm shell and the forward gunner, Trooper John Franklin, from Bedfordshire, was killed. A second B Squadron tank was also hit and the driver, Trooper Hember, seriously wounded. The gun was knocked out by Major Russell's 3-inch howitzer and several prisoners taken. On the right A Squadron worked forward but was unable to engage two enemy tanks, earlier reprieved by the non-arrival of SPGs and 17-pounders that were to have engaged them. The squadrons had to hold on until midnight as the infantry were late in getting through and, while waiting, fired their Besas at intervals at likely approaches; some parachute flares were also used to deter the enemy. Both squadrons spent the night in small laagers behind their day positions.

Trooper Hember, from Wexford, was one of the North Irish Horse's many characters. He had served with the Irish Army but 'transferred' to the British Army. Hember was wounded so badly that his right arm was shot round the back of his neck and hung down over his left pocket; he was also wounded in the left leg. Luckily there was a lull in the proceedings when he reached the casualty station and, instead of amputation, the doctor tried to save his arm with a complicated splint. Hember was sent home after various efforts to mend his arm had failed. Amputation was the final decision but there was considerable delay before this could be performed. When, at last, he was called to

Roehampton, he refused to go as he was beginning to regain some use in his arm which, eventually, became full use. But his troubles were not over; returning to Dublin, he was court-martialled for desertion from the Irish Army. However, he argued successfully that he had only been absent without leave over an extended period. This was accepted and his punishment was to be dismissed the service.

While A Squadron had been held up in the minefield that morning, Lieutenant Gardiner's tank lost a track during an attempt to bypass the mines and Gardiner was wounded while helping to repair the broken track. He completed the task before allowing himself to be evacuated. For his leadership and coolness under fire, Gardiner was awarded the Military Cross.

Lance-Corporal Craig and his driver, Trooper McCann, who were taking a party of sappers forward in a carrier to clear the minefield, were machine-gunned by enemy aircraft but were fascinated more by the tracer bullets setting fire to the tinder-dry grass than by the possible injury they might cause. When, some days later, a fire started under similar circumstances and was streaking towards a quantity of petrol cans near a parked carrier, Sergeant Lyndsay Knight saw the danger, leapt into the carrier and drove it out of danger. He was awarded the British Empire Medal.

Minelifting is one of the most unpleasant tasks imaginable, especially as mines are frequently booby-trapped. The RE officer asked for help, showing the tankmen how to go about the job, adding that any they thought to be booby-trapped should be left to him. German mines had a variety of trigger systems: the 'weight-adjusting' type allowed a light vehicle to pass before exploding under the weight of a tank; the 'ratchet' allowed a set number of vehicles to pass over before exploding. Trooper George Martin, Lieutenant Gardiner's driver, helped with the mineclearing, as well as repairing the broken track, and was awarded the Military Medal. Throughout the day there were persistent air attacks and when a Bf 110 was shot down by Besa fire its 30mm cannon was recovered. A and B Squadrons remained near Djebel Rmel until the 11th when they came under 4th Division's command.

During the night 12–13 a composite force from A and B Squadrons, led by Major Russell, was sent to support 6th Black Watch onto a forward position; this was achieved soon after first light. During the morning of 13 April Captain Leslie, the EME[3], was killed when enemy planes attacked the new workshops at Oued Zarga where he had just arrived to supervise repairs. Lieutenant Ball, Technical Adjutant, and Trooper Taylor, Leslie's batman, were wounded with Ball subsequently losing his left eye. Corporal Day and Troopers James and Newton, all B Squadron, were also wounded. Lieutenant Garner, the Recovery Officer, was appointed as EME and Lieutenant Wilson, who was commanding RHQ troop, as Technical Adjutant. On 14 April A and B Squadrons moved to a harbour near Oued Zarga and were relieved by the rejoined C Squadron to prepare for the final phase of the campaign.

Eighth Army had breached the Wadi Akarit position on 6 April, linked up with II US Corps on 7 April, took Sfax on the 10th and Sousse on the 12th and, by 19 April, was ready to attack the strong, mountainous Enfidaville position. Axis forces were compressed into a 110-mile-long perimeter arc centred on Tunis. On the Allied right was Eighth Army, from the sea to a point twenty-five miles inland; then XIX French Corps, again on about a twenty-five-mile front while First Army (reinforced by 1st Armoured Division from Eighth Army) extended for about thirty miles, from Bou Arada to the Oued Zarga heights. The remaining thirty miles, almost up to the sea, was taken over by II US Corps, now under Major-General Omar Bradley, relieving Lieutenant-General George S Patton, who had been assigned to command Seventh US Army for the planned invasion of Sicily. In ten days this corps, consisting of 1st Armored Division and the 1st, 9th and 34th Divisions, had moved over 200 miles from southern Tunisia to its new positions, passing right across the lines of communication of First Army. Superb US staff work allowed this daunting task to be accomplished without any hitches while air superiority prevented the enemy from seeing the move, thus allowing complete tactical surprise to be achieved. Lastly, on the extreme left of the Allied line on the coast, were some French units.

Meanwhile 78th Division had been assigned to capture Djebel Ang and Tanngoucha, the two 3,000-feet-high, razor-backed ridges, on the left flank, overlooking Longstop. Eleven Brigade's initial attack, supported by 6th Royal West Kents, was launched on the night of 14–15 April. Although both sides were evenly matched in numbers of men, the Allies had a distinct superiority in guns, very great superiority in tanks and, now, mastery of the air. The Axis defensive position was strong; only in the centre, the Medjerda valley and Goubellat plain, would the terrain allow relatively free movement of Allied armour. Isolated hills, Djebel Bou Kournine in the south and Djebel Bou Aoukaz in the north, had been fortified while north of the Medjerda valley the grim fortress of Longstop provided superb observation posts for the German artillery. Until Longstop was in British hands, the Medjerda valley was a 'no-go' area for tanks.

The next phase of First Army's offensive was launched on the night of 22 April. North and south respectively of the Medjerda river were 78th and 1st Divisions, with 6th Armoured and 46th Divisions farther south; the right flank pivoted on Bou Arada. Such was the change in Allied dispositions that divisions were allocated a frontage that had been tackled by a battalion five months previously. The Regiment remained with 78th Division and, on 19 April, Major-General Evelegh unfolded the plan for the attack on Longstop Hill to his brigadiers and Colonel Dawnay. Next day this was explained in greater detail on a cloth model to company and equivalent commanders; the Army Commander also spoke to the assembled officers. Once again the Regiment had the good fortune to support 36 Brigade, which was to capture Longstop; by noon on the 22nd reconnaissance and conferences had been completed.

Longstop appeared darker than the surrounding countryside, a long, dark, sullen, two-headed hump with a saddle forming the ridge between the highest features, Djebel Ahmera and Djebel Rhar. The lower slopes were covered by wheatfields, dotted with poppies, tall white lilies and sweet mustard, giving way to black juniper, gorse and camelthorn on the upper reaches, where deep ravines provided an extra hazard. To add to these natural defences the Germans dug a whole series of zig-zag trenches, with horizontal shelves deep below the surface below which they could lie safely during a bombardment and wait until the last stages of any assault. In their efficient defensive manner, they had created similarly protected, well sited machine-gun posts and had dug in mortars and artillery pieces that could be fired from below the surface. Completing the defences were barbed wire and extensive minefields. With ample water, food and ammunition, the Germans considered the hill impregnable but had not dug in any anti-tank guns since they thought tanks could not operate on such terrain. The battle for Longstop, preceded by a tremendous artillery bombardment from over 400 guns, started on Thursday night, 22 April, the eve of both Good Friday and Saint George's Day. The Buffs, on the left, and West Kents, on the right, left their start lines for Longstop's forward slopes. Ready to pass through the forward battalions to secure the entire hill before daybreak, 8th Argylls were in reserve; North Irish Horse and 1st Surreys would then exploit eastward along the Medjez–Tebourba road.

As with those of the other three divisions, the plan proved to be wildly optimistic. The Germans, superlative defensive fighters, were ready to hang on at all costs, in response to von Arnim's orders that their bridgehead must be held until August at least, to prevent an Allied landing in southern Europe that summer. Equally the Allied High Command was determined that the Tunisian campaign must be concluded not later than 15 May, a date dictated by Operation HUSKY, the invasion of Sicily, D-day for which had been set as 10 July.

The Horse left Oued Zarga on a cold and windy night at 7.30pm and all went well until near Medjez where Lieutenant Perioli's tank lost two bogies to a deeply laid mine, which many tanks had already passed over, and had to be moved off the road. Progress was slow; many mines were encountered and the route had to be altered, as many damaged vehicles had to be moved. Even so the Regiment reached the assembly point by first light, after a cold, frustrating night. The Buffs, on the left, reached their objective by 5.30am but heavy machine-gun fire, covering extensive minefields, prevented 6th Royal West Kents from getting beyond Chaibine, making it impossible for 8th Argylls to fulfil the original plan, which was revised hurriedly. B and C Squadrons were ordered to Chaibine to help the West Kents resume their advance by shooting up the troublesome machine-gun posts. This allowed the West Kents to take the ridge north of Chaibine. In retaliation, B and C Squadrons were shelled and mortared accurately but without loss.

Among the problems delaying 36 Brigade was the fact that the Germans still held the village of Heidous and the jagged, fanged Djebel Tanngoucha, high on the left flank. This allowed the enemy to enfilade attackers with mortar and machine-gun fire, and allowed excellent observation of the infantry and tanks scrambling and toiling up Djebel Ahmera. A new plan was devised: 8th Argylls, followed by the Surreys with North Irish Horse in support, would assault Djebel Ahmera, Longstop's western feature while No. 1 Troop A Squadron, under Captain Bowring, would support the Irish Brigade in clearing Heidous and Tanngoucha. As No. 1 Troop had only two tanks, Sergeant Graham's tank from 5 Troop was added to it. After a difficult journey over steep, winding tracks, Bowring reported to Brigadier Nelson Russell, the Irish Brigade commander, and was taken to Bettiour to view the enemy position. Following this reconnaissance, he was ordered to move up a valley towards Heidous but, as soon as they showed themselves, the tanks were shelled accurately and withdrew after Sergeant Graham's tank suffered a direct hit.

In his book *The Wild Geese are Flighting*, Colonel John Horsfall, then commanding D Company 1st Royal Irish Fusiliers, describes the arrival of Captain Bowring's tanks.

> It was our good fortune in having tank men by us who were not put off by the obstacles around them when most others would have been. Our cavalry regiment, The North Irish Horse, was free of inhibitions sometimes found in the traditionally minded units. They did not consider that all hunting should be over flat country, and they did not mind about their machines. Yes, they might lose a tank or two up the three thousand feet over Djebel Ang, and if they couldn't get them down again they would, no doubt, be given others. So they set off to prove it, with seventy mules behind them loaded with petrol. Two days later they had done it. Three of them, and they were the only power-driven vehicles ever to get over Ang. It was scarcely mule country. I do not think that anyone can appreciate the achievement of The North Irish Horse tank crews unless they had carried out that climb themselves, preferably in charge of a mule column. Nothing in Italy, or elsewhere in my experience, was comparable to those

trackless and precipitous mountain wastes, fit only for Berber goats and shunned even by them.

Back with the Regiment, zero hour for the Argylls' attack was 1.30pm. At 1pm the artillery bombardment increased and the hill disappeared in clouds of dust. The Germans could see the infantry forming up and mortared them heavily but the guns then switched to the enemy mortar locations. At 1.30 a flare rose out of the foothills; the attack was on. The Argylls charged with dash and determination, through heavy machine-gun and mortar fire, minefields and barbed wire and, by 3.30pm, had taken the summit of Ahmera at bayonet-point. They suffered heavy casualties; many, including their CO, Lieutenant-Colonel McNab, were killed and many more were wounded. The leader of the final assault, Major Anderson DSO, received the Victoria Cross.[4] By evening Djebel Ahmera was held by the Argylls and Surreys, both battalions very much understrength, and the West Kents, who had moved forward in support, the whole force being commanded by Lieutenant-Colonel Wilberforce DSO, of the Surreys. The Buffs guarded the left flank with the right held by a composite infantry force from various HQ companies, and anti-tank guns from 256 Battery, 64th Anti-Tank Regiment.

A Squadron had been ordered to support the left flank of the Argylls' attack and B and C the right during the attack, A Squadron worked their way round to Point 196, destroying a machine gun that was holding up the Surreys on their way to reinforce the Argylls. Captain Mackean's tank was disabled by mines but he engaged a nearby machine-gun post, resulting in the taking of five prisoners. Major Strickland pushed on and got a tank of No. 5 Troop across a difficult wadi to contact the Buffs. This tank eventually reached a spot that dominated Point 196 and the valley below and from which, despite heavy shellfire, it managed to shoot up positions indicated by the Buffs. B and C Squadrons supported the attack from near Chaibine. All tanks withdrew at 6pm, except Captain Mackean's; this was repaired and recovered after dark.

On 16 June 1943 the *Belfast Telegraph* carried a graphic account by Sergeant Bullick of No. 3 Troop A Squadron, a pre-war editorial staff member of the newspaper.

> It was very slow and therefore a most impressive assault with steel. At times the tanks almost 'stood on their heads', twisting to avoid mounds of rock and to get at right angles to the huge cracks and shell holes, but always getting nearer and nearer. Like beetles trying to climb an inverted ice-cream cone, they slipped a little, hung suspended and then went onwards towards the top. The behaviour of these tanks upset the Germans. Such tactics were untanklike, and no answer was contained in their military textbooks. Too late now to

shift the anti-tank guns from their positions, too late to make alternative arrangements to deal with this new menace. There was only one answer – retreat, and that's what the Germans did – leaving the British tanks and infantry in possession of the first slope up the heights of Longstop. So ended 23 April.

Considering the long day of heavy fighting, the casualties, none fatal – Sergeant White, and Lance-Corporal Jenkins, both B Squadron, Lieutenant Perioli and Trooper Higgins, C Squadron – were light. A feature of the day's fighting was the sight of Brigadier Howlett riding a white horse, rather incongruous in this mechanical war, but perhaps a good way to get about?

During the night the West Kents attempted to capture Djebel Rhar but failed owing to heavy mortar fire on the forming-up point. Early next morning a composite squadron, under Captain Griffith, that included RHQ Troop, to help with covering fire, assembled on the southern slopes of Longstop to support the infantry. At noon Major Welch brought two further troops forward and assumed command of the composite squadron which then took part in simultaneous operations supporting the Surreys, to clear Mosque Ridge, and the West Kents, to capture Djebel Rhar. Intense mortar and machine-gun fire fell on the infantry as soon as they moved off, the fire from Djebel Rhar stopping the West Kents' advance. A very small party of Surreys and Royal Engineers was able to reach the ridge, after tanks had cleared it. Captain Griffith then moved forward, with two troops and a FOO to the next ridge where good observation was obtained and the FOO conducted a successful shoot. A minefield had been given a wide berth but, while Captain Griffith was moving his tank, it was blown up by a lone mine, outside the main belt.

An enemy machine gun covered the tank. It was imperative an evacuation took place, whilst leaving as little as possible of use to the Germans should it fall into their hands. A groundsheet was pushed through a six-inch drain hole in the driver's compartment and the co-driver, who was on the machine gun's blind side, got out of the side door, crawled under the tank and spread out the groundsheet to catch the vital parts passed through the hole. The guns' firing mechanisms were dismantled, as were the wireless connectors while maps, orders and personal items were all passed through and collected into a bundle by the co-driver. One by one the crew left the tank, and made their way to a supporting tank. Major Welch's composite squadron withdrew just before last light but infantry patrols went forward to guard the damaged tank. During the afternoon two troops of A Squadron were sent to support the West Kents, retiring as darkness fell.

Meanwhile, in response to an intercepted message indicating a possible German night counter-attack on the Buffs' positions, a further two troops of A Squadron were sent to give support. No attack took place, but the tanks remained out during the night and the next day, being relieved at last light by two troops of C Squadron who did not rejoin their squadron until Monday morning. Captain Morton, C Squadron's second-in-command, was the day's only casualty, wounded by an anti-personnel mine while out of his tank. No. 1 Troop A Squadron remained behind Bettiour after their exertions of the previous day and in preparation for the following day.

The exhausted 36 Brigade was depleted heavily. With Djebel Rhar still a formidable fortress, supported by German positions on Tanngoucha and Kef el Tior, 78th Division's main thrust fell to the Irish Brigade, supported by No. 1 Troop A Squadron. Brigadier Russell's plan was for 1st Royal Irish Fusiliers, with North Irish Horse support, to attack Kef el Tior and Butler's Hill (named after their commanding officer), on the left, and for 6th Royal Inniskilling Fusiliers to tackle Tanngoucha on the right. Captain Bowring's troop moved forward at 10am and linked up with the Faughs (Royal Irish Fusiliers) but had to wait until a dense mist lifted. By 12.30pm they could see the crevices and crags concealing the enemy. The divisional artillery laid down a heavy bombardment on the summit. Three Churchills struggled over the crest and down the valley before them and, at very short ranges, opened up at every crag and crevice with 6-pounders and Besas. The ridge dissolved into a storm of flying chippings and ricochets. Added to artillery fire, and support from the Inniskillings' machine-guns and 2-inch mortars, this allowed the Faughs to capture both hills, although suffering many dead and wounded. The Inniskillings then took Tanngoucha, the approach to which had been unlocked by the Faughs, while 2nd London Irish occupied Heidous, which the Germans had evacuated. The Irish Brigade had cleared the left flank of the Longstop front.

The *Belfast Telegraph* of 6 July 1943 contained a further report from Sergeant Bullick.

> Captain Bowring's troop advanced over country only fit for mountain goats. One tank got bogged down to the tops of its tracks. Under heavy fire the troop towed it out and went forward only to lose another in a deep wadi. Again the crews dismounted and all the heavy work of tank towing started again. Luck was with the Ulster men once more, and out she came. In this fashion the climb was made – on and on to a position where the Germans could feel, as well as see, the menace of steel. It was not a speedy advance, nor a brilliant spectacle – just a lumbering and at times a drunken amble, but nearer, always nearer to Tanngoucha and the sites of the 'mortar men'.
>
> And if anything these deliberate elephantine antics increased the relentless threat of advancing steel. The Huns threw everything they

had at the tanks but were getting a 'bit windy' now – this was a slightly different matter to shelling unprotected infantry. At times they lost sight of the troop as it struggled through the usual interminable wadi, but sure enough they came in sight again. First one, then the other two – the 'tower' and the 'towed'. Tanks stood up to tremendous tests, crews sweated in the noon day sun.

At last further ascent became impossible and with frightening deliberation the troop settled down to blast the Germans off the mountain. Machine-guns kept firing until the fumes choked the crews, . . . Covered by this hail of fire the Irish Brigade wove their way up the rocky crags to get hand to hand with the mortar men.

Of the enemy left alive, 200 odd prisoners were taken, and it was left to one of them to coin a title that can still be seen on the side of a North Irish Horse tank. As he passed down the road to the prisoners' cage he went by the tanks. He smiled at the Commander, patted the tank and said in perfect English: 'These are iron mules you've got!' It was an absolute unbiased tribute, I think, considering the source, this is how the 'Horse' of Northern Ireland, became 'The Iron Mule of Tunisia'.

The troop remained in a counter-attack role until last light.

The North Irish Horse and 36 Brigade spent Sunday planning for the morrow, in maintenance and rest, the latter especially important for the infantry who had been in the line without relief for nineteen days. It was hoped that taking Tanngoucha and Kef el Tior might have weakened the resolve of the Germans on Djebel Rhar, and that they might abandon it during the night, but a West Kents reconnaissance patrol was shown forcibly, by machine-gun fire, that the enemy were still very much in occupation.

For the assault on the Rhar, C Squadron and a strong fighting patrol of Argylls would mount a diversion round the right southern flank from Mosque Ridge while the Buffs, with A and B Squadrons, made the main assault on the left. Brigadier Howlett fought the battle from Colonel Dawnay's tank. Uniquely the tanks were to lead the infantry and advanced at 8.30am, the Germans bringing down their usual heavy mortar and machine-gun fire which delayed the infantry's start. C Squadron pushed on to the ridge north-east of Mosque Ridge. This provided a good position for the gunner FOO in Sergeant Allen's tank, who conducted very good shooting throughout the day. Later the Argylls worked forward and cleaned out a number of snipers in the gulleys, capturing about a dozen prisoners. This most successful diversion pushed the defenders into the arms of the main attacking force on their left, and prevented an enemy withdrawal north-eastwards.

The Buffs' initial advance, with two companies forward, supported by

B Squadron, was delayed for about thirty minutes by enemy shelling. The infantry advanced on the higher ground with B Squadron pursuing a parallel course on the lower slopes of Djebel Ahmera; A Squadron moved forward by bounds, along the northern slopes, protecting the Buffs', and B Squadron's, left flank. As the advance progressed, targets were indicated successfully to the tanks by Verey lights fired by the infantry; in one case a 75mm gun was dealt with in this manner. The tanks moving in echelon along the hillside, with those higher up moving ahead of those in the valley, enabled anti-tank guns to be dealt with before they could engage the tanks in the valley. The infantry resembled a line of guns and beaters walking up grouse on a Scottish moor on the *Glorious Twelfth*. That was as far as the sport went, for suddenly a machine-gun post opened up. It was quickly silenced.

Steadily, two B Squadron troops worked forward; No. 4 Troop on the right took over the lead. Lieutenant Pope recalled that a machine gun engaged the advancing Churchills.

> Sergeant O'Hare spotted it first and silenced it quickly. I had only proceeded a short distance further, when an almighty bang proclaimed a broken track due to a mine. The driver, Trooper P. Abbot, a peacetime Irish stable lad, laconically announced over the intercom, 'That's buggered it, Sir, the old cow's spread a plate.'

Pope ordered his troop corporal, Fred White, to bring his tank alongside and changed places under machine-gun fire. Setting off at the maximum possible speed, the remaining tanks continued their upward grind. Two further machine-gun posts were engaged, their crews surrendering. Meanwhile, the Buffs steadily worked their way up the north-western slopes under constant, accurate shellfire; at times whole platoons were hidden by bursting shells. With magnificent spirit they pressed on until a machine gun on a spur checked their advance. No. 4 Troop silenced the post and put the enemy to flight. The troop immediately occupied the spur, allowing the infantry to resume their advance. Major Russell halted the troop to await fresh orders and the infantry.

By now No. 4 Troop was high on the southern slopes of the Rhar. The Buffs' commanding officer, Lieutenant-Colonel McKechnie, in consultation with Major Russell, decided to assign the final assault to No. 4 Troop; the topography dictated a single-troop attack – Lieutenant Pope on the left with Sergeant O'Hare on his right. There would be neither infantry nor artillery support; the tanks would charge forward making maximum noise, with infantry following as close as possible, to mop up prisoners as the armour advanced. As the Churchills advanced, the going became rougher and slower, at times covered by smoke caused by the enemy and the tanks themselves. The rattle of Besas and, now and then, the bark of a 6-pounder could be heard but the constant sound was that of tank tracks scrabbling for grip, and the roar of over-stressed engines as the Churchills churned their way up the precipitous slope. Lieutenant Pope's tank manoeuvred around a cluster of rocks at the head of the saddle between Ahmera and Rhar to be confronted by a 75mm anti-tank gun a few yards away. Pope yelled at his gunner, 'Anti-tank gun, twelve o'clock, give it hell!' A round of 6-pounder and Besa fire brought two pairs of hands frantically waving from a hole in the ground behind the gun. The prisoners were a ghastly sight, unshaven, tired and hungry, and obviously glad their war was over, in direct contrast to the swaggering devils met earlier. By sign language Pope learned that there were no more anti-guns on the hill.

Pope called up his troop sergeant for a progress report. The latter replied, 'Going well and taking prisoners. We've had to stop, oil pressure very low, we'll have to give her a drink'. The driver got out, revolver in one hand, oilcan in the other, to restore the problem. Sergeant O'Hare then tackled the final ascent and, on reaching the summit, took over fifty prisoners. Lieutenant Pope meanwhile, was working round to the western side of the Rhar, engaging and capturing another machine-gun post and mortar pit en route. Coming round a blind corner he met the most amazing sight: a sheer cliff about thirty yards ahead with about twenty or more cavities dug out of the rock face. Germans poured out of the holes, crammed together, holding anything white that they could lay their hands upon and presenting a pathetic sight, pleading for mercy. The holes were ancient tombs, originally walled up to conceal funerary urns and offerings to the dead, all of which had been desecrated and pilfered some two thousand years before.

O'Hare then moved down the northern slope, shepherding his prisoners and capturing another two machine-gun posts. The Buffs moved in, receiving the surrender of an embarrassing number of prisoners, including the commanding officer and his four company commanders of III/754 Grenadier Regiment. On the left, Major Russell and Lieutenant Brown's No. 1 Troop with Lieutenant Pyl's No. 2 Troop, each reduced to single tanks, joined No. 4 Troop and the depleted squadron moved on to the spur covering the plain north of the Rhar, thus preventing a German withdrawal. It is very doubtful if any of the garrison escaped. Whilst regrouping on the spur, the squadron was shelled accurately by a heavy gun. Lieutenant Pyl spotted the flashes and was able to bring the artillery to bear on it; unfortunately the FOO was killed while directing his guns. The Buffs consolidated on the Rhar, adapting the existing defences and blasting new positions, helped by sappers from 256 Field Company, who had performed magnificently throughout the four days. Whilst the Buffs consolidated, A Squadron 56th Reconnaissance Regiment, 78th Division's 'eyes', came forward to link up with C

Squadron. Major Welch was able to indicate some enemy still holding out; these were rounded up, four being killed and about thirty captured.

The final tally for the day was about 300 prisoners while the Buffs suffered forty casualties. The North Irish Horse lost Lance-Corporal William Jamieson, a Glaswegian, killed and Lance-Corporal Murray and Trooper Goulburn wounded, all of C Squadron. This was amazing, considering the ferocity of the battle and the number of tanks damaged. In the final phase alone, Lieutenant Pyl's tank was knocked out by a mine and he transferred to a second tank only to have it disabled by a direct hit on the engine cover. He finished the day in the troop's surviving tank.

Not all tank losses could be attributed directly to enemy action; Sergeant Des Kennedy's tank, No. 5 Troop A Squadron, had performed near miracles, surmounting massive boulders and wickedly deep crevices, as it climbed the northern slopes. Unfortunately, while descending at the end of the day, the tank came to that one obstacle too many; first it almost stood on its front end before, very slowly, rolling on to its side, in the manner of a mortally wounded elephant. Kennedy sent the following unforgettable message: 'We have turned over, there are some big shells coming over. If somebody does not come over and pull us over, it will be all over – Over'. Major Strickland's reply was brief: 'Sit tight Baker 5, you are in an awfully big tank! Out.'

Uncharacteristically the Germans did not counter-attack, illustrating the totality of their defeat. The northern side of Medjerda valley had been opened up. Lieutenant Pope was awarded the Military Cross and Sergeant O'Hare the Military Medal in recognition of their leadership and gallantry. David Dawnay was awarded the Distinguished Service Order for devotion to duty and outstanding leadership during operations between 5 and 26 April. An extract from the citation notes that:

> Lieutenant Colonel Dawnay's 'Churchills' accomplished feats ... previously considered impossible ... He was very largely responsible for the capture of at least three important objectives including 'Longstop' with comparatively light casualties to personnel and tanks. His own action in battle is an inspiration to his battalion [sic].

Brigadier Howlett concluded his report on these operations to Major General Evelegh: 'It is impossible to speak too highly of the support given by the North Irish Horse, or of the steady advance of the Buffs, under heavy shell fire, two factors which made the capture of Djebel Rhar possible.'

In his book *The North African Campaign 1940–43*, General Sir William Jackson writes: 'The final seizure of Longstop was notable for the surprise feat of the North Irish Horse who managed to drive their tanks up the

Djebel to help the infantry take the last and most difficult peak, the Djebel Rhar.' In itself this may not seem a great accolade but, in a very long chapter, the North Irish Horse is the only regiment named.

When questioned about his deployments the German battalion commander responsible for the defence of Longstop said:

> The Djebel Rhar is one of the strongest defensive positions that one could ever hope to occupy. I would have been prepared to hold it against a full scale British infantry brigade attack. When it was apparent that tanks were being used over the high ground I knew that all was over.

Another German officer is reported to have stated, 'When information was first received that tanks were being used on the high ground at Longstop it was not believed by the officers.'

A simple granite memorial was erected in the village of El Heri, on the railway along the northern bank of the Medjerda river, just below Longstop. This memorial commemorates the two battles.

LONGSTOP HILL
LA COLLINE du LONG ARRET
1ST ARMEE BRITANNIQUE
PRISE 23 24 DECEMBRE 1942
THE COLDSTREAM GUARDS
REPRISE 24 AVRIL 1943
ARGYLLS SURREYS KENTS
NORTH IRISH HORSE

The late Captain Jimmy Maxwell – No. 3 Troop Leader in A Squadron in 1943 – is credited as being among the first 'Horsemen' to discover this memorial – in 1959. He noted the absence of any reference to the North Irish Horse and, on returning home, contacted Major-General David Dawnay, Honorary Colonel of the Regiment, to advise him of the omission, which was rectified quickly.

The Battleaxe Division was the only British division to achieve completely its objectives in these operations. Eighth Army could make no progress at Enfidaville but II (US) Corps made significant progress in the north, entering El Aouana, beyond Sedjenane, on 26 April and taking Sidi Nsir on the 27th.

Undoubtedly the North Irish Horse's feats at Longstop were tremendous and worthy of all the praise heaped upon them. It proved that cooperation with infantry and tanks could be a winner, especially in the hills; cooperation of all arms in this battle had been superb. The artillery, as always, played their part. The sappers, especially with minelifting, and the Medical Corps, with their speedy evacuation of the wounded, had all helped to make victory possible. Longstop Hill 1943 is probably the proudest of the twenty Second World War battle honours awarded to the North Irish Horse.

Following their success at Longstop the Regiment had three relatively quiet days. The war, however, did not go away; Corporal William Manamley,[5] A Squadron, was killed and Trooper Johnston, HQ Squadron, wounded on the 28th by an anti-personnel mine, outside the A Echelon area. Fierce fighting continued south of the Medjerda river; 1st Division captured Djebel Asoud on the 26th, but was unable to capture Djebel Bou Aoukaz, the northern extremity of the mountain range dominating both the river valley and the Goubellat plain. Enemy armour launched daily counter-attacks through the Gab-Gab Gap, between Djebel Asoud and Djebel Bou Goukez, and three Churchill regiments were needed to hold the gains already made.

Seventy-eighth Division resumed its advance towards Tebourba on 30 April, a lull having occurred in the battle south of the river. At 10am C Squadron led their old friends, 8th Argylls, to attack three hills overlooking the road and were on the first two hills by 11.15, having successfully negotiated two difficult wadis. The Argylls then advanced and, in spite of machine-gun fire from the high ground, came up quickly and passed through the tanks to secure the third hill. Three MkIVs which appeared were engaged swiftly; hits scored on two made all withdraw rapidly. Half an hour later, a MkIV Special[6] appeared round the right of the middle hill and knocked out Sergeant Elliott's tank, killing the gunner, Corporal Robert Dickson, from Belfast. The tank was evacuated and the crew took cover. At much the same time, Lieutenant Richard Mann's tank was hit, wounding the driver, Trooper Neilson; the co-driver, Trooper Eastwood, although wounded slightly, managed to drive the tank out of action. Unfortunately, it overturned at the bottom of the hill. Neilson evacuated his co-driver and the injured wireless operator, Trooper Young, before making his way slowly, under constant and heavy machine-gun fire, up to Lieutenant Whelan's position, to report what had happened. His coolness and courage earned him the Military Metal.

Trooper Young was evacuated quickly but Lieutenant Mann, brother-in-law of Major Paul Welch, and Trooper Alan Whalley, from Burnley, were dead. Another MkIV then appeared over the rise and was engaged by Major Welch. The first shot hit the cupola and the tank withdrew immediately down the hill; at least one crew member was seen to bale out. No more tanks were spotted that afternoon, but heavy enemy shellfire fell on the tank positions; the only damage was to Sergeant Johansen's tank, which had a track blown off. The Argylls were ordered to withdraw, the tanks following about an hour later. Corporal Bone picked up Sergeant

Johansen and his crew and withdrew first and the squadron returned to harbour. In this action it is estimated that ten enemy were killed, fifty taken prisoner and several hits scored on three enemy tanks.

Sergeant Elliott reported in at about midnight, he and his crew having waited until nightfall before making a move. Enemy troops were encountered and the party split up: in the early hours of 1 May, Troopers Rooke and Chapman, the latter wounded, also returned. Trooper George Davies, from Warrington, was killed while trying to regain friendly lines.

Sergeant Elliott was one of those rare characters, known to all throughout the Regiment, at least by reputation, as a natural leader, a great innovator and a very practical man. The 6-pounder fitted to the Churchill was designed as an infantry anti-tank gun and the original mounting in the MkIII made removing the breach-block a tedious job. Elliott designed a modification which greatly simplified the task and which was adopted for all Churchills. In action in Tunisia, when tanks were closed down for longer periods than in training, a new problem was revealed: cordite fumes built up inside the tank causing discomfort and leading, in some cases, to acute nausea, particularly in turret crews. Realising that huge quantities of air were forced out of the engine compartment by the suction cooling fan, Elliott cut a hole between the fighting and engine compartments of his own tank which proved most effective in removing cordite fumes; this was also adopted universally.[7] The innovative sergeant also devised modifications to increase the rate of fire of the Besa machine gun and the tank's speed but neither proved practical.

Next day, 1 May, it became obvious that the final assault on Tunis was imminent. General Alexander had ordered that the attack would be on First Army's front; 4th Indian Division, 7th Armoured Division and 201 Guards Brigade were transferred from Eighth to First Army, and joined IX Corps in the Medjez-el-Bab area. Rumours circulated about the composition of the breakthrough force and the direction of the attack. At first it was thought that the Regiment would have a prominent role but this was not to be. The final plan, Operation VULCAN, was to attack from Medjez-el-Bab up the valley via Massicault and St Cyprien straight through to Tunis twenty-five miles away. A 3,000-yard front was decided upon, with two infantry divisions followed by two armoured divisions; zero hour was to be 3am on 6 May.

On 4 May the Regiment was ordered to hand over seven tanks to 145 RAC in 21 Tank Brigade and was split into three parts. RHQ and A Squadron remained with 78th Division, who were in reserve; B Squadron moved to 1st Division, still fighting to capture Djebel Bou Aoukaz, and C Squadron joined 142 RAC, in place of their A Squadron, who were also involved in the Djebel Bou Aoukaz battle. B Squadron spent 5 May on reconnaissance. At a briefing by Brigadier Maxwell, C Squadron received orders for the major attack next morning. Fourth (Indian) Division, supported by 142 and 145 RAC, would advance on the left of the main Medjez-el-Bab–Tunis road with 4th (British) Division, less 145 RAC, on the right. Their task was to break through the initial enemy positions and create a situation whereby the armour could pour through and advance on Tunis. Behind 4th Indian Division would move 7th Armoured Division, both Eighth Army formations, while 6th Armoured Division would move behind 4th Division, both First Army formations. Which Army would be first into Tunis? No love was lost between them.

On 6 May, after intense artillery and aerial bombardment, the attack was launched with C Squadron on the left flank of 142 RAC, supporting 7 Indian Brigade; 5 Indian Brigade, supported by 145 RAC, was on the right. By 6am 7 Brigade had achieved their first objectives and 142 Regiment advanced through the Gab-Gab Gap at about 8 o'clock, achieving their objective by 10am. They pushed on immediately as enemy resistance was crumbling fast. Seventh Armoured Division then began moving through the gap that had been punched, advancing north-eastwards, parallel to the main road while 6th Armoured Division streamed through on the right; an even contest so far.

During the morning C Squadron captured six 88mm anti-tank guns, two of whose crews fired not a shot. Only five enemy tanks were seen; once engaged these withdrew immediately from the Indians' final objective, which the infantry established quickly as a firm base, supported by anti-tank guns. It had been a superbly planned and executed operation; as infantry and tanks advanced they met only light opposition; the crater-pitted ground supplied evidence of the weight of artillery and air support. C Squadron suffered no casualties and by 3pm its task was complete.

The armoured divisions forged ahead; 6th Armoured was involved in a tank battle south of Furnas and drove the enemy off south-eastwards. Infantry quickly covered the exposed right flank. Despite stiffening resistance, Massicault was captured that afternoon by 7th Armoured Division and many prisoners taken. That evening, in a further tank battle north of Massicault, the enemy was driven off to the north-east. The Allied air forces supplied magnificent support and so dominated the air that their troops were unmolested by enemy aircraft. In the north the Americans made good progress and the day ended with them only nine miles from Bizerte; the French XIX Corps in the south had also made steady progress.

On 7 May the advance continued. The French captured Pont du Fahs; 6th Armoured Division reduced an enemy strongpoint in the area of La Mornaghia and St Cyprien fell to 7th Armoured Division at 8.30am. Both armoured divisions pressed on, their armoured-car regiments, Derbyshire Yeomanry and 11th Hussars respectively, entering Tunis simultaneously.

Result: match drawn. That afternoon, following severe street fighting in the suburbs, the town was entered and occupied. Bizerte and Ferryville were captured and occupied during the day. The Germans had suffered a massive defeat and were caught completely off guard by the speed of the entry into Tunis. Staff Officers were drinking coffee in city-centre restaurants while some soldiers were walking the streets arm-in-arm with their girls. A few of the bravest attempted to organise the defence of some houses but the majority surrendered quickly.

Neither armoured division was allowed to savour the fruits of victory; 7th Armoured was ordered northwards immediately to block the retreat of Axis troops retiring in front of the Americans from the Bizerte area; 6th Armoured was sent eastwards to Hammam Lif on the coast, thence southwards to Hammamet, to seal off the Cap Bon peninsula. C Squadron joined B that morning, under 3 Brigade in 1st Division; both squadrons advanced in the afternoon, B supporting 1st King's Shropshire LI into El Bathan and C carrying a company of 2nd Sherwood Foresters to the Djedeida area, fifteen miles from Tunis. Neither squadron suffered casualties and met only light opposition from isolated pockets, which had been by-passed in the armoured dash to Tunis.

Next morning, after an early reconnaissance of Djedeida by Major Welch, Brigadier Moore, commanding 2 Brigade now in the lead, decided to attack at 10am and ordered C Squadron to support his infantry across the river. Major Welch supported this attack very successfully; his own tank knocked out a pillbox and the close-support tank provided an effective smokescreen. The infantry crossed the river quickly, taking about fifty prisoners. A tank crossing was found and Captain Thomas and No. 1 troop crossed first, followed quickly by the rest of the squadron, which then deployed. As soon as the tanks appeared, about 200 more prisoners were rounded up. No. 4 troop then carried a Gordon Highlanders platoon to Sidi Abdullah and No. 3 Troop took a second platoon to Chuart; both villages were quickly captured. Captain Thomas and the other troops spent their time rounding up more prisoners in the cornfields. B Squadron arrived before dark and both squadrons harboured near Chuart.

For A Squadron, 8 May was an exhilarating day. Six months to the day after landing in Algiers, 78th Division, who had remained in reserve in the Medjez-el-Bab area, was given the honour of entering Tunis, 500 miles from the divisional starting-point. A Squadron was also ordered forward independently towards Tunis. About noon Major Strickland ordered a halt for a brew-up. The tanks had just pulled off the road when orders came over the air from Colonel Dawnay to advance urgently to Tunis; further orders would follow. Crews mounted with alacrity, the thoughts of tea quickly forgotten. Major Strickland rode on the outside of the leading tank, clutching a map in one hand and waving traffic out of the way with the other. The squadron had not gone far when two Red Caps

1. Annual camp 1910: in full-dress uniform, the Regiment marches to Magilligan Camp from Bellarena where this photograph was taken. (NIH archive)

2. The Strabane Troop of B Squadron at annual camp at the Curragh, Co. Kildare in 1905. Wearing service dress caps are Lieutenant E C Herdman, Major E A Maude and PSSM Embry. (NIH archive)

3. Lieutenant T F Cooke DL in levée dress of full-dress hat with feathers, green tunic with white lapels, full-dress belts, overalls, Wellington boots, spurs, girdle and gauntlets. (NIH archive)

4. An unknown trooper of A Squadron. The photograph is believed to have been taken in 1910 and shows the trooper still wearing the old Imperial Yeomanry breeches. (Col J T Eaton)

5. Somewhere in France: John Gillespie, who served with the Regiment throughout the Great War, looks after two four-legged members of the Regiment. (NIH archive)

6. This photograph was taken at Bethune in 1915 when the Regiment was serving as divisional cavalry to 32nd Division. The soldiers are L/Cpl G T Honer and Tpr Brennan, both of 1 Tp, B Squadron, (NIH archive)

7. On horseback is Richard Annesley West, who won the Victoria Cross with the Tank Corps in the final months of the war. (NIH archive)

8. Enniskillen 1940 and a Great War-vintage Rolls Royce armoured car of the North Irish Horse is pictured on exercise. The soldier in the foreground is Sergeant J McMorris. (NIH archive)

9. The Regiment converted to Valentine I-tanks at Ballykinlar where this photograph was taken in 1941. Wearing the white brassard is Captain The Lord O'Neill, later killed in action while commanding the Regiment, Lieutenant-Colonel Powell, Lieutenant (later Major) Sidebottom, who was awarded the MC in Italy, and Captain (later Major) Welch, who was also decorated for gallantry. (NIH archive)

10. The enemy: a knocked-out German Pz Mk VI in Tunisia. Churchills can be seen in the middle distance. (NIH archive)

11. Victory in Tunisia: A regimental Churchill taking part in the Allied victory parade in Tunis. (NIH archive)

12. Preparing for battle in the Gothic line in Italy in the summer of 1944. Lieutenant Michael Bexon, later to earn the MC, is the tank commander. (NIH archive)

13. Forli has fallen to Eighth Army and a half-track carries fitters of the Regiment through the town. (NIH archive)

14. Soldiers of HQ Squadron relax in Italy beside a Churchill that bears the name 'Donegal'. (NIH archive)

15. Churchill passing over bridging equipment in Italy. (NIH archive)

16. The shortage of conventional artillery ammunition in Italy led to tanks being pressed into service as supplementary artillery. Here six Churchills of the Regiment, five NA75s and a British 75mm-equipped tank fire a bombardment in northern Italy. (Mrs R J Griffith)

17. A Squadron fitters recover a Churchill in Italy in 1944: (left–right) Sgt Mitchell, Tpr Bailey, Sgt Jackson, Tpr Barr and Tpr Gallagher. (NIH archive)

18. Major Robin Griffith MC and Bar, the only officer in the Regiment to gain a Bar to the Military Cross; his first MC was earned in Tunisia and the Bar in Italy at the Hitler line. (Mrs K J Griffith)

19. A squadron of the Regiment marches past Her Majesty Queen Elizabeth The Queen Mother at the Jubilee Parade of the Territorial Army at Sydenham, near Belfast, in 1958. (NIH archive)

20. A Fox armoured car of D (NIH) Squadron, Royal Yeomanry on exercise with the British Army of the Rhine in 1978. The Troop commander is Second-Lieutenant R J C Eaton. (NIH archive)

21. HRH Princess Alexandra of Kent presents the Guidon to the Regiment at Balmoral, Belfast, 1960. (NIH archive)

22. Major (later Colonel) Charles Oliver Eaton, TD, DL, commanding 69 (NIH) Sqn of 32nd (Scottish) Signal Regiment but wearing Horse distinctions. Colonel Eaton was murdered by republican terrorists when he arrived at his place of business on Belfast's Springfield Road on 30 June 1976. Oliver Eaton was also a member of the Police Authority for Northern Ireland. (Col J T Eaton)

23. Colonel (now Sir) Michael McCorkell who has had the longest continuous connection with the Regiment since the Second World War. A veteran of that conflict – he served with 16th/5th Lancers in Italy – he joined the Regiment when it was re-formed in 1947 and has been associated with it ever since, commanding at squadron and regimental level and then becoming Honorary Colonel of the Regiment. (Sir Michael McCorkell)

24. Remembering other days. Jack Neilson MM and Bar and Michael Bexon MC are photographed together at Dunmore Park TA Centre, Belfast in 1990. (NIH archive)

were seen on the road, waving the tanks to stop. Nothing was going to stop A Squadron; they swerved around the MPs and carried on their way, without slowing down. A certain piquancy was added to the situation, when one irate MP was recognised as a former and most unpopular member of the Regiment.

The squadron entered Tunis to a rapturous reception early in the afternoon. Progress through the city centre was very slow, the column on many occasions being unable to move due to the throng of deliriously happy civilians blocking the streets. One seasoned warrior even had time for a haircut and shave. Men pressed wine on the troops, the ladies flowers and kisses. In the midst of this magnificent reception, orders were received to move to Carthage, ten miles farther on, to extend 7th Armoured Division's right flank. At Carthage the squadron fanned out in a defensive screen. Next morning the troop harbouring beside the tramway track, which ran along the centre of the Tunis–Carthage road, woke to the tramp of German boots marching into captivity. The tramway reminded them of Portrush days; they had come a long way since then.

On 9 May A Squadron remained in Carthage while B and C Squadron, still under 1st Division, were in the Djedeida area. The Manteuffel Group – 334th Infantry Division, 13th Panzer Division, a company of 504th Heavy Tank Battalion (Tigers) and 20th Anti-Aircraft Division, who had been defending the Medjerda valley and Goubellat plain – surrendered unconditionally with their divisional commanders and staff. Next day the Regiment was ordered to concentrate in the Ain el Asker area. A Squadron returned through Tunis and received a second ovation; the Regiment was safely united before midnight.

During the previous two days 6th Armoured Division had carried out a brilliantly executed action and occupied Hammam Lif, which the Germans considered impregnable. Tanks had been driven along the waters to avoid the massed anti-tank gun screen and then carried on to Hammamet. Fourth Division made a complete circuit of the Cap Bon peninsula, thus frustrating any slim hopes the Germans had of a Dunkirk-type evacuation. Roads were choked with hordes of enemy prisoners. Many units surrendered complete with all their equipment and were allowed to drive their own transport to the nearest prisoners' cage where they made their own cooking and sanitary arrangements. One unit arrived smartly dressed with its band; in a short time captors and captives were entertained with classical and popular music.

During the night the German 86th Regiment surrendered to 1st Royal Sussex, of 7 Indian Brigade. North Irish Horse spent the morning of 11 May quietly before receiving orders to move to the Creteville area, under command of 1st Division again. That move took place during the night and was completed before dawn. During the evening of the 11th, some 22,000 men of the Pfeiffer Group, consisting of 21st Panzer and the Italian

Superga Divisions, surrendered unconditionally. The tanks were not required during the 12th as the division's infantry units combed the countryside, rounding up many prisoners. Both Reconnaissance and Inter-Communication Troops helped marshal many thousands of prisoners, and despatch them to the hastily prepared cages that would be their homes for many months. General von Arnim surrendered at his headquarters at St Marie du Zit, south of the great rock of Djebel Ressass.

Generals Alexander and Anderson were taking no chances. Many generals had surrendered as had tens of thousands of Axis troops. All command and control of remaining enemy forces had failed; fierce opposition was maintained by those units obeying the Führer's orders to fire to the last round before surrendering. On the morning of 13 May A Squadron, with 128 Brigade, was ordered on a round-up of recalcitrant enemy in the area south-east of Djebel Ressass. No opposition was encountered and a link-up with units of Eighth Army, advancing from the south, was made. Marshal Messe surrendered unconditionally with the remainder of the Axis forces just before noon. General Alexander was able to telegraph Mr Churchill in the early afternoon

> Prime Minister, Sir, It is my duty to report that the Tunisian campaign is over. All enemy resistance has ceased. We are masters of the North African shores.

The North Irish Horse moved next day to an olive grove just west of Hammam Lif. When the other two regiments arrived, before evening, 25 Tank Brigade was complete in one place for the first time since leaving England. Two days' intensive maintenance followed before rest became the order of the day. Tunis was within easy reach, bathing facilities were magnificent and it was a most enjoyable couple of days.

Members of the Regiment returned to earth with a bump with news of the imminent victory parade, and the arrival of an Irish Guards drill sergeant, to quote one man, 'to get a grip on the Regiment'. He was of the old school, as regimental as the proverbial buttonstick. Rank meant nothing to him on drill parades; if 'Buck House' standards were not achieved he made his displeasure clear in no uncertain terms. He was not popular. Trooper George Duncan, a great mimic always in demand at regimental concerts, was able quickly to master the drill sergeant's southern Irish brogue and command mannerisms. One evening, after dark, Duncan gathered together a number of his pals and proceeded to drill them within earshot of the Sergeants' Mess. The visiting sergeant was extremely angry and demanded the name of the culprit. George Duncan was too popular for anyone to give him away.

At very short notice thirty tanks were made spotless, a regimental flag produced and a large representative party under Major Welch left for

Tunis. The victory parade, on 20 May, was an outstanding and memorable occasion held in bright sunshine. An enormous, brightly decorated saluting base was flanked by two Churchills with eighteen spotless and shining Churchills drawn up opposite the dais. The route was lined by Churchills, Shermans, guns and representatives on foot of all the units that had taken part in the campaign. Guards of honour were provided by the Grenadier Guards, the American and French Armies and the salute was taken by Generals Eisenhower, Giraud, Alexander and Anderson, Admiral Cunningham and Air Chief Marshal Tedder.

A large and enthusiastic crowd, civilians in their Sunday best, servicemen in their best uniforms, provided a carnival atmosphere. The parade was led by the French, preceded by a large band, playing stirring martial music. They were enthusiastically received by the local French population, the Goums being given a special reception by the British spectators – a fitting reward for their many exploits. A smaller party of Americans followed before the largest contingent, the British, led by General Allfrey, appeared. Pride of place in the British element of the parade, which marched past nine-abreast, was given to 78th Division. All who took part, and each regiment had a representative party, looked very proud as they marched past the saluting base to the music of many bands. The wheeled and tracked vehicles and the guns came right at the end of the procession and were turned out magnificently. Major Welch, flying the regimental flag, led the North Irish Horse Churchills. A Royal Air Force fly-past halfway through the proceedings was well executed and thrilling to watch.

The campaign was over. The Axis had been defeated comprehensively in a disaster equalled only by that inflicted by the Russians at Stalingrad. In eight days, the number of prisoners totalled 248,000, which included fifteen German and seven Italian generals. Only 648 escaped, mostly by air. The Mediterranean had been re-opened to shipping; southern Europe was now vulnerable to attack, a new threat that the Germans had to redeploy troops to counter. The Allies had gained experience in seaborne landings and in fighting in southern-European-type conditions. They had learned to fight in mountains and in valleys, over mined roads and through forests. They had blown up bridges and built new ones. They had forded rivers and fought battles in populated areas.

Churchill tanks played a notable part in both defence and attack. Their effect on the enemy and the way they gained the respect and raised the morale of their own infantry was remarkable. North Irish Horse had come through the campaign with flying colours, having been engaged in all major operations, including the capture of Point 667, Tunisia's highest peak. The Regiment served with no fewer than five divisions. Considering the severity of the fighting, casualties in personnel and tanks were remarkably light. The Regiment had fought as a team and the spirit of all ranks was wonderful. A higher tribute could not be paid than that of V Corps' commander, Lieutenant-General Allfrey to David Dawnay: 'Your Regiment has done extraordinarily well, every formation which you have served speaks well of you. I consider that a great compliment'.

NOTES

1   Medjez el Bab means, literally, 'the key to the gate'.
2   Hume Dudgeon was decorated for this work.
3   The Electrical and Mechanical Engineer (attached to the Regiment).
4   Anderson was killed in action in Italy, at the Battle of Termoli in October 1943.
5   Cpl Manamley was an Army Catering Corps cook attached to the Regiment.
6   This was fitted with a long-barrelled 75mm gun.
7   An unconnected feature of the Churchill's cooling system was that, while stationary on hard and dusty ground, the fan would blast dust under the vehicle's belly before drawing it in through the hatches, causing great discomfort to the crew, particularly the driver and co-driver. To minimise this problem, rolled anti-dust aprons were slung across the bow plates and could be lowered when tanks were likely to remain stationary for any period.

CHAPTER VII

Waiting for the Call

On 10 May, with Axis defeat in Tunisia inevitable, Hitler offered Mussolini three German divisions to assist in defending Italy. The air bombardment of the fortified Italian island of Pantelleria, midway between Cap Bon and Sicily, started that same day and continued for a month. Friday 11 June saw the virtually unopposed seaborne landing, covered by precision aerial attack, by units of 1st British Infantry Division. The Italian garrison, some 4,600 strong, surrendered quickly.

On 14 June the Italians accepted the positioning of two panzer corps in southern Italy under German command; the Germans already had reason to doubt their ally's continuing active prosecution of the war. On 10 July the Allies invaded Sicily, which was garrisoned by two Italian corps and two German divisions – Hermann Göring Panzer and 15th Panzer Grenadier.

The invasion force – Seventh (US) and Eighth (British) Armies – attacked with three and five infantry divisions respectively, each supported by an airborne brigade. Both armies broke in successfully and, after hard fighting, completed the capture of the island in thirty-eight days. Sixth Italian Army disintegrated, the majority being taken prisoner while the Germans, reinforced to the equivalent of three and a half divisions, fought with great determination and demonstrated their skills in defence and withdrawal. Their unhurried evacuation across the Strait of Messina, with all their own and much commandeered Italian heavy equipment, was successfully completed during the night of 16–17 August.

The Mediterranean sea lanes had been re-opened and German pressure diverted from the Russian Front; Operation ZITADELLE, the offensive against the Kursk salient, which started on 5 July, was abandoned prematurely on Hitler's orders on the 13th. Mussolini had been deposed on 26 July and the Italian Crown Council decided secretly to seek peace with the western Allies five days later. The stage was set for the invasion of mainland Italy.

Fifth British and 1st Canadian Divisions of Eighth Army attacked across the Messina strait in the early hours of 3 September. No Germans were encountered and the Italians offered no resistance. A firm bridgehead was quickly established and the Italian government signed an armistice that same day, although it was agreed that no public announcement would be made until the evening before the planned Allied landing on the west coast, closer to Rome. The Italians failed to make adequate arrangements for their change of sides but the Germans had prepared excellent contingency plans in the event of Italian treachery. When General Eisenhower announced the Italian surrender to the world on Radio Algiers on the evening of 8 September those German plans – Operation ALARICH – were implemented immediately; units moved into Rome and other key centres while the Italian army surrendered.

On 9 September Eighth Army was approaching the Cananzara isthmus, its first objective; 1st British Airborne Division landed unopposed, from ships, at Taranto and, in the early hours of the same morning, VI (US) and X (British) Corps of Fifth Army stormed ashore at Salerno to be met with fierce opposition. Salerno had been identified as a probable amphibious Allied landing area as it marked the extremity of the range of effective land-based fighter cover; 16th Panzer Division had moved there in late August.

The Germans knew the Allies' immediate strategy but thoughts on reaction differed among the German high command. Rommel, Supreme Commander South-West, recommended a quick withdrawal to the narrowest part of the peninsula – the Gothic Line. Kesselring, CinC South, believed a defensive line south of Rome could be held – the Gustav Line. After near disaster, the Salerno beachhead was secured on 16 September, patrols from Eighth Army linking up with the defenders the previous day. Fifth Army's breakout commenced on the 23rd. Naples was entered on 1 October, the Garigliano river reached on 2 November and Eighth Army reached the Sangro river a few days later. The mouths of these rivers marked the flanks of the Germans' winter defence line, the Gustav Line, which was based on the Garigliano and its tributary the Rapido as far as Cassino, then up and over some of the highest mountains in the southern Apennines until the Sangro was reached and followed to the Adriatic. The Germans had established outposts on the river banks with their main positions on the reverse slopes of the hills overlooking the river. Cassino was the key feature of the western half of the line; the town guarded the Liri valley, the main route northwards. The town and valley were overlooked by Monte Cassino surmounted by an ancient monastery. It is probably the most formidable defensive position in Europe.

Winter rain turned the country into a sea of thick mud that reduced the Allied advance to a snail's pace while three German infantry divisions were moved from the north as reinforcements. By mid-November Fifth Army had fought itself to a standstill. Weather and determined German resistance had thwarted the Allies' plans to capture Rome before Christmas. Three British and four American divisions were due to return to Britain at the end of November to prepare for the invasion of north-west

Europe, leaving General Alexander with only thirteen divisions. Kesselring, now CinC South West, Rommel having been moved to north-west Europe, had eleven divisions and a further seven non-committed divisions in northern Italy.

Hitherto Fifth and Eighth Armies had fought separate campaigns on either side of the Apennines but Alexander now ordered both armies to co-ordinate their attacks. Eighth Army was to smash through the Sangro river defences and take Pescara before turning due east and advancing towards Rome, while Fifth Army would break through the Mignano Gap and close up to the Rapido river in front of Cassino. The task set the two armies was to take Rome before Christmas with Eighth Army attacking on 20 November and Fifth Army on the 30th. Rain delayed Eighth Army's start until the 29th. Ortono, half way between the Sangro and Pescara, was not cleared until after Christmas and it was realised that no further major progress could be achieved on this narrow front in the appalling winter conditions. Eighth Army's activities were then limited to aggressive patrolling to prevent the Germans moving troops to another part of the line. General Montgomery handed over command of Eighth Army to General Leese on 30 December, prior to his return to England in preparation for the invasion of north-west Europe.

While all this was going on in Italy, North Irish Horse remained in North Africa. It would be several more months before it was called upon to move to Italy. In the meantime 25 Tank Brigade had moved to Ain Mokra, some twenty miles from Bône, where recreational facilities were arranged. Transport was laid on to take parties of soldiers to the coast to bathe and leave was also granted to allow men to visit rest camps by the sea. There was also training, with an exercise in cooperation between tanks and infantry planned for August. This exercise – CONCORD – was marred by the outbreak of forest fires, to the control and combating of which soldiers were diverted. Initially firefighting was carried out with long-handled shovels but the intense heat of the flames, plus the heat of summer, made this almost impossible and, eventually, bulldozers were brought in to create firebreaks. It was believed that the fires had been started deliberately by local people as the forests belonged to the French and were managed on a commercial basis.

There were also many sporting activities and the Regiment produced both soccer and rugby teams. In the former discipline the Regiment had the advantage of an English first division player, Corporal Calland, who was a professional on the books of Charlton Athletic. With a kick that could propel a ball from one end of the pitch to the other, Calland was the mainstay of the team. Soccer and rugby matches were played as 'internationals' with the Regiment representing Ireland. The rugby team included some useful players, among whom were Captains Sidebottom and Morton, Lieutenants Mahon and Irwin and Trooper Patrick.

At Ain Mokra a number of replacement officers arrived to fill the gaps left by those who had been killed or wounded in the Tunisian campaign. Lieutenants H J Hedges, J F O'Sullivan and G T Tuckey with Second-Lieutenants K W Foott, R H Horsburgh, D F Hunt and J A Watters all joined the Regiment at this time. Later arrivals included Lieutenant D Lewis and Second-Lieutenants A N McCleary, G Mahon, E D Bullick, W A Ingram and P A Garstin. In November 1943 Lieutenant G W Hutchinson was killed in a road crash while returning from hospital. Lieutenant-Colonel Dawnay was promoted Colonel and appointed second-in-command of 23 Armoured Brigade, then in Italy. Major Lord O'Neill was promoted to command the Regiment with Major Strickland returning as his second-in-command.[1]

Food improved markedly at Ain Mokra with white bread – two slices per meal – replacing the hard biscuits of campaigning days and fruit was also readily available. Lemons and oranges could be had in abundance, so much so that boxes were sent home to parents and relatives who would not have seen fresh fruit since the outbreak of war. However, few of those boxes were ever delivered to their intended recipients; it seems that they were purloined on arrival in the United Kingdom and sold on the black market.

Letters did reach home but these were censored before leaving the Regiment. This task fell to the squadron orderly officers who also doubled as censors. The job was an unpleasant one as letters could be very personal, especially when addressed to wives. No one was allowed to mention place names or divulge military information and censoring officers generally scanned letters for place names, which, if found, were crossed out. In most cases soldiers did not include such information in their letters. One soldier, however, had cause to be grateful to a censoring officer, although he may never have been aware of his debt. This man was writing to two girlfriends and placed his letters in the wrong envelopes but the duty officer noticed his error and swapped the letters about. Mail from home was a tremendous boost to morale and that was important the longer the Regiment's stay at Ain Mokra became.

That stay eventually lasted for ten months. It was said that General Montgomery, commanding Eighth Army, was not keen on the Churchill tank, which his army had used only in very small numbers at El Alamein and then only on an experimental basis. The Churchill was associated more closely with First Army and this was believed to have prejudiced Montgomery against it. It is a plausible theory, as Monty had no love for First Army or for anyone connected with it. Another plausible theory is that it was believed that the Churchill was too heavy for operations in Italy. Time was to prove this incorrect. And there are also those who consider that the British soldier had lost faith in British tanks and preferred the more reliable American products, such as the Sherman.

124

Towards the end of January 1944 the Regiment took part in Exercise PARTHIAN. This was for wheeled vehicles, of which there were sixty-nine carrying thirty officers and 260 men, and it covered many hundreds of miles, with a foray into the northern Sahara desert. It was a welcome change from the routine of life at Ain Mokra and it took members of the Regiment to some beautiful oases with their lush green grass and plants in the middle of the inhospitable desert.

One tradition from home was maintained by the Regiment while at Ain Mokra with the holding of a Twelfth celebration in July 1943. Orange 'arches' were erected and Lambeg drums were fashioned from petrol containers. On the morning of 12 July sports were held on the parade ground and the Twelfth parade itself was not held until the cool of the evening. Banners appeared on the march to 'the field' and that of 'Strickland's Chosen Few' must be unusual, if not unique, in Orange Order history; Strickland was, of course, Major Eugene Strickland, who was a Kerryman and a Roman Catholic. However, it is noteworthy that the occasion was celebrated by soldiers of all denominations, as was the case with regiments from Northern Ireland generally. The animosities of home were all left behind and an occasion that reminded everyone of home was celebrated with fervour. Sassenach members of the Regiment were given quick induction courses in Irish history and some became almost as Irish as the Irish themselves.

In such ways were the long days at Ain Mokra passed. As news of the war in Italy came back to them, the men of the Regiment longed to be with their comrades at the front once again. In the spring of 1944, after a number of false alarms, they finally learned that they would be moving to Italy.

NOTES

1   Strickland later left the Regiment to command 145th Regiment RAC and Major Paul Welch MC was appointed acting second-in-command pending the arrival of a regular officer to fill that position.

CHAPTER VIII

Italy

Now came the time to pack up and leave Ain Mokra for more serious business; during April the Regiment crossed to Italy. Sailing from Bône on 16 April the ships of the convoy carrying the main party carried out a check firing of their anti-aircraft guns resulting in an ear-shattering noise that was a grim reminder of the days in action. In contrast with the voyage to Africa, the two-day journey to Italy was very pleasant with bright warm sunshine, calm seas and excellent food that included freshly baked bread. All enjoyed the magnificent view as the convoy passed the isle of Capri, where the deep blue of the sea blended with the blue of the mountains high above. The later convoy with the tanks was not so lucky with the weather and encountered storms. With the tanks stowed below the water line, personnel had to go below and tighten the chains holding them lest they break loose and burst through the side of the ship.

Approaching Naples harbour, which had been bombed heavily by the Germans with many ships sunk, the convoy was attacked by aircraft, luckily without casualties. A sunken ship lying on its side served as a landing jetty; disembarking troops had to dash for cover as the bombers returned with an unfriendly welcome; shades of their early days in Tunisia. Lorries ferried the men out to Afrigola, a village on the outskirts of the city. Lance-Corporal Joe Lavery recalled that

> Vesuvius . . . had been up to its tricks again. As if Naples and District had not suffered enough with the war, this giant had erupted just before our arrival.[1] The massive mountain was only a few miles from the camp and tongues of flame could be clearly seen erupting from its belly. At night the sky above it was bright with the reddish hue which emerged from its gigantic mouth. The stars in the remainder of the sky glittered unconcernedly.

Joe Lavery also recalled the pathetic sight of starving men, women and children. A barbed-wire fence surrounded the Regiment's camp with metal bins along the inside perimeter to collect the residue from the mess tins. It was a common sight to see these pathetic people reaching through the wire to collect scraps, often tearing their arms on the barbed wire in the process. Since Mussolini had been deposed and the new Italian government had arranged an armistice with the Allies, the Germans had occupied the country and the people, already poor, had suffered great deprivations. As a result, Italian partisans were tough men whose only thought was to kill as many Germans as possible. Although their intentions were good, their discipline was poor and they were difficult to control as well as splintering into several political factions.

At Afrigola the Regiment received eighteen Sherman tanks and waited for their forty Churchills to arrive [2] Unloading was a long and laborious task. Daily an officer and some drivers from each squadron went down to the docks where there was much waiting about and little action. The Germans had destroyed as much commercial and industrial life as possible before they left Naples. Although the harbour was a particular target for this scorched-earth policy the extraordinary prowess of the US engineers quickly transformed Naples from ruin into a first-class harbour that now played host to many of the American Liberty ships that played a major part in the Allies' logistic chain. Unloading parties soon learned that the place to get a good meal was aboard these vessels. Famed for their hospitality and easygoing ways, American crews were happy to offer a good meal to anyone coming aboard. The trick was to pretend that one was not sure which ship carried the tanks and board that way.

When all the tanks were unloaded they were taken to the nearest railway station and loaded up for Foggia on the Adriatic coast, one of the Italian Air Force's largest pre-war bases. From Foggia 25 Tank Brigade moved into harbour just outside the small village of Lucera which, seemingly by-passed by world events, enjoyed a way of life from an earlier century. Here North Irish Horse met up with 2 Canadian Infantry Brigade to practise cooperation and tactics while 25 Tank Brigade joined 1st Canadian Division, commanded by General Vokes. The Canadians had been involved in the Sicilian campaign and the early advance in southern Italy before being rested. Their current location was a closely guarded secret, as would be their move to the Cassino area.

While at Afrigola, Lieutenant-Colonel Lord O'Neill had been taken ill and was hospitalised in Naples. Lieutenant-Colonel E V Strickland MM, from 145 RAC, assumed command, with Major Welch continuing as acting second-in-command. Popular from his previous time with the Regiment, Strickland was highly respected and a fine officer and everyone was delighted to welcome him. During the week-long stay at Lucera the local music group entertained the soldiers with their beautiful music in the evening off-duty hours.

By day the infantry and tanks trained together and in the evenings officers visited each other's messes to get to know each other better.

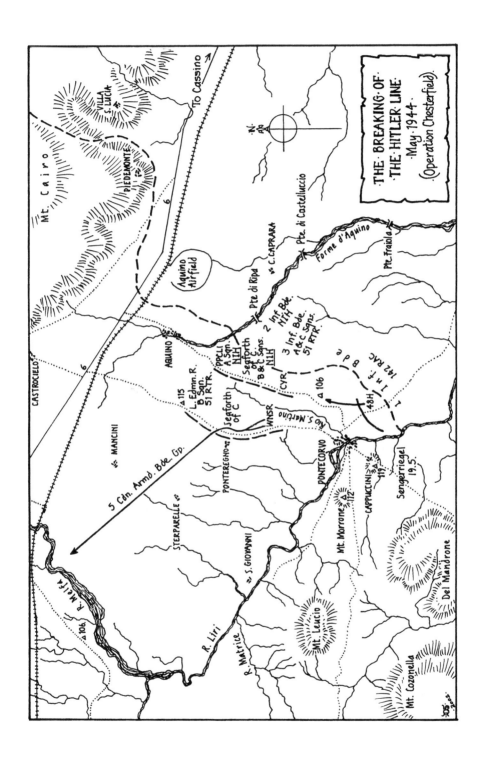

THE·BREAKING·OF·
THE·HITLER·LINE·
May·1944·
(Operation Chesterfield)

To Cassino

Mt. Cairo

PIEDEMONTE

VILLA S. LUCIA

CASTROCIELO

6

6

Aquino Airfield

Pte. di Ripa

C. CAPRARA

Pte. di Castelluccio

Forme d'Aquino

Pte. Fraiola

AQUINO

PPCLI
A Sqn.
NIH

Seaforth
of C.
B&C Sqns.
NIH

2 Inf. Bde.
NIH

3 Inf. Bde.
A&C Sqns.
51 RTR.

1 Inf. Bde.
142 RAC

L. Edmn. R.
B Sqn.
51 RTR.

△ 115

Seaforth
of C

CYR

△ 106

48H

Rio S. Martino

WNSR

PONTEREGNO

△ MANCINI

MANCINI

PONTECORVO

Mt. Morrone △ 112

CAPPUCCINI
119.

Sengerriegel
19.5.

5 Cdn. Armd. Bde. Gp.

STERPARELLE

S. GIOVANNI

R. Melfa

△ 106.

R. Liri

R. Matrice

Mt. Leucio

Del Mandrone

Mt. Cozonella

Everyone knew that they were to take part in a major attack of great importance; they had not crossed Italy to practise for something minor. A rapid bond developed between infantry and tank men, which was to pay dividends in the months ahead. Following the week at Lucera, the Regiment re-crossed Italy, and the tanks were unloaded at a station near the main Naples–Rome road, Highway 6. Riding on tank transporters they approached Caserta with its magnificent royal palace, the whole complex enclosed by four courtyards, which had housed Italy's royal family for several generations but was now General Alexander's HQ. Alex came out to see the large convoy pass by and, as it was halted for some minutes by the density of the traffic, he was able to speak to many North Irish Horsemen and hand out packets of cigarettes. This was much appreciated, especially as Alexander himself was an Irishman.

The night of 18–19 May, spent at Mignano, meant little sleep as heavy artillery was firing all night. Monte Cassino and its monastery had finally fallen to the gallant Polish Corps during the previous night.[3] Supported by 6th Armoured Division, 78th Division linked up with the Poles. The Gustav line had been smashed finally, after four months' bitter fighting. But victory was not complete. The Adolf Hitler Line, now renamed the Senger Line, six miles farther on, still blocked Highway 6. Major Griffith took a party of troop leaders to view the 'mad mile', a straight stretch of road, along which all supplies to the forward troops had been carried. Until a few days earlier this road had been in full view of the Germans on Monte Cassino and vehicles could move only at night. On first sight the Cassino area reminded them of Great War pictures; the ground was pocked with shell holes, trees were skeletal, buildings flattened, signposts and telegraph poles stood at odd angles. And overall was the continuous noise of battle, and the smell of death and destruction.

Next day the Regiment and 2 Canadian Brigade moved to an area some four miles south-east of Pontecorvo where the object of their earlier exercises was revealed; it had been preparation for an attack on the Hitler Line between Pontecorvo and Aquino, five miles apart. As always the Germans had chosen a defensive line that would be almost impossible to break. Highway 6 ran through the Liri valley and was dominated by mountains, allowing the enemy to concentrate everything in the narrow valley, with the mountains acting as a natural barrier to traffic. Telegrams between Churchill and General Alexander stressed that, with the fall of Monte Cassino, the Hitler Line was the key to the destruction of the German forces south of Rome.

The invasion of north-west Europe was imminent and Churchill wanted the Germans to be harassed on all fronts. The more German troops deployed on the Italian and Russian fronts the better the chances for the Allied invasion troops. By 18 May Kesselring was sending down reinforcements from the north as fast as he could muster them and feeding them in piecemeal in an effort to check the Allied advance. The thrust from the south drew two divisions away from Anzio.

Eighth Army was to break through the Hitler Line before the Germans had time to settle down and the breakout from Anzio was planned to coincide with the Hitler Line attack. There followed days of nervous anticipation with orders and counter orders as plans were finalised. Good aerial photographs were taken, but not always of the correct area, and it was difficult to marry up gun positions on the map with those on the ground. Bridges were scarce and approach roads narrow. Traffic jams and bottlenecks were all too common. Chaos reigned and the attack was postponed two or three times. For the troops on the ground pre-battle planning was not assisted by the frequent changes of plan.

Major A W A Llewellen-Palmer DSO, MC,[4] the newly appointed second-in-command, arrived at this time but Colonel Strickland ordered Major Welch to continue as his second-in-command for the forthcoming battle. General Leese decided that the Hitler Line could be breached only by a carefully planned major assault by the Canadian Corps, which could not take place before the night of 21–22 May. General Vokes, commanding 1st Canadian Division, had planned to use only 2 Brigade with two battalions up, supported by 51st Royal Tanks but Leese changed this to two brigades and three battalions up, supported by North Irish Horse and 51st Royal Tanks which caused more delays. H hour for Operation CHESTERFIELD was postponed to 6am on 23 May as 3 Canadian Brigade had to redeploy while new orders were issued to 2 Brigade, and North Irish Horse; 51st Royal Tanks were switched from the right to the left flank with only two hours of daylight left.

All this caused considerable frustration and a lack of detailed planning and reconnaissance – vital factors at any time but increased now by the momentous battle that lay ahead. The final plan was for 2 and 3 Canadian Brigades, supported by North Irish Horse and 51st Royal Tanks, to assault and break through the centre of the Hitler Line on a 3,000-yard front following which the tanks and infantry of 5th Canadian Armoured Division would pour through and force a crossing of the Melfa river.

Within 2 Brigade Princess Patricia's Canadian Light Infantry, supported by A Squadron would attack on the right; the Seaforth of Canada, supported by B Squadron would attack on the left; C Squadron was to support B Squadron. The Loyal Edmonton Regiment, supported by B Squadron 51st Royal Tanks, was initially in reserve. Once the Princess Pat's first objective, the Pontecorvo–Aquino road, had been consolidated, the Edmontons and their armour would push on to the final objective, the road linking Pontecorvo with Highway 6, north of Aquino.

My boys move in tonight – New boys with fear and nerves and anxiety hidden under quick smiles and quick seriousness. Old campaigners with a far away look. It is the hardest thing to watch without breaking into tears.[5]

The Germans were upset to lose the Cassino position but retained Monte Cairo and were confident they could hold the Hitler Line, which they had had six months to prepare, against all opposition. Breaking the line would open up the gateway to Rome and northern Italy. The story of the battle has never been told in full, and probably never will be but, with the help of the Battle Report and some individual memories – every crew must have had a story to tell – some of the story of this incredible assault, under almost impossible conditions, is now told.

On 21 March General Alexander, Commanding Allied Armies Italy,[6] wrote to General Wilson, Supreme Commander in the Mediterranean.

> These are not the conditions (Western Desert) I expect to encounter during the advance through Italy. Here the country is close and admirably adapted to defence. The enemy shows at every disposition to oppose our advance and inflict every possible delay upon us. The campaign to drive north is likely to start with a battle on the scale of Alamein; two such battles may be necessary before Rome falls. After that the enemy may withdraw to the Apennine position, but will do so gradually, leaving determined rear guards to dispute every mile. At the end of the pursuit we shall reach a strong defensive line, which we cannot hope to force without a heavy battle.

This was an incredibly accurate forecast of the campaign from the Gustav and Hitler Lines through to the Gothic Line.

Roads were a problem being few and far between; the narrow country lanes were inadequate for the traffic of a corps in battle. Using bulldozers, Engineers cut swathes through the countryside to build new roads and vast clouds of yellow dust from their operations made life unpleasant for everyone.

The Hitler Line positions facing the Canadians and North Irish Horse consisted of eight tank turrets, with either 75mm or 88mm guns, surrounded by steel or concrete bunkers to protect their Spandau-armed crews. Sited in depth, these intercommunicating emplacements were about 150 to 200 yards apart, each manned by twenty men. The line had another natural advantage: a wood provided natural cover. Narrow lanes had been cut through the trees and mined. Should the mines fail to detonate, anti-tank guns were sited to engage tanks and machine guns to engage the infantry. Snipers tied themselves into trees ready to fire upon anyone who moved, whether fighting soldier or stretcher-bearer. There were also ten portable machine guns with six-feet-high domed protective shields and armour from three to five inches thick. To co-ordinate all the fieldworks, observation posts and crawler trenches reinforced with concrete, or baulks of wood, provided communication and shelter. All these works were fronted by an anti-tank ditch, topped with a double row of barbed wire, plus numerous anti-tank and anti-personnel mines. A formidable array indeed.

Lyle Craig expressed his views of the feelings of some of the men before the battle.

> The clearest recollection was a feeling of foreboding. Tragically one tank crew . . . in the first wave was so affected by what lay ahead they became withdrawn and uncommunicative. Three of the turret crew lost their lives on the morning of the battle. I remember individuals on the night before the battle began engaged on simple tasks, they were to lose their lives next morning. I remember Lieutenant Brown (B Squadron) returning from the briefing, full of humour and life. He was killed by a sniper's bullet the next morning. Before darkness fell I watched Lieutenant Pyl (B Squadron) digging a narrow slit trench in which to sleep, he was also killed the next morning in the same way.
>
> On the morning of the battle we received . . . mail, which no doubt helped morale. Trooper Savage was another casualty. He came from Somerset and was a county cricketer. I recall Fred Savage being lifted up by two other members of the troop and shouting 'Good old Somerset'. He seemed only slightly wounded but died shortly afterwards. During the next morning the recce troop were called out to replenish the tanks with petrol and ammunition. We were appalled at the number of dead lying about, mostly infantry. An unusual army issue was made the night before battle [of] special field dressings, against phosphorous burns . . . to all tank personnel. Intelligence must have got hold of some information for this to be carried out; fortunately they were not required.

Zero hour was 6am and for the preceding fifteen minutes a very heavy artillery bombardment of 600 guns took place. The morning dawned bright and sunny but once the start line was crossed visibility became nil. Major Griffith recalled, 'From my position in the turret, it was impossible to see more than a yard in front of the tank!' This was caused by a smokescreen that had been laid in an attempt to hide the advance and by dust. With no wind the smokescreen was slow to clear, but the dust was much worse since the ground was baked dry by the sun; tank tracks and exploding shells provided a cloud of dust as dense as the old-fashioned London 'pea-souper' fog.

Tank commanders also found it almost impossible to have their heads out of the turret; with shrapnel, machine-gun and sniper fire such was a suicidal option. Although the attack was supposed to go in 'line abreast' this was impossible to maintain. The infantry had terrible problems. A barbed-wire maze was the first trap they encountered; they struggled to get through but became more entangled and were sitting targets for the German machine guns.

To improve communication between tanks and infantry, wireless operators from the infantry companies took the co-drivers' places in the troop leaders' tanks but this proved ineffective because of the many casualties among the foot personnel carrying the No. 38 wireless sets who made good targets for the enemy. The large number of units involved also caused frequency congestion, which made communications virtually impossible.

Mike Pope, second-in-command of B Squadron, wrote of the battle.

> Intelligence reports were contradictory and confusing. . . . However it was true there were concrete and steel gun emplacements with permanent underground living quarters. . . .
>
> Next morning at 0530 hours tanks were ready to move out of harbour. The Seaforth Highlanders whom B Squadron were supporting waved cheerfully as we went past.
>
> Now and then tank commanders opened up their turret flaps to orientate themselves as looking through periscopes with the tank turning one way and the turret traversing in another direction it was very easy to become disorientated. I was doing just that when a sharp rifle shot rang out and Graham Brown, the Troop Leader in the penultimate tank behind mine, slumped down in the turret. My fears were confirmed when Graham's wireless operator, in a grief stricken voice came over the air, 'My boss has been killed by a single shot through the head'. Almost certainly the shot had come from a sniper . . .
>
> As we advanced through the trees I told my gunner, 'Cock your Besa up in the air and keep spraying those trees until I tell you to stop'.
>
> Visibility was now practically nil from the fumes, dust and mist which lingered in the dense foliage. . . . it seemed an age before we sighted a glimmer of light, warning us of the open ground ahead. The Seaforth were striding forward with great determination.
>
> As we entered the clearing it seemed . . . all hell was let loose, so intense was the firepower that met us, I think I must have blacked for a jiffy. The next thing I heard was my driver over the intercom, 'Both tracks have been blown off and the gun turret is jammed'. I ordered [evacuation] immediately . . . I looked across at the Squadron Leader's tank and saw his crew evacuating, dragging Gordon Russell out and laying him on the engine deck. He looked completely lifeless, perhaps he was a goner too, I thought?

The scene around us was total carnage, made worse by the moaning and groaning of the wounded so close at hand, I think we all thought the end had come. . . .

Once in the crater the noise of the shells overhead was so great it felt as if one's eardrums would burst. Even worse was the noise of our tanks exploding and the blinding flashes as they went up in flames all round us.

We discussed what do to next, lie doggo or try and make a run for it? We decided to wait. At long last an eerie silence descended, making us wonder if all the terrible noise had been a bad dream, but the stench of gun powder and the carnage all around soon told us otherwise.

Our own tank was burnt out but slouched against it was a Sergeant from the Seaforth Highlanders. Without any sign of injury, his helmet tipped forward and his rifle slung across his lap. I went across to speak to him, but as I raised his helmet I realised he was dead, very dead. A nasty shock when I expected to have a chat with him. Totally dejected and drained of all feelings we started to shuffle aimlessly back in the direction from which we had come, hardly caring whether we survived or perished.

Suddenly we heard the sound of a vehicle approaching, it was the blood wagon flying a large Red Cross flag . . . As the driver pulled up we could see it was full of bodies, some strapped on to stretchers, some swathed in bandages. He cheerfully directed us to the medical aid post . . . As we approached teams of ambulances were rushing to and fro. We were relieved to catch sight of Padre Hughes, a lovely man and well respected by all ranks and religions. It was sad to see the tears in his eyes as he reeled off the names of his flock, in his warm Welsh brogue, to whom he had performed the last rites.

Apart from our pride my crew and I only had minor injuries, which were dressed by the Medical Officer. I enquired of Padre Hughes if he had any news of Gordon Russell, and was greatly relieved to learn he was about just alive, albeit in a critical condition.

A minefield and concealed anti-tank guns delayed A Squadron and Major Griffith ordered Lieutenant Hunt's No. 5 Troop to find a way round. This route was blocked by a very deep gully, into which Hunt's tank turned a complete somersault. The wireless operator recalls this episode later.

At 8am Major Russell led B Squadron out of the wood towards the objective but, with a hundred yards to go, anti-tank guns crippled five tanks including Russell's and Captain Pope's. The former was wounded seriously and the latter slightly. Russell's was no more than thirty yards from a gun emplacement, but dust made the visibility so bad that the anti-tank gun could not have been seen.

Lance-Corporal Hughes, the squadron leader's gunner, described what happened.

> Our driver, Trooper Jennings, was positioning the tank to cross a large defensive ditch when we were repeatedly hit by gunfire. Major Russell gave the order to bale out. I followed him and jumped to the ground, glancing up I saw him lying across the engine deck, with what looked like the top of his head blown off. It appeared an A.P. round had ricocheted off the turret and glanced off his head. I was down on the ground before I realised he was moving. The wireless operator, Gerry Chester, and I climbed back on to the tank, got Major Russell down and carried him to a ditch. Meanwhile Harry Jenkins, the driver, had got caught up in a tangle of metal from the track guards. Bill Wheatley, co-driver, got Harry disentangled and took him to the ditch as well.
>
> Bill Wheatley produced the First Aid kit, bandaged up Major Russell's head and made him as comfortable as possible. We decided to stay in the ditch until things calmed down a bit.

Trooper Dawson, who was in one of the two tanks to reach the objective, described the horrendous episode.

> While returning from the objective our tank was hit. Sergeant T. McAughtry saw the incident and said the turret was blown twenty feet in the air. Fatal casualties were Sergeant L Reeve, Lance Corporal H Pryde and Trooper R Ellis.[7] Sergeant McAughtry picked me up and carried me back to the dressing station. A little later on he returned with a Sergeant tank commander, and four of them carried Major Russell to the Sergeant's tank, which was positioned in a ditch some way off. They were able to drive him to the First Aid post at the rear where the Medics took over. Some months later Major Russell was able to visit the [Squadron] and we were all delighted to see him again.

Alan Hughes and Bill Wheatley were both Mentioned in Despatches for their efforts.

No praise can be too high for the medical team. The doctor, Captain Lush, and Corporal Gleghorn worked wonders, going about their business with calm efficiency and sympathy although almost overcome by the number of casualties. Corporal Gleghorn, a man respected throughout the Regiment, was subsequently awarded the Military Medal.

Meanwhile the battle went on. Lieutenant Pyl, on B Squadron's left, reached the objective with the Seaforth, who pointed out a house to him about 200 yards ahead from which they were being engaged heavily. Pyl's troop immediately silenced all opposition from the house and returned to the remainder of B Squadron, now under Captain Mackean. Soon afterwards Mackean advanced slowly into the clearing and was immediately engaged by anti-tank guns. Using smoke to extricate himself, his tank was quickly knocked out by another anti-tank gun and he and his crew baled out but were pinned down by machine-gun fire. It was at this point that Lieutenant Ronald Horsburgh, from Edinburgh, was killed by yet another sniper's bullet.

With so many tanks knocked out, a composite squadron was formed from B and C Squadrons, under Captain Thomas. Unfortunately this force was situated in one of the killing ground areas and was very heavily bombarded, three more tanks being hit by high-calibre shells, probably 210mm. They had reached the objective but were unable to find any trace of the Seaforth. Captain Thomas displayed great coolness when the CO ordered him to withdraw to a feature where he could dominate the objective. Whilst trying to do so, he came under more direct fire from many anti-tank guns. Seven tanks, including his own, were destroyed. Meanwhile Lieutenant Mahon's troop destroyed a Panther turret and a 75mm anti-tank gun. The Sherman's 75mm and the 6-pounder of the Churchill of his composite troop penetrated easily the armour of the two guns while Besa fire killed the crew of the 75. The range was about 200 yards. However, Mahon's tanks were then knocked out.

Captain Thomas was awarded the Military Cross. The citation gives a greater insight into these events.

> Captain Thomas was supporting the Seaforth of Canada. Early in the fighting in the course of which both his Squadron Leader and that of the flanking Squadron were knocked out . . . he took command and re-organised the remaining eleven fit ones. He did this on foot under heavy fire and full view of the enemy. Having re-organised this force . . . , he carried out the original plan . . . and against all opposition fought his way to the objective, losing three more tanks on the way, to emplaced anti-tank guns at 100 yards range. In the course of this action he destroyed one Mk V Panther emplacement, one Mk IV Special, one 75mm anti-tank gun, one 20mm anti-tank gun and overran a complete enemy infantry strong point. The fact of his force penetrating the enemy line was largely instrumental in the rolling up of the complete Hitler Line. Whilst holding the objective his own tank and five others were destroyed. Despite this, Captain Thomas would NOT leave the objective until ordered to do so. His coolness, daring and determination were an inspiration to all his officers and men.

Among the countless brave actions on this particular day that of Sergeant John Maxwell, who was awarded the Military Medal, allows a greater insight to some of the incidents that occurred. The citation for his award reads:

> Sergeant Maxwell, a Troop Sergeant, was supporting a platoon of the Seaforth Highlanders of Canada. At 1300 hours his tank was hit by a heavy calibre anti-tank gun and put him out of action. The area around the tank was subjected to very heavy shelling and mortaring. Sergeant Maxwell ordered his crew to dismantle the Besa machine gun and set it up in a firing position on the ground. When this was done Sergeant Maxwell ordered . . . his crew to take cover in the tank, while he continued to fire the Besa . . . His action was instrumental in pinning down a complete enemy strong point. This so angered them that a heavy concentration was put down on his position as a result of which his Besa was put out of action and he himself severely wounded. His devotion to duty has been an inspiration to the Regiment and his courage outstanding.

Meanwhile, on the right flank, Major Griffith reported a number of tanks and anti-tank guns forming up near the road on the bank of the Forme d'Aquino. After a reconnaissance he decided it was too dangerous to use artillery fire against them owing to the presence nearby of Canadian troops. The only way forward was to ask the Sappers to gap the minefield. This they did despite losses. Sergeant Best led two Churchills through the gap only to be knocked out by two concealed anti-tank guns. Sergeant Walter Best, a Belfastman, was killed.

In Major Griffith's report of the battle he tells of another amazing incident.

> Major 'Snipe' Watson of the PPCLI lay all day under the muzzle of an 88mm anti-tank gun. Every time it fired (and this often) he suffered the heat and blast from the discharge. It was a long day. He was wounded twice by shrapnel, once in the arm, secondly in the head by a piece of his helmet and then by a Schmeisser bullet in his forehead. He was found next day by an old friend, Colin McDougal. An eyewitness swears the entire conversation went thus:
> 'Hullo, Bucko'.
> 'Oh, Hello, Colin'.

Major Griffith continued.

> The PPCLI took possession of a deep and well-appointed German dugout about 100 yards in front of my own position. In the fog of war it became clear we had over-run a well organised defensive position. The danger from anti-personnel mines and anti-tank mines was ever

present, minimum movement was the order of the day. This was confirmed the next day when the RSM of the PPCLI left the bunker and trod on an S-mine and was killed. I and many others had used those steps many times to go in and out.

Trooper Farmer recalled the extraordinary episode that befell his tank. As mentioned earlier, soon after the attack went in, No. 5 Troop A Squadron were ordered to try and find a way round the minefield, which was holding up the attack.

Visibility was almost nil. As wireless operator in the Troop Leader's tank, I heard him say 'Driver, left a little'. All of a sudden we seemed to be falling upside down as the six-pounder fired! Little Harry Freer, the gunner, had his finger on the trigger, ready for any emergency. The unexpected movement caused him to fire. All was chaos. Ammunition and everything that had been carefully stowed, was all over the place. We landed with an almighty thump on the turret, the force being so great we rolled over onto the tracks! Fumes from the discharge of the gun filled the turret, everything was scattered, the wireless torn from its mounting, bodies lay about the turret. Silence. After a few moments a voice called out our names. It was the Troop Leader doing a sort of roll call. Everyone answered. The next thing a bottle of whiskey was thrust towards me. I took a swig. I had never drunk the stuff before, and nearly choked as the fiery liquid went down. The bottle was passed round.

We discovered our driver, Davy Graham, had the presence of mind to switch off the ignition as we fell, thus avoiding a fire, I'm sure. The Troop Leader called for Davy to meet him under the tank to examine the tracks. When they got back in they reported neither were broken. I tried to get the 19 set going again, but without success. The Troop Leader said he would have to find Major Griffith and report to him on foot.

It seemed ages before he returned. We feared the worst. At last he got back and told us where we were. Apparently we had gone over the side of a very deep ravine, luckily landing on a plateau about fifty feet down. The ravine itself was shaped like an inverted Dunce's cap and must have been at least 300 feet deep. We now had to get back to the defensive line.

Davy Graham set off at a very, very steep angle to get to the bottom before climbing up the other side. It was a superb piece of driving requiring the greatest skill. At last we got to the top on the other side only to be met by a sheer ten-foot climb to get out. We required three attempts to master it. It was the finest piece of driving I had ever seen, no words can describe his skill, at any minute it seemed the tank might run head over heels, the angle was so steep.

Later in the day Major Griffith was ordered to form a base with A Squadron, the PPCLI and the Loyal Edmontons, while the remainder of B and C Squadrons rallied near the start line with Captain Mackean, who had returned on foot, in charge. The Canadians had not fought with the Horse before. Lieutenant-Colonel Wade, PPCLI, was delighted when he heard they would stay with the infantry for the night; he had not expected this. That night proved uncomfortable for A Squadron, the tanks having to remain closed down because of machine-gun fire and German patrols that came very close.

Another aspect of the battle can be gleaned from the citation for the award of a Bar to Major Griffith's Military Cross. It is noteworthy that the squadron leader was the only officer in the Regiment to be so honoured.

On 23 and 24 May 1944, in action against the Hitler Line, Major Griffith's squadron supported a battalion of an infantry brigade. 600 yards from the start line his squadron was held up by obstacles and an extensive enemy mine field. Visibility was 10 yards and the squadron came under very heavy shelling and mortaring, which continued incessantly for 28 hours. Touch was lost with the infantry and a battle commenced against powerful anti-tank defences. Major Griffith controlled the battle on foot despite the heavy enemy fire, and besides accounting for several snipers himself, his tanks destroyed two Mark V tanks (Panthers), 2 75mm anti-tank guns, one 88mm anti-tank gun and inflicted severe casualties on the enemy infantry. Four of his Churchill tanks were destroyed in the action. As it was found impossible to by-pass the minefield and all attempts at gapping were unsuccessful, Major Griffith consolidated his gains. To do this, he left the safety of his tank and for many hours, on foot and under intense fire, directed the forming up on a strong point. He helped considerably in the reorganisation of the infantry and directed the clearance of casualties. He held this position against constant enemy action throughout one day and one night and would only leave the area when ordered to do so the following morning when the battle had been won. His clear appreciation of the situation, his complete disregard for his personal safety, his coolness and daring were an inspiration to all the troops and there is no doubt that his action in pinning down powerful elements of the enemy defences helped considerably in the forcing of the Hitler Line.

Near nightfall C Squadron was unlucky when a stray Nebelwerfer shell landed near the squadron and RHQ refuelling area causing much damage and casualties. The regimental spirit and its will to win were exemplified by the Bar to the Military Medal won by Trooper Neilson. His first Military Medal had been won at Longstop in North Africa. The citation for his Bar reads:

On 23 and 24 May 1944, in action against the Hitler Line, Trooper Neilson's tank was knocked out by enemy anti-tank guns. . . . this soldier refused to leave the battlefield and on his initiative undertook the task of collecting the wounded. Under very heavy fire and full view of the enemy, Trooper Neilson organised and directed the evacuation of the many wounded. Three times he carried men safely back and each time he returned to the battlefield for more. He seemed to bear a charmed life, and for more than twenty hours remained under fire collecting the wounded. It was not his duty, and on two occasions he went to help wounded men when stretcher-bearers were unable to do so owing to heavy enemy fire.

His unfailing calmness under these conditions [was] an inspiration to all troops in the area.

On 24 May some volunteers returned to the battlefield to collect dead comrades and bring them back for burial. Next day a burial service took place at the Canadian cemetery, where a plot of ground was reserved for the North Irish Horse. The Canadian dead were buried on three sides of a square and those of the North Irish Horse on the fourth. The moving service was made more poignant when Canadian pipers played a lament, the skirl of the pipes drifting across the now deserted battlefield. Everyone present was visibly moved; the loss of so many friends deeply affected those left behind. As the *Last Post* was played it signalled a farewell to friends who had made the ultimate soldier's sacrifice. Friends left behind in that Italian cemetery will never be forgotten; brave men and true.

Trooper Dick Dawson recalled when the cupola was blown off his tank and he himself was wounded and sent to hospital. In hospital in Naples he heard that Kitchener Hanna would like to see anyone from the Horse. Kitchener had received terrible wounds at the Hitler Line, losing an eye and an arm as well as being very badly burnt. Those who knew Kitchener were well aware of his indomitable spirit at the best of times; it would take more than the Germans could do to break that spirit.

Sister Mitchell from Portadown thought Kitchener would be lucky to survive the night. The surgeon asked her to pay special attention to him, especially as she was from his area. During the night she went away to make tea and while she was away she heard terrible screams. Rushing back she found Kitchener's heavily bandaged arm on fire. With great presence of mind she dealt with it. Apparently he had come to and tried to light a cigarette; the loss of his eye and arm made the operation particularly difficult and he succeeded only in setting fire to the bandages.

Kitchener had the will to fight, and the will to live. When Dick Dawson visited him he found he was not on his last legs at all, but quite chirpy. Kitchener informed Dawson that he did not want a false arm but a spike instead, adding that he would march forward making holes in the ground

141

while the man behind put the potatoes in. Needless to say he recovered and secured post-war employment as a security guard on a military base.

A letter received after the battle gives further detail some of B Squadron's wounded.

> Tony Drew[8] is coming on fairly well now and certainly looks better than when he came in with two black eyes, his upper lip very swollen and blue, one side of his face three times the size of the other and the rest of him covered in bandages. The Sisters call him 'Black Eyes'. However his head injuries are nearly OK now but his left leg is still in plaster.
>
> Ray Dixon's legs are still a mass of bandages, with little rubber tubes projecting through where the penicillin is introduced to his wounds. The 'Big Wigs' reckon that penicillin now reduces the recovery time to about three weeks, where before it would have taken about three months to achieve the same result. So Ray may be moved sooner than expected, although his legs still have a long way to go.
>
> Johnny Cook was in a pretty bad way when he came in. For adding to the burns he received, he caught malaria on the way up, arriving with a temperature of 105F. However he is fairly good now and should be on the road again soon.

With the loss of the Hitler Line, Kesselring's army was now in disarray, menaced by the British advancing towards the Melfa and the French, who had fought tremendously well in the mountains, and were nearing Route 6. Allied forces were pushing inland from Anzio and Kesselring had to bring in his last reserves, which had been intended for France, vindicating the Allied strategy of extending Hitler's resources to the full on all three fronts.

During the battle 1st Canadian Division had 879 casualties from one brigade – the highest single daily casualty toll for any brigade in Italy – while the North Irish Horse lost thirty-six officers and men killed, including two who died later from their wounds, thirty-six wounded and thirty-two tanks lost, representing sixty per cent of regimental strength. This led to a reforming of the Regiment, squadrons reduced to four fighting troops: A and C Squadrons disbanded their No. 5 Troops and B Squadron its No. 3 Troop.

Hitherto, all losses had been light, but this was an instance of participation in a set piece attack with little room to manoeuvre; it was a case of 'Into the valley of death rode the six hundred'. All ranks displayed the greatest devotion to duty throughout and their determination to support the infantry whatever the cost won the highest praise from many sources as indicated by the citation for the award of the Distinguished Service Order to the commanding officer.

On 23 May 1944 the North Irish Horse was in support of 2nd Canadian Brigade. The line was strongly organised and firmly held. The nature of the terrain and vegetation favoured anti-tank defence and the enemy had taken full advantage of the facts in preparing his positions. Numerous anti-tank weapons, cleverly sited and minefields disposed in depth, took heavy toll of the North Irish Horse tanks. The Regiment however pressed on, determined to support the infantry, who were meeting strong resistance and murderous fire from artillery and mortars.

Lieutenant Colonel Eugene Victor Strickland, the Regimental Commander, was almost continuously in the forward area organising and inspiring the repeated tank attacks in support of the infantry. When the situation was critical ... Lieutenant Colonel Strickland personally organised a tank force in the forward area to assist the elements of two companies of the Seaforth Highlanders of Canada isolated on their objective.

In reorganising the armour, this officer, on several occasions, found it necessary to dismount from his tank to assist in the forming up.

His personal example of coolness, determination and indifference to heavy enemy fire was an inspiration to both his own men and the infantry alike.

The Canadian GOC 1st Canadian Division added his own personal recommendation: 'This officer's conduct during the battle was an outstanding example of personal bravery and determination to win, in the highest traditions of the service.'

Many tributes were paid to the Regiment and, significantly, they were granted the honour of wearing the Maple Leaf on their sleeves, a distinction shared by all units of 25 Tank Brigade, and a constant reminder of true Canadian friendships which remain evergreen.

In retrospect it is easy to criticise the preparation for CHESTERFIELD. Perhaps the higher command did not appreciate fully the strength of the emplacements as the pre-battle artillery bombardment did little damage; 7.2-inch howitzers would have been necessary for this. A set piece tank attack had never before been taken on with so little room for manoeuvre and where the plan for the deployment of armour was changed less than twenty-four hours before H-Hour. It would have been better to advance under cover of darkness. However, many lessons were learned, which were applied in later battles. Thereafter greater skills in fighting were developed as the campaign moved up Italy.

This tremendous achievement by the gallant Canadians and Ulstermen was not accomplished without cost. Close to the scene of the bitter fighting rest those who paid the price of victory with their lives and on a plaque bearing the words 'Canadian Infantry Brigade Group, Adolf Hitler Line,

May 23 1944' the names of four regiments are inscribed, three Canadian and The North Irish Horse. That day left a deep impression upon everyone. In 1952 Lieutenant John Allen of B Squadron North Irish Horse (TA) started a commemoration in Londonderry for those who fell at the Hitler Line. He had served with A Squadron throughout the war, becoming Squadron Sergeant Major. This commemoration has been carried on every year by successive North Irish Horse Squadrons based in the North West and is currently held in Limavady by 69 (North Irish Horse) Squadron Royal Signals. The Fiftieth Anniversary held in 1994 in Shackleton Barracks, Ballykelly was a memorable weekend, attended by a large gathering, including many who had served at the Hitler Line. Brigadier-General D M Dean CD of the Canadian Forces was also present, representing the Canadian Army.

That the Hitler Line battle should have been chosen as the 'Regimental Day' is hardly surprising. The bloodiest day in the history of the North Irish Horse was 23 May 1944; more men lost their lives on that early-summer day in Italy than in any other single day in two world wars. But it was not sacrifice alone that was being commemorated; the Regiment had done sterling work and its achievements were recognised by General, later Field Marshal, Alexander. In the early 1950s Alex was Minister of Defence in Churchill's government and Colonel Strickland was appointed as a special military aide as a result of which he travelled a lot with Alex and 'had many long conversations with him'. Alex told Strickland that 'the breaking of the Hitler Line was due to those two Churchill Tank Regiments and gave him his most satisfactory day of a long and very distinguished military life'.[9]

Strickland went on to recall that:

> Alamein had been a glorious day for [Alexander], and then had come the taking of Tunis and his famous telegram to the war-time Prime Minister. But, the Field Marshal added, Cassino had caused him nightmares, as had the Anzio affairs, and the final break-through by the Churchill tanks on that day in the Liri Valley, as a result of which Kesselring's great defiance was ended and Alex's own fears demolished, would remain for him the most potent reminder. He insisted on the two Commanding Officers being awarded immediate DSOs.
>
> . . . you won't find the above in any biography or history but it is the truth. You see, the relative failure of Anzio and the inability to break the Hitler Line had placed Alex on a knife-edge. What might have been the breaking of his reputation was saved that day by the crews of those Churchill tanks, so many of whom now lie in that huge Cassino cemetery. Kesselring had to withdraw and was chased back to his next great line of defence – the Gothic Line.

... I had no idea how he (Alex) thought about these things until years later ... when he talked to me in the terms I have indicated above. You know that the Army Tank Brigades were never glamorised like some of the Armoured Divisions.

NOTES

1   Vesuvius erupted on 19 March 1944. Gunners of 25 HAA Battery, 9th (Londonderry) HAA Regiment had marked St Patrick's Day by climbing to the top of the mountain to look down into the crater.

2   With the arrival of the Shermans, the squadron establishment altered to three Churchills in SHQ, three troops each of three Churchills and two troops of three Shermans.

3   When the Poles made their final attack they hit thin air; the Germans had already evacuated the monastery. The leading Polish soldiers, of the Podolski Lancers, ran up a hastily made regimental flag.

4   His own regiment was the King's Dragoon Guards.

5   A quote from the chaplain of the Seaforth of Canada.

6   During the Italian campaign the army group was known as 15 Army Group before becoming Allied Armies Italy and then reverting to the original designation.

7   Sergeant Leslie Reeve was a Londoner, Corporal James Pryde came from Antrim and Trooper Reginald Ellis was from Hertfordshire.

8   Tony Drew was a great character, who had inherited a small fortune before the war and gone through it in next to no time. He was an excellent tank driver.

9   Letter from Colonel Strickland to Gordon Bradley, dated 23 August 1982.

CHAPTER IX
The Chase Begins

The Germans began retreating from the Hitler line during the night 23–24 May, abandoning much heavy equipment. On 29 May the North Irish Horse rejoined 2 Canadian Brigade and during the following night the Edmontons, with C Squadron, established themselves at Frosinone; by first light on the 31st B Squadron had linked up with the Seaforth of Canada and A Squadron with the Princess Patricia's, respectively north and south of the town. The brigade was to advance and hold Monte Radicino, thus securing the right flank of 1 Canadian Brigade, advancing along the western side of the Liri valley. The Edmontons, supported by C Squadron and with A Squadron providing right-flank protection, would carry out this attack. A section of 25 Tank Brigade's Royal Engineers' troop arrived at 11.30am and a battery of Royal Devon Yeomanry provided artillery support. While preparations were being made, all movement in the valley was shelled and mortared by the Germans. At 11.45 the advance began with B Squadron pushing two troops forward to secure the vineyard feature from which they could control the left flank.

At 1.00pm, after slow progress in very difficult country, C Squadron was stopped by a large demolition on Route 6. Major Welch asked the sappers to make a crossing east of the demolition. Once this was complete, with help from infantry pioneers, C Squadron crossed the stream about ninety minutes after starting. Some opposition was encountered on the right of the objective, fire coming from a convent situated on a small, steep knoll; an infantry company and two C Squadron troops deployed to take this feature while tanks from A and C Squadrons bombarded the convent. Although a C Squadron Sherman turned turtle in a deep hole no one was hurt, nor were any casualties sustained that day. The Edmontons captured and consolidated Monte Radicino in the afternoon while the historic town of Ferentino on Route 6, eight miles north-east of Frosinone, was cleared next morning. With the enemy in full retreat the remainder of the day was devoted to essential maintenance; the Regiment would not be involved in further operations until mid-June.

On 4 June, the day Rome fell, Lieutenant-Colonel Strickland DSO, MM[1] handed back command to The Lord O'Neill, and returned to command his own regiment, 145 RAC, while 25 Tank Brigade bade farewell to the Canadians on coming under command of 4th British Division. The Regiment was allotted to support 28 Brigade. On 6 June the long-awaited news of the landings in Normandy caused considerable elation and a feeling that the war was now in its final phase. Since 28 Brigade was in reserve the Regiment did not move forward to join it in Valmontone until the 7th. But when 8th Indian Division took over the advance from 4th Division on 10 June, 28 Brigade had still not been committed and the Regiment came under command of 17 Indian Brigade, now some eighty miles to the north. With no tank transporters available and 8th Division operating in country unsuitable for large numbers of tanks, 51st Royal Tanks were withdrawn from the advance on the divisional handover. North Irish Horse had no immediate role as only 142 RAC was required to support 8th Division.

Since Valmontone is little more than twenty miles from Rome, visits to the Eternal City were arranged daily and enjoyed thoroughly by all. The city was still enjoying liberation 'fever' with streets thronged with delighted Romans and happy servicemen. Shops, cinemas and hastily, but well organised, canteens were great attractions and gifts, mostly underwear for wives and sweethearts, were bought and posted home. Many visited Saint Peter's and even stolid Ulstermen were impressed; the vast, quiet, cool interior and the basilica's magnificent splendour contrasted markedly with the heat, noise and squalor outside.

On 15 June the Regiment was ordered to form a composite squadron of all its available Shermans which would move north next day to join 8th Indian Division, relieving 142 RAC's composite Sherman squadron. The latter regiment had been advancing in contact with the enemy for eleven days and the pace had become too hot for its Churchills, which needed urgent maintenance; with the Churchills withdrawn, 142's Shermans continued supporting the Indians. The composite North Irish Horse squadron, which included all the Sherman troops plus the Recce Troop, was commanded by Major Welch with Captain Thomas as second-in-command. With no transporters available, the tanks set off at 7.30am next day on a drive of 138 miles.

Trooper Farmer, of A Squadron, recalled the

> mammoth effort which took three days; it started in glorious sunshine and ended in pouring rain. It was never intended to be so long, but the enemy kept retiring before we could make contact, it developed into a chase until we caught up with him. It was fortunate that we had Shermans at this time as they were faster on the road than Churchills. . . . I remember answering a call of nature one night . . . and was horrified to see the whites of a pair of eyes peering at me from the other side of the bush. It proved to be a member of a Gurkha

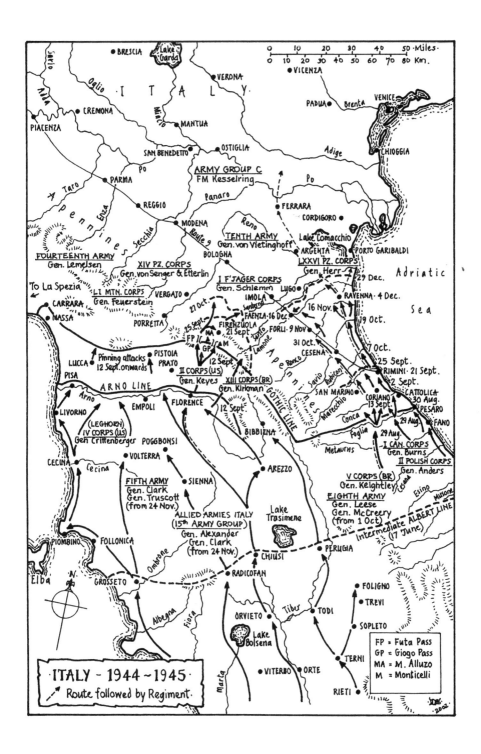

ITALY - 1944 ~ 1945 ·
Route followed by Regiment.

FP = Futa Pass
GP = Giogo Pass
MA = M. Alluzo
M = Monticelli

patrol. A few moments later a grinning face appeared. It was uncanny how quietly they could move at night.

As the squadron advanced, signs of the routed enemy could be seen; unburied bodies, knocked-out tanks – mostly Mark IVs – and wrecked artillery pieces littered the route. Whenever the tanks halted, starving Italians rushed out to greet the crews and were grateful for any food the troops could offer. The language barrier was eased by the many Italians who had lived in the USA and spoke English with a pronounced 'Yankee drawl'; 'sonofabitch' was used to describe one and all.

Lyle Craig recalled one incident in a vineyard.

> We . . . were sitting on the grass waiting for the evening meal to cook. Some Italians tentatively approached and asked if we would rise. It was the family orchard. The troops did as they were asked and were surprised to see the family set to and start digging up the family valuables. The troops in question regarded this as a great compliment as they had been hidden away from the Germans but not from the Allies.

The squadron spent the second night at Massa Martana, twenty miles behind the front. A withdrawal over twenty-five days and some 150 miles had taken the Germans back to the Trasimene line where they had established a continuous, cohesive line across the country for the first time since 11 May. This new line was some forty to fifty miles short of the Gothic Line which Kesselring proposed to hold throughout the winter. From now on the Allies would pay heavily in men and in time for every mile of their advance; the terrain lent itself to the classic German defensive tactic of holding a position long enough to force the attackers to deploy and mount an attack before falling back to the next position where the pattern would be repeated.

Eighth Indian Division had been advancing westwards towards Perugia, capital of Umbria, which fell to 6th Armoured Division on the 20th. After a sharp skirmish on the morning of the 17th, 1st Argyll and Sutherland Highlanders entered Assisi, birthplace of Saint Francis, Italy's patron saint. Route 75 crosses the Chiasco river at Bastia where the Germans had blown the bridge and sited anti-tank guns to cover the demolition. Following a stiff fight, 3/8th Punjab Regiment crossed the river during the night and went on to take the airfield, three miles to the north-west. On 18 June, in pouring rain, the composite North Irish Horse squadron entered Bastia and relieved 142 RAC's composite Sherman squadron. The latter moved back to Narni, fifty miles north of Rome, having spent their last day supporting 1/5th Gurkhas of 17 Brigade,[2] and a squadron of 6th Duke of Connaught's Own Lancers,[3] against a determined rearguard action just north of the town. Two North Irish troops, under Lieutenants Hunt and Rogers, moved up that afternoon to join the Lancers; RHQ arrived that evening to harbour in Petrignano, three miles north of Bastia.

The clearing of the Ripa ridge, running for five miles between the Tiber and Chiasco rivers and rising to a thousand feet, was 17 Brigade's next objective; the ridge takes its name from the village of Ripa, which, with Civitella, is perched upon its crest. In Civitella a tower provided excellent observation of the surrounding countryside. Two troops advanced at 5.30 next morning with B Squadron 6th Lancers to support 1/5th Gurkhas as they attacked along the ridge towards Ripa. An earlier incorrect report had indicated that Civitella had fallen at 4.00am and that the Gurkhas were advancing but the village remained in German hands and the Gurkhas were stalled under heavy shell- and mortarfire. Anti-tank weapons immobilised two tanks of Rogers' troop at about 9 o'clock, killing Lance-Corporal William Hill, a driver from County Tyrone, and wounding seven others; Rogers and Corporal Ham were the only two unscathed. The troop leader ordered evacuation of both tanks and the crews reached cover in spite of heavy mortaring and machine-gun fire. However, Trooper Linton was missing and Corporal Ham volunteered to join Lieutenant Rogers in a search for him. After crossing ground swept by machine-gun fire and mortars, the pair found the injured trooper, unable to move, beside the tank, placed him on a groundsheet and began to crawl back, dragging him along. Deciding that this was too slow and tiring, Rogers returned to bring his remaining tank forward. Ham and Lance-Corporal Archibald Jackson, that tank's driver, tried to lift Linton into the vehicle, but Jackson, a Londonderry man, was hit by enemy fire; the wound proved fatal. Rogers and Ham eventually got Trooper Linton into the tank, strapped Jackson on to it and withdrew; Rogers and Ham rode on the outside.

However, a shell then hit the Sherman, injuring Rogers and Ham and blowing them off the hull. Having lost radio contact with Rogers' tank, Lieutenant Hunt set out to look for his fellow troop leader and found him with a serious arm wound. Hunt took both Rogers and Ham to a cottage occupied by terrified Italians where he dressed the men's wounds, applying a tourniquet to Rogers' arm and giving him morphine for his pain. Hunt then left with Corporal Ham, having told the Italians to loosen the tourniquet every twenty minutes, an instruction that he believed they understood. Back at his own tank, he radioed for medical assistance for Rogers and arranged for Ham's evacuation. When medical help reached Lieutenant Rogers, at around noon, it was found that the Italians had not understood Hunt; the tourniquet had not been loosened and, as a result, Rogers' arm had to be amputated. For his part in this action Lance-Corporal Ham received the Military Medal.

151

At 11 o'clock Civitella was finally secured and D Company of the Gurkhas, supported by the troops of Lieutenants Behr and Garstin, with Captain Thomas in overall command, began edging along the ridge towards Ripa. Superb support came from both tanks and artillery, the latter providing the strange, perhaps unique, and certainly surreal spectacle of a FOO directing his guns while perched on a step-ladder in the open under pelting rain. Among targets destroyed by the tanks was an enemy OP in a church tower. The Gurkhas worked their way past well prepared defensive positions on all the approaches to Ripa and, as the doughty little hillmen infiltrated their positions, the Germans were forced to withdraw, a withdrawal that Lieutenant Hunt's troop encouraged with fire from their tanks. At much the same time, Lieutenant Hubbard's troop supported 1st Royal Fusiliers' attack on Palazzo ridge above the Chiasco river, following which the fusiliers joined the Gurkhas in Ripa. For the rest of that day, tanks continued to engage targets indicated by the infantry.

The brigade now pushed on with Behr's troop supporting 6th Lancers as, at first light, they tried to advance northwards from Ripa. Stiff enemy opposition stopped the Lancers but an attack by the Frontier Force Regiment, supported by the troops of Lieutenants Irwin and Garstin, reached the ridge south of the Grande river, where the Germans were making a stand. The ridge was to be attacked at 6.30pm under cover of smoke and an artillery bombardment. However, the smoke was too heavy, making it difficult for both troops to link up with the companies they were to support; but this was finally achieved with the help of a Frontier Force Regiment liaison officer. A successful attack saw the ridge in Indian hands by dusk. North Irish Horse tanks remained with the infantry throughout the night and the Frontier Force commanding officer arranged for a reconnaissance with Major Welch; at 5 o'clock next morning they would reconnoitre for an attack on the Colombella feature on the far side of the Grande.

At first light on 21 June Lieutenants Irwin and Garstin advised Welch that their respective companies wished to carry out mopping-up operations north of their positions. Those operations uncovered a significant number of Germans still in the area. Irwin was told to deal with them; in the ensuing action between thirty and forty Germans were killed and six captured. Garstin's troop, also in action, knocked out two machine-gun posts. An hour before noon, 17 Brigade's commander decided to switch the axis of his advance to a road farther east as Colombella was heavily defended. In this new assault, Major Welch was to support the Royal Fusiliers with his other four troops. However, at 3.00pm, it was decided to postpone the attack until the next day, due to a shortage of artillery ammunition. That delay also meant that the complete composite squadron could be deployed since the troops then with the Frontier Force Regiment would be back in the squadron fold.

The Lord O'Neill used this lull to relieve Major Welch and Captain Thomas by Major Mackean and Captain Morton while the tanks came back, singly, to replenish. At last light Lieutenants Irwin's and Garstin's troops withdrew and rejoined the squadron, having been in their tanks for twenty-six hours. Next morning brought further postponement of the attack and news that the composite Horse squadron would be relieved by 3rd King's Own Hussars. With a complete armoured regiment the divisional commander could carry out a deeper penetration than would be possible with a single squadron. However, the day of the delay was not wasted; a harassing shoot was arranged with the battalion commanders and 1,000 HE rounds were fired at enemy strongpoints, causing severe casualties. Four parties of Germans appeared under Red Cross flags at various points to collect wounded.

A further shoot took place on the 23rd, the day that RHQ moved back to Narni. At first light next day, 3rd Hussars relieved the composite squadron. The Shermans were left at Bastia with Captain Pope while their crews moved to Narni in trucks. Churchill NA75s were to replace the Shermans left at Bastia and North Irish Horse was to have a three-week period for maintenance, training and shooting. During this period forty-eight-hour leave passes to Rome were granted. However, those weeks were not without their tragedies; in mid-July, Trooper Harry Freer, from Birmingham, a gunner, was killed when his tank fell off a bridge in training; two other crew members were injured.

The Reconnaissance Troop was also re-organised with a troop of three Shermans for close support while the remaining eight Honey tanks formed three patrols and provided the commander's and rear-link vehicles. Major Welch became second-in-command of the Regiment, succeeding Major Llewellen-Palmer, who was posted back to his own regiment; Captain Morton, to be promoted Major, took over C Squadron.

The Churchill NA75 (North Africa 75mm), a Mark IV Churchill with a 75mm gun and mantlet taken from Shermans damaged in Tunisia, was the brainchild of Captain Percy Morrell, REME. In late 1943, as second-in-command of a tank workshop in Algeria, Morrell had noticed that, in bright sunlight, the Churchill's recessed mantlet cast a deep shadow, which provided an excellent aiming point. He was also aware that the shortage of 6-pounder HE rounds in Tunisia was a problem when dealing with anti-tank guns and believed that both problems could be resolved by the simple expedient of fitting a Sherman gun and mantlet in a Churchill. The idea worked although it met a further complication: in British tanks the gunner sat on the left while he was on the right in US tanks. Morrell cured this problem by turning the gun through 180 degrees. Range trials with the new installation were successful, 200 Churchills were converted and Morrell was promoted to major and appointed MBE. The 75mm gun, firing a round weighing 14.9 pounds, was a less effective anti-tank weapon than the 57mm 6-pounder and was outclassed by the German 75 and 88mm weapons, but the bigger HE round was much more effective and the availability of smoke rounds, and indirect fire capability, produced a tank that was much more useful in the infantry support role. Troops initially included two NA75s and one 6-pounder-equipped Churchill to retain dual capability.

The Besas in the turret and the bow were also replaced by Brownings. On the NA75s' first time in action the replacement of the turret Besa resulted in a 'near miss' for Lance-Corporal Moore, a gunner in No. 2 Troop A Squadron.

> During a lull in the fighting we were ordered to pull out while another troop took our place. The usual procedure was to clear our guns before this happened. The quickest, although not the official way, with the Besa was to take the belt out and press the trigger. As no one had told us any different, I followed this procedure with the Browning. As I did this, to my horror, there was a loud bang. I remember taking a cautious look out of the turret. Fortunately the other two tanks had their engines running, thus drowning the noise of the shot, and no one appeared to have heard anything.
>
> Immediately, Major Griffith came on the air, enquiring whether anyone had seen any movement in the houses opposite, which we were supposed to have cleared, as a sniper's bullet had just passed over his head. We kept quiet.

The North Irish Horse was the first regiment to receive the new tanks and, while the extra road speed of the Shermans had been appreciated on the drive to Bastia, crews were glad to have their favourite Churchills back again. Their hillclimbing ability would be as useful in Italy as it had been in Tunisia and the thicker armour was an extra comfort. By contrast, petrol-engined Shermans were prone to burst into flames when hit; the Germans called them 'Tommy cookers' and their crews dubbed them 'Ronsons' from the claim by the eponymous cigarette-lighter manu-facturers that their product 'lit first time'.

On 17 July 25 Tank Brigade reverted to command of 4th Infantry Division with North Irish Horse again supporting 28 Infantry Brigade. Early on the 18th the tanks left on transporters for Arezzo, some seventy-five miles to the north; the wheeled vehicles followed the next day. Colonel The Lord O'Neill and the squadron leaders reported to Brigadier Montague Douglas-Scott, commanding 28 Brigade, at Pogi, a dozen miles west of Arezzo, on the 20th.

The breakthrough following the fall of Rome had lost its impetus and now the Allies had pulled out seven divisions – four Free French and three

American – for Operation DRAGOON, the invasion of southern France, planned for mid-August. By this stage, the advance had reached the mountainous Tuscan countryside, which further slowed progress. Despite splendid work by Royal Engineers, blown bridges and demolitions increased the difficulties of bringing forward sufficient supplies to maintain the momentum; everything had to come by road since railway repairs were incomplete as was the extension to the petrol pipeline. This problem was compounded by the increasing distance from the main bases, now several hundred miles to the south. Delays occurred increasingly on narrow mountainous roads, made treacherous by unseasonable rain. Crashed, or broken-down, vehicles had to be shoved off the roads to keep the supply lines open; fortunately road movements were unhindered by enemy air attack as the Allies had complete control of the air. German resistance, increasingly helped by the terrain, was determined; rearguard actions intensified as they withdrew while their supply problems decreased as their lines of communications shortened. Kesselring planned to delay the Allied advance at every opportunity, and for as long as possible, with the time being used to complete his next prepared position north of Florence, the Gothic Line.

Brigadier Scott explained the divisional plan to the North Irish Horse officers: 4th Division was to advance through Chianti country, west of Route 69, the road running northwards through the Arno valley, and capture Florence. At first, in this difficult country with few roads, 12 and 28 Brigades would lead, with 10 Brigade in reserve; 28 Brigade was so constrained by lack of roads that Scott planned to attack initially on a single-battalion front, normally supported by only two tank troops. A Squadron would support 2nd King's Regiment (Liverpool), B Squadron 2nd Somerset LI and C Squadron 2/4th Hampshires. That night C Squadron and the Recce Troop moved to the area of Bucine just north of Pogi, before linking up with 2/4th Hampshires.

Next morning Major Morton reported to Lieutenant-Colonel Mitchell, commanding the Hampshires. C Squadron was to concentrate south of Montevarchi, five miles to the north-west by 4.00pm; an infantry patrol would go westwards through the mountains to Meleto, six miles away, during the night of the 21st–22nd and, if found unoccupied, No. 2 Troop under Lieutenant Hubbard would support A Company the following morning through Meleto and northwards up the brigade axis. During the day RHQ moved forward to 28 Brigade Headquarters and A and B Squadrons moved forward to Bucine.

C Squadron was fortunate to have a Royal Italian Army liaison officer attached for the forthcoming operations. The indefatigable Teniente Gian-Carlo Stacchi Prinetti was very helpful in gathering intelligence from partisans and local people about destroyed bridges and blows, locations of minefields and enemy positions, their strength and likely intentions.

When on the move, he rode in the co-driver's seat of the leading tank. Should the tank be disabled, he was the first to be rescued and evacuated as the Germans shot captured Italians out of hand. He showed the greatest gallantry; nothing was too much trouble and he was always cheerful. His family owned the prestigious vineyards of Badia Colti, near Montevarchi and the squadron was sorry when the time came to bid *Arrivederci* to their new-found friend.

Meleto was found still to be in enemy hands. Nos. 1 (Lieutenant McCleary) and 2 Troops were ordered forward, ready to cross the start line at 6.00am. The gully crossing, on the start line, was difficult; County Down man Sergeant Terence McQueen, Recce Troop, was killed while on foot guiding tanks across. All six tanks surmounted this obstacle safely before being confronted by a blown bridge. Finding a diversion proved difficult and further delay occurred when Lieutenant Hubbard's tank overturned while crossing. Colonel Mitchell decided to press on without the tanks and A Company reached and consolidated their first objective. C Squadron succeeded in getting all its tanks across by noon. Lieutenant Irwin, in a Sherman from the Recce Troop, had taken over command of No. 2 Troop.

B Company was ordered to pass through A Company towards their objective, Fiazzoie, on the western edge of the Meleto ridge. Nos. 2 and 4 (Lieutenant Bexon) Troops and Captain Thomas, in his close-support tank, took up positions on the ridge held by A Company, and gave accurate and effective fire support to the advancing infantry, who quickly attained their first objective. No. 3 Troop (Lieutenant Foster) had great difficulty in finding a crossing of a river, thus slowing his move to join B Company. During the reconnaissance to find a suitable crossing, Corporal Cunningham's tank was heavily engaged by a 75mm gun, located in Meleto but, although hit three times, it was not penetrated and no serious damage or casualties ensued. When at last a crossing was found, Nos. 2 and 3 Troops joined the infantry but further progress was impossible due to heavy machine-gun and self-propelled anti-tank-gun fire. Brigadier Scott decided to consolidate the positions achieved; the tanks spent the night with their infantry.

Supported by A Squadron, 2nd King's resumed the attack on Meleto at first light on the 23rd but the squadron found great difficulty in moving over the three river crossings used and damaged by C Squadron the day before; forty-ton Churchills caused severe damage to unmade crossings. This new problem was to be a constant menace thereafter; great driving skill was required as tanks skidded and slewed down the approach, followed by the scrabbled climb out on the far side; with the driver's view restricted greatly by the Churchill's tracks, good understanding between commander and driver was essential. The Lord O'Neill had to ask for H-hour to be put back.

Originally the King's had planned a single approach attack from the south-east but reconnaissance revealed no tank crossing from that direction. A two-pronged attack plan was adopted. At 5.30am on the 23rd, it was learned, from partisans, that the Germans had evacuated Meleto during the night; two companies of the King's, supported by the newly arrived A Squadron, entered the village unopposed. Success was short lived; tanks and infantry were subjected to intense shelling, mortar and machine-gun fire from three sides as they took up positions while SPGs appeared and, from close range, set about the tanks. Sergeant Barbour knocked out one of them. Lieutenant Watters, in a Sherman, was about to engage another when his tank was hit by a HE shell and his wireless-operator wounded. By the time his vision had cleared the SPG had gone. Any move forward was impracticable. Counter-attack positions were taken up by the infantry and tanks, who suffered a day of constant enemy fire. Unusually, however, no counter-attack was mounted.

During the night, infantry patrols found many enemy still in the area with strong defensive positions on at least two hilltops. A Squadron, joined in the afternoon by C Squadron's NA75 Churchills and the three Recce Troop Shermans, engaged potential enemy positions, strongpoints and buildings to very good effect, causing considerable damage. Brigadier Scott decided to shift the axis of the next day's advance as the country north-east of Meleto was even more unsuitable than the ground gained so slowly, at considerable cost to the infantry and wear and tear on the tanks, during the last three days.

It was now the Somersets' turn, with B Squadron, to lead the advance northwards towards Gaville with their first objective an east–west track and their second the riverline. An afternoon route reconnaissance revealed a track thought to be passable. At last light Nos. 1 and 2 Troops B Squadron, Lieutenants King and Fleming respectively, and two close-support tanks, moved forward into harbour. Infantry patrols sent out by 2nd King's during the night found the enemy gone, their objective of delaying the advance achieved. At 5.30am on 25 July Lieutenant King's troop moved to support a Somerset company. The going proved more difficult than expected and the tanks had to be guided on foot behind the leading infantry but the first objective was reached without opposition. King then supported his infantry towards the second objective while Fleming's troop and one close-support tank moved up the route blazed by No. 1 Troop.

Initially the advance to the second objective met no resistance until a prominent hill was reached where the infantry met machine-gun fire and were forced to take cover. No. 1 Troop engaged suspected localities with machine-gun and HE rounds which brought enemy fire down on the tanks. The rear tank broke a track while manoeuvring, blocking the narrow road, which was little better than a track. Lance-Corporal Hughes was sent for, but by the time he arrived with his ARV the hapless tank had become a target for every enemy gun in the area. Undaunted by shells landing all around him, Corporal Hughes set to work with complete unconcern and in thirty minutes the track was mended. The troop then took up counter-attack positions at the nearby road junction. By last light the infantry had secured the ridge to their immediate front and No. 2 Troop moved to a covering position on the Camporeggi ridge.

No. 1 Troop was not engaged next day but No. 2 Troop with their 75mm tanks fired at enemy-occupied buildings in the Poggio Secco area which were causing problems for 2nd King's in their resumed advance from Meleto. No. 2 Troop obtained good results, air-bursts being particularly effective, and the enemy were seen to evacuate casualties. Direct fire from A Squadron finally forced them to withdraw. During the afternoon the Somersets learned from partisans that the bridge ahead had been blown and were told of a possible crossing. A strong infantry patrol, accompanied by Captain Sidebottom and Sergeant Ridley of the Royal Engineers' detachment, went out at last light on a reconnaissance and reported that, after some demolition work, the crossing was possible, although difficult. At 5.30 next morning, the Somersets advanced and soon had two companies across the river. With the bridgehead secured, Sappers moved down to the waterside and quickly carried out the necessary demolitions. No. 2 Troop advanced first, taking up fire positions covering the crossing. No. 1 Troop then moved down but both leading tanks broke tracks, completely blocking the approach, and becoming targets for enemy mortars. Corporal Hughes and his ARV were quickly on the scene and, over four hours in the open, under constant mortar fire, including a salvo of Nebelwerfer, repaired and recovered the tanks. Hughes was awarded the Military Medal, the citation for which concludes, 'This NCO's complete disregard for his own safety and his determination to get the tanks mended, in spite of enemy fire was an inspiration to all.' It was mid-afternoon before No. 1 Troop crossed, to be joined quickly by No. 2 Troop. Both troops moved forward to join the Somersets and advanced to Ponte. No further progress was possible that day due to demolitions and what the Battle Report describes as impossible country.

On the 28th the Hampshires and C Squadron took the lead; their objective was San Martino, 1,500 yards to the north, and the surrounding heights. The attack went well as far as Pavelli where yet another bad gully was encountered but, after an hour's hard work by the sappers, four tanks crossed before it became unusable. Those four tanks successfully supported the Hampshires to Fata Palagio while the remainder of the squadron took up position overlooking San Martino ready to support the next phase. Intense fire from the high ground of San Lucia made further progress towards Point 531 impossible. Colonel Mitchell decided to attack

Point 505, which was occupied and consolidated after heavy fighting. During this attack C Squadron, less four tanks, engaged targets in San Martino. Nos. 3 and 4 Troops then advanced to San Andrea, in an attempt to reach Point 531, but the ground proved impossible and they were ordered to halt for the night. A Squadron moved forward to conform with the movement of the King's.

The Hampshires probed forward next morning, seeking a way up to Point 531, but heavy machine-gun and mortar fire prevented any progress and the attack was postponed until the following morning. Meanwhile, Nos. 3 and 4 Troops shot up targets in the San Martino area and, during the afternoon, the FOO of the Royal Devon Yeomanry, equipped with 105mm SPGs, directed his guns on to the same area. The Germans were not yet ready to withdraw and put down an effective counter barrage, which resulted in the tanks withdrawing to cover for the night. A Squadron again moved forward with the King's.

The Hampshires' determined aggression paid off and by 6 o'clock next morning, after almost forty-eight hours' fighting, the Germans had been driven off Point 531. This indicates both the German determination to give up ground slowly and the harsh nature of the ground over which the battalion was fighting. The King's took over the attack, passing through the Hampshires, who went into reserve. A Squadron was unable to support the King's since the tanks could not pass the San Andrea area as San Martino, with its mortars and SPGs, was still in enemy hands.

The last day of the month saw the capture of San Martino, so long a thorn in the flesh; the Somersets and B Squadron had finally completed a most difficult task. San Martino's fall released A Squadron from their confinement near San Andrea and, with two Recce Troop Shermans, the squadron passed forward through B Squadron to Point 531. Ahead the country was so totally unsuited to tanks that it was impossible to catch up with the King's but Point 531 provided excellent observation of the far river bank under attack by 6th Armoured Division, advancing on 4th Division's right.

All the Churchill NA75s, and both Shermans, engaged targets across the river in front of 6th Armoured Division. Their shooting was most effective, targets including a headquarters location, two guns and a Nebelwerfer position as well as transport on Route 69, and was so valuable that, after consultation with 6th Armoured Division, Lieutenant Waters with his two Shermans remained there for three days, liaising with 6th Armoured's FOO and flash spotter. Excellent work was done, each Sherman firing an average of 200 rounds per day – hard work for crews and A Echelon alike. A Squadron harboured nearby that night, C Squadron moved up to the San Martino area and RHQ and Brigade Headquarters also moved forward. Slow and painful progress was being maintained, the Germans still fighting tenaciously for every yard.

Tuesday 1 August was a day of comparative respite for the North Irish Horse, providing an opportunity for maintenance and repairs. Sergeant Ridley and his Royal Engineers section repaired three demolitions in preparation for the planned advance. C Squadron moved forward to Poggio alla Croce and, that evening, A Squadron shelled the area north of Incisa. The brigade axis was about to enter a long, steep-sided pass through the mountains leading towards San Polo, which promised to be a punishingly difficult line of advance. Wednesday was spent planning the next day's advance through the pass. The right flank, an area that had been troubling the King's during the day, was shot up by moonlight.

Next morning the Somersets, supported by B Squadron, advanced towards San Polo and, to their surprise and delight, found the enemy gone and the dreaded valley undefended. Major Griffith's jeep was the sole casualty, running over a Schu-mine and suffering a buckled wheel. That afternoon, in glorious sunshine, the Hampshires and C Squadron passed through the Somersets and reached San Donatino unopposed. To regain contact, Lieutenant Irwin with a troop of Honeys and a section of the Hampshires' carrier platoon was ordered forward to locate the withdrawing Germans. A small party of Germans, mostly in houses, was found in Belmonte, where the 'point' Honey was knocked out by a Panzerfaust,[4] the driver, Trooper Bloer, being seriously wounded. Corporal Brown, the commander, and Troopers 'Sandy' Powell and Whitehurst were wounded by shrapnel from a near miss while evacuating the driver under mortar fire. Lieutenant Irwin asked for artillery support which was refused as the position of 12 Brigade's forward infantry, west of Belmonte, was uncertain. Irwin was ordered to shoot up the German positions and then withdraw, his task of contacting the German rearguard complete.

On the morning of 4 August C Squadron, Recce Troop and Hampshires set off, led by Captain Thomas in a jeep, and made good progress throughout the morning, again in glorious sunshine and now through beautiful countryside. It was strangely quiet with not a shot from either side. Undefended demolitions were encountered but cleared quickly and the advance continued until Captain Thomas, still in the lead and a little ahead of the leading tank, came upon another demolition just around a sharp bend. This time there were Germans. Thomas reversed quickly before the Germans could do anything. The opposition was quickly removed, three prisoners, members of 104th Panzer Grenadier Regiment, being taken. By 12.15pm, the infantry reached La Croce, overlooking Florence. The advance was not to continue beyond Vicchio, one and a half miles south of the Arno as tacit agreement had been reached that Florence, with its beautiful buildings and priceless works of art, would be treated as an open city. Despite this agreement the Germans destroyed all the city's bridges over the Arno except the Ponte Vecchio, which they blocked by demolishing and mining houses at both ends. C Squadron and the Recce Troop were ordered to withdraw due south and rejoin the Regiment near Le Carti. As they moved back they came under heavy shellfire that killed Sergeant James Clulow, from Armagh, and Trooper Bertie Coote, from Bedfordshire, and wounded six Recce Troop members and one C Squadron man.

Night-time infantry patrols reported a strong enemy presence and the sound of digging-in on the high ground; the Germans were preparing for a stand in the mountainous country guarding the Arno east of Florence. Incontro was the dominating feature barring the divisional advance. An ancient monastery with thick walls, surrounded by a ten-foot-high perimeter wall, was perched on the summit. The Germans could observe the advance not only of 4th Division from the south, but also 6th Armoured Division as they advanced along the Arno's right bank to the east. The position could be compared to a miniature Cassino.

Next morning the Somersets captured Monte Pilli, a mile and a half south of Incontro, which they were ordered to take that night. In the afternoon two C Squadron troops bombarded enemy targets; the other two troops were to provide a fifteen-minute diversion before the attack went in, by firing their Besas on fixed lines. Two troops of B Squadron moved out before last light into fire positions to give moonlight fire support. However, the Somersets' leading companies were unable to reach their objectives in the face of heavy machine-gun fire and withdrew.

On the 6th the divisional commander ordered 10 Brigade to take over from 28 Brigade, capture Incontro and clear the country south of the Arno. Since 10 Brigade's affiliated regiment, 51st Royal Tanks, could not move due to road restrictions, A and B Squadrons North Irish Horse came under 10 Brigade command; A Squadron would support 2nd Bedfordshire and Hertfordshires and B Squadron 2nd Duke of Cornwall's LI. C Squadron remained with 28 Brigade's Hampshires. During the morning No. 2 Troop C Squadron moved to positions commanding Point 431 to provide fire support for Hampshire patrols probing forward to the left of Incontro. In the early afternoon a Spandau opened fire on a Hampshire ambulance jeep near La Croce. No. 2 Troop observed the incident and engaged the position successfully. The enemy were seen to have suffered casualties, a tribute to the effectiveness of No. 2 Troop's direct fire. At 2.00pm the Recce Troop Shermans went into action at Antella and shelled the Incontro area.

The Lord O'Neill reported to Brigadier Shoesmith at 10 Brigade HQ early on 7 August to learn that 2nd Duke of Cornwall's LI would attack Incontro at first light the next morning. He was asked for initial tank support from the area of Point 516 and for suggestions on any possible further support. The Lord O'Neill and Major Mackean carried out a reconnaissance and reported that tanks could give excellent support from Point 516; it was also thought that tanks could climb to Incontro, though this could not be guaranteed. The Lord O'Neill placed the three Recce Troop Shermans under Major Mackean's command to provide right-flank observation and protection. In addition, an A Squadron troop was to provide further right-flank protection and a composite 75mm troop from C Squadron would take up positions from which targets on Point 436 to the left of and behind Incontro could be engaged.

Major Mackean then reported to Lieutenant-Colonel Musson, commanding 2nd Duke of Cornwall's LI, and the battle plan was explained. The infantry would attack at daybreak, 4.30am, from south-west of the monastery; the tanks were to be in position by 5.00am. Incontro would be pounded throughout the night by the divisional artillery, fire being concentrated on the two possible alternative routes to create the impression that the assault would come from one of those. Once the attack started, the artillery would switch to the chosen route and provide a creeping bombardment up to the monastery wall before concentrating on two likely places from which the Germans might attempt to reinforce the monastery. B Squadron harboured for the night, except for No. 1 Troop (Lieutenant King), which was separated from the rest of the squadron by an impassable cliff just behind the start line. The A and C Squadron troops detailed for the morrow also moved to their positions.

At daybreak on the 8th, B Squadron moved forward. Lieutenant Foott's No. 4 Troop led, followed by No. 5 Troop, Lieutenant Fleming, two tanks from SHQ, the FOO's tank and the Recce Troop Shermans at the rear. No. 2 Troop, Lieutenant Behr, was in reserve. By 5.00am the troops were in position; No. 4 was on a ridge 150 yards north-east of Point 516 and No. 5, the FOO tank and a close-support tank on Point 516. The Shermans were on Point 508 observing the right flank with No. 1 Troop on the left. Before long the sound of battle was heard. B Company's advance towards the south-eastern corner of the outer wall was delayed. Observing the enemy forming up, just around the corner, for a counter-attack, No. 1 Troop opened fire with HE and machine guns, making the enemy disperse; twelve dead were later found in the area. At one place the fire put down by the tanks was only fifty yards ahead of their own infantry, a feat possible only because of excellent communications, Captain Sidebottom's being able to report the infantry positions on the tank wireless net and the accuracy of the shooting of the tank commanders and gunners. Meanwhile C Company entered the monastery grounds through a narrow gap in the southern perimeter wall and fought their way to within fifty yards of the monastery before being pinned down by intense fire, suffering heavy casualties. The survivors withdrew and dug in, just inside the wall at the south-east corner.

By 7.30am deadlock had been reached; further progress was impossible and casualties mounted. D Company was given the task of recapturing the south-east corner, which had been retaken by the Germans some time earlier. About 10.30am the infantry reported an enemy machine-gun post in the monastery tower which was swiftly demolished by No. 1 Troop. The counter-attack, planned for 10.50am, started on time. A supporting bombardment was called for between 10.45 and 10.50 and Colonel Musson asked that, once the counter-attack started, a troop of tanks should try to reach the monastery. D Company recaptured the south-east corner just before noon, broke into the grounds and worked their way round the inside of the eastern wall to capture the entrance lodge soon after 1.00pm; the lodge, in the northern corner, guarded the single road approach. They broke into and had cleared the main buildings, taking many prisoners, before No. 4 Troop arrived. The monastery was firmly in British hands, but already subject to heavy artillery fire.

On receiving Colonel Musson's request for support, Major Mackean ordered No. 4 Troop to attempt the descent and climb up to the monastery. Lieutenant Foott, after a foot reconnaissance, reported that he had found a way, but the going was difficult and very exposed on the right. Mackean then went forward with Foott, and discovered a way further to the left which provided right-flank protection. Lieutenant Foott then manoeuvred his troop down the precipitous slope, under only spasmodic fire. Sergeant Bullick's tank disposed of a sniper operating from a trackside well with a burst of Besa fire. The troop leader's gunner, Trooper Fitzgerald, finished off the well with a single HE round for good measure. Eventually the valley floor was reached and the troop picked its way along until it was able to swing left and start the slow, agonising climb under the watchful eyes of No. 5 Troop. The outer wall was reached with comparatively little opposition and the leading tank entered the monastery grounds by pushing the wall down. The depleted DCLI gave the tanks a warm and appreciative welcome; the infantry were busy preparing to repel the expected counter-attack. Very hot tanks took up defensive positions. The climb had been carried out without the tanks having fired a shot or suffering any damage. There were no anti-tank guns; the Germans had not imagined tanks operating in such country. It is a coincidence that it again fell to No. 4 Troop of B Squadron, as at Longstop, to prove the outstanding mountain-climbing capability of the Churchill, a further demonstration of the ability and determination of the North Irish Horse to support their infantry regardless of terrain.

An extract from the Narrative of Operations of 25 Tank Brigade for the period notes that:

> The capture of Incontro by tanks of the North Irish Horse, up what appeared to be an almost unscaleable height for tracked vehicles, completely disorganized the enemy . . . The capture of this position undoubtedly forced the enemy to abandon his positions south of the Arno.

During the period of No. 4 Troop's climb the FOO, Captain Sedgwick, was wounded by a mortar bomb while out of his tank. No. 2 Troop was then ordered to advance to the monastery, No. 5 Troop remaining to provide covering fire. No. 2 reached the monastery by the trail blazed by No. 4 Troop and also completed the hazardous journey without damage or loss. No. 2 Troop had not been in the monastery for long when Lieutenant Behr and Trooper Fuller were wounded while out of their tanks, Fuller receiving a shrapnel wound in his back that required evacuation. He was placed in a No. 2 Troop tank, commanded by Corporal Reynolds, to return the way they had come. Sergeant Verso of No. 5 Troop, who had come forward to assist the wounded, was guiding the tank while standing on the outside of the turret. They were surprised in the dusk by a party of Germans armed with a Panzerfaust who missed the tank at very short range although the projectile passed between the heads of the sergeant and corporal. Verso suffered a cut cheek and jumped off the tank and took cover. Corporal Reynolds' jaw was fractured and a number of teeth were knocked out, removing part of his lower gum. He fell down in the turret. He recalled:

> I vaguely remember the driver, Lance-Corporal 'Darkie' Gault shouting, 'They're coming for the tank'. Fortunately 'Darkie', to whom I shall always be indebted, crawled into the turret, climbed over me and shut the hatches. He then with the advice of the wounded Trooper Fuller fired the main armament and ordered the co-driver to fire the front Besa, thus creating a hell of a noise and frightening the Germans off. He then climbed back into the driver's compartment, turned the tank around and took us from the danger zone.
>
> In due course the stretcher bearers extracted me from the floor of the turret and carefully carried me along a difficult route to a forward dressing station. Incidentally, although I was only semi-conscious at the time, I was very impressed by their courage and devotion to duty, although encountering heavy mortar fire, they never failed to place me gently on the ground, [and] get down beside me until it was safe for them to continue. My great regret was not being able to thank them for their thoughtfulness and undoubted courage – sadly I have no way of tracing them.

No. 5 Troop had observed the successful climb of the tanks to the monastery without any requirement for offensive action on their part. About 5.30pm Lieutenant Fleming saw a signal flare rise out of the wood situated to his right of the monastery and alerted his gunner and the other two tanks. Guns were trained on the edge of the wood. Seconds later German troops swarmed out; the tanks fired as they charged. Many were cut down well before they reached their objective and the remainder raced back to the cover of the wood, suffering more casualties on the way. From the rising of the signal flare to the retreat into the wood all was over in little more than a minute.

This was the last German counter-attack on the monastery although the captors suffered a night of constant bombardment. Trooper Martin was injured by shell fragments while out of his tank; thereafter crews remained closed down. The tanks withdrew to harbour next morning; the battle was over and German resistance broken south of the Arno. Some seventy Germans, including three officers, were taken prisoner and twenty killed; 2nd Duke of Cornwall's LI lost nineteen killed and eighty wounded while B Squadron suffered five wounded.

Next day information was received that 25 Tank Brigade would be withdrawn and, by midnight on 10 August, 4th Division had been relieved by 1st Division. The Regiment concentrated in pouring rain east of San Donato prior to moving farther south. Unbeknown, at that time, to the Regiment and to most of Fifth and Eighth Armies, the plan of campaign had been changed. The original plan called for both armies to assault straight up the centre of Italy through the Futa and Il Giogo passes, seize Bologna and cross the Po river north of Ferrara.

The decision to abandon this plan was probably the most controversial taken in the Italian campaign. Attacking forces and reserves had been assembled, logistic arrangements were almost complete and an elaborate deception plan had been initiated to make the Germans believe the attack would take place on the Adriatic side. General Alexander issued his orders to both armies on 26 July. Speed was vital as only two months of summer remained. General Leese did not like the orders he received and was unhappy with the thought of having to fight through the mountains without the assistance of the French, the experts in mountain fighting; Allied superiority in armour and artillery would count for little in the coming battle. Leese was also reluctant to fight a battle alongside Fifth Army as this would undoubtedly lead to invidious comparisons in each nation's press. General Clark loved publicity for himself and his army and, in Leese's experience, cooperation with Clark had never been easy. Matters had not been helped by Clark's dash for Rome and glory in defiance of Alexander's orders at the end of May.

Leese now sought a meeting with Alexander to voice his fears and objections. Alexander, accompanied by his Chief of Staff, General Harding, flew to Orvieto where the three men met, sheltered from the blazing sun by the wing of an aircraft. Leese stated his objection to his orders and proposed that Eighth Army should move, secretly and swiftly, across country and attack on the Adriatic coast where the hills were at their lowest. A breakthrough to Rimini would open up the Lombardy plain and his armoured divisions could, for the first time, fight free of the mountains. Harding was not convinced; the planners had considered this proposal and rejected it in favour of the shortest route, as now ordered. However, Alexander was attracted by the idea of a two-fisted approach: first a right hand and, when Kesselring's reserves had been committed, a straight left through the mountains. In the words of an official account, 'Realising how impolitic it would be to persuade an Army Commander to fight a battle against his inclination and judgement, General Alexander acceded to General Leese's new proposal'.

Matters other than the seemingly eternal battle against blown bridges and steep ravines, climbing even steeper hills and avoiding the dreaded 88s were part of daily life. Tomatoes were plentiful and made a welcome addition to army rations. Breakfast, taken before dawn when in action, usually consisted of fried tomatoes and bully beef with a mug of strong tea. Many did not enjoy a fried tomato, or, for that matter, bully beef, for years after returning to civilian life. A 'brew-up' as often as possible was essential; the method of preparation varied depending upon the circumstances. When the tank was closed down, the co-driver made the brew in the issued dixie on the tank's portable stove. On the move, he had to grip the stove between his feet and hold the dixie handle with both hands. In the open, water was boiled on an empty 'flimsy', the name given by the troops to the one-trip petrol containers used before jerrycans became available. The flimsy, part filled with gravel or soil, had petrol poured on and set alight; the water boiled quickly.

During a lull in a battle three men were out of their tank, two watching the driver make the brew. The driver, Trooper Jack Cowley, was a character. His mother who, as the Irish say, 'had the sight', told him that he would survive the war unscathed. He believed her and he did survive. (He frightened his crew by driving in action with his vision port open while all around had theirs closed; he could only be persuaded to close down on receipt of ever-increasing threats from the tank commander, concerned for the safety of the other crew members.) The water on this particular day was coming to the boil when an approaching shell was heard. Both watchers dived for cover under the tank but Cowley stood fast. The shell landed, the blast blew the dixie into the air, the water descending on four disappearing legs. The immediate thoughts of one, as he felt a warm dampness soaking his legs was 'Good, back to the lovely nurses'; he had just returned from hospital following wounds received at the Hitler Line. The second, who had received most of the water, thought momentarily that both his legs had been seriously injured and called out to Jack, still standing unconcerned in the open, 'Quick, take a look! Have I any legs left?'

One afternoon Lieutenant Hunt was ordered to attend an O group summoned by the commanding officer of the infantry battalion A Squadron was supporting. Machine-gun posts and a concealed 88mm anti-tank gun were holding up infantry and tanks alike and would have to be dealt with. The rendezvous point was quite a distance from his location and Hunt set off on foot, forgetting, in his haste, to take his gunner's personal weapon, a Tommy gun, which would have been much more effective than his own pistol. The O group was held in a farmhouse looking across the valley towards the enemy positions. It was built into the side of a hill and had a basement under the back of the house.

The troop leader was the last to arrive and found senior officers discussing matters that did not concern him directly. He was at the back by an open window, minding his own business, when he heard voices below. 'Excuse me, Colonel,' he said, butting in, 'I hear voices below.' 'Oh, there's nothing there,' came the reply. 'But Colonel, I'm sure I can hear voices.' 'Oh very well,' retorted the slightly irritated colonel, 'If you are sure, go and have a look, probably only some Eyeties jabbering.' Off he went round the side and carefully round the back, pistol in hand. He listened and clearly heard German voices. He went a bit farther and, poking his head round a corner, surprised ten or twelve grey-clothed figures. 'What the hell are you doing here? Hande hoch!,' he bawled. They came out with their hands up. He hurled a few oaths at them to attract the attention of those above. The colonel and others looked down to see what was happening. Hunt was ordered to march the prisoners back to the infantry and get back as quickly as possible. It transpired later that the prisoners were demoralised Austrians. Had they been a German fighting patrol, the outcome could have been very different. While Hunt was away, the positions of the anti-tank gun and the machine-gun positions were located. He returned just as the O Group was breaking up. The enemy positions were dealt with and the advance resumed.

NOTES

1 Strickland retired from the Army in 1969 as Major-General Strickland CMG, DSO, OBE, MM.
2 The brigade's other two battalions were 1st Royal Fusiliers and 1/12th Frontier Force Regiment. Indian infantry brigades usually included one British battalion, as well as two Indian battalions.
3 The reconnaissance regiment of 8th Indian Division, equipped with Humber armoured cars and carriers.
4 A shoulder-mounted light anti-tank weapon, the German equivalent of the American bazooka.

CHAPTER X
The Gothic Line

On 12 August in bright sunshine the Regiment moved some fifty miles eastwards to the Arezzo area amidst tight security. Identifying signs were removed or covered up. B Squadron took the opportunity to 'dress up' using an assortment of garb, some even discarding their uniforms, resulting in a similarity to partisans. Lieutenant Foott donned a German tunic which caused consternation among the Italian population during one halt. Told that he was a prisoner, the Italians hissed and booed him until he broke 'free' and chased them – they ran for their lives. Next day transporters carried the tanks to the brigade concentration area, five miles west of Perugia, where the Regiment stayed for six days. The secrecy and deception continued with priority given to camouflaging vehicles and tents; movement was kept to an absolute minimum. From dawn to dusk, maintenance was carried out, conferences were held, liaison visits made and rest taken whenever possible. A Churchill replaced the last Sherman remaining in squadron service and, for the first time since arriving in Italy, the Regiment was equipped fully with Churchills. Regiments in 21 Tank Brigade retained two Sherman troops per squadron.

On 15 August Operation DRAGOON took place on the French Riviera, east of Toulon; Seventh US Army and the French Expeditionary Corps[1] achieved surprise against little opposition. Advancing rapidly up the Rhone valley, Seventh Army linked up with Third US Army at Dijon on 11 September and the liberation of France was almost complete. Although the French Mediterranean ports would ease Allied supply problems in north-western Europe, a shortage of supplies prevented maximum exploitation of Allied successes in August. A manpower shortage also affected the Italian theatre; Alexander's command had been reduced to provide manpower for DRAGOON, an operation opposed by Churchill. However, Churchill's advice went unheeded on this occasion, probably due to the terminal illness of Field Marshal Dill, Britain's principal liaison officer in Washington. Alexander lost an American corps and General Juin's French corps who, with their mountain fighting skills, would have been a great asset in Italy. The loss of these formations, and reduced air support, were significant factors in the change of plan for the assault on the Gothic Line. An unexpected bonus was Kesselring's misappreciation of the intentions of Seventh Army, which he expected to land in north-west Italy to outflank his positions. Kesselring moved reserves to meet the threat and took his eye off the Adriatic coast where II Polish Corps, opposed by two German divisions, were the only Allied troops involved in the eastern approach to the Gothic Line.

The change of plan, Operation OLIVE, created tremendous adminis-trative and logistical problems, not least because assault divisions were in the wrong places, as were the stocks of ammunition and supplies built up for the attack. Only two roads across the Apennines to the Adriatic were in Allied control for their entire length but the Germans had blown bridges and carried out demolitions along both as they withdrew. Neither Route 76 nor 77 had been rebuilt or repaired; scarce engineering resources had been devoted to re-opening and improving the routes linking Florence to the south, these being Eighth Army's main supply routes. There was a serious bottleneck at Foligno whence both roads started; the shorter Route 76, to the north, needed bridging, widening and repairing to class-70 standard to carry Churchills and SPGs on transporters while the longer Route 77, to the south, had to be rebuilt and repaired to class-30 standard since most of the Shermans and Honeys would travel on their tracks. New locations were also needed for hospitals and workshops that were already being moved forward. And the main logistical railhead, almost complete at Arezzo, would have to move to Ancona on the Adriatic coast. All of this had to be planned and completed quickly to allow the attack to take place before the autumn rains.

Planning was complete and movement orders were issued on 13 August. The sappers accomplished their mammoth task, including building sixteen Bailey bridges by the scheduled date of the 15th. Movement of V and the Canadian Corps – an armoured and four infantry divisions – began that night, amidst strict security. Those two corps, with all their armour, artillery and supporting arms and services, passed through Foligno to their new concentration areas; over eight nights 60,000 tanks, guns and vehicles travelled under cover of darkness and without lights. All were in position, briefed and ready to attack on D-day. The move had been planned and carried out in only eighteen days, a truly remarkable achievement. However, it can be argued that the time spent in this move was time lost before the onset of wet weather and that keeping to the original plan may well have brought the Italian campaign to an earlier conclusion.

While at Perugia the Regiment learned that 25 Tank Brigade would move to the Adriatic sector and 46th Division (Major-General Hawkesworth) in V Corps. With the Canadian and Polish Corps, V Corps would take part in a massed offensive planned to start on 25 August with the initial objective of smashing through the Gothic Line. Venice and Vienna by Christmas were stated to be the ultimate objectives.

The Regiment did not move until late on the 20th; 25 Tank Brigade's move to Ferrato, some fifteen miles south of the Metauro river, was complete by the evening of the 22nd. The Germans, roughly handled by the Polish Corps on the coastal sector, had completed their withdrawal behind that river by the evening of the 23rd. North Irish Horse came under command of Brigadier Kendrew's[2] 128 (Hampshire) Brigade; A Squadron was affiliated with 2nd Hampshires, B with 1/4th and C with 5th. Defence overprints, aerial photographs and tank-going maps were issued and final maintenance carried out. Finally, the tanks and echelons moved to Fratte Rosa, a few miles south of the Metauro.

The main Gothic Line defences in the V Corps area were on steeply rising ground, reaching to 1,000 feet, north of and overlooking the Foglia river. The river ran between high steep banks and could be crossed without difficulty by infantry in the dry August weather but tank crossing places were few and hard to find. To strengthen these natural defences, the Germans had constructed deep concrete emplacements for artillery pieces or anti-tank guns, well protected from shell fire with firing slits just above ground level and only a few feet of structure visible. Panther turrets, as used in the Hitler Line, had also been installed, supplemented with interconnected machine-gun posts, barbed-wire entanglements and minefields; there were over 2,300 machine guns, 479 anti-tank, mortar and gun emplacements and some 12,000 yards of wire. An anti-tank ditch had been dug from the Adriatic coast to Montecchio, but not in front of the defences to be attacked by 46th Division; the steep river banks, overlooked by high hills, were considered an adequate obstacle. Shortage of time, labour and materials meant that little attempt had been made at defence in depth; the defended area was not more than eight hundred to a thousand yards deep, except in the Montecalvo area. There was, however, an obstacle zone that was about ten miles wide and Italian civilians had been evacuated from an area that was some twelve to fourteen miles in depth.

Eighth Army was to attack with the three corps in line, with V Corps in the more difficult terrain of the left flank. General Keightley, commanding V Corps, planned a three-phase attack beginning with an assault by 46th Division on the right and 4th Indian Division on the left, over the twelve miles of hilly country between the Metauro and Foglia rivers, where the Gothic Line defences started. This would be followed by the breaking of the line while the final phase was to be the breakthrough by 1st Armoured Division, supported by 4th Division, to exploit northwards towards the Po with the aim of destroying the left wing of the German Tenth Army. The latter, defending the eastern flank, initially consisted of LXXVI Panzer Corps on the coastal sector with LI Mountain Corps on its right; Hawkesworth's 46th Division was opposed by the German 71st Division.

Second Hampshires launched 46th Division's attack, crossing the Metauro at 11.00pm on 25 August, a starlit night with the moon down before midnight. To attain maximum surprise, there was no artillery bombardment. Following an unopposed crossing, a creeping bombardment helped them forward through olive groves. A Squadron moving from Fratte Rosa as the Hampshires started to cross, the tanks reached the river without incident at 4.00am to find the approach would not bear a Churchill's weight. A fresh crossing was located and the squadron joined their infantry at Monte Felcino at 6.20am, an advance from the river of two miles and a climb of 600 feet. Further progress by the tanks was blocked by a ravine, and although extensive foot reconnaissances discovered a crossing well off to the right flank, the tanks did not cross until 5.30pm, too late for the Hampshires to reach that flank to attack with tanks that evening. That night the squadron harboured south of Monte Bartola and B and C Squadrons moved to the Monte Felcino area in readiness for the next day's advance.

During the night 1/4th Hampshires took Monte Bartolo and 5th Hampshires swung left to take Monte Guidoccio and Monte Grosso. At dawn B Squadron crossed the ravine that had delayed A Squadron the previous day and supported 1/4th Hampshires from Monte Bartolo's lower slopes. Some enemy-held houses were dealt with by the tanks' guns, allowing 2nd Hampshires to pass through and, with A Squadron in support, the battalion made steady progress until the road junction one and a half miles south of the hilltop village of Monte Gaudio. The intention had been to keep the squadron on the high ground but, as the going was slow, No. 3 Troop was ordered down to the road to join the infantry. By-passing two craters blown by the retiring Germans the tanks were eventually held up by a blown bridge. Progress in the hills continued to be very slow and the tanks were unable to provide flanking fire to support the infantry still south of Monte Gaudio. Accordingly, The Lord O'Neill ordered them down to the road and arranged for a bulldozer to be brought up which pushed enough material into the river to create a crossing. No. 3 Troop resumed its advance but three more blows were encountered and filled by the bulldozer before the squadron linked up with the infantry stalled by the Germans holding the foothills of Monte Albullo, an awkward 1,500-foot-high feature. A Squadron drenched the whole area with HE and machine-gun fire, enabling their infantry to capture it by 10.30pm. The squadron endured heavy shelling and mortaring; enemy opposition was stiffening.

At 10 o'clock next morning (28th), B Squadron, supporting 1/4th Hampshires, passed through A Squadron and 2nd Hampshires en route to Monte Gaudio and the high ground to the west. Further blows were encountered and the bulldozer was again employed. Germans occupied the village and fought stubbornly before it fell at 6.00pm; the Hampshires' company commander was killed and thirty prisoners taken. Intense mortaring prevented the left-flank company advancing towards point 414. Nos. 1 and 4 Troops tackled the fearsome ascent, with covering fire from Nos. 2 and 5 Troops but, although two machine-gun posts were knocked out during the climb and the mortaring diminished, the infantry were still unable to advance.

Disaster then struck No. 4 Troop's leading tank, which slipped and crashed 200 feet down the mountainside into a ravine, turning over six times during its fall. Miraculously, only one man, London-born Trooper James Bradfield, was killed. Trooper Parkinson, of the Recce Troop, on wireless watch halfway up the slope saw the tank climb slowly to the skyline, turn right, hull-down, and begin traversing the mountainside, a dangerous practice that was frowned upon. Watching with alarm, Parkinson saw the right track on the low side begin to plough a furrow. Suddenly the tank lurched, the left track having encountered a rock, and shuddered before starting to roll and fall, crashing down the hill within twenty to thirty yards of Parkinson's tank. As it passed, the turret separated from the hull, Trooper Bradfield, the gunner being hurled high in the air. The turret eventually came to rest with Corporal McCalmont trapped with the turret ring across one leg; the injured operator, Trooper Dorman, lay nearby. The tank continued its fall with the driver Lance-Corporal Moore and co-driver Trooper Holt still inside. The Recce Troop tank crew rushed to help the injured. Morphine was injected, and Corporal McCalmont was eventually pulled clear of the turret after soil had been dug from around the trapped leg, it being impossible to move the heavy turret. When the wrecked tank was reached, the driver and co-driver were found trapped inside, terribly battered, bruised and concussed but alive. Corporal McCalmont made a complete recovery and walked without a limp; after the war he was able to resume his interest as a scout leader.

The infantry could make no further progress despite the efforts of the tanks, which were now being shelled and mortared heavily; one was hit by an anti-tank gun but suffered no casualties. To maintain the impetus, both 128 and 139 Brigades continued during the night. By 6.45am next morning 5th Hampshires had reached Monte Busso, the western extremity of the German stop-line to find this strongly prepared position abandoned. C Squadron was ordered across the river at first light to support 5th Hampshires. In spite of very bad going, two tanks got forward. The remainder of the squadron was about to move by a more attractive route when orders were received for the Regiment to revert to 25 Tank Brigade and concentrate near Monte Grosso with a promise of twenty-four hours' rest and maintenance. In four days V Corps had advanced twelve miles and closed up to the southern banks of the Foglia.

During the night 29–30 August, infantry and tank representatives carried out extensive reconnaissance of the approaches to the Foglia north of Colbordolo, finding only one crossing suitable for tanks. At 5.00am the commanding officer joined Brigadier Kendrew at Colbordolo for a joint reconnaissance. Viewed from this position, the Gothic Line presented a formidable appearance. A regimental officer is quoted thus, 'It looked like an elaborate killing ground. All houses had been razed to the ground, trees and vines felled and avenues prepared between extensive minefields for a hail of machine-gun fire.'

The first ridge rose steeply from the river for 900 feet while Mondaino village could be seen on the skyline behind on a higher ridge. Obviously, Monte Gridolfo, the key defence bastion on this part of the front, would have to be taken before infantry or tanks could cross the lower slopes. The Lord O'Neill was summoned to a planning group at 11.00am to learn that the Gothic Line had been penetrated by the Canadian Corps and that 2nd Hampshires would attack across the river at 2.00pm that day. Desert Air Force aircraft had carried out a morning-long strafe of the far bank with hundreds of anti-vehicle and anti-personnel mines. When Brigadier Kendrew asked for North Irish Horse tank support, the commanding officer explained that the Churchills were stripped for maintenance, but that the Reconnaissance Troop would be available; this troop was ordered to move forward in an hour's time. The CO also undertook to have the Churchills back on the road without delay. Recce Troop was so delayed by congested roads that Brigadier Kendrew decided not to use the tanks until the next day; traffic problems were causing more difficulties than the Germans. However, 2nd Hampshires crossed the river unmolested, finding the formidable prepared positions virtually unmanned and by nightfall had established a firm bridgehead. The Regiment, less the Recce Troop, was ordered forward to the Ripe area at 5.00pm to join 25 Tank Brigade.

At 5 o'clock next morning, 31 August, North Irish Horse was again under 128 Brigade command. A and B Squadrons crossed the Foglia after a Sherman dozer made a crossing and A Squadron was ordered to support 2nd Hampshires' attack westwards on Monte Le Vecchie, commanding the lower ground south of Monte Gridolfo. A direct ascent to the village was thwarted by an extensive minefield and the squadron was ordered to advance up the road which was also found to be mined; sappers had to be brought forward. An unlocated SPG then opened fire. Further progress on the road was impossible; the hillside was so jagged and steep that not even Churchills could climb it. A Squadron was ordered to remain in place. This attack was supported by a force including 46th Reconnaissance Regiment, 5th Hampshires and North Irish Horse Recce Troop, commanded by Brigadier Kendrew in the borrowed North Irish Horse 'Gin-Box', the commanding officer's armoured command vehicle. The attack lay across the lower ground to the right, the objective being to outflank Monte Gridolfo. Meanwhile, 2nd Hampshires had made steady progress. Supported by B Squadron, 1/4th Hampshires took over the lead and captured Monte Gridolfo, just before 6.00pm, an advance of almost two miles from the river. The Gothic Line had been cracked in two days' hard fighting but the enemy had yet to be destroyed.

Hawkesworth, charged with seeing 1st Armoured Division safely on its way to the Po and the Lombardy plain, now hustled his troops forward to open the gate guarded by the Coriano ridge – three and a half miles from the coast – the last high feature before the more open country beyond. The advance was complicated by the terrain, rising as it did westwards into the Apennine foothills. The Canadians and 46th Division would make better progress than 4th Indian Division in the more mountainous country of the left flank.

On 1 September 46th Division attacked with all three brigades up. Supported by 142 RAC, 138 Brigade, both previously uncommitted to the battle, attacked over the more open rolling country on the right; 128 Brigade, and North Irish Horse, was in the centre and 139 Brigade on the left with 51st Royal Tanks. North Irish Horse had a relatively quiet two days; A Squadron supported 5th Hampshires on to the high ground west of Monte Gridolfo and then, before noon, helped them and 1/4th Hampshires mop up the entire Monte Gridolfo area. Soon enemy SPGs were seen approaching from the east and moving southwards towards Meleto. Five more SPGs were seen entering the Colle Longhi area; one was engaged at long range by Major Griffith's tank. Artillery support was called for and heavy fire directed on the area. No further movement was seen until late in the evening when one SPG appeared on the road and was engaged and destroyed by Lieutenant Hunt's No. 3 Troop. At about 2.00pm, 5th Hampshires reported a SPG in Meleto; this was engaged and driven off. The squadron remained in observation throughout the day. At 2 o'clock next morning an enemy counter-attack, supported by two or three tanks, on 5th Hampshires' positions was beaten off. A Squadron remained firm in the Monte Gridolfo area but were not called to action before being ordered to rejoin the Regiment near Monte Busco.

Intelligence reports indicating that the badly shaken Germans were going to stand on the Conca river, to allow time for reinforcements to be transferred across the excellent lateral Highway 9 – Via Emilia – linking Bologna with Rimini, meant a change to 46th Division's plan. The enemy, and two days' hard going, had imposed such strain on 142 RAC, that it had to be relieved and North Irish Horse was ordered to the area of Maria del Monte, A and C Squadrons coming under 138 Brigade while B remained with 128 Brigade. Other factors influencing the new plan were the imminence of the early autumn rains and the commencement of 1st Armoured Division's move forward. Therefore, 46th Division was to advance quickly, clear Coriano ridge and form a left-flank protective screen across the Marano river to permit 1st Armoured Division to break out into the Romagna. Initially, 128 and 138 Brigades would advance northwards towards Coriano and 139 Brigade north-west along the axis Saludecio–Croce.

Brigadier Harding, of 138 Brigade, issued his orders at 9.00pm. During the night 2–3 September, 2/4th King's Own Yorkshire LI was to form a bridgehead over the Ventena; 6th York and Lancasters, supported by C Squadron, were to pass through, cross the Conca and secure the high ground beyond Morciano on the river's east bank. No.2 Troop, C Squadron, with a section of the Brigade RE Troop, moved down the road in moonlight to the KOYLI's positions across the Ventena and opened fire on enemy locations in Morciano at 6.00am. The remainder of C Squadron moved at 5.00am and had joined the York and Lancs south of the Conca by 8 o'clock. No.3 Troop, with two of its own tanks and one from No.1 Troop, was ordered across the river, supported by Nos. 2 and 4 Troops on the right and left respectively. At 8.30am, at the crossing, overlooked by high ground north of the river, the tanks came under accurate fire from a SPG in a cemetery some 800 yards behind Morciano. Two tanks were knocked out and the infantry heavily stonked, forcing them to seek cover. Artillery support was called for by the FOO and directed upon the high ground around the cemetery after which No.4 Troop was ordered to move to their right and support No.2. During this move the troop leader's tank was knocked out, and the other two pinned down. He described what happened in detail.

> It was a dull, overcast day and I had been quietly watching the left flank from high ground some way short of the river. After some time . . . I was ordered to move my troop into a position nearer the river from which I could continue to cover the left flank. We moved forward and by this time everything had quietened down, there being no traffic on the squadron net and no sign of any shooting. I arrived on a small ridge overlooking the river and . . . I could see Churchill tracks leading down to the river and the rear of a Churchill under some trees at the bottom of the slope. I decided to leave two tanks turret down on the ridge and nip down to the river to find out what was going on.
>
> We advanced over the ridge and at a cracking pace crossed a little track when suddenly there was an enormous bang and the tank shuddered to a halt on the forward slope. I ordered the driver, Corporal Charlie Hamilton, to reverse but he calmly informed me over the intercom that he couldn't as the gear lever had come away in his hand. There was nothing for it but to order '[bale] out' and I was propelled out of the turret, despite still having my headset on, by the gunner's head in my crutch as he smartly evacuated.

At this point, which in fact had only taken seconds, machine guns and mortars opened up and we dashed for the little track . . . which seemed to offer the only cover. We were all out before the tank, which was brewing up in the engine compartment at the rear, was hit again. We had a quick check only to discover that Trooper Bertie Gore, the co-driver, was missing. Corporal Hamilton and I noted that the sponson door on his side of the tank was open and we hared back to the tank. I looked inside . . . to see an empty co-driver's seat with a large round hole in the seat back. The first round fired at us had hit and penetrated the front glacis plate (around 102 mm thick and angled) passed through the seat between the gunner's and my legs and through the bulkhead into the engine compartment from which flames and a lot of smoke were now issuing.

Turning round to run back, we suddenly came on Gore lying in the grass and bleeding profusely from a large wound in his right buttock. We dragged him into what little cover there was on the track which consisted of about six inches of earth with some grass on top. After a whip-round for shell dressings we set ourselves to bandaging but each time one of us reared up to wind the dressing over the wound, a burst of fire ensued. Soon to our delight we saw a couple of infantry stretcher bearers with a Red Cross flag coming over the ridge. We loaded Gore onto the stretcher and hastily attached ourselves to the party under the flag to beat a retreat into cover!

Afterwards Gore swore that he had seen the flash of the SP firing and had instinctively turned to his left to open the sponson door thus presenting his right buttock to the incoming round. I am afraid none of us believed this story but it is curious that it fitted in with his escape from certain death.

The squadron leader's tank now came under fire from an 88mm gun. Major Morton went forward on foot, located the 88 disguised in a haystack and, on his return, directed 75mm HE Churchill fire on to the area. In setting the haystack alight the 88 was disclosed and destroyed.

Since the enemy were holding excellent positions on the high ground covering the river, a halt was called and fresh plans made. The cemetery area was shelled heavily and when the infantry were ready the right flank was smoked. Two companies, supported by fire from the five remaining tanks, crossed and secured the high ground on the far side after which Major Morton ordered the remnants of his squadron to cross. One tank would not start and the movement of the others attracted heavy shelling. When Morton reached the broken-down tank he dismounted under fire, attached his tank's tow rope to the cripple, calmly remounted and, head out of the turret, towed the broken-down tank until it started. The five tanks crossed without further incident and climbed to join the York and

Lancs but were soon relieved by A Squadron. Major Morton was awarded the Military Cross for his courageous and energetic leadership.

On the right, B Squadron crossed the Conca at midday to support 2nd Hampshires and made considerable progress. Point 167, 2,000 yards north-east of San Clemente, was taken and consolidated and enemy positions on the ridges to the north were engaged by the tanks, which remained overnight in a counter-attack role. A Squadron had a good day supporting the York and Lancs on to their objective, San Clemente and the ridges to the north-west. Towards sunset, a SPG in the area of Cevelo, opened up on A Squadron but caused no damage. 'Uncle' targets were engaged by 25 Tank Brigade's affiliated gunners, 142 Army Field Regiment (Royal Devon Yeomanry) RA, equipped with Priests[3].

The bridge at Morciano had been harassed by artillery fire throughout the day to prevent the Germans placing demolition charges and destroying it. At 10.00pm the KOYLI entered the town and captured the bridge intact. Enemy rearguards on the Conca had been driven back some one and a half miles in the day. The North Irish Horse had forced two river crossings and advanced seven and a half to eight miles in three days.

The day of the planned coup de grace by 1st Armoured Division was to be 4 September. Equipped with Shermans and commanded by Major-General Hull, the division started moving on the 2nd from a staging post near Senigallia on the coast north of Ancona, some thirty-five miles from Coriano. It was an appalling approach march; the roads were congested and the tracks north of the Foglia were so bad that low gear had to be used most of the time. Many tanks broke down, while others were kept going but were in no fit mechanical state for battle. Constant delays tired the crews and left little time for rest before the division crossed the Conca at 10.30 that morning.

General Hawkesworth called for one last effort from the exhausted and understrength 128 Brigade. The brigade's first objective, with support from 46 Recce Regiment and B Squadron North Irish Horse, was to clear Coriano village, at the northern end of the ridge that bears its name. The second objective was to capture the bridges over the Marano river at Ospedaletto, some 4,000 yards north-west of Coriano and form a flank facing west. With A Squadron, 46 Recce was then to pass through Coriano and block all approaches from the south-west. These screens were to prevent the outflanked enemy interfering with 1st Armoured Division's movement. On the right, B Squadron started at dawn in support of 1/4th Hampshires, with 5th Hampshires on their left, two miles north of San Clemente. It was a slow advance; isolated machine-gun posts had to be dealt with. At the crossroads less than a mile east of the village, a SPG on the ridge opened up on the Hampshires and the tanks. Captain Hern's tank was hit, killing Trooper Douglas Loxdale, a Londoner, and wounding the other three crewmen; Hern, the acting second-in-command, escaped uninjured. Coriano Ridge was held in much greater strength than anticipated. The fire now brought down on the two Hampshire battalions was so heavy and casualties so high as to make further progress impossible.

A Squadron and 46 Recce started later than B Squadron and reached the southern edge of the ridge unmolested where 46 Recce bade farewell to the tanks and set off around the ridge's western edge. A Squadron prepared to climb the ridge only to be withdrawn to form a firm base back on San Clemente Ridge. Major Griffith recalled.

> By 0730 hours things were very quiet at the southern end of the Coriano Ridge, 46th Recce Regiment had gone about its own business. I ordered A Squadron to advance, this was in the 0800/0900 hours region, two troops up, followed by me, leaving two troops in covering positions on the San Clemente Ridge. We were doing fine, no opposition – Coriano seemed to be ours. Then Lord O'Neill came up on the air and said that the armour was going to go through and I was to return to the San Clemente Ridge to make a firm base. Unfortunately I had forgotten about Nelson at Copenhagen and heard the message. We turned about and were in our defensive positions, this must have been about 0930 hours. We sat there until noon and saw no activity on the Coriano Ridge. No British armour had arrived but we then saw the Germans return with tanks and self-propelled guns. The smoke from their exhausts was quite obvious. This was reported back.
>
> At about 1500 hours Lieutenant-Colonel Douglas Kay, commanding 10th Hussars, arrived at my position. I explained the situation and said I had reported it back. He replied, 'I have had my orders', and off he went. The reason the armour was late was due to absolute chaos on the route up, administrative traffic was running about all over the place and river crossings and bottlenecks not properly managed. Later we heard from German POWs that the Coriano Ridge had indeed been evacuated and they only returned following British inactivity during the morning.

The delay in the advance of 1st Armoured Division, which had been briefed for pursuit across the flat coastal plain, may be attributed more accurately to an enforced last-minute change in plan. The inability of the exhausted, and substantially reduced, 46th Division to reach its objectives, meant that 1st Armoured Division had to assault the ridge and did not start their attack until 3.45pm. By then the sun was low and shining into British eyes but the Germans had perfect visibility; their tanks and SPGs, brought up during the day, inflicted very heavy casualties on the advancing Shermans. The attack failed and, that night, two further German divisions arrived in the area, from Fifth Army's front.

As the leading tanks of the armoured brigade moved up, A Squadron observed an enemy tank moving on Coriano Ridge. It was knocked out by No. 3 Troop. Three more tanks were engaged, one being knocked out and another damaged. Both squadrons rallied back behind San Clemente Ridge for the night. While coming into harbour, shelling started and tanks were parked in the lee of protective features for maximum protection. Lieutenant Hunt dismounted to report for orders but had only covered about ten yards when a HE shell hit his tank's turret. Shrapnel flew all over the place, Hunt was blown off his feet and severely wounded and Trooper James Tweedie, from Armagh, who was also in the open, was killed.

That night 25 Tank Brigade was relieved from immediate operational commitments, but the congested state of the roads made it impossible for the Regiment to move back and it suffered heavy shelling which daily increased in intensity. To add to this discomfort, heavy rain fell on 6 and 7 September. The Regiment was not sorry when ordered to move to a more comfortable area on the 8th.

Major-General Hawkesworth issued a special order in which he noted:

> In one week's fighting we have advanced 25 miles and have broken the Gothic Line. We have defeated the greater part of two German divisions, capturing prisoners and inflicting on the enemy casualties which cannot be less than 3,000. This is a remarkable achievement and a notable victory. The Army Commander and the Corps Commander have both asked me to tell you they consider the performance of the Division is marvellous. They have asked me to congratulate and thank you.

An extract from 128 Infantry Brigade's account of the battle reads:

> A special tribute must be paid to squadrons of the North Irish Horse. Day after day their Churchills forced positions and supported our infantry over appalling tank country. Undaunted, squadron leaders on foot led their tanks up seemingly impossible slopes. One tank actually slipped over and crashed 200 feet.

On 8 September both North Irish Horse and 51st Royal Tanks moved to Tomba di Pesaro, near the coast, where both regiments were assigned to support 4th Division, newly brought forward from Army reserve in place of the Polish Division in I Canadian Corps. Once again North Irish Horse was to support 28 Brigade with squadrons affiliated to the battalions they had supported a month earlier south of Florence; 51st Royal Tanks were to support 12 Brigade while 142 RAC remained with 46th Division in V

Corps. There was a fresh plan to capture Coriano Ridge and establish bridgeheads over the Marecchia river; the Canadian Corps was to attack with two divisions up, 1st Canadian Division on the right, 4th British Division on the left. Before the main attack 5th Canadian Armoured Division was to capture the northern end of Coriano Ridge, by now heavily defended with innumerable tanks, including Tigers and Panthers, SPGs and anti-tank guns. Eighth Army was opposed by five German divisions.

Responding to Eighth Army's threat to his left flank, Kesselring ordered his troops in the central mountains to begin withdrawing to their Gothic Line positions. Vietinghoff's Fourteenth Army on the Mediterranean sector was pulled back some six miles north of the Arno, thus shortening his line and compensating somewhat for the transfer of three divisions to oppose Eighth Army.

On 5 September Alexander judged that the time had come for Fifth Army to land its left-hand punch to coincide with Eighth Army's renewed offensive, and ordered Fifth Army, now including two American and one British corps, the British on the right, to close on the Gothic Line positions. The army moved forward on the 10th and drove the Germans back into their prepared positions within two days; II (US) Corps launched its attack on Bologna via the Futa and Il Giogo passes on the 13th as planned.

Eight days later, 5th Canadian Armoured Division captured Coriano. On their left, 1st Armoured Division took Passano village, midway along the ridge, only to have further progress held up by flooded water courses. At 6.30am on the 14th, 12 Infantry Brigade, with 51st Royal Tanks, crossed their start line and attained their objectives, Points 106 and 113, by 5.00pm. During the night 1st Royal West Kents of 12 Brigade established a bridgehead over the Marano in the Ospedaletto area.

At 1 o'clock next morning A, followed by C, Squadron North Irish Horse advanced to meet their respective infantry. A Squadron, with 2nd King's, were across the river by 6.30am, quickly followed by C Squadron with 2/4th Hampshires. On the left the Hampshires and C Squadron were on their objective, the Bagli Ridge, by 7 o'clock; the King's and A Squadron had a more difficult time but were on their objective farther along the ridge by midday from where they looked down on the Ausa, the first of many rivers to be stoutly defended by the Germans. The lead was then taken by 2nd Somersets who captured Point 137, the highest feature in the area, only to be counter-attacked and driven off. However, they succeeded in holding an adjoining slightly lower peak, Point 126, for the rest of the day. A and C Squadrons remained in position throughout the day supporting their infantry in the counter-attack role. Any movement brought down immediate heavy enemy fire. Lieutenant Michael Bexon described what the simple phrase 'to remain in support of the infantry in the counter-attack role' actually entailed that day.

It was a hot day, the high ground had dried since the rains of the previous week. Dust swirled up every time a tank moved or a shell landed. The day was marked by the heaviest continual shelling that I had experienced. The whole area was under observation from high ground and for hours we played a sort of blind man's bluff with the German artillery who on that day seemed to have no shortage of ammunition

The Germans would select one tank and ... range on it. The technique was to allow them to bracket it and at the right moment to move off one hundred yards or so to one side or fore or aft, allowing the stonk to arrive at the spot one had just vacated. It got hotter as the sun climbed the sky and so much dust was being kicked up that it got inside the tanks, one's clothes and eyes – most unpleasant! It was unhealthy to dismount from the tank so, as usual in these circumstances, an old 75-mm round was passed round the crew. When it was full it was handed to the tank commander whose job it was to empty it over the side of the turret. This meant he had to stick his head out to make sure there were no friends in the vicinity.

Although there was no counter attack in our sector the shelling continued unabated all day. It was particularly heavy when an artillery FOO in a White scout car arrived to set up his FOP. It was unpleasant to see shrapnel from the shell bursts going straight through the thin armour of his vehicle.

As darkness fell thoughts turned to being withdrawn and ... a cooked meal. We had been kept going since dawn on hard tack biscuits and tea brewed up on a tommy cooker between the co-driver's legs. No such luck, we were ordered to remain with the infantry throughout the night and didn't leave until next morning.

B Squadron, in reserve, were not called upon until last light when Nos. 4 and 5 Troops relieved A Squadron, who returned to the Poggio area. Nos. 1 and 2 Troops moved forward at 10.00pm to Patrignano for the planned first-light attack on Cerasola, a village atop an almost sheer cliff. Next morning they returned to their previous day's positions, as Point 137 had not been retaken during the night.

Fourth Division's attack had lost momentum; all hopes of Venice by Christmas had gone. The many peaks which the Germans now held tenaciously gave magnificent observation over the surrounding country-side while their artillery, anti-tank and machine guns made movement by day increasingly difficult and costly for the attacking infantry who, by now exhausted, had suffered the highest daily casualty rate to date of the Italian campaign. With no reserves available, battalions had been re-organised on a three-, rather than four-, company basis, greatly reducing both effectiveness and offensive capabilities. In 56th Division one brigade had been reduced to cadre and its manpower redistributed while 1st Armoured Division was being disbanded, only 2 Armoured Brigade remaining as an independent formation.

The next day was relatively quiet. New plans had to be made following the failure to gain control of the high ground, an essential prerequisite to the assault crossing of the next river, the Ausa. B Squadron's Nos. 4 and 5 Troops were the only tanks actively engaged, providing cover on the still untaken Point 137. Again they spent the day in the counter-attack role under incessant heavy shelling. Despite evasive action, Lieutenant Mahon's tank (5 Troop) received a direct hit and had to be abandoned. Trooper Raymond Mitchell, from Gloucestershire, was wounded seriously and died next day; the damaged tank was recovered after dark. C Squadron was ordered to Patrignano late that evening prior to supporting 2/4th Hampshires' attack on Cerasola, where the Germans were still holding up the divisional advance.

Arriving at Patrignano, it fell to Lieutenant Bexon to do the job that many troop leaders disliked most: go out with an infantry recce patrol to the bottom of the ravine and find a suitable tank crossing place of the inevitable river.

I was given a large and conspicuous roll of white tape to mark the approach to the exact location of the chosen crossing place. I married up with the patrol and handed in documents and badges (the latter being impossible when wearing a beret with a sewn-on embroidered badge) so I stuffed it in my pocket where it remained until after we had moved off!

After passing through the FDLs the patrol adopted a diamond formation with me in the middle where they hoped I could do least harm. We set off down the forward slope cautiously, stopping from time to time to listen. I was aware that we (or rather I) were making too much noise as we moved through a field of maize, brushing against the ripe heads produced a distinct crackling sound which I felt could be heard for miles. Our stop and go progress had taken us about half way down the steep slope to a ditch. The far bank was higher than ours and at this moment the patrol leader ordered us to freeze, which we did with me caught between steps in a most uncomfortable position. There was a rustling sound in the grass on the far bank and in the bright moonlight (artificial, I think) a couple of German heads appeared and we stared at each other.[4] Nobody in my patrol seemed unduly worried although I was acutely aware that I was standing rather like a heron and that I only had a Smith & Wesson with six rounds securely fastened in my holster. After a little while the enemy heads withdrew and they moved off up the hill while we continued down. 'Another recce patrol,' whispered the nearest infantryman to me.

The rest of the night passed uneventfully although blundering around looking for a fording place in a river in the early hours is tedious when you know in a few hours you will be leading the squadron down and expected to find the way to your white tapes. This I duly did although it did cross my mind that the returning German recce patrol might have found them on their way back and moved them to a quite unfordable place covered by Panzerfausts!

During the night 17th–18th, the King's relieved the Somersets and went on to capture Point 137. No. 1 Troop, B Squadron, under Lieutenant B E S King, moved forward before first light at 4.30am to join the King's, engaging and destroying three machine-gun posts en route; the troop arrived just below their objective after first light. With No. 2 Troop in covering positions, King dismounted to reconnoitre on foot and contact the infantry, who had advanced on a different axis. Reaching the crest he came under shell fire and was slightly wounded. He then spotted a MkIV Special and called his two tank commanders forward to make a plan to engage it. While manoeuvring to take up fire positions, two of his tanks were knocked out almost simultaneously by armour-piercing rounds[5] but King smartly reversed his own tank behind the ridge without suffering damage and the MkIV was knocked out by No. 2 Troop. Having ascertained the fate of his two crews and arranged their evacuation King went forward again on foot to the crest and quickly confirmed that the MkIV offered no further threat. Believing that there must be a second tank, he eventually located a Panther concealed by a house, slightly behind and to his right of the damaged MkIV. He directed sustained and accurate fire on to the Panther from No. 2 Troop which forced the crew to bale out and surrender.

King again advanced on foot under fire to the infantry and arranged to support them from his remaining tank while they moved forward to destroy the already damaged MkIV with PIATs.[6] The plan worked and the tank was destroyed. Not content with the damage he had already inflicted, King went forward on foot for a fourth time, now under heavy shelling, and spotted enemy men and vehicles moving westwards from a T-junction due north of Point 137. Running back to his tank, he called for artillery support and observed and corrected this fire by running backwards and forwards between his tank and his FOP on the crest. When he returned to leaguer he was evacuated through medical channels. Lieutenant King was awarded the Military Cross for his courageous leadership and aggressive spirit.

C Squadron, supporting 2/4th Hampshires on B Squadron's left, started to advance at 5.30am and quickly found the white tapes marking the chosen crossing place below Cerasola. An uneventful crossing was made and, incredibly, the infantry were on their objective by first light, many prisoners being taken. Nos. 1 and 4 Troops covered the division's left flank, while No. 2 looked after the right, leaving No. 3 Troop by the village with the infantry to spend another long day under constant shelling; any movement on foot attracted sniper fire. The infantry were unable to make progress northwards as the village of La Pastoro was heavily defended. Lieutenant McCleary on the extreme left acted as a FOO for 343 Battery, Royal Devon Yeomanry and conducted several good shoots. The squadron remained with the infantry until relieved by 9th (Yorkshire Dragoons) King's Own Yorkshire LI, of 18 Brigade, 1st Armoured Division, at 2 o'clock next morning. A Squadron was ordered to move to Ospedaletto during the afternoon, in preparation for the Ausa crossing.

Fourth Division's plan to cross and exploit beyond the Ausa called for the three battalions of 10 Brigade on the right, with the Royal West Kents of 12 Brigade on the left, to secure bridgeheads on the enemy-held bank during the night of 17th–18th. At first light the three 51st Royal Tanks' squadrons were to cross and support 10 Brigade on to the high ground beyond the river before advancing northwards. The Royal West Kents and A Squadron North Irish Horse, on the corps boundary, were to cross separately, advance to the high ground and secure the division's left flank thus permitting 10 Brigade to advance unimpeded by enemy interference from the south-west. On 10 Brigade's right, 2nd Bedfordshire and Hertfordshires, supported by A Squadron 51st Royal Tanks, met very determined opposition on the east bank and had not reached the river by first light. A day's hard fighting gained little ground and the force was withdrawn at 11.00pm. The Duke of Cornwall's LI, supported by C Squadron Royal Tanks on the left, had an easier task, the enemy thoughtfully retiring behind the river when first attacked. A bridgehead was established quickly and an Ark[7] crossing for the tanks provided; they and the infantry got to within 200 yards of their objective before being forced to give ground by a counter-attack. Thus by nightfall none of the objectives on 10 Brigade's front had been achieved. The only bright spot of the day was the West Kents' attack, supported by A Squadron. The infantry crossed the Ausa during a night of confused fighting, communications with the tanks being virtually non-existent. At 5.00am the squadron was ready to move, but no information was available as to where a bridgehead suitable for tanks had been established. Major Griffith decided a move must be made before first light.

The second-in-command, Captain Finch Noyes, went forward down the slope followed by guides and Lieutenant Norris's No. 2 Troop, to find a crossing. This proved easier than expected. Nos. 2 and 4 (Lieutenant Reid) Troops crossed at first light under accurate high-explosive and small-arms fire to marry up with their infantry companies and support them on to their objective, a 1,200-yard stretch of road atop a ridge; some sixty prisoners were taken. As the first part of this operation was carried out in darkness without prior reconnaissance and under heavy fire, its remarkable success is a tribute to all concerned. However, the success of the day was marred by the death of Corporal Peter Asprey, from Hertfordshire, commander of No. 2 Troop's point tank. The tanks remained with the West Kents throughout the day and night.

The divisional priority now became the crossing of the wide Marecchia, some five miles north of the Ausa, before the threatened rains made it impassable. Neither North Irish Horse nor 28 Brigade were to be involved in phase one and would not be required until the night of the 21st–22nd. On the 20th B Squadron moved south of San Aquilina for phase two of the divisional attack. C Squadron moved to marry up with 2nd Royal Fusiliers of 12 Brigade, but this operation was cancelled by the onset of heavy rain that evening. With rain persisting throughout the next day, all tank operations were abandoned on this the day that the Canadians captured Rimini and Fifth Army broke through the Futa Pass. Supported by 51st Royal Tanks, 11 Brigade had achieved the two stages of phase one of the divisional plan.

During the night of 21–22, 28 Brigade moved up and passed through 11 Brigade's positions, pushing infantry patrols forward over the small Mavone river to secure the high ground around Vergiano which they found unoccupied. The Germans had taken advantage of the bad weather to withdraw behind the Marecchia and the brigade formed a bridgehead over that river. B Squadron, supported by No. 2 Troop of C Squadron with Captain Thomas and Lieutenant Irwin with the Reconnaissance Troop Shermans, was ordered up to Vergiano in the early afternoon. The tanks provided an initial bombardment and then covering fire while the infantry crossed the river. Captain Sidebottom, with Nos. 2 and 4 Troops, crossed before last light covered by a smokescreen provided by the SHQ support tanks. The other twelve tanks covered the assaulting tanks as they crossed, fire being directed particularly on likely observation posts, as the infantry were suffering heavy shelling. The Somersets and the half squadron created a strongpoint in the village of San Giustina on Route 9. No. 2 Troop, temporarily under command of Sergeant Tommy McAughtry, were the first tanks to reach the vital Route 9; during the night the tanks remained in the Somersets' forward defence locations. Sergeant McAughtry spent most of the night out of his tank liaising with the infantry and provided great assistance in driving off repeated enemy counter-attacks. The tanks were subjected to heavy shelling during their two-day stay in and around the village.

The final phase of the divisional plan had worked like clockwork; 28 Brigade maintained its bridgehead until 5th Canadian Armoured Division could renew the advance. At first light on the 23rd, Nos. 1 and 5 Troops of B Squadron were sent to support 2/4th Hampshires at Bornacino, west of the other two troops. Both villages, as usual, were heavily shelled throughout the day; the enemy had no shortage of ammunition. Sergeant White of No. 4 Troop recalled his stay in San Guistina clearly.

> We had no sooner reached the village when the shelling started, we were ordered to move out to the left and disperse. Lieutenant Foott and Corporal Malseed promptly did so. We couldn't, our tank had broken down, we were stuck! We quickly became the target of the day. The C.O. the Lord O'Neill, visiting Captain Sidebottom on a hill overlooking the village, was able to see our predicament and gave permission by wireless to evacuate if we wished. Dick Dawson and Les Fennell were with me in the turret, we all thought it safer to remain. In the event of an evacuation the C.O. ordered us to retrieve the guns, wireless etc. Captain Sidebottom lightened the tension by slyly asking if that included the 'big gun' too? We spent the longest day I ever remember, I smoked 80 cigarettes and Dick the same (all we had), whilst Les continuously smoked his pipe, we were not concerned with the dangers of smoking in those days and all survive some fifty years later! We were glad when darkness came and we and our tank were recovered.

A Squadron relieved Captain Sidebottom and Nos. 2 and 4 Troops. The next night Nos. 1 and 5 Troops were relieved by Lieutenant Irwin's Shermans and No.1 Troop A Squadron. Although torrential rain hampered the Canadians' takeover this was complete by last light on the 25th, allowing the North Irish Horse to be released from operations after thirty-two days of almost continuous fighting. The various scattered tanks were collected; many had fallen foul of the ground, the weather or mechanical problems. During a short break in the weather, the Regiment moved back to concentrate at Aquilina for much needed repairs, maintenance and rest. The Marecchia, ankle deep on 21 September, was a wild brown torrent, twelve feet deep, a week later. It rained continuously from 29 September until 2 October and every ford became impassable.

The failure of 1st Armoured Division to achieve a decisive break-through on 13 September meant that the Allies were committed to another bitter winter in the mountains. The Italian campaign ceased to have any relevance to the ultimate defeat of Germany, other than the retention and destruction of German forces away from the northern European battle-ground.

The Coriano battle, following the cracking of the Gothic Line, bears a marked resemblance to the Hitler Line battle four months earlier, illustrating the continuing inability of the British high command to sustain a battle, after the carefully planned and well executed break-in. It demonstrated again the willingness to throw armour into a setpiece battle without adequate preparation or planning, regardless of cost; 2 Armoured

Brigade – Queen's Bays, 9th Queen's Own Lancers and 10th Royal Hussars – fought with the utmost bravery and suffered horrendous casualties, but unlike 25 Tank Brigade did not have the solace of success.

General Leese handed over command of Eighth Army on 1 October, to take up a new appointment in Burma and was succeeded by General Sir Richard McCreery, commander of X Corps, who had first-hand knowledge of the hill-fighting abilities of the Indian divisions. McCreery, late 12th Royal Lancers, was the first cavalryman to command Eighth Army.

NOTES

1   Later expanded into First French Army and creating 6 Army Group with its US partner.
2   Brigadier Andrew Kendrew was commissioned into The Leicestershire Regiment in 1931 and served with his battalion in Londonderry's Ebrington Barracks in the mid-30s. While stationed in Londonderry, he met and married Miss Nora Harvey of Malin Head in Donegal. His address is given as Malin in the *London Gazette* in one of his DSO citations; he received three Bars to the DSO. He later became a major-general and was Governor of Western Australia from 1963 to 1973.
3   The Priest was based on the American M3 Grant tank and mounted a 105mm gun. It was called Priest in British service because of its pulpit, with its .5in Browning machine gun for anti-aircraft and local defence.
4   Artificial moonlight was a recent innovation that involved directing the beams of searchlights onto low clouds thereby providing the equivalent of moonlight.
5   Sergeant Maxwell and Lance-Corporal Gifford, the operator, had been injured and the driver, Trooper David James, from Edinburgh, killed when their tank was hit. The other crew, fortunately, sustained no injuries.
6   PIAT: Projector, Infantry, Anti-tank, the British personal anti-tank weapon, a spigot-operated equivalent of the American bazooka.
7   A modified Churchill tank with hinged metal trackways fitted to the superstructure which was used by driving the vehicle into the obstruction and opening the trackways, fore and aft, by cable-operated winches. Obstacles up to fifty feet wide could be bridged by a single Ark while wider rivers could be bridged by driving two or three Arks into the river to create a causeway. Deep narrow obstacles could be crossed by driving one Ark into the obstruction and then driving a second on top of the first, piggy-back fashion.

CHAPTER XI

From river to river

With 2nd New Zealand Division about to relieve 4th Division there were indications that 25 Tank Brigade might be allowed some much needed rest and refitting. Apart from thirty-two days' continuous operations, the unrelenting heavy rain had placed an additional strain on man and machine. It was not to be; on 25 September the Regiment was ordered to leave 4th Division and come under 10th Indian Division, then transferring to the Adriatic from the Arno–Tiber front. North Irish Horse alone was to support 10th Division throughout the forthcoming operations. The employment of a single tank regiment in support of a division was justified by the mountainous terrain across which 10th Indian Division was to attack and the difficulties faced by tanks in traversing such country in the rainy season. By contrast, 142 RAC were not to be called forward until the 17th while 51 RTR would not be called upon until 20 October.

Tenth Indian Division was to relieve 4th Indian Division on the left of V Corps' sector on 1 October and to attack westwards through the Apennine foothills to secure a bridgehead over the Fiumicino river, close to its source at Sogliano. This was a prerequisite to Eighth Army's main assault with two corps during the night 6–7 October – the Canadians on the right along the coast towards Ravenna and V Corps in a north-westerly direction, parallel with Route 9, in the direction of Bologna. The initial task was assault crossings of the Fiumicino by both corps and then the securing of bridgeheads over the Savio, the next major river obstacle, some eight miles to the west.

Torrential rain, which made roads difficult and tracks virtually impassable, delayed the takeover by 10th Indian Division. C Squadron, which was to support 25 Brigade[1] on the right flank and thus the first to arrive, was not ordered to move to Poggio Berni until 2 October where, next day, it relieved 6th Royal Tanks. Liaison was effected with the infantry in the Cormacchiara area, east of Borghi, a troop with both the King's Own and the Punjabis and the other two troops with the Garhwalis. The changeover, in heavy rain, was observed by 721st Jäger Regiment and shelling, the inevitable welcome to newcomers, took place but no casualties resulted.

The remainder of the Regiment reached Poggio Berni on the 4th, A Squadron to be affiliated with 20 Brigade[2] to operate on the left flank and B Squadron with 10 Brigade in the centre. The divisional line ran from north to south and was little more than ten miles from the sea at one point. The area to be attacked was heavily populated and densely cultivated; invariably villages were on summits and the many farm buildings provided strongpoints. With main roads practically non-existent heavy traffic led quickly to serious damage to the sodden secondary roads.

Tenth Division's attack commenced during the night 4th–5th with a two-brigade assault on a narrow front. On the left, two battalions of 20 Brigade, supported by A Squadron, struck into the west at 11.00pm to capture Strigara and Sogliano. Lieutenant Watters with No. 3 Troop supported by Lieutenant Irwin and three Recce Troop Shermans moved forward at the same time at 'clickity-clack' speed.[3] The tanks were roadbound, due to the previous heavy rain, entailing a long detour that kept them at least a couple of miles north of the Gurkhas' centre line. Captain Finch Noyes, A Squadron's recce captain, marched with the Gurkhas, with a No. 22 wireless set on a mule to maintain contact. The tanks were to rendezvous with the Gurkhas at a road junction one mile east of the objective at first light and support them in their final attack on Sogliano. Finch Noyes' mule slipped, fell and rolled over, smashing the 22 set, some two thousand yards short of the rendezvous. Communications were not re-established until he moved across country on foot in pouring rain to contact the tanks. Just before reaching the rendezvous, the leading tank was blown up on a mine, blocking the road and preventing any further advance. The remaining tanks took up fire positions and opened fire on selected targets with excellent results. The Gurkhas stormed into Sogliano, only to find the Germans gone; they had been beaten to it by fighting patrols of the Punjabis from their left. On being held up on their approach to Strigara, the Punjabis had turned north towards Sogliano and established themselves there. Better still, they had pushed north-westwards, down a road which descends seven hundred feet with seventeen hairpin bends in less than a mile, to seize two bridges over the river. The tanks remained in support in full view of the enemy still in San Martino and suffered heavy shelling throughout the day without incurring any casualties. At last light, the Churchills withdrew to harbour; the Shermans moved only a short distance as they were to support another attack later that night. The mined tank was recovered after nightfall by Lance-Sergeant Jackson with the A Squadron ARV.

The King's Own, 25 Brigade, supported by Lieutenant Hubbard's C Squadron troop did not start their attack towards the important village of San Martino, some two and a half miles north-east of Sogliano, until 3.00am on the 5th. As they did not have as far to travel as the Gurkhas the final attacks on the two objectives were to be simultaneous, but the attack on San Martino, aided by artificial moonlight and tanks firing on fixed lines, met fierce opposition from an enemy alerted by the Gurkhas' approach to Sogliano. Both leading companies burst into the village only to be driven out again by heavy counter-attacks. At first light they were still being held on the outskirts where they stayed, beating off counter-attack after counter-attack. A second attack just after full darkness was planned, this time supported by No. 4 Troop C Squadron and the three Shermans used in the successful attack on Sogliano. This attack, again aided with artificial moonlight, was successful; by 9.00pm the village was securely in the King's Own's hands. Lieutenant Bexon described the part the tanks played in this attack.

> San Martino was the usual Italian village for these parts, straddling a ridge and separated from us by a deepish valley. To give covering fire for an infantry attack at night, even with artificial moonlight, was generally hazardous not only because of the poor visibility but also the complete lack of direct contact with the infantry. In this case I took my troop along a narrow dirt road running just below the top of our ridge on the forward slope, until we got into a position where we could see the houses of San Martino huddled on the ridge in front of us.
>
> The plan was extremely simple as far as we were concerned: to shoot up the village and anything that moved in it and to stop firing before our troops entered it; frankly easier said than done under these circumstances but as H-hour approached we loaded HE and at the right moment all the tanks opened up. The results were quite spectacular as at the same time Harry Irwin and the Recce Troop's Shermans further along our ridge opened fire and we saw clouds of white dust rising from the whole village.
>
> The problem now was to know when to cease fire. Visibility was in no way good enough to see our infantry and I believe that it was purely by guess and by God that we stopped at the right time. The attack was a success and we were thanked for our part in it, but I never admitted how unscientific was our action.

Later, in thick fog and pouring rain, the Punjabis renewed their attack on Strigara, but again without success. Reinforced by two companies of the Baluch Regiment from 10 Brigade, the attack was resumed immediately after dark next evening and, following ninety minutes' fighting, Strigara was in Indian hands. In two days' hard fighting, the division had cleared the five-mile ridge from Strigara and was up to the Fiumicino. It was poised and ready to play its part in the main offensive.

Tenth Indian Division was to attack on a seven-and-half-mile front in a north-westerly direction to create bridgeheads over the Savio and outflank the German defences opposing the advance of 46th Division parallel with Route 9 on the Indians' right. Facing the left of the Indians' front, two high bare hills blocked the way. On the right, Monte Farneto, 1,600-feet high was protected by a maze of deepcut watercourses. Some 2,000 yards to the west stood Monte Codruzzo, an abrupt buttress with steep, trackless slopes which rose 1,300 feet above the plain. Its crest marked the beginning of a long ridge stretching northwards towards Aquarola, some two miles south of Cesena, the summit of which was marked by a series of hamlets, guarded by precipitous slopes and difficult approaches along the razor-backed crest while, beyond Monte Farneto, a similar system of ridges also led to Aquarola. Two German divisions, 114th Jäger to the north and 356th Infantry, responsible for the Monte Farneto area, opposed 10th Division. To help in this inhospitable and strongly defended country, and in an attempt to balance the scales, 43 Gurkha Lorried Infantry Brigade was placed under 10th Division command but their lorries would be of little use in the coming attack.

Tenth Division planned to attack with two brigades up during the night of 6 October; 25 Brigade, on the right, supported by C Squadron, was to cross the river and capture San Lorenzo and Roncofreddo. On the left 20 Brigade, now supported by B Squadron, was to capture Monte Farneto. Both squadrons spent the day liaising with their infantry and, in C Squadron's case, reconnoitering for suitable crossing places. B Squadron was fortunate in that one of the two bridges captured by the Punjabis could carry a Churchill. Lieutenant McCleary and Sergeants Thacker and Williams, with patrols from C Squadron, spent a fruitless day searching for a suitable crossing place, which failure led to a twenty-four hour postponement of 25 Brigade's attack. C Squadron's troop leaders spent the night searching for a crossing and, although provided with infantry escorts, invariably found themselves alone as their escort glided off on more exciting and usually profitable missions. McCleary eventually found a crossing place judged to be suitable due east of Roncofreddo. Preparations were put in hand for 25 Brigade to attack that night.

In the meantime, A Squadron, now affiliated to 10 Brigade, was not engaged actively but carried out the necessary and important liaison with the infantry with whom they would soon be operating. A mobile force for left-flank protection was required and No. 4 Troop, under Lieutenant Milne, was to be prepared to support Central India Horse, the divisional reconnaissance regiment, which had been given this task and began moving to Strigara at 3.00am on 8 October.

To take Monte Farneto, 20 Brigade used two battalions, the Gurkhas on the right with Lieutenant Fleming's No. 2 Troop and Lieutenant Irwin's Shermans under command of Major Mackean. Captain Sidebottom, with Nos. 4 and 5 Troops, was to support the Mahrattas in their attack on the left of the feature. At 8.00pm both battalions trudged off on a long night march into the north and, by the early hours, had closed up on the objective. The tanks left harbour at 11.00pm in heavy rain and pitch darkness and moved to Sogliano, ready to cross the Fiumicino at first light. Such pelting and impenetrable rain served the Indians well, for the enemy apparently had decided that hostilities were impossible in such weather. His forward positions were unmanned and the two battalions swept over the objective. Monte Farneto was firmly in Indian hands by 5.30am with little loss. Led by Captain Sidebottom, the tanks moved forward from Sogliano in the dark down the steep winding road, crossed the bridge at first light and immediately came under heavy shelling. Sidebottom's force turned left and had joined up with the Mahrattas by 6.30am – a magnificent performance for tracked vehicles over such terrain according to the exultant Mahrattas. Major Mackean's force, which was to go straight on, found their way blocked by a blown culvert. Extensive foot reconnaissances by the squadron leader and Captain Hern revealed there was no way round and the tanks had to retrace their tracks, a slow process, until the track used by Captain Sidebottom was reached; Mackean's tanks linked up with the Gurkhas just before midday.

Dumbfounded by the capture of Monte Farneto, the enemy took a surprisingly long time to react to this major setback. The routine counter-attack was not mounted until early afternoon by which time the Indian infantry were well dug in with B Squadron in support and the divisional machine-gun battalion, 1st Royal Northumberland Fusiliers, was moving forward to consolidate the defence of this key feature. The divisional artillery had ranged and the Desert Air Force was alerted. A battalion-strength first counter-attack was beaten off, tanks and artillery playing an effective role in breaking it up. As a second counter-attack developed the air weighed in with fighter-bomber attacks and the attempt failed. That evening the Northumberlands' machine guns helped smash the third and final counter-attack of the day. At 6.30pm B Squadron suffered a severe loss: Major Mackean, transferring from his tank to a jeep to attend evening orders was wounded by a shell splinter. Although taken immediately to the Regimental Aid Post, he died soon after admission.[4] Command of B Squadron passed to Captain Sidebottom, to be promoted Major.

As further counter-attacks during the night were expected, the tanks remained with the Indians, slightly behind the leading companies, for a sleepless night. As the day's heavy rain made it impossible for the normal re-supply vehicles to reach them, Captain Hern commandeered all available jeeps and trailers and, under heavy fire, completed the replenishment by 4.00am. Enemy patrols were active throughout the night but failed to break in; the tank crews repeatedly 'stood to'. At first light the tanks moved forward to take up positions in close support of the Indians but remained static throughout the day to give valuable support to the Gurkhas of 10 Brigade, who were advancing north-eastwards towards San Paolo, a village lying between Monte Farneto and Roncofreddo. The Germans defended the village stubbornly and although Gurkhas managed to reach the outskirts, they were unable to clear it. The tanks used their main armament with HE rounds and machine guns to good effect on targets indicated by the Gurkhas.

B Squadron was to remain on Monte Farneto until the 11th. On the 8th they helped beat off two determined counter-attacks. Next day saw the final counter-attack which the tanks helped repulse; the Germans had finally admitted defeat. Infantry and tanks had been subjected to heavy and continuous shelling during these two days. Sergeant McAughtry, again temporarily in command of No. 2 Troop, despite heavy and continuous shelling, spent much time out of his tank, liaising with the Gurkhas and fighting his troop in an exemplary manner. The shelling continued the following day while the relief of 25 Brigade by 43 Gurkha Brigade[5] was being completed. B Squadron, now supporting 43 Brigade, was allowed to withdraw to harbour that night and would not move before the road to Monte Codruzzo, lying west of Monte Farneto, was open.

The Gurkha Brigade – 2/6th, 2/8th and 2/10th Gurkha Rifles – was to strike due west for the eastern bank of the Savio; 2/6th Gurkhas started the advance during the night 11th–12th and, in an amazing feat, captured and consolidated Monte Codruzzo, the key feature, by first light next morning. Here, after a long and arduous march, they were joined by 2/10th Battalion, who were immediately pushed forward towards Monte Del Erta. Tenacious resistance along the approach ridge slowed down progress, but after bitter fighting, which included beating off several counter-attacks, the village was secured; 2/6th Battalion then passed through to overrun Monte Guzzo during the night 13th–14th. By dawn they had reached Monte Chicco, the last high knoll and dominating feature above the Savio, where the triangle of high ground approached its apex. Here they were assailed by furious assault from all three sides and an increasingly fierce and bitter battle ensued. Both 2/8th and 2/10th Battalions rushed companies forward. All the divisional gunners were involved in a box barrage programme to protect the flanks and front of the heavily engaged hillmen and fighter-bombers from the corps' 'cab-rank' were called in. When night fell a heavy shoot by Spandaus and mortars seemed to indicate a continuation of the struggle but turned out to be cover for a German withdrawal. By first light 43 Brigade held the high ground above the deep valley of the Savio. They had achieved their objective in outstanding fashion, in an amazingly short time. To prevent damage to the brigade supply route, B Squadron had not been permitted to move in support.

On 14 October the weather was fine and the terrain starting to dry. B Squadron, back with 10 Brigade, now operating north of 43 Brigade, was ordered to move at 2.30pm north-west to Monteleone. Owing to the state of the roads, and almost impossible off-road going, progress was very slow. The squadron harboured for the night two miles short of the village. Next morning Lieutenant Fleming's No. 2 Troop made a gallant attempt to reach Adriano, north-west of Monteleone, to link up with the Gurkhas advancing along the bed of a small river. Some 350 yards beyond Monteleone, the leading tank was attempting a most difficult stream crossing. Just short of the far bank a track broke. Up to his waist in water and mud and under heavy fire, Sergeant McAughtry, assisted by his crew, repaired the track and completed the crossing. Very shortly, his and the troop leader's tanks became bogged. After much hard work they were extricated. No further attempt was made to advance up this route and no alternative tank route was possible. No. 4 Troop meanwhile had moved forward to Monteleone to follow the leading troop to Adriano but, in view of the fate of No. 2 Troop, both troops were withdrawn. Sergeant McAughtry was subsequently awarded the Distinguished Conduct Medal in recognition of his outstanding determination to support the infantry, without regard for his own safety and as an acknowledgement of his outstanding activities as a leader.

In heavy rain and thick mist, C Squadron started their move forward to the selected crossing place over the Fiumicino at 3.00am on the 8th. The intention was that the squadron would be on the infantry objectives by first light; 25 Brigade with two battalions up had crossed the river the evening before. On the right the Garhwalis were to capture San Lorenzo and the spur of high ground northwards from Roncofreddo village, supported by Nos. 1 and 2 Troops under Major Morton. On the left the Punjabis were to take Roncofreddo, one of the bastions of the enemy defences, south of the proposed crossing, in an attack supported by Nos. 3 and 4 Troops under Captain Thomas.

The approach march was a nightmare, carried out in pitch blackness and torrential rain on a steep and narrow track made slippery by the rain. When the leading tanks reached the river they found that rain had so swollen it that what was always going to be a difficult crossing had turned into an almost impossible one. To quote from *The Narrative of Operations of 25 Tank Brigade*, however, 'With the never say die spirit of the Irish . . . the crossing was attempted and by 0700 hours several tanks had crossed'.

The journey down to the river was described by a troop leader.

It was not long before my tank slid off the narrow track in darkness as the edge gave way and in trying to extricate ourselves and regain the path the left track broke. I transferred to another tank and pushed on down the sodden slope. It then became a case of tow-ropes out as tank after tank got stuck. When the river was eventually reached after dispiriting hours of travail we found it rising rapidly. We watched several tanks make the crossing to the far side, but then one got stuck in the middle of the river. We had the rare sight of the crew [baling] out before the water finally came right up to the turret. No further tank crossing was attempted. The tanks that had got across found their way forward blocked by a steep and slippery slope at which even Churchills balked.

C, immediately renamed by the other squadrons 'Sea' Squadron could go no further. The Garhwalis, however, beat down the opposition and quickly cleared San Lorenzo but the Punjabis ran into almost impossible ground; enfiladed by fire from a strongly fortified church on their left, they could make no more progress during the day. They succeeded brilliantly in a second attack, carried out during the night of 9th–10th and swept through Roncofreddo in dashing style to advance to the high ground north-west of the town. C Squadron spent a miserable and frustrating day de-bogging tanks and repairing broken tracks under shellfire and the ever-present rain. During this messy business Trooper George King, a squadron fitter, was killed while in the open working on a tank. One of three brothers from Strabane who joined at Enniskillen, he was the only one to serve overseas with the Regiment. Despite every effort no further progress was achieved and the tanks remained in and around the crossing until darkness called a halt to recovery work. The echelon had great difficulty in getting supplies down to the river, and once again had to employ jeeps and trailers, floating supplies across the fast-flowing river on improvised rafts, which Major Morton likened to the coracles of the ancient Britons. The morning brought no respite from the rain; the river rose still farther and flooded what had previously only been sodden ground, adding to the already considerable problem faced by the squadron, and to the discomfiture of the beleaguered crews, who were beginning to wonder if they were on combined operations.

Little was achieved next day despite intense efforts, especially by Lance-Sergeant Stewart. The first tanks did not reach the San Lorenzo road until the 11th. By the evening of the 12th the squadron was in better mood as twelve tanks had reached Roncofreddo. The drowned tank was a write-off and had to be abandoned; two remained to be recovered. Roncofreddo, being a hilltop village, provided shelter at last from the rain and good standing for the tanks which, because of the condition of the roads, were not allowed to move until the 14th when, as a very welcome change, the weather was fine. The squadron moved out east of the town and escaped the shellfire directed on it. They were to remain in this position for a further week, until allowed to move forward for the crossing of the Savio. The days spent in and around the Fiumicino were the Regiment's worst experience of weather and ground combined throughout the war.

The only battalion of 10 Brigade involved in the division's initial attacks towards San Paola, north-east of Monte Farneto, was 2/4th Gurkhas. A Squadron took advantage of the opportunity to liaise with and get to know the other two battalions with whom they would be operating. The division's left flank was open as the planned arrival of the Polish Corps had been delayed. In the last few days of September, rain washed away many of the temporary bridges on Eighth Army's line of communication, which there had not been enough time to weatherproof. This led to a twenty-four-hour postponement of General McCreery's main attack. The Polish Corps had been under orders to move on 29 September, but this was cancelled due to the loss of bridges on its route forward.

Ten Brigade next committed the Baluchis westwards towards Monte Codruzzo on the division's southern flank. The battalion was to advance along slopes slashed by innumerable streams and quite impossible for tanks. Meanwhile, 2/4th Gurkhas were making good progress towards San Paola, north-east of Monte Farneto, now held firmly by 20 Brigade. The Durhams, supported by A Squadron, were to take Monte Spaccato on the next ridge north-west of San Paola and the neighbouring village of Monteleone. A Squadron, less No. 4 Troop, started their approach march from Borghi in the by now appalling weather at 11.00pm on 9 October. By first light they had one troop roadbound, five hundred yards south-west of San Paola and the other two troops just north of Sogliano in positions to provide fire support for the Durhams who, during early morning ground mist, had found several gaps in the defences of Monte Spaccatto. When the sun broke through the Germans going about their morning chores found C Company in their midst. Fierce hand-to-hand fighting ensued resulting in the enemy being evicted. The tanks provided effective support in driving off counter-attacks. A number of machine-gun posts were eliminated and one gun on the left flank, the cause of much trouble for supply vehicles, was destroyed. The gun crew was captured by the Punjabis of 20 Brigade. The tanks remained throughout the day and supported the Durhams into Monteleone, their second objective. Roncofreddo on the right flank was captured early the same morning by 25 Brigade and 10th Division was now master of the forelands of the peninsula of high ground that blocked the way to the plains. Only on the extreme left, where the Baluchis had encountered tough going, did the enemy hold ground below the main crests.

Nos. 2 and 3 Troops moved forward next morning to support the Durhams, now ready to push on north-westwards to Monte del Vacche, the knoll at the extremity of the high ground. Roadbound, the troops had to move through San Paola, which had been reported clear. However, the enemy had filtered back overnight, re-occupying houses to the north and north-east of the village. Good shooting by No. 2 troop helped the Gurkhas to clear them out. As the road northwards from San Paola was heavily mined and as sappers were not available to clear it, the tanks took up fire positions in and around the village and supported both Durhams and Gurkhas as required. The squadron was not allowed to move throughout the next day as the road had not yet been repaired.

No. 4 Troop away on the divisional left continued to wind its difficult and tedious way along narrow roads through the hills in support of Central India Horse and were finally held up by a bad blow in the road, about one and a half miles south-east of the small village of Santa Maria Riopetra. The village stands on a road running down to Route 71, the main road running south-west from Cesena. It was impossible to by-pass the blow and the troop had to wait for the road to be repaired. A Squadron was not allowed to move the next day as the road had still not been repaired.

During the 13th, a better day weatherwise, the three A Squadron troops were permitted to move forward to Monteleone. At 11.00pm, in only light rain for a change, they moved forward again a short distance over very difficult country and took up positions in the area of Point 345, north-west of Monteleone. Called forward early next morning, when the weather again was fine and the tracks starting to dry, the tanks were ordered up to Sorrivoli, which had been cleared during the night by the Durhams; they were to support the Baluchis in their attack on the important village of Dio La Guardia, a couple of miles farther north-west. No. 2 Troop, followed by No. 3, crossed a ford only to be held up by a blow in the road three hundred yards farther on. No. 1 Troop remained on Point 345 with a troop of M10 SPGs, waiting to cross when the opportunity arose. Despite intense effort with pick and shovel, it was not possible to negotiate the blow. To make matters worse, the road behind had collapsed under the weight of tanks on a surface weakened by previous continuous heavy rain. They were trapped and perforce had to occupy the best defensive positions available. No. 1 Troop and the M10s were refused permission to move, to avoid further damage to the roads. The Durhams were advised on foot and the Baluchis by wireless of the squadron's predicament. Although unsupported, the Baluchis overcame heavy enemy resistance and occupied Dio La Guardia by first light.

Meanwhile, No. 4 Troop, still supporting Central India Horse, had negotiated the blown road that had barred their progress for days and moved forward with great difficulty to rejoin the Indians westwards of Santa Maria on the 14th. Central India Horse then pushed out patrols towards the Savio, their objective being the two bridges over that river north of Cella. During the night Royal Engineers re-opened the collapsed road and filled in the blow blocking the advance of Nos. 2 and 3 Troops. In the morning both troops resumed their difficult advance, but owing to the narrowness of the road and yet another crater, were unable to get into Dio La Guardia itself. The Royal Engineers worked through the night again but it was not until 1.00pm next day that the two troops, commanded by Lieutenant Reid, reduced to three tanks by mechanical failure, struggled the short distance up and into the village. All had to have Royal Engineers assistance, a small bulldozer providing essential help. While the tanks had been struggling to get forward, the infantry continued their steady, if slow, progress and were closing up on the Savio. On 10 Brigade's left flank the Gurkhas had cleared Monte del Vacche on the northern extremity of the high ground and the Baluchis had pushed on and captured Monte Reale, one and a half miles to the north-east. From this newly won position they overlooked the Savio at Roversano to the west. Looking northwards, above the diminishing ridges, could be seen the spires and high buildings of Cesena on Route 9, less than three miles away. By now Cesena was almost in the grasp of 46th Division, advancing from the south-east on the plain below. During this day extensive foot reconnaissances were carried out by Lord O'Neill, the second-in-command and B and C Squadron leaders together with the battery commander of 383 Battery Royal Devon Yeomanry to find tracks and second-class roads leading forward from Roncofreddo and Monte Farneto as all movement of tanks on supply routes would make them unusable for the rest of the division prior to the now imminent assault crossing of the Savio. The divisional commander had relieved 10 Brigade, less their leading battalion, the Baluchis, with 25 Brigade and ordered the Baluchis, as already related, to capture Monte Reale and the Punjabis Aquarola a mile nearer Cesena. Lieutenant Reid's troop moved forward in the early hours of the 17th with orders to marry up with the Baluchis and then support the Punjabis in their attack on Aquarola. The tanks had a nightmare journey in the darkness over tracks which were barely 'jeepable'. Some quarter of a mile short of Monte Reale their progress was finally halted by yet another blow, carried out by the retreating enemy. Here they were to remain for thirty-six hours and were constantly shelled, fortunately without casualties.

Infantry patrols probing the approaches to the Savio reported that the tracks were heavily cratered. The country between Monte Reale and the river was impassable to tanks because of deep ravines, in some places with sheer sides, and steep riverbanks. No. 4 Troop, continuing to plod on with the unit searching for fords, crossed the Savio during the night at shallows in the area of Cella and by first light were on Route 71, pushing northwards. A thousand yards north of Cella they took up defensive positions around the bridge and were heavily shelled throughout the day.

During the 18th the commanding officer and second-in-command reconnoitred approaches to the Savio in the Cella area following reports that no suitable tank crossings were available to 10th Division any farther downstream. All available Arks had been allocated to 4th Division who would be operating on 10th Division's right, across what was assumed to be better tank country. On the 19th the only tanks to move were Lieutenant Reid's three which, finally, were able to join the Punjabis who had cleared Aquarola the previous day and carried on to seize Point 157, 1,000 yards farther north. The tanks took up defensive positions; 10th Division's final task had been fulfilled by securing the left flank of 46th Division during their final assault on Cesena. The division's mission had been accomplished, the extremely difficult country between the Fiumicino and the Savio had been cleared, and the width of the Eighth Army front doubled. Cesena was entered and cleared up to the Savio by 46th Division on the 19th.

The Regiment's most notable achievement while supporting 10th Indian Division was its decisive part in assisting 20 Brigade to hold Monte Farneto, the key to the enemy defences and to establish that feature as a firm base for the division in the ensuing operations. The struggle had been mainly against the elements. It had been a heartless task for the crews trying to get their forty-ton tanks over bad and narrow tracks, up and down hills, over soft and boggy country and across streams and fast-flowing rivers in appalling weather. Hours were spent with pick and shovel, repairing broken tracks, and towropes were in constant use. The infantry, superb mountain fighters, admired greatly the tenacity of their supporting armour and the determination shown by them in their efforts to keep up with their advance.

Fourth Division, supported by 51st Royal Tanks and 142 RAC, relieved 46th Division on 10th Indian Division's right during the night 18–19 October for the next phase of Eighth Army's offensive, the advance to and crossing of the Ronco river ten miles to the west. North of Meldola, the Ronco is protected by substantial flood banks that form a major obstacle, twelve feet high and about fifteen feet wide at the base. Tenth Indian Division, still supported by the North Irish Horse, was to continue the V Corps battle without relief.

On being relieved from operations at Monte Farneto on 11 October, 20 Indian Brigade went into reserve. The successful crossing of the upper reaches of the Savio and establishment of a bridgehead during the night 17th–18th by Central India Horse created a new opportunity. The lack of Arks and easy, natural tank crossings on the divisional front led to a change of plan. Supported by C Squadron, 20 Brigade was to move south to Cello, cross the Savio and advance northwards to Borello, some three and three-quarters miles downstream, clearing the west bank in the process. They would then swing into the north-west and capture Monte Cavallo on the watershed separating the Savio and Ronco valleys. The brigade, with the division's three field regiments under command, but without C Squadron, quietly and unobtrusively crossed the river on 20 October. Moving quickly against light opposition but through difficult country, the leading patrols were approaching Monte Cavallo by next afternoon. C Squadron was ordered to Cello on the 21st. It poured all day and the route was very difficult, despite which the squadron reached and crossed the Savio before darkness fell and the river rose. The squadron harboured for the night, with orders to move forward to Barello on the morrow.

No. 4 Troop A Squadron, which had been in the area for three days, was now placed under C Squadron's command. The troop had spent those days supporting Central India Horse on reconnaissance and found that Route 71, which ran northwards on the Savio's east bank until it crossed the river 800 yards east of Borello on the west bank, was impassable to tanks due to blows and demolitions. On the west bank the ground was soft and boggy and rose quickly into trackless hills before the higher slopes of the Apennines were reached. Lieutenant Milne, a tough, wiry farmer from Argentina, who had returned home to serve in the war, wore the BLAV (British Latin-American Volunteer) flash on his uniform and had volunteered to transfer from 25 Tank Brigade HQ to the Regiment at the end of the Tunisian campaign, proved to be a dedicated and resourceful troop leader who fitted in very well with the North Irish Horse. The only possible route forward for the tanks that he could foresee was the most unusual one of driving them down the bed of the river where there would be no mines.

As early as the night 18th–19th, and as ostentatiously as possible, elements from both 25 and 43 Brigades on the north and centre respectively of the divisional front had been probing the defence of the Savio with strong fighting patrols. During the night 20th–21st the Garhwalis created a bridgehead on the far bank in the area of San Carlo opposite Castiglione, five miles south of Cesena; 2/6th Gurkhas crossed against lighter opposition three miles farther upstream. A Squadron, supporting 25 Brigade, despite the earlier dismal prognostications of the Indian infantry, had found a route down to a potential crossing place at Castiglione.

At dusk on the 21st 25 Brigade began crossing the Savio. Monte della Rovere was its first objective after which it was to cross the watershed and capture Tessello. The night was dark and the weather appalling as the dogged infantry slogged through squelching mud. None of the three battalions was able to reach their objectives, being savagely counter-attacked and driven back by a newly arrived assault battalion. The Gurkhas of 10 Brigade had advanced simultaneously up the slopes westwards towards Formignano, a village on a ridge crest some two miles east and half a mile north of Monte Cavallo. They also met fierce opposition and, by dawn, were no more than halfway there. A Squadron, supporting 25 Brigade, had planned to cross at first light but the river had risen overnight and was now too deep for tanks, forward movement of which was then prohibited by the Commander Royal Engineers; the squadron was eventually stood down in the area of Aquarola where it would remain until early November.

Twenty Brigade launched its attack on Monte Cavallo three hours after the start of 25 Brigade's crossing at San Carlo. Monte Cavallo, the first of the German fortified positions west of the Savio, marked the watershed. Gurkhas and Mahrattas initially made progress but opposition stiffened and they were pinned down on the slopes, unable to advance.

It was imperative that C Squadron get forward. Major Morton had been briefed on the difficulties that lay ahead by Lieutenant Milne who reported on the lack of available conventional routes, but suggested that it might be possible to use the river bed. Morton carried out a reconnaissance and accepted Milne's offer to lead the tanks down the river. Amazingly, all the tanks reached Borello before nightfall. It was a magnificent effort; Milne walked the four and a half miles leading the tanks with, at times, ice-cold water up to his chest. This most unpleasant and very exhausting example of leadership and dedication to duty was acknowledged by a Mention in Despatches. While C Squadron was waterbound, 20 Brigade's third battalion, the Punjabis, moved up to reinforce the fighting line and 2/6th and 2/10th Gurkhas of 43 Brigade crossed the Savio under temporary command of 20 Brigade to fill the gap between 20 and 10 Brigades.

That evening, for the first time in Italy, 20 Brigade staged a setpiece attack behind a heavy bombardment by the three supporting field regiments; 10,000 rounds rained down upon enemy positions on Monte Cavallo and Formignano. A co-ordinated assault went in all along the line. On Monte Cavallo's slopes, 2/3rd Gurkhas crept forward and, with a swift dash out of the dark, won ground; strong German parties were either killed or taken prisoner. The Mahrattas then passed through the hillmen to close up to the crest after confused and bitter fighting. Although the defenders struck back in reckless counter-attacks, they achieved nothing and, by first light on the 23rd, Monte Cavallo was firmly in Indian hands. Suffering reverses all along the Indians' front the defeated Germans were so disorganised that, for once, they failed to muster sufficient strength for the customary counter-attack.

Indian Sappers and Miners erected two Bailey bridges across the Savio and supplies and support weapons were rushed to the fighting men in the hills. The third battalion of 43 Brigade, 2/8th Gurkhas, crossed and the brigade retrieved its two battalions lent to 20 Brigade the previous day before leapfrogging north-westwards for Tesselo on their left, some 2,000 yards north of Monte Cavallo and Monte della Revere on the right. C Squadron, now with 43 Brigade, moved towards Monte della Revere; B Squadron was ordered forward to Borello under 20 Brigade in lieu of the departed C Squadron.

C Squadron, less No. 4 Troop, again moved by means of the river bed to avoid the still unopened Route 71 and reached Castiglione with surprisingly little difficulty – practice makes perfect – and regained terra firma. The squadron crossed Route 71 but the leading troop had covered only about half a mile of the track to Monte della Revere when it was confronted by a large demolition. The brigade Royal Engineers' Troop arrived quickly and reopened the track using a small bulldozer. However, the resumed advance was halted some 800 yards farther uphill, a thousand yards short of the objective, by a second major demolition. The sappers reckoned they would be unable to clear the way before dark and C Squadron returned to harbour leaving them hard at work. Meanwhile, No. 4 Troop had moved up to Monte Cavallo with the intention of getting across country by the track running from there to Tesselo. B Squadron arrived at Borello and contacted 20 Brigade.

No. 4 Troop leader described his arrival at Monte Cavallo and the subsequent advance to Tesselo.

> The first problem was to get up Monte Cavallo by the dirt track that led to the right-hand side of the top and our luck held so that we got all the tanks over a little bridge that politely fell in after the last one had crossed. There were now the customary demolitions and blows accompanied by mines but a Royal Engineer detachment with their ubiquitous bulldozer arrived and were invaluable in helping us get to the top where we were able to take up position.
>
> The view was superb and one could clearly see across the valley to the other side and to the left the ridge bending round to point straight ahead to where we knew the last hills before the plain lay. So good was it that I was joined by the Brigadier and his three Gurkha commanding officers who had chosen this spot to hold an O-Group. For the first and only time in my career as a troop leader I was invited to participate in a brigade O-Group and asked from time to time 'What does the Armour say about that?' A plan was made for the next day and I was to recce a possible track down the valley and up the other side to Tesselo and attempt to support them into it and further.
>
> As soon as it was dark Sergeant Kennedy, MM, and I set off into the night, he with a tommy gun, down the track to see if it was tankable. After some time I asked him what was the overall width of a Churchill; he wasn't sure and neither was I, so we agreed to assume that it was around eleven feet. [Actual width was 10ft 8in.] If the Germans had been watching us they would have been amused to see Sergeant Kennedy and I continually putting one foot before another to see whether eleven of them would fit on the track or go through an opening. We returned after going about a quarter of a mile or so and felt that there was a chance we could get through. I reported

accordingly. Although the distance on the map was just over a mile, on the ground it was at least double that.

During that same night 43 Brigade continued its northwards attack. On the left flank, Tesselo was cleared with great élan and the battalion advanced north-westwards towards Monte Palareto which stands guard over Meldola, an important town and road communication centre on the Ronco's west bank. To the right, Monte della Revere had been cleared and the battalion on this flank was advancing on Colinello, on the northern extremity of the watershed ridge, which overlooks the plain and Route 9, over which 46th Division had just started to advance.

At first light No. 4 Troop C Squadron set off to join the Gurkhas in Tesselo but the troop spent a frustrating day working their way down and then climbing up the other side of the valley. Towropes, picks and shovels were the order of the day. It took fifteen hours to reach Tesselo where the Churchills were refuelled from cut-down Honeys that had followed the troop's tracks. The remainder of the squadron experienced many difficulties in their endeavours to reach Monte della Revere and their infantry.

Supported by B Squadron, 20 Brigade also attacked on the morning of the 24th from their Monte Cavallo positions north-westwards towards Teodorano, situated on the only road directly linking the Savio to the Ronco in 10th Division's sector. It was not known at the time that, on 20 October, Kesselring had ordered his three mobile divisions, 29th and 90th Panzer Grenadiers and 1st Fallschirmjäger, opposing Eighth Army, to counter Fifth Army's threat to Bologna. As a consequence, he ordered his troops on the Adriatic Front to withdraw to the Ronco on the 24th, thus shortening his line. Little did Kesselring know that Fifth Army had shot its bolt and was to halt its offensive on the 27th nor, of course, could he know that he would be injured in a vehicle crash on the 26th and that command of German forces in Italy would pass to von Vietinghoff.

At first light B Squadron started the climb to Monte Cavallo and, on arrival, Nos. 4 and 5 Troops were ordered to support the Mahrattas advancing parallel with the road towards Teodorano. When the infantry were held up by unexpectedly determined opposition short of the village, Major Sidebottom and the leading company commander devised a plan. No. 4 Troop, with a platoon of infantry, reached Ardiano some 700 yards short of the village, took up hull-down positions and called upon the Royal Devon Yeomanry battery for fire support before renewing the attack. The Lord O'Neill and Major Sidebottom roared up in a jeep during this lull and stopped some fifty to seventy yards away from the troop sergeant's tank. Both officers walked forward to a small stone barn on a nearby hill to observe the impending attack. The tanks and the Devons' Priests engaged the village and surrounding area before the Mahrattas' advance and No. 4 Troop's move over the crest and down the forward slope. This activity evoked strong enemy reaction and the tanks were shelled heavily in return. B Squadron's leader suggested that he and the colonel might take shelter in the lee of the barn but The Lord O'Neill wished to have a clear view of the impending attack and they remained in the open, smoking cigarettes. Following the order to advance, Sergeant White in the leading tank had not travelled very far when he was aware of a heavy round passing close by his tank and landing by the barn. Lord O'Neill was killed and Major Sidebottom wounded seriously. The death of Lord O'Neill was a tragic loss for the Regiment he had joined as a captain on 20 September 1939. His pride in the North Irish Horse was enormous and his death was universally mourned as a great loss to the Regiment and Ulster, both of which he had served so well.[6]

Sergeant White's tank was struck shortly thereafter and had a number of bogies blown off, although no one was injured, and could only provide supporting fire for the Mahrattas; it remained under fire throughout the afternoon. The infantry were unable to take Teodorano and had to go to ground. At last light No. 4 Troop withdrew a short distance while the remainder of the squadron harboured farther back. Major Welch assumed temporary command of the Regiment with Captain Finch Noyes, of A Squadron, taking over B Squadron. Sergeant White got his damaged tank back over the crest after nightfall and found a comfortable farmhouse for the crew where they remained until the fitters came forward with spares to repair his tank. His was the last B Squadron tank to rejoin the Regiment in Cesena on 3 November.

During the night 24th–25th the Punjabis relieved the Mahrattas, captured Teodorano and pushed on towards Monte Palareto. B Squadron followed at first light and were quickly in Teodorano. No. 5 Troop moved forward to Monte Palareto but, after slow progress due to mines in the road, were eventually halted by an impassable hogsback bridge. It then started to rain heavily and in the late afternoon the squadron concentrated in Teodorano, unable to advance farther. C Squadron, less No. 4 Troop, spent a frustrating day moving from Monte della Revere to Polenta on a heavily mined road. Sappers had to clear the length of the road and found eight different types of mine, including the new non-magnetic type, on a one-mile stretch.

No. 4 Troop, starting from Tesselo, set off at first light to join the Gurkhas who had cleared Polenta during the night. The dirt-surfaced road ran along the side of a ridge just below the crest, so that there was generally a bank on one side and a drop on the other. Slow but steady progress was made until, rounding a bend, there was a loud bang and the leading tank stopped, blocking the road with its left track off. Lieutenant Bexon went forward on foot to find out what had happened, cautiously taking a length of aerial rod as a probe and sticking to the right-hand track marks. He found that a mine, which must have been two linked Teller mines, had not only blown off the track and a couple of bogies but had cracked the floor plate, wounding the co-driver, Trooper Tattersall. Having summoned help for Tattersall, and engineers for the mines, he told the troop to make for the nearby church if they were able to move before his return. Bexon then set off again on foot to reach the Gurkhas and explain the situation. Luckily, he was able to keep to the infantry's footmarks and give a prod with his aerial if anything looked very suspicious. There were quite a few dead Germans around but it looked as if they had been shot up from the air. Eventually, he reached the Gurkhas to be rewarded with a magnificent mug of tea, served in the silver beakers with which they were issued, strong and so sweet that the proverbial spoon would stand up in it.

On his return to his troop, Bexon was able to get the two mobile tanks and the knocked-out crew into the church courtyard where they were able to shelter from the heavy rain which was to last for days. Luckily they had a good stock of rations including emergency compo with them. The troop spent the next two days sheltering from the rain as best they could and rounding up German prisoners before moving forward to Polenta and rejoining the squadron.

The, by now, constant rain made re-supplying B and C Squadrons very difficult; B could be reached with great difficulty by jeeps, but C was isolated for two days. On the 26th, the rain reached a new intensity and the mud became deeper and more liquid. The infantry depended completely upon mules and the muleteers, Indian and Italian, often sank waistdeep in mud while the poor beasts frequently collapsed, enforcing the abandonment of their loads. The jeephead was about five miles behind the leading companies; B and C Squadrons were stuck in Teodorano and Polenta; the Ronco was now a turbulent torrent twelve feet deep and every valley bottom was swilling with water. Despite the atrocious weather, both 4 and 20 Brigades closed up to the river, north and south of Meldola and, during the night 25th–26th, 43 Brigade put patrols across. The Nabha Akal Infantry[7] got two companies across and immediately sent out strong fighting patrols, which contacted leading elements of 15th Polish Cavalry Regiment, 3rd Carpathian Division, advancing from the south, thus closing the front. Tenth Division quickly established a firm bridgehead two and a half miles on either side of Meldola.

Recces were carried out by B and C Squadrons on both the 26th and 27th but 10th Division would not allow the tanks to move. On the 29th came welcome orders: B and C Squadrons would concentrate in Cesena where blocks of flats had been taken over for the Regiment; A Squadron was to remain in Acquarola, where they had been for eight days and had already made themselves comfortable. The Regiment reverted to 25 Tank Brigade with the promise of approximately sixteen days' rest and refitting. A workshops programme was arranged for the overhaul of the tanks and arrangements made for crews to be sent off on very well earned leave.

Meanwhile, 10th Indian Division continued to thrust westwards beyond Meldola. On the 28th the Nabha Akals drove the enemy off the heights between the Ronco and the next river, the Rabbi, which flows through the western suburbs of Forli to join the Montone three miles to the north-west. Then 43 Brigade pushed across open fields towards Forli and, on the 30th, a wireless intercept revealed that the Germans were withdrawing everywhere. British, Indian and Polish troops were all converging on the airfield south-east of Forli but the Indians, in the centre, were soon squeezed out and withdrawn.

On 3 November A Squadron rejoined the Regiment in Cesena where a simple but moving memorial service was held two days later for those members of the North Irish Horse and its supporting units who had been killed since the Hitler Line battle on 23 May. Later that day leave parties departed for Rome and Pesaro.

Winter was approaching rapidly and Allied defeat of Germany in 1944 was no longer a possibility. Alexander's forces in Italy had suffered some 35,000 casualties, mostly infantrymen, in the preceding two months, but no British reinforcements had been received from the United Kingdom since July which led to the disbandment of 18 and 168 Brigades. American losses had not been fully replaced. To make McCreery's task more difficult, Eighth Army had been weakened further by Churchill's insistence on sending troops to Greece following the start of the German withdrawal and the outbreak of civil war in early October; instead of returning to Italy, 23 Armoured Brigade was diverted to Greece while 2 Parachute Brigade was the first formation to be transferred from Italy. These were followed, before the end of October, by 4th Indian Division and 3 Greek Mountain Brigade while 46th and 4th British Divisions and the King's Dragoon Guards would follow before the end of the year.

In an attempt to balance the scales, many anti-aircraft regiments had been disbanded and some 15,000 gunners retrained as infantrymen. Two armoured car regiments, 9th and 27th Lancers, and 2nd Lothians and Border Horse, an armoured regiment, were dismounted to serve, in the short term, as infantry. In addition, 16th/5th Lancers and 1st Derbyshire Yeomanry found the former being used as stretcher bearers and breakers of stones, the latter in airfield construction.

NOTES

1   The brigade included 1st King's Own Royal Regiment, 3/1st Punjab Regiment and 3/18th Royal Garhwal Rifles.
2   The brigade included 1/2nd Punjab Regiment, 3/5th Mahratta Light Infantry and 2/3rd Royal Gurkha Rifles.

3 Tanks moved in first gear using the lowest possible engine revolutions to minimise noise and maintain the element of surprise until contact was made.

4 William Mackean MC was a native of County Antrim who had transferred to the Regiment from the Royal Artillery in the early days of the war. As a Gunner officer, he was responsible for what was almost certainly the British Army's first shot in anger of the Second World War.

5 The second infantry brigade of 1st Armoured Division, which was then being disbanded.

6 The names of Lieutenant-Colonel The Lord O'Neill, and Major The Earl of Erne, together with the regimental badge are incorporated in a stained glass memorial window installed in the Palace of Westminster. Their sons both served with the Regiment in the 1950s and 60s

7 A States Forces unit raised in the Punjab in 1757, which had rejoined 20 Brigade on 23 October.

CHAPTER XII

More rivers to cross

Those members of the Regiment not on leave on 7 November welcomed back their former second-in-command, now Lieutenant-Colonel Llewellen-Palmer, as the newly appointed commanding officer to succeed the late Lord O'Neill. This happy event, and visions of a long rest, were shattered by the arrival of Brigadier J N Tetley, 25 Tank Brigade, who ordered the immediate formation of a composite squadron to move forward at first light to support 12 Brigade, which would relieve 10 Brigade. The squadron, to be known as A Squadron, was formed with difficulty as many crews were on leave and there was a shortage of serviceable tanks due to the major overhaul programme. Major Griffith was to command the squadron, which included four Churchill troops from the tanks of A, B and C Squadrons, plus a troop of three Shermans from regimental headquarters.

By 1 November 4th Division had established bridgeheads over the Ronco on Route 9 and closed up to the outskirts of the airfield, both some three miles east of Forli. Very heavy rain that night washed away the Class 9 Folding Boat Equipment bridge over the river and demolished the canal crossing on the bridge approach. Temporary bridges across the Savio farther back were also washed away, leading to a temporary halt in the division's advance. Bridges over the Savio were quickly replaced but a Class 40 Bailey bridge over the Ronco was not completed until late on the 5th. Improved weather conditions permitted aircraft, including rocket-firing Typhoons, which had just entered service in Italy, to resume operations. Bombs were dropped on the town and Typhoons rocketed the airfield defences. Fourth Division resumed its attack during the night 7th–8th: 10 and 28 Brigades were to capture the airfield, advance through Forli and take Faenza, ten miles farther on, where Route 9 crosses the Lamone river.

The airfield had been cleared by dusk on the 8th and 12 Brigade relieved 10 Brigade that night. At 7.00am on the 8th the composite A Squadron moved to Forli, staying there all day under command of 12 Brigade. Here the squadron was split: Major Griffith, with two troops, was to support 6th Black Watch on the left, with Captain Irwin and the remainder of the squadron supporting 1st Royal West Kents in their attack parallel with Route 9. The immediate task for 12 Brigade was to clear the area between Route 9 and the airfield and advance on Forli. Brigadier Tetley informed Colonel Llewellen-Palmer that 142 RAC had been ordered to place two troops of their B Squadron under command of the composite squadron and that North Irish Horse would have to provide a commander for the enlarged force. The commanding officer decided that he would act as force commander.

The terrain across which the force was about to fight was completely different from anything previously experienced. Except for the floodbanks, the reclaimed land was absolutely flat, and intersected by numerous canals and countless drainage ditches, now overflowing after the recent rain. Movement by men or vehicles over the rich soil quickly converted it into deep, glutinous mud, making off-road going for tanks almost impossible. The landscape was cultivated intensively, with farmhouses and their outbuildings every few hundred yards, each a potential defensive position. Vines in rows, supported on wires up to ten feet high attached to poplar trees, about fifty feet apart, greatly restricted tank commanders' vision. This was ideal defensive country and the enemy fought for every yard of ground with more infantry on the ground than Eighth Army. Every road was covered by tanks or anti-tank guns which had to be located and knocked out or forced to move by tank gunfire, artillery or, weather permitting – which it seldom did – fighter-bombers or rocket-firing Typhoons. Methods used to deal with enemy-held buildings varied considerably, the most usual being for one tank, covered by another, to engage at point-blank range. On a pre-arranged signal infantry would then rush the building; the surviving Germans usually surrendered. Sometimes the infantry led, covered by fire from the tanks. The capture of each building or house, ditch or canal required a separate plan. Not surprisingly, a day's fighting seldom resulted in more than a few hundred yards' advance.

A Squadron left Forlimpopoli at a minute past midnight on 9 November and linked up with the infantry despite heavy ground mist that reduced visibility to as little as five yards. Forli was entered without opposition save for shelling; the infantry cleared the town and encountered real opposition only on the western and northern outskirts. On the left the Black Watch came under heavy Spandau fire as they approached the crossroads leading to the level crossing on the north-west exit while the West Kents, at about the same time, came under fire on reaching the Canale di Ravaldino north of the railway on the Roncadello road.

Major Griffith ordered No. 1 Troop under Lieutenant Mahony forward to shoot up the surrounding buildings. Fierce hand-to-hand fighting ensued with the Black Watch unable to reach the crossroads. Captain Irwin could not reach the West Kents as the bridge over the canal that they had crossed had been blown. Obviously the Germans were now going to make 12 Brigade fight for every yard of ground. The brigade's third battalion, 2nd Royal Fusiliers, was brought forward to the area of the cemetery on the Ospedaletto road to provide right-flank protection. A night attack by the Black Watch and West Kents was planned but preliminary probing attacks met such intense fire that it was decided to postpone a full-scale attack until next day. The tanks withdrew to the southern half of the town and joined RHQ. Throughout the night Forli was heavily shelled and the tank crews suffered two commander casualties, including Lieutenant Mahony.

The next day's attack was delayed until noon due to the difficulties experienced by 1st RAC/RE Assault Regiment's detachment in placing an Ark over the canal behind the West Kents. Captain Irwin's leading troop was then able to provide welcome and accurate fire support that inflicted casualties on the enemy and relieved the burden on the hard-pressed infantry. The West Kents, supported by both troops, made limited gains during the afternoon. Each farmhouse or barn had to be attacked individually. During this action the leading tank, crewed by C Squadron members, was knocked out, wounding Corporal Cunningham and Trooper Yates.

Probing attacks by 6th Black Watch early in the day found no weakness in the defences of the opposition, an assault battalion of Kesselring's Grenadier Regiment. Both commanding officers and Major Griffith decided that, as contact with the enemy was so close, artillery support was not feasible; the only way to clear the houses was for the tanks, supported by the infantry, to fight their way forward. Lieutenant Maguire, with No. 2 Troop, supported by two Shermans and B and C Companies was ordered to clear the crossroads and then turn right down the street, believed to be mined, to the level crossing. The tanks engaged the houses one by one, firing HE and armour-piercing rounds and belts of Besa into each building; as soon as they stopped firing, infantry entered and cleared each house. The tanks had great difficulty in manoeuvring to bring their guns to bear and the very short range required maximum depression. Eventually, the crossroads was reached and Sergeant Barbour took his tank round the corner under intense fire to find the approach to the level-crossing blocked by fallen trees and wire. He charged the obstacles regardless of the threat of mines; had he stuck or been mined, the chance of escape at such close-quarters would have been minimal. His tank surmounted the fallen trees, ran over a mine that failed to detonate and then blew down the remaining enemy-held house at point-blank range. Such was the effect of Barbour's attack that the Black Watch was able to clear the remaining houses. Sergeant Barbour was awarded the Military Medal for his skill and daring. By 3.30pm the level-crossing was secure and patrols were pushing out towards Casa Fortis[1]. Fighting had been gruelling for both tanks and infantry with many tanks exhausting their ammunition. One house was later found to contain ten Spandaus, one at each window. The Black Watch suffered some forty casualties, including a company commander fatally wounded. A complete enemy company had been annihilated; only six surrendered. The tanks, amazingly, suffered no casualties and were allowed to return to the centre of the town in the late afternoon.

Colonel Llewellen-Palmer said afterwards: 'Some of the most ferocious fighting I have seen, with the battlefield so small as to be almost pocket handkerchief size,' while the Black Watch described the action as its most bitter fighting experience since its fight with Heydrich's paratroopers at Cassino.

The two troops with the West Kents remained in close support throughout the night as anti-tank guns had not yet been brought forward and the situation in this sector had deteriorated and seemed vulnerable to German counter-attack. That night the Germans attacked but were repulsed. The tanks engaged a Panther which fired rounds through the building where the wounded were being cared for, fortunately causing little damage and no additional injuries. Only one of the two B Squadron troops of 142 RAC managed to cross the Ark behind Captain Irwin's position before last light; only one tank was fit, one had mechanical trouble and the third became bogged. The second troop harboured south of the canal and came under heavy fire during which the troop leader was wounded.

Little ground was gained on the 11th as 12 Brigade, to be reinforced by 2nd King's Regiment of 28 Brigade, redeployed and planned for the morrow. The Black Watch spent the morning consolidating its newly won ground and in the afternoon pushed a patrol forward to occupy Point 27, 250 yards north of the level-crossing. A strong West Kents fighting patrol took Casa Fortis early in the day. The ground north of the Ark crossing had become almost impossible. C Company, supported by Captain Irwin's two troops, was given the task of opening up the southern road to Casa Fortis to permit tanks to advance the next day. Enemy opposition was quelled effectively by accurate tank shooting and the objective attained. The tanks were then ordered south to Point 27 to support the Black Watch in anticipation of possible counter-attack, a threat that did not materialise. The tanks returned to Forli at dusk.

Effectively supported by the 142 RAC tanks, 2nd Royal Fusiliers passed through the West Kents that afternoon and fought their way some five hundred yards to their objective, a vital road junction. One tank was knocked out by what was believed to have been a Tiger, which appeared from the west and just as quickly disappeared, and 142 RAC suffered further loss when a broken-down tank was attacked by an Allied aircraft, killing two men. The surviving tanks were held forward throughout the night.

The Black Watch, supported by Major Griffith's two troops and all four mortar platoons of the enhanced brigade, launched their attack at 7.00am on the 12th. The battalion on the brigade centre line was directed towards San Martino di Villafranca, a small town on the Montone's east bank. Initially the attack went well; Casa Pettina, the first bound, was reached quickly. Despite being mostly roadbound due to the soft muddy ground, the tanks provided excellent support for the advancing infantry. The advance continued with B Company on the right supported by No. 2 Troop, towards the Villa Manuzzi. A Company, supported by No. 1 Troop, commanded that day by Sergeant Donaghy in place of Lieutenant Mahoney, advanced towards a group of houses south-west of Villa Manuzzi.

B Company met increasingly heavy resistance the closer it got to the villa which was cleared after stiff hand-to-hand fighting, helped by accurate HE and much machine-gun fire from the tanks, and A Company on the left. B Company then had to fight for every yard of the way forward until the link-up with the left-flank company of 2nd King's was achieved south-west of Casa Guardia. Excellent tank and infantry cooperation allowed A Company to clear quickly the houses south-west of Villa Manuzzi, killing ten Germans and capturing a further ten. On the resumption of the advance to the day's final objective, a T-junction just south-west of San Tome, air observation reported the presence of enemy tanks in the village. Air and artillery support was called for and, under cover of smoke provided by No.1 Troop, a platoon reached the beginning of a row of houses, two hundred yards short of the objective as dusk approached. Here they came under a hail of murderous Spandau fire.

The road approaching the houses and onwards to the road junction was straight and guarded by an anti-tank gun and was the only way forward to assist the infantry but had not been swept for mines. Sergeant Donaghy made a most gallant attempt to reach the platoon. As soon as he moved, his tank came under fire from enemy tanks and the anti-tank gun but he continued until, just before he reached the house around which the platoon had taken cover, his tank was disabled by a large mine. It was then hit, wounding Sergeant Donaghy in the face but he refused to be evacuated. After dark, under fixed-line Spandau fire, he repaired his tank sufficiently to be towed back to a defensive position. He manned his tank and commanded the troop throughout the night and did not go to hospital until ordered to do so next day. Uniquely, the recommendation to 12 Brigade for the award of his Military Medal was made not by his own commanding officer but by the commanding officer of the Black Watch. The final paragraph of this citation reads:

> Sgt Donaghy's grim determination at all costs to carry out his task of supporting the infantry and his success in carrying out this task in

face of strong opposition and in spite of his own wounds, showed devotion to duty and personal courage which were quite beyond praise.

That night the Black Watch fought their way forward, clearing houses as they went, and captured the road junction. Just before first light they were relieved by the West Kents. Major Griffith and his two troops were also relieved once the changeover had been completed and rejoined the Regiment, which had moved forward to Forli the previous day.

The initial attack by 2nd King's, on the right of the Black Watch, supported by the two 142 troops still under North Irish Horse command, had immediate success with the German positions overrun quickly and many prisoners taken. Good progress was maintained throughout the day, again with effective cooperation between the two arms. By 11.00am Casa Guardia, five hundred yards north-east of Villa Manuzzi, still the scene of heavy fighting, had been cleared. The day's final objective, the road junction at Point 21, two thousand yards east of San Tome, was firmly in their hands by 3.00pm. Anti-tank guns arrived before dark and the tanks withdrew after a good day's work.

The two troops of 142 RAC rejoined the King's at first light on the 13th and continued the drive on the brigade's right flank. During the morning a party of twenty Germans located behind a haystack were either killed, wounded or taken prisoner when Besa fire from a Churchill set the haystack alight. Good progress was maintained until A Company approached the cluster of houses around Casa Pasi in the early afternoon where a ditch forced the supporting troop south-westwards to cross by an Ark. On rejoining the infantry, the attack was pressed home and Casa Pasi secured. This troop remained with A Company throughout the night in a counter-attack role. The left-flank King's company, with 142's other troop, took the day's objective, San Martino di Villafranca where they were joined at 6.30 next morning by the troop which had spent the night with A Company. Both troops were soon joined by the two previously uncommitted B Squadron troops, making it a complete squadron under North Irish Horse command, and continued supporting 12 Brigade.

Major Griffith and his two troops had been relieved by two fresh troops plus, for the first time, a fascine-carrying Churchill, commanded by Captain Bowring, the A Squadron echelon commander. A fascine is a large-diameter (7–8 foot) bundle of 12–14 foot faggots bound together, which could be carried on the front of a modified Churchill. A ditch or canal that was previously uncrossable, except by Ark, could now be crossed by dropping a fascine from the tank to form a platform over which the carrying tank and others could cross. Having dropped the fascine the tank resumed its normal role. The limited resources of 1st Assault Regiment, RAC/RE, shortage of equipment and trained manpower in

Italy led to the conversion of twenty-four of 51st Royal Tanks' and 142 RAC's Churchills, twelve as fascine carriers and twelve as Arks. Crocodiles – flame-throwing Churchills – arrived from the UK at the same time; these were Mark VIIs with flame guns in the co-driver's position, the flame fuel being carried in a trailer behind the tank. The Arks, Crocodiles and fascine carriers were held by 25 Tank Brigade headquarters and allocated to regiments or to infantry divisions as circumstances dictated.

The West Kents, supported by the North Irish Horse troops, resumed their advance westwards towards the Montone on the left of the King's, with one troop providing left-flank protection for D Company in their advance on San Tome. Approaching their first objective, a ditch, the battalion's leading elements met a hail of Spandau fire and the tanks, which were on the opposite flank, had to move round to their right before being able to bring down intense machine-gun and HE fire, which quickly silenced the opposition. Covering fire was provided for the West Kents as they crossed the ditch and resumed their advance on San Tome, which was soon in their hands. The advance on Casa Goberti, the day's final objective, was supported by Lieutenant Milne's troop and the fascine tank; the big ditch west of San Tome was made passable by dropping the fascine. Catching up with the infantry, the tanks supported them into Casa Goberti and remained during the night. Forward elements of 12 and 28 Brigades were now some 500–600 yards short of the Montone, a mile and a half north of Route 9.

Next day, the 14th, both squadrons remained with their infantry with no other task than to shell all likely enemy escape routes on the west bank. Apart from enemy shelling, they spent a quiet day and moved back to harbour late in the afternoon. The enemy had been pushed back to the east bank of the Montone along the entire V Corps front and a small bridge-head over the river had been established on Route 9. This bridgehead had been formed by a skeleton brigade group of 56th Division, consisting of 1st London Irish Rifles and three Shermans of 51st Royal Tanks' Recce Troop, 56th Division having entered the battle in a deception role to make it appear that a fresh division was attacking astride Route 9. To aid this deception all radio rear links of 25 Tank Brigade on 4th Division's radio net were closed down and re-opened on 56th Division's net.

The commanding officer and Captain Bowring's force returned to Forli next day to rejoin the regiment and three days were spent on maintenance in preparation for the next phase, the crossing of the Montone north of Route 9. To widen V Corps' front, 10th Indian Division had been brought back into the line and was taking over that part of the line held by PorterForce[2] on 4th Division's right. The Indians' task was to force a crossing of the Montone north of Villafranca di Forli before advancing westwards towards the Lamone river, simultaneously clearing both banks of the Montone northwards as far as the 30 Northing line, thereby giving the Canadian Corps enough room, and a good start, for their attack on Ravenna and subsequent advance to the Lamone. North Irish Horse was to support 10th Indian Division and, on the 18th, the Regiment was placed in support of 10 Brigade; A Squadron was affiliated with 2/4th Gurkha Rifles and C Squadron with 2/10th Baluch Regiment; B Squadron, commanded by acting Major Finch Noyes, and 1st Durham Light Infantry were in reserve. During the 19th 10 Brigade took over a four-mile front on the division's right in a somewhat fluid situation. The enemy occupied a number of houses, well defended with Spandaus on both sides of the river and a number of positions dug deep into the thirty-feet-high eastern floodbank, which were immune from all forms of fire. Those banks were formidable tank obstacles and formed the basis of the German defences. Forward positions in the northern sector occupied by the Baluchis were as little as two to three hundred yards from the eastern floodbank. On the Baluchis' left, the Gurkha positions, by contrast, were more than a thousand yards short of the river. The eastern floodbank had been breached, flooding the countryside, and the only approaches available to tanks were along the few elevated roads, which had been cratered in many places and had all culverts blown.

Colonel Llewellen-Palmer, accompanied by Majors Griffith and Morton, visited 10 Brigade HQ early the next morning to reconnoitre the unpromising terrain over which the attack was to be made. Before C Squadron could follow up any significant gain a canal east of the river would have to be crossed to allow the tanks to take up new firing positions but it was currently impossible for A Squadron to get anywhere near the Gurkhas' positions. Major Morton and two C Squadron troops moved forward to the Filetto area and, next morning, reconnaissance of the area revealed a likely canal crossing place. The remainder of the squadron joined late that afternoon. Among the tanks brought forward was a fascine-carrying Churchill but it was without a fascine, as one was not immediately available. Both battalions probed forward next morning against fierce opposition but cleared some of the houses east of the river, the Baluchis benefiting from supporting fire by C Squadron's leading troop. During the night, 43 Gurkha Brigade came into the line on the left of 10 Brigade and A Squadron was ordered forward in readiness to exploit.

A fascine was delivered to C Squadron early on the 23rd and fixed to Sergeant Kennedy's tank. The fascine would be dropped into the canal for No. 4 Troop, temporarily commanded by Lieutenant Corrie, to cross and support a platoon in clearing houses on the flat ground north of their start line. When this had been accomplished, the troop was to support two fresh platoons in a westward attack on houses on the river bank. Unfortunately, the fascine tank became bogged in almost impassable ground just short of the canal and had to drop the fascine. Under cover of smoke and heavy machine-gun fire from the tanks, the fascine was broken up and the individual logs dropped into the canal by a reserve infantry platoon, enabling No. 4 Troop to cross, link up with the waiting platoon and shoot them into the houses that were their objective. By then daylight was fading rapidly and the Baluchis' commanding officer postponed the attack towards the river bank until the next day; No.4 Troop was allowed to withdraw. Enemy shelling and mortaring had been intense throughout the day indicating that the intention of the armour-supported 356th Division was to hold their well prepared and deeply dug positions in the eastern bank for as long as possible.

Air support was arranged for the next morning and Colonel Llewellen-Palmer arranged to borrow two Crocodiles from Colonel Peyton, CO of 142 RAC, in the belief that flame was the ideal weapon to deal with the deep enemy positions. The promised air support was not as effective as had been hoped due to heavy rain, which had started during the night, and the two Crocodiles became bogged before reaching the fascine crossing. It was early afternoon before No. 4 Troop re-crossed the canal to support the delayed attack towards the houses sheltering the defenders beneath the eastern flood bank. At first, the attack went well and Lieutenant Cumming's No. 1 Troop arrived to support No. 4 Troop. However, as the infantry reached the houses they came under heavy shelling directed from an observation post in a church tower on the far side of the river as well as Spandau fire from the dug-in positions on the near bank. The infantry took cover but the tanks were unable to silence the Spandaus and could do nothing about the artillery fire. An enemy tank then appeared atop the far bank but disappeared before it could be engaged. Due to the lateness of the hour, the commanding officer decided to withdraw but had no communication with his leading platoon. Lieutenant Cumming dismounted and went forward in search of the platoon commander whom he found in one of the houses and gave him his orders to withdraw. No. 1 Troop covered their withdrawal and both troops were then allowed to rejoin the squadron, which had just passed to 43 Gurkha Brigade command, this brigade having assumed responsibility for the division's northern sector. The Gurkhas and Durhams on the Baluchis' left had secured lodgements on the eastern bank in their respective sectors and during the night 24th–25th attempted to put patrols across the river but were unable to force a crossing due to its depth and the opposition offered by the enemy.

Operating on the Indians' left, 28 Brigade of 4th British Division had seized a bridgehead over the river south of Route 9 the previous day and, during the night, attacked north-westwards towards the next river obstacle, the Lamone. Route 9 was crossed and Corleto, a mile north of the highway, was securely held by 10.00am on the 24th. The brigade now struck westwards and 4th Reconnaissance Regiment, providing the division's right-flank protection, pushed two patrols, each supported by a troop of B Squadron, 142 RAC, some three miles to the north where they took up defensive positions.

Supported by 6th Royal Tanks, of 7 Armoured Brigade, 20 Indian Brigade was ordered to pass through 4th Division's bridgehead and clear the west bank as far north as Casa Boschi before assisting 10 Indian Brigade's planned crossing of the river that night north of Villafranca de Forli. During the day, 10 Brigade brought forward assault boats and finalised the plan for the night's crossing, to be led by the Durhams. The enemy was alert and laid down heavy artillery fire, supported by Spandaus, on the line of the river which led to delays, damage to the boats and casualties among the leading platoons. It was not until the Mahrattas of 20 Brigade with armour support attacked the right rear of the German positions on the west bank that the Durhams were able to cross and establish a bridgehead. By noon both brigades were represented in an expanding perimeter west of the river. B Squadron moved that morning in darkness through Forli and up the newly opened Route 9 as far as Cosina before turning north to link with the Durhams' bridgehead. Major Finch Noyes established his tactical headquarters at San Bernardo. Enemy shelling of both 10 and 20 Brigade areas was intense throughout the day and despite fire support from the tanks the Durhams could make no significant advance. C Squadron, still on the east bank, supported 43 Brigade's Gurkhas in their nibbling advance towards the river. The FOO of the Royal Devon Yeomanry succeeded in knocking down the church tower that had been so useful to the Germans.

During the night, 2/4th Gurkhas crossed the river and joined the Durhams. Seven Armoured Brigade (2nd, 6th and 8th Royal Tanks), relieved 51st Royal Tanks and 142 RAC, and 20 Brigade, supported by 6th Royal Tanks, resumed their westward attack toward Alberto, a mile east of the Lamone, while 10 Brigade struck northwards. To begin with, 10 Brigade made good progress with the Gurkhas on the Durhams' right supported by Nos. 2 and 5 Troops of B Squadron respectively. Stiff resistance was met from the enemy who, as usual, had reacted quickly and established a defensive line based on Casa Bettini[3], just north of the village of San Giorgio, on a strategic east–west road. Despite fire support from the tanks, which included the first recorded employment of a Churchill Mark V close-support tank mounting a 95mm howitzer, which proved quickly to be very effective against buildings, the infantry could make no further significant progress that day. C Squadron remained with 43 Gurkha Brigade for the next two days, aiding them in beating off a series of determined counter-attacks. A Squadron, commanded by Captain Bowring as Major Griffith had departed on home leave to Ireland, moved forward on the 29th and crossed the Lamone to come under command of 10 Brigade's 2/4th Gurkhas, prior to the start of the major Eighth Army two-pronged offensive aimed westwards up Route 9 towards Faenza, to facilitate the forthcoming American attack on Bologna, and northwards to Ravenna. The objective of both Allied Armies was to achieve comfortable billets for the winter.

Eighth Army was to attack with the Canadian Corps on the right of V Corps[4] in the centre and the Polish Corps on the left. At 5.45am on the 30th, 10th Indian Division launched the offensive; both Indian brigades with five battalions up attacked outwards from Migliara, the individual thrusts diverging outwards in spoke fashion. On the right the Gurkhas, with Nos. 2 and 3 Troops of A Squadron, attacked north-eastwards towards Lamisoria. No. 2 Troop led as the tanks were confined to the road. The first objective, a crossroads, was reached quickly, several prisoners being taken on the way, and the area was consolidated under shellfire. No. 2 Troop and C Company were then ordered forward to the final objective, which was reached after a stiff fight on the final approach, more prisoners being taken en route. The sole incident of note during this second phase was the destruction by the tanks of one SPG and the capture by the infantry of a second, the crew of which had baled out under the weight of the tanks' attack. The presence of these guns had been indicated to Lieutenant Reid by track marks leading off the road towards some buildings. No. 3 Troop and the remainder of the battalion came forward and the position, now under heavy shellfire, was consolidated by early afternoon, an advance of 2,000 yards. The tanks withdrew at last light. Supported by B Squadron, the Durhams smashed their way to their objective, a road junction north-west of Casa Bettini after sharp fighting in and around San Giorgio, an advance of over a mile. This day marked the first occasion on which a regimental Ark, commanded by Lieutenant Bullick of HQ Squadron, was used in direct support of the fighting tanks. It permitted the squadron to cross quickly an otherwise impassable canal and for Nos. 2 and 5 Troops to keep up with A and B Companies throughout the day. Farther west, 20 Brigade, supported by 6th Royal Tanks, attained all their objectives, as had the New Zealanders on the Indians' left.

During the night the Baluchis relieved the Gurkhas. The initial attack supported by Lieutenant Mahoney's No. 1 Troop went well, the tanks engaging a number of defended houses that were taken swiftly against light opposition. No. 3 Troop, Lieutenant Maguire[5], in support of C Company, continued the advance, two prisoners being taken early on. Sixteen prisoners were captured farther up the road in house-to-house fighting near Casa Palacci. The next cluster of buildings was held in strength and it was decided to consolidate and dig in, the tanks taking up defensive positions. About 4.00pm the Germans mounted a counter-attack preceded by a heavy shell and mortar attack. This was beaten off with artillery support and machine-gun fire from the tanks. At dusk the tanks thinned out and were finally withdrawn at 7.00pm.

During the evening of 1 December, 3 Canadian Infantry Brigade relieved 10 Indian Brigade with orders to break out of the Indian bridgehead next morning and exploit north-westwards towards Russi and the Lamone. A Squadron, now supporting the West Nova Scotia Regiment, was on the right and B Squadron supported the Royal 22ème Regiment, the *Van Doos*, raised in French-speaking Canada. Nos. 2 and 4 Troops A Squadron advanced at 9.15am and shot the West Novas into numerous groups of houses which were cleared quickly, a number of prisoners being taken. Steady progress was maintained until the Scolo Via Cupa, halfway to Russi, was reached, where the bridge had been blown and the canal proved impassable to tanks. A platoon succeeded in forcing a crossing under covering fire from the tanks, which then engaged targets north of the canal, allowing the leading companies to cross and resume the advance. German counter-attacks were beaten off with the aid of artillery and the tanks, which remained in support until the reserve company crossed and the leading platoons had advanced beyond visual range. A Squadron was relieved by C Squadron, 12th Royal Tanks on the morning of the 3rd and withdrew.

The *Van Doos*, supported by a composite No. 5 Troop, attacked at 9.00am parallel with the country road leading to Prada and on to its junction with Route 302, the Via Ravenna, which links Faenza with Russi. The initial assault was successful and the advance went well, the Germans withdrawing in bounds. Prada was cleared quickly but, on approaching the junction with Route 302, enemy resistance stiffened and it became obvious that a plan was required to clear houses that were firmly held. Sergeant Verso, commanding the point tank, was ordered to move off to the right flank while Lieutenant Mahon and Sergeant Burns in a 95mm close-support tank continued up the road to engage the houses that were holding up the Canadians. Both tanks were knocked out by an anti-tank gun, probably an 88mm, killing the turret crew of the close-support tank, Sergeant Hugh Burns, from Belfast, and Troopers Robert Stafford, a Liverpudlian, and John Wood, from Lancashire. Trooper Norman Corbin, from Hampshire, co-driver of the troop leader's tank, was also killed and the driver, Lance-Corporal Wallace, and Trooper McClay wounded when their tank was hit. Sergeant Verso jumped out of his tank and, with his tommy-gun, covered the survivors back to safety before going forward under fire to the now burning tanks to see if he could do anything for the others. Unfortunately, he could not. He returned unharmed to his own tank in time to help beat off a fierce counter-attack which by-passed his tank and reached the company headquarters' position before being checked and beaten back. By staying put and fighting it out, Sergeant Verso played a major part in frustrating the enemy. He remained in position for the rest of the day under heavy shell and mortar attack supporting A Company, whose wireless sets had either been damaged or gone useless so that all orders had to be relayed through him, which meant countless journeys under fire backwards and forwards between his tank and company HQ. His bravery, initiative and the clear concise messages he passed throughout the afternoon were recognised by the award of the Military Medal. The Regiment was later awarded the battle honour Lamone Crossing.

B Squadron was also relieved at first light by A Squadron, 12th Royal Tanks, of 21 Tank Brigade, and returned to Forli. C Squadron, still supporting 43 Gurkha Brigade, was relieved at first light on the 4th by C Squadron, 48th Royal Tanks, also of 21 Tank Brigade, and ordered to rejoin the Regiment in Forli.

On 26 November 4th British Division was relieved prior to moving to Greece to deal with the threat of civil war there following the German withdrawal. It would be followed before Christmas by 46th Division.

NOTES

1 Casa Fortis was later awarded as a regimental battle honour.
2 Commanded by Colonel H Porter, CO of 27th Lancers, PorterForce included 12th and 27th Lancers, both dismounted, as well as 145 RAC, Popski's Private Army and a miscellany of British and Canadian units.
3 Subsequently awarded to the Regiment as a battle honour.
4 Now including 2nd New Zealand, 10th Indian and 56th (London) Divisions.
5 Lieutenant Michael Maguire MM had recently rejoined the Regiment, having been commissioned in England.

CHAPTER XIII
The end in Italy

Between 4 December and 11 January the Regiment was 'resting' in Riccione. However, the daily round of duties, maintenance and the many chores of military life meant that there was little real rest, although there were 'great Christmas and New Year celebrations' and, once the Regiment had settled in its new billets, leave parties to Rome were organised while cinemas and clubs were provided as well as the usual round of sports activities. There was even a present of ten horses from the King's Dragoon Guards when that regiment was sent to Greece.

On 4 December the Regiment left 25 Tank Brigade, with which it had served since September 1942, when the brigade re-formed as an assault engineer brigade. A new home for the Regiment was provided by 21 Tank Brigade in which it replaced 145th Regiment RAC, which was disbanded. It was a happy posting for the North Irish Horse since 21 Brigade's commander was none other than Brigadier David Dawnay. Alongside the Horse in 21 Brigade were 12th and 48th Royal Tanks.[1]

The rest, such as it was, came to an end on 12 January when the Regiment moved to Ravenna to support the Italian Gruppo Cremona, which was responsible for the right flank of the Canadian Corps; C Squadron relieved New Brunswick Hussars as the armoured support for an Italian brigade from Route 16 to the Reno river. Next day, A Squadron took over from the Governor General's Horse Guards in support of another Italian brigade, holding the sector from the Senio river to the sea. Ravenna was home to B Squadron, Headquarters Squadron and RHQ.

By this stage of the war, Italian troops were fighting alongside the Allies in Italy; no longer a surrendered enemy, they were now co-belligerent. However, the soldiers of Gruppo Cremona, now part of Eighth Army, were not yet fully trained and were very excitable. The Germans took advantage of this by sending in strong patrols at night to create alarm; this placed a heavy burden on the Horse who, invariably, had to drive out these infiltrators in the morning. In one such action, on 17 January, Lieutenant Reid earned the Military Cross for his part in evicting German troops from a position that they had captured from the Italians. During this sharp skirmish, Reid was wounded slightly.

Since the Italian troops were not fully reliable, North Irish Horse squadrons created protective troops from their own echelons for the twin purposes of guarding the tanks at night and holding the line. Gruppo Cremona had neither the manpower nor the experience to carry out the task assigned to them and, when this was realised at corps level, the group was stiffened by the return of 2 Canadian Infantry Brigade who took over from Route 16 to the Bonificio canal; thereafter a definite improvement was noted in the situation.

During this period of static warfare, half of 21 Tank Brigade was held in reserve. The two Royal Tank Regiments, supporting the longer and strategically vulnerable left flank of the corps front, took it in turn to support their infantry. North Irish Horse was required to provide two squadrons in direct support and, to provide relief for these two squadrons, a fourth, composite, squadron, named the Reconnaissance Squadron. The reconnaissance troop[2] provided a Sherman and a Honey troop while the squadron was completed by three 6-pounder command Churchills drawn from RHQ, and a Churchill 95mm troop, formed by taking one tank from each of the HQ troops of A, B and C Squadrons. The Reconnaissance Squadron relieved A Squadron on the coast on 25 January.

Between 27 January and 3 February the Canadians launched several small attacks to take posts that had been seized by the Germans from the Italians and these were supported by fire from B Squadron. The Canadians did not have a clear run at regaining the posts; on 3 February a platoon suffered thirty casualties when it was caught in an explosion in a booby-trapped house. Offensive action in this sector more or less came to an end at this time. There continued to be incidents – Lieutenant Maguire MM escaped with only minor injuries when he stepped on a Schu-mine – and alarms; the Italians were prone to exaggerating the strength of German attacks, especially at night. Although their skills were improving, Gruppo Cremona's soldiers were sometimes apt to claim that an entire German army was attacking a single Italian platoon. When a strong German attack was put in against the Italians on the coast on 6 February, the Honeys of the fourth squadron pushed the Germans back at daylight after a hectic night.

Several quiet days followed in which there was 'nothing to report'. On 12 February C Squadron took possession of eleven Shermans that had been left by the Canadians, who were preparing to leave Italy for north-west Europe. These Shermans had been deployed in an anti-tank role from Route 16 to the Bonificio canal and, allegedly, were dug in, although only one proved to be so. All were badly sited and of little value to C Squadron although the crews could be used to strengthen the infantry posts. C Squadron bade farewell to the 'dug-in' Shermans on 21 February. Next day 2 Canadian Brigade was relieved by 17 (Indian) Brigade in B

Squadron's sector; within days the Canadians would be gone, their presence sorely missed in Italy and especially by the soldiers of the North Irish Horse with whom the doughty Canadians had worked so well.

Routine changeovers took place along the front but there was virtually no activity for the rest of the month. Then, on 1 March, plans were made for an attack by Italian infantry to clear the base of the strip of land, known as the Spit, between Lake Comacchio and the Adriatic; C Squadron was to support the Italians in this operation. The operation was preceded by air attacks on the river bank and the point north of Casa Venti on which the artillery were to put down a concentration; counter-battery fire was to be available throughout the operation while a 'cab rank' of fighter-bombers would be on call for two hours after H-hour.

Under cover of the air and artillery bombardment, the leading infantry, from 9th Company 21st Regiment, left Casa Senza Nome at noon, H-hour, and advanced to a position some two hundred yards north of Fillopine where they made their first contact. No. 3 Troop C Squadron was advancing with a platoon of 11th Company 22nd Regiment on the right flank, while No. 2 Troop was on the left, moving through a wooded area; both troops were accompanied by flame-throwers. No. 3 Troop carried their platoon forward, debussing them short of Fillopine where they were briefed on the situation while No. 2 Troop, with a platoon of the reserve company, took up a position covering Casa Venti and No. 4 Troop covered the canal bank. The flame-throwers were told to find a position near Fillopine, in readiness for the assault, and the 95mm Churchills were assigned targets in the area. However, one flame-thrower was blown up on a mine; the other joined No. 3 Troop on the beach. The latter troop advanced about five hundred yards up the beach and found positions from which to bombard buildings around Casa Venti.

Mines dogged the infantry in their advance and the sappers who tried to clear the mines were engaged by machine guns and mortars. The Germans were putting up a typically stout resistance, which was brought home forcefully to both infantry and armour. No. 3 Troop and its flame-thrower were ordered to return and move towards Venti but, as they came off the beach, two tanks and the flame-thrower fell victims to mines. Although the Royal Engineers' troop attempted to clear the mines, enemy shelling intensified and any movement brought down fire, making movement impossible. A German counter-attack along the beach was beaten off with some casualties. All the while aircraft were supporting the attack and, at times, were strafing within two hundred yards of the leading troops.

With the infantry held up and so many tanks damaged, the attack was called off and the assaulting troops consolidated north of Fillopine. Late that afternoon both flame-throwers and one of No. 3 Troop's tanks had been repaired and the tank troops returned to Borsetti for the night. The attack was renewed next day at 11.15am with reduced air support, and, on this occasion, Nos. 2 and 3 Troops provided very close support to their infantry colleagues, shooting up targets indicated to them by a liaison officer. No. 3 Troop destroyed three pillboxes and almost fifty enemy troops surrendered. At the same time, on the left flank, No. 2 Troop was causing similar consternation to the enemy around Casa Venti; as the tanks stopped firing the infantry went in and over sixty prisoners were taken. Slowly but surely the area around Casa Venti was being cleared of enemy troops. About two hundred prisoners were taken, most of whom were not German but either Mongolian or Turcoman. Although some resistance persisted, the remaining enemy were steadily worn down and by early evening the battle was over and the infantry were consolidating their newly gained positions.

After this flurry of action routine returned with the tanks continuing their supporting role. The long-expected major enemy counter-attack never materialised and, save for some minor incidents, there was little to report. By now, however, Eighth Army's plans for a spring offensive were nearing completion and changes in frontline infantry formations seemed to be constant; this was partly due to re-organisation for that offensive and partly to mislead the Germans about Allied intentions. Such was the lack of fervour on the part of the enemy that the Regiment was able to celebrate St Patrick's Day in some style. Next day, however, it was learned that the Regiment would lend support to a feint attack by the Jewish Brigade – which had arrived in the sector in early March – on the 20th.

No. 4 Troop A Squadron supported the Jewish Brigade operation in which two enemy-occupied houses were captured and eight prisoners taken. The pace of activity seemed to be increasing; on the 21st B Squadron were told that they would be working with 2 Commando Brigade in an attack on the Spit and the squadron began training with No. 43 Commando a day later. That night the Reconnaissance Squadron's tanks had fired a direct-fire support programme for 12th Lancers whose positions covering Alberto had come under attack.

The long period of static warfare was almost over. On 25 March A and C Squadrons were assigned to 8th Indian Division for the forthcoming offensive to support 19 Brigade – A Squadron with 1st Argylls and C Squadron with 6/13th Royal Frontier Force Rifles. In the early days of April the squadrons moved to training areas; B Squadron was back with the Italians and A and C were with their assigned battalions and an intense training programme was carried out. Both squadrons trained and practised with their infantry colleagues, each getting to know the other and their ways of working. Many nights were devoted to night marching across country, something that Royal Armoured Corps' experts held to be impossible but which the Horse, in typical fashion, proved 'quite practical under certain conditions'. In the battle to come this training paid great dividends, as did the aerial reconnaissances made by many officers; flights in observation aircraft allowed a clearer picture to be built up of the ground over which the Regiment would fight. For the assault the Regiment asked for considerable assets in specialised armour, which led to much argument; the final allocation was two Churchill bridgelayers, giving a thirty-foot bridge, two Sherman dozers, two Arks and two fascine tanks. Such a reduced allocation might have sufficed had other formations not borrowed at will, often to be used improperly.

The German left flank lay on the Spit between Lake Comacchio and the sea. Comacchio is a shallow lake with deep mud and the Spit is less than a quarter of a mile wide. B Squadron were to support an amphibious operation by the commandos, the opening move of the spring offensive by both Fifth and Eighth Armies. The commando operation had a twofold objective: to seize the Spit, drawing in German reserves, and to distract the Germans from the main operation. Should the operation be very successful it would be continued around the north of the lake.

The plan was for an amphibious crossing by the commandos from the lake coupled with an assault crossing of the Reno river at its mouth, thus coming at the Germans from both east and west. Naval patrols reported the Reno to be seven feet deep at its mouth and so two troops of B Squadron were waterproofed for the assault crossing. However, they were unable to carry this out as the river proved to be twelve feet deep. The other two troops of the squadron were to cross on rafts to an area in British hands in the west of the Spit, whence they would attack along a narrow track between the river's floodbank and the lake, supported by two commando platoons.

Such was the nature of the ground that the commandos' boats stuck in the mud, but the situation was soon retrieved and, a little late, the attack went in as planned. Both troops crossed the Reno at night but they, too, met a complication, being held up by a dyke; this was crossed with the aid of a fascine and by 4pm that day, 2 April, Easter Monday, the tanks were behind the enemy's floodbank positions and engaging the Germans at close range. Some forty prisoners had been taken. However, a mine stopped the leading tank just before it reached the Spit, blocking the track, but the last elements of German resistance ended when the tanks opened fire on their positions; the occupants surrendered. B Squadron's other two troops had been firing across the mouth of the Reno and had knocked out several enemy posts; the commandos captured or killed about 2,000 enemy troops. On 3 April all of B Squadron was rafted across the Reno and followed the commandos who had advanced almost as far as Porto Garibaldi where there was a strong German position. Although struck by a shell, one of the tanks was recovered immediately. At the end of the day, 10th Hussars relieved B Squadron.

The scene was set for Eighth Army's final assault, Operation BUCKLAND, which was to begin on 9 April. The Regiment was ready for its role, with A and C Squadrons under 19 Indian Brigade and B Squadron supporting Gruppo Cremona. Eighth Army's task was to smash the enemy defensive positions and seize crossings over the Senio and Santerno rivers, then race through the Argenta gap and into the plain of Lombardy where the German forces south of the Po would be destroyed.

Preparations for BUCKLAND had been thorough and far-reaching. Morale in Eighth Army was high, with the number of soldiers reported absent from duty the lowest for any month since September 1943. General McCreery issued an order of the day in which he stated that the enemy 'must not be allowed to use his Armies in Italy to form a garrison for a Southern German stronghold . . . We will destroy or capture the enemy south of the Po'.

Ten minutes before 2 o'clock on the afternoon of 9 April, Allied aircraft opened Operation BUCKLAND with a massive bombardment of enemy positions. For an hour and a half, 825 heavy bombers – B17 Fortresses and B24 Liberators – of the US Fifteenth Strategic Air Force unleashed 125,000 fragmentation bombs on the German artillery lines and reserve areas facing Eighth Army's assaulting corps. The bombing was assisted by a bomb, or marker, line of smoke shells fired by 3.7-inch heavy AA guns and the bombers 'completely drenched' their targets. As the heavies pounded their targets, more than 600 medium bombers were assaulting defensive locations and troop concentrations back towards the Santerno, an area the heavies would attack the following day. Simultaneously, the tactical air forces, the British Desert Air Force and US XXII Air Support Command, with over 700 planes, attacked German positions on the forward edge of their line. Command posts, mortar and machine-gun positions, and other strongpoints felt the full brunt of this Allied onslaught. The brutal reality of Allied air superiority manifested itself in incidents such as a single German tank being attacked by up to fifteen aircraft; there could be no doubt about who controlled the air over the battleground.

Artillery and mortars took over when the air assault subsided and, for forty-two minutes, 1,500 guns bombarded German positions. As the guns fell silent the Germans waited for the inevitable ground attack but, instead, the fighter-bombers returned again, strafing river banks before moving on to the area behind the river, at which point the guns and mortars re-opened their bombardment. For five and a half hours Allied artillery and aircraft sustained this storm of fire. During that time the Germans experienced four 'false alarm' bombardments. Then, at 7.20pm, came another false alarm, this time from fighter-bombers that swooped to strafe the river bank but did not open fire. Instead, Wasp and Crocodile flame-throwers opened their jets to belch a flood of flame across the river.

This spectacular display may not have done much physical harm to the Germans but it can have done little good for their morale, already sapped by the experiences of the previous six hours and more. But the flame attack was a morale-booster for Eighth Army's soldiers who now awaited the command to attack. After ten minutes of flame-thrower assault, that command came and Eighth Army moved forward to battle once more.

In V Corps, the assault divisions were 8th Indian and 2nd New Zealand, each attacking with four battalions across the Senio in a purely infantry assault. The Indians were on the right, with 19 and 21 Brigades leading, the former on the divisional right; 1st Argylls and 6/13th Royal Frontier Force Rifles led for 19 Brigade and 1/5th Mahrattas and 3/15th Punjabis for 21 Brigade. Initial objectives, on the forward floodbank, were taken quickly but the defending 362nd Division began to recover its poise and its soldiers left their dugouts to man defensive positions. In spite of spirited resistance, the Indian soldiers crossed the Senio. Two men, Sepoy Ali Haidar of the Frontier Force, and Sepoy Namdeo Jadhao, of 1/5th Mahrattas, earned the Victoria Cross in this battle; both survived to receive the award.

In some areas, fighting continued throughout the night but dawn saw 8th Indian Division about a mile and a half beyond the river. The sappers had erected three bridges that allowed 21 Tank Brigade's Churchills to cross and support their infantry. A Squadron's tanks moved forward to link up with 1st Argylls and C Squadron's with the Frontier Force Rifles. Before the link-ups had been completed one Horse officer, Lieutenant Michael Bexon, had won the Military Cross while another, Captain J S Milne, had laid the foundation for a later award of that decoration.

Crossing the Arginello canal, C Squadron was faced with a stout anti-tank defensive location on the Tratturo canal where houses had been demolished, trees felled, mines sown and anti-tank guns dug in. Under enemy fire, Lieutenant Bexon removed the charges from the Arginello canal, which saved several hours, knocked out a self-propelled anti-tank gun and led the advance to the Tratturo. For this work he received the Military Cross. Although Nos. 3 and 4 Troops, which had halted on the Lugo canal, engaged the enemy and knocked out that anti-tank gun, they could not cross the open ground in daylight.

Captain Milne had been charged with guiding C Squadron forward and it was for this, as well as exceptionally good reconnaissance work on the subsequent advance to the Santerno, that he was awarded his Military Cross. That night 6/13th Frontier Force were relieved by the Punjabis who, with C Squadron, then advanced to the Santerno against sparse opposition; most German troops had been pulled back. A Squadron had crossed the Lugo canal where, with their infantry partners, they had created a small bridgehead from which two troops roved out on reconnaissance missions, with a view to exploitation if possible. After considerable progress the advance was held up by a German SPG which, however, withdrew under fire from the Churchills. Thereafter a dismounted troop of 6th Lancers – 8th Indian Division's reconnaissance regiment – joined No. 1 Troop and made for the Arginello where enemy tanks and defensive positions were engaged and a crossing point was sought.

A lack of bridging with the Italian troops of Cremona made for a most frustrating time for B Squadron who were unable to support the Italians for much of the day. Although two troops crossed on a Bailey bridge of 19 Indian Brigade, they still could not marry up with the Italians west of the Senio due to blown bridges and canals and were ordered to withdraw over the same bridge. They were, at last, able to cross when a Bailey arrived for the Italians. That crossing took place at 1am on the 11th; the rest of the squadron crossed later in the day. Nos. 2 and 5 Troops joined the Italians to cut Route 16 while the soldiers of Cremona entered Alfonsine. Frustration had not ended for the squadron; Major Sidebottom found it very difficult to get information from the Italians; the three generals commanding the Italian brigade were arguing amongst themselves but, in spite of this divided command, the Italian soldiers performed well.

On that day also, C Squadron were relieved by a Sherman squadron of 4th Hussars, under the Regiment's command, and linked up with 21 Indian Brigade. The 4th Hussars' squadron led an advance towards the Santerno, which was stopped after little over a mile by an anti-tank gun that knocked out the leading Sherman, killing four crewmen. The Hussars were withdrawn that afternoon and rejoined their own regiment. Meanwhile A Squadron had spent the day making ready for a night advance. That night A Squadron, without infantry, crossed some 6,000 yards of difficult country using their own bridging devices, an operation that earned two gallantry awards, a Military Cross for Lieutenant Maguire MM and a Military Medal for Sergeant W Ballard. Dawn found A Squadron at the Santerno, three miles from C Squadron to the south. However, once again the Germans had pulled out. By 8 o'clock on the morning of the 12th, three troops had reached the confluence of the Reno and Senio rivers. The country in front of the advancing Italians was now clear of Germans but the Santerno was held in strength and all bridges across the river had been demolished. To avoid any misunderstandings with the Italians, A Squadron was recalled. C Squadron made a northward movement to link up with A, and captured a few enemy stragglers en route. B Squadron drove along Route 16 as quickly as bridging work would allow and was in contact with patrols of A Squadron by last light.

Both A and C Squadrons had a break from operations on the 13th as 19 Indian Brigade was pulled out for a much-needed rest. However, B Squadron was to continue supporting the Italians, who were to make an assault crossing of the Santerno. At 6.30am No. 5 Troop drove up Route 16 and Lieutenant Pope took his tank to the top of the floodbank from where he opened fire on the opposite bank. A retaliatory Panzerfaust round struck, but did not pierce, the tank which reversed out of the position over several mines that failed to explode. The Italian infantry, pinned down by mortar and machine-gun fire, were unable to cross.

No. 4 Troop advanced without infantry support, the foot soldiers not being ready, entered La Pastorello unopposed and then reached the Santerno over a damaged railway bridge. Although heavily mortared, they shot up every enemy post that they could see. At noon the troop collected the Italian infantry and launched another attack that reached the river bank but was stopped there. A further attempt four hours later was successful and the Italians crossed the river. During this action Lieutenant Foott earned the Military Cross for his efforts in rallying and leading the Italian soldiers on his feet; no Italian officers were present. Although a tank crossing was completed during the night of the 13th–14th, B Squadron was no longer needed since 2 Armoured Brigade had reached the Argenta bridge from the south. In this fighting, some 250 prisoners were taken and Sergeant J C Buchanan won the Military Medal. Back in the regimental fold, B Squadron settled down in La Pastorella.

During the following four days, the North Irish Horse was in army reserve. This fortunate, though unusual, break provided an opportunity to catch up on lost sleep and carry out maintenance on the tanks. On 20 April the Regiment moved to a concentration area near Consondola to be ready to support 8th Indian Division in its advance along Route 16 to Ferrara. Next day, B Squadron and 17 Brigade moved up the road against minimal opposition, continuing the advance with the Punjabis the following day. Stiffer opposition was encountered when they were some two miles from Ferrara. At 4pm A Squadron and 1st Argylls passed through to reach the canal south of Ferrara. As the leading troop approached, the canal bridge was blown up and, with no crossing equipment available, the tanks had to stop and wait. However, C Squadron, with 21 Brigade, reached the south-western outskirts of the city, having raced along a road parallel to Route 16. As they probed into the edge of the city, they met several German tanks, which held them up until dusk when the Panzers withdrew into Ferrara, blowing the bridge behind them.

As day dawned on the 23rd, C Squadron was ordered to advance to the Po to prevent the Germans using a ferry-point on the river. No. 3 Troop, under Lieutenant David King, was the first Eighth Army unit to reach the Po, arriving at 10.45am. There they captured a large haul of enemy vehicles and stores but, more importantly, almost guaranteed that the German force in Ferrara would now be cut off and forced to surrender. Lieutenant King was subsequently awarded the Military Cross for this and 'previous excellent work'. Nos. 1 and 2 Troops with 1st Mahrattas cleared the country up to the Po di Volano, overcoming some determined opposition in so doing.

B Squadron had pushed into Ferrara with the Jaipurs, meeting considerable opposition from enemy tanks in the industrial area to the west of the city. The sole crossing over the canal around Ferrara was covered by tanks and SPGs under cover in factory buildings. Not until darkness did B Squadron cross the canal to clear the factory area before advancing into the city to join A Squadron which had entered with 1st Argylls. The night assault achieved complete surprise and eight German tanks and two SPGs were captured. During this action Major Bertie Sidebottom earned the Military Cross.

The Po was the next objective and orders were received on the 24th to move up to the river for a crossing by rafts, although it was not entirely clear who would be providing these. Some fighting continued in Ferrara, but the city was finally cleared that day allowing North Irish Horse to move to a concentration area on the 25th, ready for the crossing. Here recces were carried out and a series of plans made, each being superseded in turn. In spite of much German propaganda to the contrary, there was no opposition to the crossing of the Po; the forces that might have provided such opposition lay shattered south of the river.

Rafts finally appeared and C Squadron was first to cross. Most of the squadron was over the river by 10am on the 26th but A Squadron's crossing was delayed by very heavy rain, although two troops were rafted over. It was left to C Squadron to advance to the next river, the Adige, which was reached by a circuitous route over bridges that were still intact. At the end of the day the squadron was just over a mile short of the Adige where it linked up with 17 Indian Brigade. By then the rest of the Regiment had crossed the Po.

The Regiment's final action of the war fell to C Squadron. On the 29th the squadron caught a very large column of German tanks, artillery and soft- and hard-skinned vehicles trying to cross the Adige. The countryside thereabouts was littered with the detritus of a defeated army; there was more abandoned equipment than there had been along the Po. It was clear that the end of the Italian campaign was in sight.

And so it was to be. On 30 April North Irish Horse received the order 'Stand down' for the last time in the Second World War. Four days later all German forces in Italy surrendered. The long slog that had begun in Tunisia over two years earlier was over at last. The price had been high: North Irish Horse had lost seventy-three dead, including a commanding officer, Lord O'Neill, two squadron leaders and several troop leaders, although there had been no deaths and only very few casualties in the April fighting. But the Regiment's skill and daring had been of the highest standards, as was its leadership at all levels. The long weeks and months of training had paid off in the months of action. North Irish Horse ended the war with a reputation second to none in Italy, and with few equals in the armoured regiments of the British Army. This was a tremendous achievement for a unit that had existed only on paper in early 1939 and says much for the quality of both officers and men.

But that achievement was due not only to the men in the front line who manned the tanks. A great debt was acknowledged to those who ensured that the tanks were fit for action, as was noted in the regimental battle report.

> The remarkable achievement of having every tank in the regiment still going when the Campaign ended was due to first-class recovery and repair work by the regimental fitters and the light aid detachment. No other tank regiment has ever achieved this, even with Shermans. Churchill tanks are by far the most difficult to keep on the road.

There were also the men of the echelons who kept the fighting troops supplied with all that they needed and who brought their soft-skinned vehicles into areas that were decidedly unhealthy for such vehicles and performed all the myriad tasks essential to keeping an armoured regiment in the field. They did so knowing that their contribution was vital but that there were few rewards other than the satisfaction of knowing that they had done their duty. Among them were men such as Corporal J Drummond, a Sherdozer driver attached to the Regiment, who received the Military Medal, a distinction also awarded to Squadron Sergeant-Major L C Bumstead of C Squadron. The concept of duty nobly done sums up not only the men who manned the tanks of North Irish Horse but all those who were the Regiment in the Second World War and who earned it the tremendous reputation that it gained.

NOTES

1   The senior unit of 21 Brigade was the Horse. This is disputed in some circles where 12th Royal Tanks is held to be senior, as it was a regular unit. However, it was a wartime-raised regular regiment whereas the Horse was a cavalry regiment in the Supplementary Reserve prior to transfer to the Royal Armoured Corps in September 1939. Page 58 of the official account, *21 Tank Brigade Operations in Italy, August 1944–May 1945*, lists the regiments serving in the Brigade as North Irish Horse, 12th and 48th Royal Tanks. The nominal roll of officers dated 9 June 1945 lists North Irish Horse after Brigade HQ and before 12th Royal Tanks. There is a parallel with other Northern Ireland-raised Supplementary Reserve units: 8th (Belfast) and 9th (Londonderry) Heavy Anti-Aircraft Regiments took precedence over all but the seven pre-war regular HAA regiments of the Royal Artillery.

Two troops in each squadron of the brigade's regiments were still equipped with Shermans but Churchill VIIs were to replace the Shermans before the start of the spring offensive.

2   From July 1944 to mid-January 1945 the establishment of the Recce Troop included three Shermans and eight Honeys.

CHAPTER XIV
The post-war era

Peace did not come immediately in May 1945. The shooting and the killing may have stopped, but the scars of war were all too obvious; personnel still suffered from wounds, the dead were mourned and all around was a country ravaged by war. Nor would there be a swift return home for the Regiment and its men. The demobilisation system meant that many would still be in uniform twelve months later.

In the meantime the Regiment held a Service of Thanksgiving for victory. There was to be no move north of the Adige and within days came news of a new role, that of guarding prisoners of war. Tanks were handed in, save for three per squadron, and the Regiment moved to Rimini and the PWs. Routine was broken by sports, including race meetings, the first of which was held at Ravenna on 12 July with the band of the Royal Norfolk Regiment in attendance; proceeds went to the regimental benevolent fund. Two officers who were to become household names in racing circles – Dick Hern and Mike Pope – played important roles in the organising of race meetings.

In late October guard duties came to an end and North Irish Horse moved to Austria to join 78th Division as its reconnaissance regiment, equipped with armoured cars – a return to its 1939 role. The Regiment absorbed many personnel from 56th Reconnaissance Regiment, which was about to be disbanded and which had been 78th Division's 'eyes'; the new armoured cars were Greyhounds, sleek, six-wheeled American vehicles, built by Ford and capable of 55mph – a far cry from the Rolls Royce cars of just over five years earlier. While in Austria squadrons were detached for other duties, including garrison duty in Vienna where escorts were provided for the GOC. By the end of January 1946 Horsemen were busy on woodcutting duties, there being a great shortage of fuel in post-war Austria. Guard duties on the Yugoslav frontier were also performed.

During January the Regiment moved to Germany and absorbed personnel from yet another reconnaissance regiment, 53rd (Welsh) Regiment on joining 53rd (Welsh) Division. Over the next five months North Irish Horse carried out internal security duties in the Wuppertal area until, in May, came news that these responsibilities would be handed over to 14th/20th Hussars and the Regiment would disband. By now demobilisation was taking more and more men home and the final disbandment process began on 7 June. A month later the Regiment's disbandment was complete. However, its time in limbo was to be short.

In 1947 the Territorial Army was re-formed and, for the first time, the organisation covered Northern Ireland.[1] Included in the new TA were twenty-eight yeomanry regiments, among which was the North Irish Horse.[2] There were also six Royal Tank Regiments, while the Warwickshire Yeomanry joined the order of battle of Yeomanry RAC regiments in 1950. Since 1947 the Regiment has been in continuous existence, the longest such period in its history but one marked by a number of re-organisations of the Territorial Army from which the Regiment has emerged considerably reduced and changed in character, but still firmly part of the Army's order of battle. At the beginning of the history of the post-war TA there were thirty-four TA armoured regiments, the majority of which were equipped with tanks. In 1956 the TA lost its tanks, three of the Royal Tank Regiments were disbanded, two were amalgamated with each other and a third amalgamated with the North Somerset Yeomanry and twelve yeomanry regiments amalgamated to form five reconnaissance regiments. North Irish Horse survived this re-organisation as an armoured-car unit and it did so again in 1961 when only three armoured-car regiments remained in the TA. By now the thirty-four RAC regiments of 1947 had reduced to eighteen. As we shall see the Horse was to survive the most swingeing cuts of all – in 1967 when only one armoured-car regiment was retained in the TA, one squadron of which was provided by the Horse. The story of the Regiment in this period is a remarkable one.

That story began when recruiting for the reborn North Irish Horse started in autumn 1947. The first squadron formed in Londonderry, at Caw Camp, built for 9th (Londonderry) HAA Regiment[3] in 1939 and within one and a quarter miles of the pre-1914 squadron headquarters. Major R H S Sidebottom, who had served with the Regiment throughout the war, commanding B Squadron in Italy from October 1944, was squadron leader. Sir Michael McCorkell recalls recruiting at the Creggan roundabout, a practice that could hardly be recommended today. Numbers built up quickly, possibly assisted by the civilised practice of not inviting a signature until several drinks had been consumed and a suitably rosy picture of the Regiment formed in the recruit's mind.

Soon afterwards A Squadron was raised in Belfast under Major E D Bullick, another regimental veteran of the late war; RHQ and A Squadron were co-located at Dunmore Park, also within a short distance of the original headquarters in Skegoniel Avenue. In 1948 C Squadron, commanded by Major R H Carryer, was raised in Lurgan; a troop was also formed at Ballynahinch and two further troops at Enniskillen, known as C/E Squadron. Two troops, known as A/B Squadron, were raised at Ballymoney in 1950 and, finally, HQ Squadron was raised at Dunmore Park Camp in 1954, commanded by Captain W R C Moore. Lieutenant-Colonel Llewellen-Palmer, who had commanded the Regiment in Italy, was the first post-war CO and the sponsor unit was 1st King's Dragoon Guards, Llewellen-Palmer's parent regiment. In this early phase, and for many years thereafter, many wartime veterans continued to serve, including Major Tommy McAughtry DCM, MBE and Lieutenant (QM) J C Buchanan MM, both of whom had served throughout the war and would do so until 1969.

As part of the Chester-based 23 Armoured Brigade (TA) the Regiment was equipped with Daimler armoured cars, Dingo scout cars and soft-skinned vehicles ranging from trucks to the ubiquitous jeeps. Although there were many experienced drivers it was found that driving a scout car in Hillsborough required quite different skills from those needed in a Churchill in Italy. A one-week camp at Ballyedmond was attended by all the newly raised units in Northern Ireland with some 684 personnel present, including 200 from the North Irish Horse, which was the best-recruited unit in the TA. An order that there should be central messes somehow failed to reach the Horse who ran an all-ranks' canteen, which, in common with the Windmill Theatre, never closed and kept the echelon fully exercised on re-supply.

Recruiting continued steadily and throughout the 1950s the Regiment was usually at full strength with attendance at annual camp rising to a record 530 in 1959. It was a stirring sight to see the Regiment move out on exercise, a convoy of almost 100 vehicles stretching for some miles. The North Irish Horse developed a great spirit and pride and achieved training standards and efficiency that were second to none. The Daimler armoured cars were the Regiment's basic equipment until they were replaced by the Alvis Saladin six-wheeled armoured car in 1961. The new complement of vehicles, Saladins, Saracen armoured personnel carriers and Ferret scout cars, was completed in 1962. (Twelve Saladins were allocated to each of the three yeomanry regiments that remained as armoured-car regiments and were pooled prior to annual camp so that each had its full quota for training and exercises.)

On 15 July 1950 the Regiment took part in its first major ceremonial occasion in Northern Ireland when Her Majesty The Queen was present at a Review of the Territorial Army at Balmoral. Two years later a service of Commemoration and Rededication was held to mark the regimental fiftieth anniversary; Reverend Elwyn Hughes, regimental chaplain throughout the war, gave the address. Major-General Sir David Dawnay

KCVO, CB, DSO, the Regiment's distinguished commanding officer from Tunisian days and Honorary Colonel from 1947 to 1971, took the salute at the parade. The year also saw the Regiment adopted by the City of Belfast, a distinction shared with other units.

That same year B Squadron held a parade in Londonderry to commemorate the Hitler Line battle, beginning a tradition that continues today. Held annually on the Sunday closest to 23 May, this parade, with its Church service and associated dinners, has become second in importance only to the Old Comrades'[4] weekend held each autumn. To mark an eventful year, 1952 also saw the formation of the North Irish Horse Band under Bandmaster WOI Francis.

For the coronation of Her Majesty Queen Elizabeth II in Westminster Abbey in 1953 the Regiment provided a marching party under Major McCorkell as well as a street-lining party under Captain Irwin. North Irish Horse parties also lined streets in Belfast and Londonderry when the Queen visited Northern Ireland later that year.

On Christmas Day 1957, her 21st birthday, HRH Princess Alexandra of Kent was appointed Honorary Colonel and paid her first visit to the Regiment at camp at Lulworth on 4 May 1959 where she addressed the parade on the lawns of Lulworth Castle and was presented with a diamond regimental brooch.

As part of the Territorial Army Golden Jubilee celebrations Her Majesty Queen Elizabeth The Queen Mother reviewed 3,000 men and women in No. 1 Dress at Sydenham on 10 May 1958; two composite North Irish Horse squadrons were present. This was the first occasion on which officers wore crossbelts, in most cases over the incorrect shoulder, a situation that has now been resolved: officers wear crossbelts over the right shoulder although, in a decision which others may find baffling but which comes naturally to the Horse, the Guidon Party wears crossbelts over the left shoulder, an idiosyncrasy enshrined in Regimental Dress Regulations.

As 1958 came to an end so, too, did the Regiment's affiliation to 1st King's Dragoon Guards; thereafter sponsorship was provided by two Irish cavalry regiments, 5th Royal Inniskilling Dragoon Guards and the newly amalgamated 4th Queen's Own Hussars and 8th King's Royal Irish Hussars, now known as the Queen's Royal Irish Hussars.

In a ceremony during a parade at Balmoral Showgrounds on 15 May 1960, Princess Alexandra of Kent presented a Guidon to the Regiment and when the Princess married the Honourable Angus Ogilvy at Westminster Abbey on 24 April 1963, General Dawnay, together with a number of officers and senior other ranks, attended. The Regiment provided four junior officers to act as ushers, one of whom did nothing to enhance his military prospects by placing General Dawnay behind a pillar that blocked his view of the proceedings. As a wedding gift, the Regiment presented HRH with a silver statuette of a horse. Princess Alexandra, the Honourable Lady Ogilvy, visited RHQ in February 1965

The Earl of Shaftesbury, who had raised the Regiment, as the North of Ireland Imperial Yeomanry, in 1902 and who had been Honorary Colonel from 1913 to 1946, died in 1961. His grandson, the present Earl, was to tell how the raising came about at a lunch at Belfast Castle in 1992 to commemorate the ninetieth anniversary of this event. His grandfather, he said, bumped into the Prince of Wales, shortly to be King Edward VII, as he came out of his club in Saint James's. The conversation went something like this: 'Mornin' Shaftesbury, doin' anything much these days?' 'Well, er . . .'. 'Good, be a good chap and go and raise a yeomanry cavalry regiment for me in the north of Ireland.' So he did.

On 28 October 1962 a regimental memorial window was unveiled in Belfast City Hall in memory of those who lost their lives during the Second World War. Commissioned by the Old Comrades' Association, the window, beside that for the First World War, was unveiled by General Dawnay and consecrated by the Archdeacon of Raphoe, the Reverend Louis Crooks, Regimental Chaplain, who had served throughout the Second World War as chaplain to 9th (Londonderry) HAA Regiment. The address was given by Reverend Elwyn Hughes who said that those who looked at the window should consider the meaning of the light that shone through it: the light of sacrifice; young men had laid down their lives and no one could offer more than that. After the service General Dawnay took the salute at the march past outside the City Hall.

During the 1950s battle honours were allocated for the Second World War and regiments were invited to submit their nominations for inclusion in the list of units involved in each action that was to be honoured. These nominations would be examined by a War Office committee, the Battle Honours Committee, which also decided which battles were to be commemorated and the names by which they were to be described.[5] The Regiment submitted its list and most were approved although General Dawnay had to engage in debate with the committee to ensure this; one nomination, for Forli, was not allowed as the committee decided that this should be officially 'Capture of Forli' and averred that the Regiment's involvement in the capture of the town was peripheral. By way of compensation, however, the Battle Honour 'Casa Fortis' was granted.[6] This honour commemorated the clearing of the north-western outskirts of Forli after its capture and was awarded to four regiments. The Regiment had also applied for the award of the battle honours 'Rome', 'Trasimene Line' and 'Cosina Canal Crossing' in Italy and 'Mine du Sedjenane' in Tunisia. None of these were granted; 'Rome' was for award only to units that had been at Anzio and the committee considered that the Regiment's involvement in the Trasimene Line battles had not been sufficient for recognition. However, 'Liri Valley' and 'Casa Bettini' were awarded in place of those and the committee also agreed to 'Monte Cavallo' and 'Valli di Comacchio' which had been rejected previously. The full list of awards was included in a letter to General Dawnay, dated 21 May 1957.

The post-war forces have been subject to many re-organisations and reviews, generally heralded as intended to provide greater effectiveness or efficiency but usually reducing strength. In the first such major review, in 1956, twelve TA yeomanry regiments underwent amalgamation to form five armoured-car regiments.[7] Other armoured-car regiments, including the Horse, were to convert to the light reconnaissance role, equipped with scout cars. However, the Regiment's standing and efficiency led to a reversal of this decision; it remained an armoured-car unit. The Chester-based 23 Armoured Brigade (TA) was disbanded as part of the reduction but the Brigadier RAC Western Command remained responsible for training the Regiment. Administration was assumed by 107 (Ulster) Independent Infantry Brigade (TA) but the Regiment never went to camp with 107 Brigade. As if by way of compensation for the reduction in TA strength, 1956 also saw a start to building new centres at Belfast, Enniskillen and Londonderry. The Enniskillen centre was blown up by the IRA in December 1956 and finally opened in May 1963.

That attack was part of a terrorist campaign that would last until 1962, one immediate result of which was that TA personnel took over guarding centres from early 1957 until April 1958 when those duties were assumed by civilian armed watchmen.

On 2 November 1958 new buildings for RHQ and A Squadron were officially opened at Dunmore Park Camp by Lord Wakehurst, governor of Northern Ireland. The TA centre at Lurgan was designed by Major E W Beaumont TD, second-in-command of the Regiment and was opened by Major-General T P D Scott CB, CBE, DSO, Colonel of The Royal Irish Fusiliers and commander of the Irish Brigade during the Italian campaign. C Squadron shared the centre with B Company, 5th Royal Irish Fusiliers.

In 1961 the TA underwent further re-organisation with the yeomanry reducing to three armoured-car regiments; the remainder became armoured reconnaissance regiments. It was a particular tribute to the Regiment's continuing excellence that it was chosen to be an armoured-car unit.[8]

When the IRA campaign ended in 1962 and the security situation returned to normal, there was a relaxation of guarding requirements on TA centres. Major W T Gleghorn MM, TD, who had unbroken service with the Regiment since 1939, was awarded the MBE in the New Year's Honours list and Major John Allen retired from commanding the Londonderry Squadron after twenty-one years' service.

Lieutenant-Colonel Weston-Simons' period in command witnessed a raising of the regimental standard of living in the field which prompted B Squadron's officers to devise the *Typewriter*, a portable drinks cabinet, suitably disguised. The two officers of A/B Squadron, which customarily joined B Squadron at Ballymoney station en route to camp, were much impressed by this adjunct to civilised living and invented their own *Oxygen Box* which served a similar purpose. Though the original has long since disappeared, acquired, no doubt, by some collector of military arcana, a more sophisticated model still exists.

In January 1964 the CIGS, General Sir Richard Hull GCB, DSO, visited Dunmore Park Camp and in the same month Padre Louis Crooks left the Regiment. The two events were not connected. The new padre was Louis' brother, Sammy, later to become Dean of Belfast and originator of the Black Santa, a reference to his cloaked figure during his annual pre-Christmas vigil outside Saint Anne's Cathedral in Belfast that raised huge amounts for charity. The practice continues today. Another well known regimental figure to retire was WOI Francis, founder bandmaster who was succeeded by WOI Callen.

In 1967 the Territorial Army was again subjected to massive re-organisation. Although heralded for several years, the final announcement was made in such a way as to mislead the public into believing that the TA was being disbanded. In 1965 total TA strength was about 120,000 but the strength of the new force, known as the Territorial and Army Volunteer Reserve (TAVR), was set at a much-reduced 65,000.

As part of this re-organisation, North Irish Horse relinquished its armoured-car role on 31 March 1967 and the drill halls at Lurgan, Ballymoney and Enniskillen closed; only RHQ at Dunmore Park Camp and B Squadron's camp in Londonderry remained. The TAVR was divided into two principal groups, TAVR II and TAVR III. The former had a role with the British Army of the Rhine (BAOR) but TAVR III units were lightly armed, assigned to home defence duties and had a lower training commitment. For those familiar with bureaucratic parsimony, the future for TAVR III did not look rosy, and so it proved.

On 1 April 1967 the Regiment was designated North Irish Horse (T), an AVR III unit with a diminished role and very little equipment. Yet again, however, the Regiment's qualities were recognised and it was selected to provide a squadron of the sole armoured-car regiment in the re-organised TA, the Royal Yeomanry, an AVR II unit. D (North Irish Horse) Squadron was commanded by Major The Lord O'Neill, who had commanded C Squadron at Lurgan. Raised mainly from the old A and HQ Squadrons in Belfast and A/B Squadron in Ballymoney, the squadron retained complete North Irish Horse uniform, badges and insignia although a Royal Yeomanry shoulder title was adopted subsequently.

Equipped at first with Ferret scout cars and Land Rovers as an air-portable squadron, D (NIH) Squadron met the other Royal Yeomanry squadrons for the first time at Westdown Camp, Salisbury Plain, in May 1967. Those other squadrons were formed from the Royal Wiltshire Yeomanry (A Squadron), Sherwood Rangers Yeomanry (B Squadron), Kent and County of London Yeomanry (The Sharpshooters) (C Squadron) and the Berkshire and Westminster Dragoons (HQ Squadron); the band was from The Inns of Court and City Yeomanry.

In April 1968 further pressure was applied to AVR III units when they ceased to be paid, although training continued with an inadequate permanent staff of two. Every effort was made to keep going, many being prepared to train without pay. However, when all allowances were stopped and petrol and rations had to be bought, the end was clearly in sight. Princess Alexandra visited the Regiment in May and was escorted from Aldergrove airport to Dunmore Park Camp by four Ferret scout cars. Later in the year the Princess officially opened the Ulster offices in London, with regimental personnel forming a lining party.

On 25 September 1968 the Museum of Irish Cavalry Regiments – 5th Royal Inniskilling Dragoon Guards, Queen's Royal Irish Hussars and North Irish Horse – was opened in Carrickfergus Castle by Northern Ireland's Prime Minister, Captain Terence O'Neill. The three regiments formed a Guard of Honour supported by trumpeters and three regimental bands. This museum continued in existence until 1987 when the local council required the castle for other purposes and it had to close. A new location could not be found for the combined regimental collections and the North Irish Horse Museum is now housed at Dunmore Park.

Early in 1969 RHQ and A Squadron were finally stood down. B Squadron in Londonderry became 69 (North Irish Horse) Squadron of 32 (Scottish) Signal Regiment (V) and continued to wear North Irish Horse dress, except for a Royal Signals cap badge and lanyard. The Band, AVR IV, suffered a drastic reduction in authorised training time but remained in being and, though designated as part of the North Irish Staff Band, retained complete independence and stayed at Dunmore Park. A new element was the Cadre, a small organisation, eight-strong, with, amongst other tasks, the role of forming the base upon which to raise any further units demanded. In summary, therefore, as a result of the 1967 upheavals, the North Irish Horse continued to exist in several separate manifestations: the North Irish Horse Cadre, of which Princess Alexandra remained Honorary Colonel, administered by and closely identified with D (NIH) Squadron Royal Yeomanry; 69 (NIH) Squadron Royal Signals and the Band. At the annual Old Comrades' Reunion all units paraded with the Guidon. It was not a bad outcome in the end.

One positive result of the re-organisation was that AVR II units received a full complement of vehicles and equipment, a situation that had not existed before. With no further need to pool vehicles before annual camp, training standards were raised. In 1969 D (NIH) Squadron went to camp in Germany for the first time, to Wolfenbuttel near the East German border. Major The Lord O'Neill TD, DL had assumed command of the Cadre and Major J F Leslie JP, DL, now commanded the squadron. The approach march to camp was 450 miles via Liverpool, Harwich and Bremerhaven; all vehicles got there and back with no problems, which spoke volumes for the LAD. Later in the year, IRA activities once again required the provision of guards on TA Centres; these guards were provided from the squadrons.

The new parent regiment of 69 (NIH) Squadron, 32 (Scottish) Signal Regiment, was formed by reducing TA signals regiments, 51st (Highland), 52nd (Lowland) and 61st (City of Edinburgh), to squadron strengths. With the new role of providing Scottish home defence communications the Scottish squadrons were based at Glasgow, Edinburgh and Aberdeen; 69 Squadron's role was to provide Northern Ireland regional communications. The squadron had to develop a completely new range of skills but, under the command of Major C O Eaton, it set about the conversion and within two years was a fully operational unit.

In 1970 D Squadron reverted from being air-portable to an armoured-car role, equipped with the familiar Saladin armoured cars and Saracen APCs. Time was spent on the necessary conversion training, the first week of camp being at Warcop, as a squadron, doing gunnery, and the second week with the rest of the Royal Yeomanry at Thetford. The build up of regular forces in Northern Ireland had required a force of at least company strength to be stationed at Dunmore Park Camp since 1969. Initial problems were relieved by the construction of a self-contained set of accommodation within the compound. Training in the Province had been able to continue fairly normally, D Squadron being the only TA unit allowed to train outside MOD property.

Major-General Sir David Dawnay, Honorary Colonel since 1947, died in 1971. Four serving officers, from the Cadre, D Squadron and 69 Squadron, attended his funeral in County Waterford. A year later he was succeeded by Colonel His Grace The Duke of Westminster, a former commanding officer.

D Squadron attended a second camp in Germany in 1972, driving via Harwich and Hamburg to Paderborn to take part in a large exercise. This was good training since their role, at that time, was that of an armoured-car covering force on the East German border. Their attachment to BAOR could be rated a success as not one Warsaw Pact soldier dared put a foot across the border while they were there! The following year D Squadron returned to Westdown Camp on Salisbury Plain where it was visited by Princess Alexandra, Honorary Colonel of the North Irish Horse as represented by the Cadre, and by The Queen Mother, Royal Honorary

Colonel of the Royal Yeomanry. The complete Regiment paraded with all its armoured vehicles, a stirring sight as they advanced in review order and a spectacle that will be long remembered by those present.

By now 69 (NIH) Squadron was firmly established as part of 32 (Scottish) Signal Regiment and Major C O Eaton became second-in-command of the Regiment on leaving 69 Squadron. In 1972 he was appointed Deputy Commander of 2 Signals Group in the rank of full Colonel. Four years later Colonel Eaton was murdered by terrorists in Belfast and the following year another former B Squadron Officer, Major J P Hill, serving with 5th (Co. Londonderry) Battalion, Ulster Defence Regiment, was murdered in Londonderry. The Drill Hall at Clooney Base to which 69 (NIH) Squadron moved in 1979 was dedicated to Colonel Oliver Eaton and on a subsequent move to Limavady in 1992 the Drill Hall at the Camp at Edenmore Road was similarly dedicated.

Initially 69 Squadron was equipped with D11 HF radios mounted on K9 Austin one-ton vehicles. This equipment remained in service until the mid-1970s when it was replaced with long range PRC321 HF radio equipment. Towards the end of the 1970s the squadron was carrying out trials on the prototype of the national radio communications system then known as Conrad. The squadron maintains the strong historical link with its antecedent, the North Irish Horse, and continues the old B Squadron practice of commemorating the Hitler Line battle with an annual parade. In 1988 squadron members followed the Regiment's campaign route through Italy, from Pescara northwards. The tour culminated with a memorial service at the Commonwealth War Graves Cemetery at Cassino attended by the Honorary Colonel, Lord O'Neill, whose father was killed commanding the Regiment in Italy.

In 1994 the Fiftieth Anniversary of the battle of the Hitler Line was marked by a series of events, starting with an all-ranks dinner on the Friday evening, attended by over 150, and continuing with a well supported garden party on Saturday, where the Commander Land Forces, Northern Ireland, Major-General Leask, was chief guest; Sir John Wheeler, Minister at the Northern Ireland Office, represented the Secretary of State. On Sunday 22 May events were brought to a close by a Drum Head Service and Parade. Among large numbers of past and serving members, families and friends was Padre Hughes who had served as regimental chaplain throughout the war. Colonel M W (now Sir Michael) McCorkell, Lord Lieutenant for County Londonderry, took the salute, supported on the rostrum by three other Lord Lieutenants, all previous members of the Regiment, in uniform, an event unique in the annals of the Lieutenancy. The other Lord Lieutenants were Colonel the Lord O'Neill TD, County Antrim, The Earl of Erne, County Fermanagh and Colonel J T Eaton CBE, TD, City of Londonderry. All the events were held at Ballykelly, as there was insufficient space at the Limavady TA Centre. Many veterans of the battle came from Britain and farther afield and the Canadian government and armed forces were represented by Brigadier-General Darrell Dean CD, of the Canadian Defence Liaison Staff in London.

Further changes were now taking place in the armed forces. In 1994, as a result of Options for Change, the government's restructuring of the armed forces following the collapse of the Warsaw Pact, 69 Squadron left 32 (Scottish) Signal Regiment to assume a new role in 40 (Ulster) Signal Regiment, equipped with Land Rover-mounted 321 HF Radios and 521 HF sets. They retrained quickly, were declared fit for role some six months ahead of schedule and had a most successful camp at La Courtine in the Massif Central in France in 1995.

The squadron has very quickly become an integral part of 40 (Ulster) Signal Regiment but retains the same affiliation to the North Irish Horse as it did while part of 32 (Scottish) Signal Regiment; there has been no alteration to the uniform. One officer and six soldiers of 69 (NIH) Squadron have been called up for operational service with IFOR in Bosnia, each undertaking a minimum tour of six months, and two having elected to serve for a further six months.

On 1 April 1976 the Cadre was disbanded as part of further defence cuts. During its existence it gave much assistance to D Squadron and the Band by training recruits, administering accounts and providing a link between D Squadron and 69 Squadron as well as being a focus for regimental pride and traditions. A ceremonial stand-down parade, with three officers mounted, was held at Shane's Castle on 4 May. The Cadre trooped the Guidon through two guards, one from D (NIH) Squadron Royal Yeomanry and one from 69 (NIH) Squadron 32 (Scottish) Signal Regiment, before handing it over to a composite Guidon Party from the two squadrons. It was a splendid parade with an excellent turnout of old comrades and friends of the Regiment.

At this time the Duke of Westminster felt unable to continue as Honorary Colonel due to ill health and handed over to Colonel M W McCorkell, a former commanding officer and Colonel TA, but not before the Band had the honour of providing two trumpeters for the wedding of his daughter, Lady Leonora Grosvenor, to Lord Patrick Litchfield in Chester Cathedral. HRH Princess Alexandra was appointed Deputy Royal Honorary Colonel of the Royal Yeomanry.

1977 saw the end of an era, when D Squadron's Saladins and Ferrets were replaced by the new Fox armoured-car, a highly complex item of equipment to which the squadron converted remarkably quickly. In this year the Royal Yeomanry became part, first, of 16 Parachute Brigade and then of 7 Field Force, a predominantly regular formation with a BAOR role. Thus the pattern was set for the future – a role compatible with the Regular Army, which meant not only equipment to the same scale, but also similar training standards. The Regular Army vacated Dunmore Park in October 1977, handing back the camp and responsibility for its security to D Squadron. This year was also the seventy-fifth anniversary of the raising of the North of Ireland Imperial Yeomanry and the Old Comrades' weekend in October saw the best turnout for many years. Finally 1977 saw the squadron exercising in Northern Ireland for the first time for four years.

The late seventies through to the mid eighties saw changes in both vehicles and role. Saracens finally departed in 1984 and tracked vehicles were added to the Fox, namely Spartan, Sultan and Samaritan (the ambulance). The Rarden 30mm automatic cannon replaced the old 76mm gun and Clansman radio replaced Larkspur. Equipment, though more sophisticated in design, became simpler to use: no longer was there an opportunity for a virtuoso performance of 'sweetening' a 19 set, or demonstrating the correct use of a small piece of silver paper. Colonel The Lord Dunleath TD DL, the last commanding officer of the Regiment, succeeded as Honorary Colonel in 1981.

In 1982 D Squadron took part in the Lord Mayor's Parade in Belfast, with a mounted officer leading a Saladin, a Ferret and two Foxes. Occasions to parade in public had been somewhat limited and participation in the event was a useful aid to recruiting.

During this period the normal pattern was for each alternate camp to be held in Germany. Opportunities for training in Northern Ireland were limited and squadron exercises were often held in Scotland, crossing from Larne to Stranraer, and sometimes in England. Vehicles were often sent ahead in containers, an unsatisfactory practice from the training point of view, which, fortunately, ceased in 1990. Guarding TA Centres was taken over by Non-Regular Permanent Staff, or NERPS, which was a relief. In 1985 the Band was fully integrated into the Northern Ireland Staff Band and moved to Lisburn, thus ending the 'gentlemen's agreement' which had enabled them to remain for so long at Dunmore Park. That year also saw the appointment of Colonel The Lord O'Neill as Honorary Colonel.

The most unusual event of 1987 took place in Dublin. In 1922 the South Irish Horse was disbanded and their flag laid up formally in Dublin's Saint Patrick's Cathedral. When that flag was destroyed by vandals in 1986, the Adjutant, Captain N Lamb, 5th Royal Inniskilling Dragoon Guards, had a replacement made and, following considerable work on both sides of the border, permission was granted for a party to go to Dublin to lay up the new flag. The ceremony was performed by a Ceremonial Party in No.1 Dress; a party of officers and senior ranks also attended in uniform. After the ceremony the party went to a reception given by the British Ambassador. All those attending had a close Garda escort throughout the visit which was most appreciated.

The Royal Yeomanry celebrated its twenty-first anniversary in 1988 and included among the events in which D Squadron participated were receptions at Regimental Headquarters in London attended by the Queen Mother and Princess Alexandra.

In 1991 the TA was subjected to another upheaval under Options for Change. Northern Ireland suffered very severely with a cut of thirty-six per cent in TA strength, compared to an average seventeen per cent across the United Kingdom. The logic for this disparity was one that only a politician could advance: it was to bring the Province's hitherto much higher percentage of volunteers into line with the rest. So much for our naive notion that it was a good thing to recruit volunteers for the Reserve Forces. In the first draft there was no mention of the North Irish Horse, but intense lobbying brought changes, and with effect from 1 April 1993, D Squadron became The North Irish Horse independent medium recon-naissance squadron under command of 107 (Ulster) Brigade. Thus ended the squadron's happy association with the Royal Yeomanry and the North Irish Horse was re-established in the Army List in its own right. A parade was held at Dunmore Park Camp on 5 June 1993 to mark the occasion.

Colonel J F Leslie succeeded Colonel The Lord O'Neill as Honorary Colonel in 1991 and a very sad event during 1993 was the death of Colonel The Lord Dunleath, last commanding officer of the Regiment and a previous Honorary Colonel. His funeral in Down Cathedral was attended by many serving and past members and Princess Alexandra was represented by the Lady Moyra Campbell CVO.

1994 saw two significant events. The first, in April, was a Royal Review on Smith's Lawn in Windsor Great Park before The Queen, The Duke of Edinburgh and The Queen Mother to celebrate the 200th anniversary of the formation of the yeomanry. This year had been christened 'The Year of the Yeomanry' and it involved the Squadron in numerous fund-raising and charity events. The Horse provided the largest single yeomanry and regimental association contingent on parade. The second event was the fiftieth anniversary of the Battle of the Hitler Line, which has already been described.

Camp in 1995 was in Gibraltar where the squadron made such a good impression and held such a successful Officers' and Sergeants' Mess cocktail party that the officers were invited to dinner at Government House – twice! Everyone visited, including the GOC Northern Ireland, the Brigade Commander, the Honorary Colonel and the Colonel Yeomanry. Dunmore Park Camp was completely refurbished for the first time since being built in 1958. Though the squadron lost its armoured recon-naissance vehicles and re-equipped with Land Rovers as a light reconnaissance squadron, it had a full complement of officers, was well recruited and retained the same spirit that was always a hallmark of the North Irish Horse.

Hardly, it seemed, had the squadron settled into its new routine than another defence review was announced. In this grandly styled Strategic Defence Review, or SDR, the role of 69 (NIH) Squadron seemed to be in little danger but there was apprehension about the future of the reconnaissance squadron, as there was for the other yeomanry units in the TA. Colonel D M Christie TD, DL had no sooner succeeded Colonel Leslie as Honorary Colonel than he was thrown into the battle for the survival of the Squadron. A first draft plan from the Director Royal Armoured Corps envisaged the Horse becoming part of a reconstituted Northern Yeomanry but this proposal was later reversed due to the alleged 'remoteness' and resultant additional costs of maintaining a squadron in Northern Ireland.

In August 1998 the Horse set in motion a lobbying campaign that led to a timely intervention in the debate by Her Majesty Queen Elizabeth The Queen Mother as well as a debate in the House of Lords that was devoted to the North Irish Horse – shades of the Commons debate on the 'one man regiment' of sixty years earlier. As a result the Squadron was saved from possible suspended animation or disbandment, or whatever description the Ministry of Defence might apply. In November, when the review had been completed, the North Irish Horse yeomanry squadron had been saved and would take its place in the new TA organisation due to come into effect in July 1999. From that date the Squadron was redesignated B (NIH) Squadron, Queen's Own Yeomanry, with RHQ in Newcastle upon Tyne. The Squadron's role is that of a support squadron and it is equipped with Spartan CVR (T),[9] Sultan and Samaritan.[10]

In a letter to the Honorary Colonel following the Squadron's successful campaign for survival, the permanent under secretary in the Northern Ireland Office wrote: 'If the North Irish Horse fight the enemy as well as they fought this campaign, we can rest quietly in our beds.'

Between 1947 and 1969 the Regiment had eight commanding officers, three of whom came from regular regiments and had wartime experience. The first two commanding officers, Lieutenant-Colonels Llewellen-Palmer and Cairns, both came from the King's Dragoon Guards, then the Regiment's sponsor unit. The other regiment that provided a commanding officer was the Queen's Royal Irish Hussars. When Lieutenant-Colonel Lord Robert Grosvenor TD, DL, took over as commanding officer he was the first TA officer to command the Horse.

Perhaps the longest post-war connection with the Regiment is held by Colonel Sir Michael McCorkell who served with 16th/5th Lancers during the war and with the North Irish Horse since 1947. He took over command on 1 June 1961 and when he retired in 1964, after eighteen years' service with the Regiment, he was appointed OBE in the Birthday Honours List and gazetted Brevet Colonel. Subsequently he became Honorary Colonel and retains his link to the Horse to this day.

*

Sport has always played an important part in Army life and TA units are no different. The Regiment has had a healthy sporting tradition. In 1952 Trooper D Campbell, C/E Squadron, won the TA light-welterweight boxing championship and in the late 50s and early 60s the North Irish Horse team dominated the Northern Ireland Command Motorcycle Trials for six years, winning from 1957 to 1962. The team represented Northern Ireland in the Army Trials while Lieutenant F C, later Sir Christopher, Bland competed as a Pentathlete in the Olympic Games in Rome in 1960. The boxing team were runners up in the Northern Ireland TA Championships and Trooper Neill won the lightweight title in the TA Championships in London.

In February 1964 Trooper Hunter, A/B Squadron, won the TA Section of the Northern Ireland Command cross-country championships at Ballykinlar, later running as a member of the TA team against the Regular Army. The boxing team won the Northern Ireland Command championships in April and Corporal McIlvenny and Trooper Garrett were members of the Northern Ireland Command team that won the TA Championships. Finally, Trooper Neill, winner of the Boxer of the Year Trophy for Northern Ireland in 1963, was selected at light-welterweight to represent Ireland at the Olympic games in Tokyo.

The Adjutant, Captain N G P Ansell, 5th Royal Inniskilling Dragoon Guards, won the 1965 Grand Military Gold Cup at Sandown on his horse Threepwood and was so pleased with this success that he christened his son after the horse. Next year Lieutenant Buchanan, B Squadron, was selected for the TA Rugby XV which beat the Regular Army at Twickenham in March. Major J Moore, commanding 69 (NIH) Squadron, played for the TA Cricket XI against the Regular Army in 1990.

For TA units the climax of the year's training programme is the annual camp where the full range of skills is put into practice in a more realistic setting and often alongside other units who would be wartime partners. It is worth noting some of the highlights of the Regiment's camps over the years.

Most camps have been held in Britain but there were occasional exceptions, as we shall see. In 1959 camp was held at Lulworth to which the Regiment moved with 530 personnel, the largest number since its reforming, and a full complement of Daimler armoured cars. It was at this camp that HRH Princess Alexandra of Kent paid her first visit to the Regiment as its Honorary Colonel. Both 1960's and 1966's camps were held in Northern Ireland as shipping strikes precluded a sea crossing. In 1960 camp was held at Magilligan. The following year's camp brought a report that is alleged to have included the following comment: 'This Regiment set itself impossible targets. It achieved them.'

Chickerell near Weymouth was the venue in 1963, although firing of the main armament and machine guns took place on the ranges at Lulworth, which entailed driving some thirty miles from Weymouth to Lulworth each morning. It rained most of the time. However, as compensation, the Regiment was entertained magnificently by the Inniskilling Dragoon Guards at Tidworth on Salisbury Plain. A contemporary newspaper report notes: 'It was Irish weather too, and the North Irish Horse arrived in camp very wet but very cheerful.'

Annual camp in 1964 was held at Thetford where good accommodation, reasonable weather and the presence of the Warwickshire and Worcestershire Yeomanry to provide 'enemy' during the second week's exercise ensured a most successful camp. The following year's camp was held at Proteus Camp near Ollerton with an attendance of 472. The final camp as a TA unit was held at Saint Lucia Barracks in Omagh in 1966 instead of the planned venue of Warcop. A lack of vehicles meant that most of the exercising was done on foot. However, in September thirty members of the Regiment spent a fortnight at Wolfenbuttel with the Queen's Royal Irish Hussars and put two troops in the field who took a full part in the first five days of a three-week corps exercise, acquitting themselves very well. Four years earlier thirty-seven warrant officers and sergeants visited 5th Royal Inniskilling Dragon Guards at Sennelager in Germany. That visit took place in March, allowing the party to attend the Saint Patrick's Day celebrations.

As the Regiment marks its centenary, the North Irish Horse of 2002 consists of B (NIH) Squadron of the Queen's Own Yeomanry and 69 (NIH) Squadron of 40th (Ulster) Signal Regiment (V), the latter providing command and control communications for its regiment from its Land Rover 110s and VRC321 HF radios. The passage of a century has seen many changes and two world wars. Long gone are the days of the horse and the equipment of the ordinary soldier has changed out of all recognition from that of 1902. Whether the North Irish Horse will ever go to war again is a moot point. No one wishes to see war but the Horse's soldiers, both Yeomanry cavalrymen and Signallers, are well trained and ready for any eventuality. They share one common factor with their forebears of a hundred years before: they have a tremendous pride in their Regiment, a pride that is arguably greater than that of the Horseman of 1902 for today's soldier is very much aware of the achievements of his Regiment in two wars. Today's soldier has much to live up to but is determined that the North Irish Horse will always do its duty to the best of its ability and to the standards set by its soldiers of yesteryear at Mons, the Somme and Selle or at Longstop, the Hitler Line and the Advance to Florence.

NOTES

1 The first TA soldiers in Northern Ireland were members of two sub-units created in 1937, followed by 102 Heavy AA Regiment, which was raised in August 1939.

2 Frederick's *Lineage Book of British Land Forces* gives the date of the Regiment's reconstitution as 1 January 1947 (p. 32).

3 9th (Londonderry) HAA Regiment was another Supplementary Reserve unit.

4 The Old Comrades' Association is now the Regimental Association.

5 This led to some anomalies: most authorities agree that there were three battles for Cassino but the nomenclature committee recognised only two and units that took part in the final battle were awarded the honour 'Cassino II'.

6 Another inconsistency of the Battle Honours Committee's work was the refusal to assign battle honours to the Reconnaissance Corps, a wartime formation, on the grounds that, in common with the Royal Artillery and Royal Engineers, the Corps had been involved in all the Army's battles and, therefore, should be treated in similar fashion. This ignored the fact that the Corps became part of the Royal Armoured Corps in 1944 and that the same ruling could have been applied to the RAC. Perhaps the fact that the Reconnaissance Corps had been disbanded in 1947 had an influence on the committee's decision.

7 The greatest reduction in TA strength at this time came with the disbandment of Anti-Aircraft Command and most of the TA anti-aircraft regiments.

8 The others were the Royal Wiltshire Yeomanry and the Westminster Dragoons.

9 Combat Vehicle Reconnaissance (Tracked).

10 Spartan, Sultan and Samaritan are all members of the Scorpion family of light armoured fighting vehicles. Spartan was designed as an armoured personnel carrier (APC) but is used as a special purposes vehicle while Sultan is a command vehicle and Samaritan the ambulance version.

APPENDIX I

Jack Neilson MM and Bar: Soldier and Poet

Trooper Jack Neilson MM and Bar was born in southern Ireland but settled in Northern Ireland after the war. He was one of the best known soldiers of the Regiment and, as well as his obvious courage, a man with a love for poetry and words who put some of his thoughts into verse during the Tunisian campaign. Two of his poems are reproduced here, the first written on 7 April 1943 at Ksar Mezouar station and entitled *The Observer*.

At Kasar Masour Station in Wog Hut Watching
Silent stand in Observation post,
Field glasses focused on form opposite,
Two miles of undulating greenness
On skyline, red roofed white buildings,
And nearer the broken fuselage of a Focke-Wulf.
Intensely aware of singing birds,
See love-sick storks, building nest.
By soft breeze over valley drifting
The sickly scent of death.
Quietness suddenly shattered
By Wheow – Wheow – Whumph!
Of German Six Inch Mortar
Hastily our Five Fives
Quickly send screaming
Their hazard messengers of death.
In hut on far farm watching
Stands silent some German boy,
Wistfully thinking of Gamerisch–Partenkirchen.
Brain war weary asking 'Why?'
So, watching, invisible to each other
Mutually wonder 'Why?'
And the stork builds on.

The second poem was written in 36th General Hospital, Algiers on 13 May 1943 when he was recovering after he had been shot through the arm 'beyond Longstop Hill (Hill 202 to be precise)'. Axis forces in North Africa had just surrendered and in introducing the poem, *African Victory*, Jack Neilson noted that:

> In the flush of Victory I noticed that every soldier in Hospital wore a wristwatch or ring, 'presents from loved ones'. One thought of the cost of victory, the dead at Sedjenane and Longstop, each dead soldier wearing some token of love and so representing not a mere individual, but a person whose manner of living influenced others, who thus became poorer because of that death. Thus victory for the soldier is not something to be lightly celebrated: to the soldier, victory and dead friends are bracketed together.

Rommel's rout,

Church bells peal gaily,

Victory's price paid freely

From Greenhill to Longstop –

All the Medjerda Valley –

From Bizerte to Tunis –

Ours by conquest.

Paid for yard by yard,

With dead soldiers

Men and boys

Wearing wrist watches,

Presents from loved ones.

Through mud and through blood,

To the green fields beyond.

Beyond the green fields,

And lurking round the bend

Death, the inevitable friend

Freedom's cost –

Paid by us!

Freedom's Torch –

Yours to keep flaming!

Remember the dead soldiers

Men and boys,

Wearing wrist watches

Presents from loved ones.

APPENDIX II

HONOURS AND AWARDS

First World War

Victoria Cross
Lieutenant-Colonel Richard A West DSO*, MC, attd Tank Corps (6th Tank Bn)

Cross of St Michael and St George
Lieutenant-Colonel Viscount J H M Cole

Bar to Distinguished Service Order
Lieutenant-Colonel R A West DSO, MC, attd Tank Corps

Distinguished Service Order
Major R A West, attd North Somerset Yeomanry
Lieutenant-Colonel A K M The Lord Farnham, attd R. Innisk Fusiliers
Major A E Phillips, R West Kents, commanding V Cyclist Regiment (NIH)
Lieutenant-Colonel N G Stuart-Richardson, for service in Middle East

Military Cross
Captain J V Adair, attd 12th Lancers
Lieutenant E A Atkinson, V Cyclist Bn
Captain W Bookes, V Cyclist Bn
Lieutenant W Buchanan, Army Cyclist Corps, attd V Cyclist Bn
Captain H S Dean, attd 9th (NIH) Bn R Irish Fus
Lieutenant J K Greer
Lieutenant B O'N Hodson, V Cyclist Bn
Lieutenant J Knox, attd R Irish Rifles
Lieutenant J A MacClean, attd Royal Field Artillery
Second-Lieutenant J F E McFarland, attd 4th Bn R Irish Fus
Lieutenant H E L Montgomery, V Cyclist Bn
Major R D Ross
Captain E Sinton, attd Royal Field Artillery
Captain R R Smart, 2nd NIH
Lieutenant G W Vesey, attd 9th (NIH) Bn R Irish Fus

Lieutenant-Colonel R A West, attd Tank Corps (6th Tank Bn)
Second-Lieutenant J B Young, attd 9th (NIH) Bn R Irish Fus

Bar to Military Medal
SSM H Boyd MM

Military Medal
Corporal J Armstrong
Corporal J Bailey
L/Sergeant R C Blair
SSM H Boyd
Corporal W Brown
SSM R J Carmichael
Sergeant J Clancey
Private J Close
Private D Connolly
Sergeant W H Glendinning
SSM F R Harding
Sergeant T Jamison
Corporal W J Johnston
Private H V Kearon
Private J J McLoughlin
Corporal W McMurray
Sergeant S Rainey
Sergeant W Scott
Corporal W Stevenson
Corporal R C Stewart
RSM J Wright DCM

Meritorious Service Medal
Corporal F Ferguson
Corporal R Hassard
Sergeant S Rainey

Croix de Guerre
Major R D Ross

Medaille Militaire
Trooper J McArow

The Medaille Militaire was awarded to one other member of the Regiment but no record of his name has survived.

In addition, twenty-one Mentions in Despatches were awarded to the Regiment.

Second World War

Distinguished Service Order
Lieutenant-Colonel D Dawnay
Lieutenant-Colonel E V Strickland MM

Distinguished Conduct Medal
Sergeant T C McAughtry

Member of the Order of the British Empire
Major W W G Lavery
Captain A D Wilson
RQMS W Dockey

Bar to Military Cross
Major R J Griffith MC

Military Cross
Major G P Russell
Major R D Morton
Major P Welch
Major R S H Sidebottom
Captain R J Griffith
Captain C M Thomas
Captain A K E Finch Noyes
Captain W M Mackean
Captain R B M King
Captain J S Milne
Lieutenant M B Pope
Lieutenant G E Gardiner
Lieutenant B E S King
Lieutenant K W Foott
Lieutenant G C Brown
Lieutenant H E Irwin
Lieutenant W A L Reid
Lieutenant M L Bexon
Lieutenant D R King
Lieutenant A Maguire MM

Bar to Military Medal
Trooper J D Neilson MM
Trooper S Johnston MM

Military Medal
SSM L Bumstead
Trooper A B Church
Sergeant E O'Hare
Sergeant J Maxwell
Sergeant J E Barbour
Sergeant T W Donaghy
Sergeant F Verso
Sergeant G Ballard
Sergeant J C Buchanan
L/Sergeant J Stewart
Corporal R B Cox
Corporal W T Gleghorn
Corporal J J Cunningham
L/Corporal A Maguire
L/Corporal F D Kennedy
L/Corporal C M Moriarty
L/Corporal F J Ham
L/Corporal W Hughes
Trooper A B Church
Trooper S Johnston
Trooper J D Neilson
Trooper G E Martin

British Empire Medal
Sergeant D L Knight

Silver Star (USA)
Captain G Mahon

Bronze Star (USA)
Sergeant F D Kennedy

In addition, sixty-three Mentions in Despatches were awarded to the Regiment.

Post-war

Commander of the Order of the British Empire
Colonel R F M Windsor DL   1972

Officer of the Order of the British Empire
Lieutenant-Colonel A J H Cramsie TD, DL   1958
Lieutenant-Colonel M W McCorkell TD, DL   1964

Member of the Order of the British Empire

WO II (RQMS) J E McCausland	1955
Major W T Gleghorn MM, TD	1961
WOI (BM) J Francis	1963
Major T C McAughtry DCM, TD (NIHT)	1968
Major W B S Buchanan TD 69 Squadron	1975
Major R J Moore 69 Squadron	1988
Major G M Wylie 69 Squadron	1996

British Empire Medal

Sergeant J A Smith	1953
Staff Sergeant H McCrory REME D Squadron	1979
Staff Sergeant W Redmond D Squadron	1980
Sergeant S J Lyle 69 Squadron	1986

APPENDIX III

Uniforms of the North Irish Horse

The early uniform of the Regiment has been the subject of much inaccurate description over the years and this Appendix is an attempt to correct such inaccuracies. Soldiers were issued with an all-purpose khaki uniform embellished with a white clover leaf on the tunic cuffs and a white welt on the seams of the Bedford cord pantaloons. Leather buttons were worn on the tunic but were later replaced with brass, and collar badges of the harp and crown with the regimental title were also worn; the cap badge was a larger version of this badge. The headdress was a slouch hat with a cloth patch on the upturned brim. A full-dress uniform was issued for ceremonial occasions and for walking out by other ranks. It was a lancer-style uniform featuring a green tunic, described as being lighter or brighter in colour than that worn by rifle regiments, with black overalls with a single wide white stripe, and a unique headdress – a bowler-style with cloth on the underside and black patent leather on the upper, adorned with a green plume and a silver badge on a white corded ribbon rosette with a half-inch green border on its outer edge.

During the two world wars the Regiment wore the standard service dress of the Army – in the Great War – and battledress – in the Second World War – with regimental embellishments. For most of the Army distinctive ceremonial uniforms became a part of history after the Great War but, in the wake of the Second World War, a dress uniform in dark blue was introduced for use on special occasions. This has been worn by the Horse with its own distinctions while 69 (NIH) Squadron Royal Signals has worn the uniform of its parent corps with certain North Irish Horse distinctions.

APPENDIX IV

Award of the Maple Leaf

Belfast Telegraph, Saturday 24 June 1944

NORTH IRISH HORSE at THE HITLER LINE

The North Irish Horse, an Ulster Regiment, which in North Africa and Italy added fresh honours to its proud battle record, achieved its greatest triumph in the assault on the Adolf Hitler Line.

The smashing of this formidable defensive line was one of the grimmest tasks confronting the Allies and the action proved one of the bloodiest of the campaign. The final assault . . . was carried out by The North Irish Horse and three Canadian regiments.

The magnitude of the undertaking and the courage and will to win of these gallant Ulstermen and Canadians was recognised by the award of the Maple Leaf to the Tank Brigade to which The North Irish Horse is attached.

> The Special Orders of the Day issued after the smashing of the Hitler Line contain these eloquent tributes.
>
> (1) From the Commander First Canadian Corps to Commander Tank Brigade: 'Canadians owe a debt of gratitude to your Brigade which has fought so magnificently with us today. The courage and determination of all ranks has been beyond praise.'
>
> (2) From Commander a Canadian Division to Commander Tank Brigade: 'Canada will be proud for ever of a battle which a Canadian Division has won today. Through the courage and determination of all ranks of the Division and their British comrades of a Tank Brigade Hitler Line has been broken in the face of bitter opposition and the enemy has been dealt a blow from which he will not soon recover. The final victory is near; let us press on and finish our task.'
>
> (3) GOC a Canadian Infantry Division to the Tank Brigade: 'Well done. We have won a resounding victory. This victory is the fruits of your magnificent courage, endurance and will to win. Now we have them on the run we must keep them running. All we need to do is to keep cracking. Good luck. I am the proudest man in the world.'
>
> (4) Commander the Tank Brigade to his Brigade: 'By the great

courage and determination which you have shown today and by the magnificent way in which you have faced the most difficult task you have ever met, you have made a great page in history.

Many experienced soldiers might have thought that your task was impossible in such country and with such skilled and determined defence. I thank you all for the great job you have done.

Officer Commanding the Infantry Division (Canadian) intimated that he would be pleased if all ranks of the Tank Brigade would wear a Maple Leaf in token of the part they played in breaking the line. I have accepted with thanks.'

BIBLIOGRAPHY

Austin, A B, *Birth of an Army* (London, 1943)

Blaxland, Gregory, *The Plain Cook and the Great Showman – The First and Eighth Armies in North Africa* (London, 1977)

——, *Alexander's Generals – The Italian Campaign 1944–1945* (London, 1979)

Doherty, Richard, *Clear The Way! A History of the 38th (Irish) Brigade, 1941–1947* (Dublin, 1993)

——, *A Noble Crusade. The History of Eighth Army 1941–45* (Staplehurst, 1999)

Graham, D & Bidwell, S, *Tug of War – The Battle for Italy, 1943–45* (London, 1986)

Horsfall, John, *The Wild Geese are Flighting* (Kineton, 1976)

Hunt, Donald F, *To the Green Fields Beyond* (Durham, 1993)

Jackson, W G F, *The Battle for Italy* (London, 1968)

——, *The North African Campaign* (London, 1975)

Joslen, Lt-Col H F, *Orders of Battle Second World War* (London, 1960)

Macksey, Kenneth, *Kesselring – German Master Strategist of the Second World War* (London, 1978)

Marshall, Howard, *Over to Tunis* (London, 1943)

Molony, C J C, & Jackson, W, *The Mediterranean and the Middle East, Vols V & VI* (London, 1973 & 1988)

Nicholson, G W L, *The Canadians in Italy 1943–1945 (Official History of the Canadian Army in the Second World War, Vol 2)* (Ottawa, 1956)

North, John (ed), *The Memoirs of Field Marshal Earl Alexander of Tunis, 1940–1945* (London, 1962)

Playfair, I S O et al, *The Mediterranean and the Middle East*, Vol IV, *The Destruction of the Axis Forces in Africa* (London, 1966)

Pope, Michael, MC, *Fighting for Freedom and Fun* (London, 1999)

Ray, Cyril, *Algiers to Austria – The History of 78 Division 1942–1946* (London, 1952)

Stevens, G R, *The Tiger Triumphs* (London, 1946)

Strawson, John, *The Italian Campaign* (London, 1987)

Tanner, Michael, *The Major. The biography of Dick Hern* (London, 1991)

The Army at War: Tunisia (London, 1944)

North Irish Horse Battle Report (Belfast, 1947)

Unpublished

HQ 15 Army Group, *Finito! The Po Valley Campaign 1945*

Supreme Allied Commander, Mediterranean, *Report on the Italian Campaign, Pts I–III*

British Historical Section, Central Mediterranean, *Narrative of Operations 25 Tank Brigade 1 Aug–2 Dec 1944*

——, *21 Tank Brigade Operations in Italy Aug 1944–May 1945*

Public Record Office, Kew

WO32/15949 North Irish Horse: Battle Honours and Distinctions

WO175/294 War Diary, January–June 1943

WO169/9335 War Diary, July–December 1943

WO170/846 War Diary, 1944

WO170/4633 War Diary, 1945

Roll of Honour

(N.K. = not known)

Name	Date died	Cause of death	Buried/ Memorial	Comments
Cpl W H Adams	8 Aug 1917	KIA	France	10 Innisks
Lieut W Anderson	20 Oct 1918	KIA	France	15 RIR
Sec.Lieut R H Andrews	25 Sep 1915	KIA	France	RIR
Tpr R G Armstrong	27 Mar 1918	KIA	France	Cyclist Regt
Tpr W F C Arthur	22 Jul 1918	KIA	Belgium	9 (NIH) RIrF
Tpr J Baxter	16 Aug 1917	KIA	Belgium	1 RIR
Tpr W Beattie	30 Sep 1917	DoW	Belgium	174 Coy, Machine Gun Corps
Tpr J A Bell	19 Apr 1918	KIA	Belgium	9 (NIH) RIrF
Tpr V N Bell	26 Oct 1917	KIA	France	9 (NIH) RIrF
Tpr J Best	3 Oct 1918	DoW	France	9 (NIH) RIrF
Tpr W Biggart	3 Apr 1918	DoW	France	9 (NIH) RIrF
Tpr A Blair	2 Sep 1918	DoW	France	Cyclist Regt
Tpr J A Bowden	19 Apr 1918	KIA	Belgium	9 (NIH) RIrF
Cpl R I Bradley	20 May 1917	KIA	France	1 NIH
Tpr H Brennan	3 Nov 1918	DoW	France	Cyclist Regt
Tpr W Brown	12 Aug 1918	DoW	France	9 (NIH) RIrF
Tpr T Bryson	21 Aug 1918	KIA	France	Cyclist Regt
Cpl E Buchanan	23 Oct 1914	DoW	Surrey	Either A or C Sqn
Tpr T Cartmill	29 Mar 1918	KIA	France	9 (NIH) RIrF
Lieut S B Combe	1 Oct 1914	DoW	France	C Sqn
Tpr J Connell	16 Aug 1917	KIA	Belgium	1 RIR
Tpr F St G Cooke	19 Apr 1918	KIA	Belgium	9 (NIH) RIrF
Tpr F T Cordwell	19 Sep 1917		France	1 NIH
Tpr A S Crawford	29 Mar 1918	KIA	N. K.	9 (NIH) RIrF
Tpr J Culley	4 Nov 1918	DoW	N. K.	Cyclist Regt
Tpr A Davey	19 Apr 1918	KIA	Belgium	9 (NIH) RIrF
L/Cpl J Deery	11 Oct 1918	KIA	Belgium	9 (NIH) RIrF
Lieut J R Dennistoun	9 Aug 1916	DoW	Germany	No. 23 Sqn RFC
Sec.Lieut J Denny	23 Oct 1918	KIA	Belgium	1 RIrF

Name	Date died	Cause of death	Buried/ Memorial	Comments
Tpr W H Dundas	1 Oct 1918	KIA	Belgium	1 RIrF
Tpr J J Durneen	26 Mar 1918	KIA	France	Cyclist Regt
Tpr C Elder	7 Nov 1918	KIA	France	Cyclist Regt
L/Cpl A Erskine	11 Oct 1918	DoW	Belgium	9 (NIH) RIrF
Tpr J Evans	25 Oct 1918	DoW	France	Cyclist Regt
Tpr W J Finlay	23 Jun 1916	KIA	France	? 1 NIH
L/Cpl H Flanagan	22 Nov 1917	KIA	France	9 (NIH) RIrF
Tpr J Forbes	29 Mar 1918	KIA	France	9 (NIH) RIrF
Tpr J Forde	3 Nov 1917	KIA	N. K.	9 (NIH) RIrF
Tpr G Galbraith	24 Nov 1917	DoW	France	9 (NIH) RIrF
Tpr G M Gibson	N. K.	N.K	N.K.	
Tpr G Gill	26 Aug 1918	KIA	France	Cyclist Regt
Tpr T S Gillespie	13 Nov 1915		Belfast City Cemetery	NIH Cav Sqn
Lieut G K M Greer MC	3 Oct 1916	DoW	France	Irish Gds
Tpr M Haggan	17 Oct 1918	Died	N. K.	Staffs Yeo (Middle East)
Tpr N H Hale	16 Aug 1917	KIA	N. K.	1 RIR
Tpr T Hall	7 Mar 1917	KIA	France	1 RIR
L/Cpl R J Hanna	20 Apr 1918	DoW	France	1 Innisks
Tpr G Harper	24 Apr 1915		Hampshire	A or C Sqn
Tpr T Harper	18 May 1918	DoW	N. K.	9 (NIH) RIrF
Tpr R Heathwood	3 Nov 1917	KIA	France	9 (NIH) RIrF
Tpr T N Henderson	7 Sep 1918	KIA	Belgium	1 RIR
L/Sgt G A Henry MM	26 Mar 1918	DoW	France	9 (NIH) RIrF
L/Cpl R H Hill	10 Nov 1918		France	Cyclist Regt
Tpr W Hillocks	10 Nov 1918		France	Cyclist Regt
Cpl C E Houston	2 Oct 1918	KIA	Belgium	2 Innisks
Tpr A Huggins	30 Aug 1918	DoW	France	6 Dgn Gds (Carabiniers)
Tpr R J Hull	1 Oct 1918	KIA	Belgium	9 (NIH) RIrF
Sgt R Irwin	3 Nov 1917	KIA	France	9 (NIH) RIrF
Tpr W Irwin	2 Mar 1915		France	A or C Sqn
Tpr A Johnston MM	16 Aug 1917	KIA	Belgium	1 RIR
L/Cpl J Johnston	12 Nov 1918	DoW	France	Cyclist Regt (CWGC register shows as 9 (NIH) RIrF
Tpr T Johnston	24 Mar 1918	KIA	France	2 RIR
Lieut H P Kellock	6 Oct 1918	DoW	France	Attd Royal Field Arty
Tpr A G Kelly	26 Aug 1918	KIA	N. K.	Cyclist Regt
Tpr J Kelly	5 Sep 1918	DoW	France	9 (NIH) RIrF
Tpr J D King	3 Nov 1917	KIA	N. K.	9 (NIH) RIrF

Name	Date died	Cause of death	Buried/ Memorial	Comments
Tpr A J Knox	16 Aug 1917	KIA	Belgium	1 RIR
Lieut J Knox MC	23 Oct 1918	DoW	N. K.	? RIR
Cpl W Leckey	11 May 1918	KIA	Belgium	1 RIR
Tpr W G Leinster	19 Apr 1918	KIA	Belgium	9 (NIH) RIrF
Tpr F Livingstone	21 Aug 1918	KIA	N. K.	Cyclist Regt
Sec.Lieut R V Lyons	24 Mar 1918	KIA	France	14 RIR, attd 23 Entrenching Bn, RIR
Tpr T Lyons	29 Mar 1918	KIA	France	9 (NIH) RIrF
Lieut A W McLaughlin	9 May 1915	KIA	Belgium	3 RIR (attd 1 RIR)
Capt D McCausland	22 Nov 1917	KIA	France	12 RIR (served with Irish Horse in Boer War)
Sec.Lieut A McClelland	13 Oct 1917	DoW	France	5 RIR
Lieut R J McCullough	22 Oct 1917	KIA	N. K.	16th Cheshire Regt
Sec.Lieut J F E McFarland MC	22 Jul 1918	KIA	N. K.	4 RIrF
Lieut J A MacLean MC	30 Sep 1917	KIA	N. K.	RFA
Tpr J Magill	6 Jun 1918		France	9 (NIH) RIrF
Tpr G Mark	4 Sep 1918	KIA	Belgium	9 (NIH) RIrF
Tpr A Martin	20 Nov 1917	KIA	France	10 Innisks
Lieut E M Meredith	13 Apr 1918	KIA	Belgium	No. 21 Sqn RAF
Tpr R G D Montgomery	31 Aug 1918		France	2 Innisks
Tpr J Moon	29 Mar 1918	KIA	France	9 (NIH) RIrF
Lieut A Moore	26 Mar 1918	KIA	France	13 RIR attd 22nd Entrenching Bn
Tpr R Moore	6 May 1917		Co. Down	1st or 2nd HIH
Tpr W Moore	15 Sep 1914	KIA	France	C Sqn
Tpr A Morrison	16 Aug 1917	KIA	N. K.	1 RIR
Tpr W Morrow	9 Apr 1918	KIA	France	Cyclist Regt
Tpr H Mortimer	10 Aug 1917	KIA	Belgium	9 (NIH) RIrF
Tpr W M Murphy	12 Feb 1917		France	1st or 2nd NIH
Tpr G T Murray	12 Dec 1917	KIA	France	7 (SIH) R Irish Regt
Tpr J McArow	27 Apr 1916	KIA	France	A Sqn. Awarded Medaille Militaire (France).
Tpr W J McAuley	11 Apr 1918	DoW	Belgium	9 (NIH) RIrF
Tpr W McClelland	16 Aug 1918	KIA	N. K.	Cyclist Regt
Tpr R McConnell	19 Apr 1918	KIA	Belgium	9 (NIH) RIrF
Cpl T J McCormick	27 Mar 1918	KIA	France	Cyclist Regt
Tpr J E McCready	6 Aug 1918		Egypt	Notts Yeomanry (Sherwood Rgrs) attd Staffs Yeo in Egypt

Name	Date died	Cause of death	Buried/ Memorial	Comments
Tpr C H McDaniel	15 Oct 1918	Died	Syria	NIH, Attd 1/1 Staffs Yeomanry
L/Cpl J McSparran	6 Mar 1917	KIA	France	1 RIR
Tpr J McVea	26 Aug 1918	KIA	France	Cyclist Regt
Tpr M McVeigh	25 Oct 1918	KIA	Belgium	9 (NIH) RIrF
Lieut H R Nixon	26 Oct 1918	KIA	N. K.	Wiltshire Regt
Tpr W Nixon	6 Mar 1917	KIA	France	1 RIR
Tpr R O'Hara	1 Apr 1917	KIA	Lanarkshire	1 RIR
Tpr R Park	19 Apr 1918	KIA	Belgium	9 (NIH) RIrF
Tpr A Pepper	12 Aug 1918	KIA	Belgium	9 (NIH) RIrF
Tpr W J Petty	22 Nov 1917	KIA	France	9 (NIH) RIrF
Lieut W L Reavie	16 Aug 1917	KIA	Belgium	3 R. Dublin Fus
L/Cpl W J Reid	14 Oct 1918	KIA	Belgium	1 RIR
Tpr R Richmond	20 Oct 1918	KIA	Belgium	9 Innisks
Tpr J E Riddle	3 Aug 1918	KIA	N. K.	9 (NIH) RIrF
Cpl D W Ritchie	17 Mar 1915		France	A or C Sqn
Tpr J Roberts	21 Aug 1918	KIA	N. K.	Cyclist Regt
Tpr S Robinson	9 Aug 1917	DoW	Belgium	1st or 2nd NIH
Tpr R Ross	21 Aug 1918	KIA	France	Cyclist Regt
Tpr C Russell	24 Mar 1918	KIA	N. K.	1 RIR
Lieut R C Russell	31 Aug 1918	DoW	Turkey	N Staffs Regt
Capt S T Saunderson	22 Apr 1918		Shropshire	RAF flying instructor
Lieut T J Savage	11 Nov 1918	KIA	France	3 Rifle Brigade
L/Cpl F Scanlon	23 Nov 1917	KIA	France	9 (NIH) RIrF
Tpr Hon. H StG L Scott	8 Oct 1914	KIA	France	C Sqn
Tpr J Scott	8 Oct 1918		France	19 Hussars
Tpr G M Shannon	25 Oct 1918	KIA	Belgium	9 (NIH) RIrF
Tpr S Shiels	10 Oct 1918		Co. Monaghan	9 (NIH) RIrF
Tpr P Sheridan	9 Dec 1918	DoW	Co. Cavan	9 (NIH) RIrF
Capt E Sinton MC	21 Aug 1918	KIA	France	Royal Field Arty attd R. Engineers
Tpr T Sittlington	21 Mar 1918	KIA	France	9 (NIH) RIrF
Tpr J Sleator	23 Nov 1917	KIA	France	9 (NIH) RIrF
Tpr J Smith	6 Sep 1917	KIA	Belgium	1 RIR
Tpr J Smyth	1 Dec 1917	DoW	France	9 (NIH) RIrF
Tpr E A Stevenson	16 Aug 1917	KIA	Belgium	1 RIR
L/Cpl T Stevenson	16 Aug 1917	KIA	Belgium	1 RIR
Tpr G W Strange	8 Jul 1918		N. K.	9 (NIH) RIrF
Tpr W P Stuart	30 Mar 1918	DoW	France	9 (NIH) RIrF
Tpr J Talbot	7 Jun 1917	KIA	Belgium	10 Innisks
Tpr F Tate	21 Mar 1918	KIA	France	9 (NIH) RIrF

Name	Date died	Cause of death	Buried/ Memorial	Comments
Tpr W Thompson	6 Dec 1917	DoW	N. K.	9 (NIH) RIrF
Tpr W F Timbey	4 Sep 1918	KIA	Belgium	9 (NIH) RIrF
Tpr C D Turner	20 Jul 1917	DoW	Belgium	1st or 2nd NIH
L/Cpl S Turner	20 Jul 1917	KIA	Belgium	1st or 2nd NIH
Capt G W Vesey MC	26 Mar 1918	DoW	France	9 (NIH) RIrF
Maj H Waring	15 Apr 1918	DoW	Belgium	12 RIR
Lt-Col R A West VC, DSO*, MC	2 Sep 1918	KIA	France	Attd 6 Tank Bn
Lieut L C Wise	2 May 1917		India	Serving in India
Tpr C R Woodside	8 Nov 1918		France	Cyclist Regt
Tpr T Wright	28 Jul 1916	DoW	France	2nd NIH
Tpr W Waller	16 Aug 1918	DoW	France	Attd 9 Lancers
Sgt R A Wylie	26 Jun 1917	DoW	Belgium	1st NIH
Cpl P Asprey	18 Sep 1944		Italy	
Tpr H J Barwell	25 Sep 1944		Italy	
Tpr A E Bateman	23 May 1944		Italy	Hitler Line
L/Cpl W J Benson	23 May 1944		Italy	Hitler Line
Sgt W J Best	23 May 1944		Italy	Hitler Line
Sgt R E Bone	15 Aug 1944	DoW	Italy	Hitler Line
Tpr J E Bradfield	28 Aug 1944		Italy	
SQMS A Brown	21 Mar 1943		Tunisia	
Lieut G C Brown MC	23 May 1944		Italy	Hitler Line
Sgt H McI Burns	2 Dec 1944		Italy	
Lieut A D C Butler	14 Jul 1943		Sicily	No. 3 Commando
L/Cpl A J Cantwell	23 May 1944		Italy	Hitler Line
Tpr J A Cartmale	23 May 1944		Italy	Hitler Line
L/Cpl T S Chambers	23 May 1944		Italy	Hitler Line
Sgt J E Clulow	4 Aug 1944		Italy	
Tpr A Codd	23 May 1944		Italy	Hitler Line
Tpr B G Coote	5 Aug 1944		Italy	
Tpr N Corbin	2 Dec 1944		Italy	
L/Cpl S Cox	23 May 1944		Italy	Hitler Line
Tpr R J Currie	9 Mar 1943		Tunisia	
Tpr W Currie	23 May 1944		Italy	Hitler Line
Tpr F A Davage	28 May 1944	DoW	Italy	Hitler Line
Tpr G Davies	30 Apr 1943		Tunisia	
Cpl R Dickson	30 Apr 1943		Tunisia	
Tpr T L L R Dunne	23 May 1944		Italy	Hitler Line
Sgt A G Elliott	23 May 1944		Italy	Hitler Line
Tpr R C Ellis	23 May 1944		Italy	Hitler Line

Name	Date died	Cause of death	Buried/ Memorial	Comments
Major J H G The Earl of Erne	23 May 1940		France	Attached XII R. Lancers in BEF
Tpr John J Franklin	10 Apr 1943		Tunisia	
Tpr H Freer	14 Jul 1944		Italy	
Tpr J Galloway	23 May 1944		Italy	Hitler Line
Sgt E A Harrison	5 Oct 1943	Killed in road crash	Algeria	
L/Cpl R S M Hazeldine	4 Mar 1943		Tunisia	
Sgt N Hewitt	9 Mar 1943		Tunisia	
L/Cpl W J Hill	19 Jun 1944		Italy	
Lieut R M Horsburgh	23 May 1944		Italy	Hitler Line
Lieut G W Hutchinson	1 Nov 1943	Killed in road crash.	Algeria	Noted as RAC on Army Roll of Honour
L/Cpl H Hutchinson	9 Mar 1943		Tunisia	
Tpr L Isherwood	4 Mar 1943		Tunisia	
L/Cpl A Jackson	19 June 1944		Italy	
Tpr D G James	17 Sep 1944		Italy	
L/Cpl W C Jamieson	26 Apr 1943		Tunisia	
L/Cpl H Jenkins	23 May 1944		Italy	
Cpl H Kennedy	16 Dec 1940	Killed in road crash.	Co. Down	
Tpr G King	8 Oct 1944		Italy	
Tpr F T H Leach	21 Nov 1943		Algeria	
Captain D A Leslie REME	13 Apr 1943			EME attd to NIH
Tpr U G Love	23 May 1944		Italy	Hitler Line
Tpr D V Loxdale	4 Sep 1944		Italy	
Tpr D McFaul	28 Mar 1943		Tunisia	
Maj W M MacKean MC	7 Oct 1944		Italy	OC B Sqn
Sgt J McLaughlin	23 May 1944		Italy	Hitler Line
Sgt T J McQueen	22 Jul 1944		Italy	
Cpl W Manamley	28 Apr 1943		Tunisia	ACC attd to NIH
Lieutenant R P M Mann	30 Apr 43		Tunisia	
L/Cpl R Milliken	23 May 1944		Italy	Hitler Line
Tpr R T Mitchell	17 Sep 1944		Italy	
Tpr N Moss	23 May 1944		Italy	Hitler Line
Tpr T R Mould	22 Feb 1946		Cologne	Formerly of 56th Reconnaissance Regt
Tpr R A H Newton	23 May 1944		Italy	Hitler Line
Tpr J R Nursey	28 Feb 1943		Tunisia	

Name	Date died	Cause of death	Buried/ Memorial	Comments
L/Cpl D J O'Farrell	4 Mar 1943		Tunisia	
Lt-Col S E R The Lord O'Neill	24 Oct 1944		Italy	Commanding Officer
Tpr T Price	23 May 1944		Italy	Hitler Line
L/Cpl J H M Pryde	23 May 1944		Italy	Hitler Line
Lieutenant J J H Pyl	23 May 1944		Italy	Hitler Line
Sgt L N Reeve	23 May 1944		Italy	Hitler Line
Major J Rew	4 Mar 1943		Tunisia	OC B Sqn
Tpr J W Rutherford	23 May 1944		Italy	Hitler Line
Tpr J H Ryan	4 Mar 1943		Tunisia	
Tpr C J F Smith	23 May 1944		Italy	Hitler Line
Tpr B L Squires	23 May 1944		Italy	Hitler Line
Tpr R A Stafford	2 Dec 1944		Italy	
Tpr J A Stewart	23 May 1944		Italy	Hitler Line
Tpr M S Strong	23 May 1944		Italy	Hitler Line
Lieut T G Tuckey	23 May 1944		Italy	Hitler Line
Tpr J T Tweedie	6 Sep 1944		Italy	
Sgt P J Walters	28 Feb 1943		Tunisia	
Tpr J A Wasson	27 May 1941	Killed in road crash.	Co. Tyrone	
Tpr A Whalley	30 Apr 1943		Tunisia	
Tpr J W Wilson	23 May 1944		Italy	Hitler Line
Tpr J J Wood	2 Dec 1944		Italy	
Tpr R H Wright	21 Jul 1943		Algeria	

At the going down of the sun, and in the morning
We will remember them.

Index

271